PARTY FOOD
& APPETIZERS

PARTY FOOD
& APPETIZERS

how to plan the perfect celebration with over 400 inspiring appetizers,
snacks, first courses, party dishes and desserts

EDITOR
BRIDGET JONES

HERMES
HOUSE

This edition is published by Hermes House, an imprint of Anness Publishing Ltd
Hermes House, 88–89 Blackfriars Road, London SE1 8HA
tel. 020 7401 2077; fax 020 7633 9499

www.hermeshouse.com; www.annesspublishing.com

If you like the images in this book and would like to investigate using them for publishing, promotions or advertising,
please visit our website www.practicalpictures.com for more information.

Publisher: Joanna Lorenz
Managing Editor: Linda Fraser
Project Editor: Jennifer Schofield
Editor: Linda Doeser
Production Controller: Wendy Lawson
Editorial Readers: Jane Bamforth and Richard McGinlay
Designers: Nigel Partridge and Jonathan Harley
Illustrator: Anna Koska
Recipes: Catherine Atkinson, Alex Barker, Angela Boggiano, Carla Capalbo, Kit Chan, Jacqueline Clarke, Maxine Clarke, Andi Cleverly,
Roz Denny, Matthew Drennan, Joanna Farrow, Rafi Fernandez, Christine France, Silvano Franco, Sarah Gates, Shirley Gill, Brian Glover,
Nicola Graimes, Rosamund Grant, Carole Handslip, Deh-Ta Hsing, Peter Jordan, Lucy Knox, Elisabeth Lambert Ortiz, Ruby Le Bois,
Clare Lewis, Sara Lewis, Christine McFadden, Leslie Mackley, Norma MacMillan, Sue Maggs, Sally Mansfield, Sallie Morris, Jane Milton,
Keith Richmond, Rena Salaman, Marlena Spieler, Jenny Stacey, Liz Trigg, Linda Tubby, Oona van den Berg, Hilaire Walden, Laura Washburn,
Steven Wheeler, Kate Whiteman, Elizabeth Wolf-Cohen, Jeni Wright
Photographers: Karl Adamson, Edward Allwright, Caroline Arber, Steve Baxter, Martin Brigdale, Nicki Dowey, James Duncan, Gus Filgate,
John Freeman, Ian Garlick, Michelle Garrett, Peter Henley, John Heseltine, Amanda Heywood, Janine Hosegood, David Jordan, Maris Kelly,
Dave King, Don Last, William Lingwood, Patrick McLeavy, Michael Michaels, Roisin Neild, Thomas Odulate, Spike Powell, Craig Robertson,
Simon Smith, Sam Stowell, Polly Wreford
Food for photography (chapter openers): Becky Johnson

ETHICAL TRADING POLICY
Because of our ongoing ecological investment programme, you, as our customer, can have the pleasure and reassurance of knowing that a
tree is being cultivated on your behalf to naturally replace the materials used to make the book you are holding. For further information
about this scheme, go to www.annesspublishing.com/trees

© Anness Publishing Ltd 2003, 2011

A CIP catalogue record for this book is available from the British Library.

Previously published as *Appetizers, Finger Food, Buffets & Parties*

PUBLISHER'S NOTE
Although the advice and information in this book are believed to be accurate and true at the time of going to press, neither the authors nor
the publisher can accept any legal responsibility or liability for any errors or omissions that may have been made nor for any inaccuracies nor
for any loss, harm or injury that comes about from following instructions or advice in this book.

Bracketed terms are intended for American readers.
For all recipes, quantities are given in both metric and imperial measures and, where appropriate, measures are also given in standard cups
and spoons. Follow one set, but not a mixture, because they are not interchangeable.
Standard spoon and cup measures are level. 1 tsp = 5ml, 1 tbsp = 15ml, 1 cup = 250ml/8fl oz.
Australian standard tablespoons are 20ml. Australian readers should use 3 tsp in place of 1 tbsp for measuring small quantities.
American pints are 16fl oz/2 cups. American readers should use 20fl oz/2.5 cups in place of 1 pint when measuring liquids.
Electric oven temperatures in this book are for conventional ovens. When using a fan oven, the temperature will probably need to be
reduced by about 10–20°C/20–40°F. Since ovens vary, you should check with your manufacturer's instruction book for guidance.
Medium (US large) eggs are used unless otherwise stated.

contents

Introduction

Party-giving should be enjoyable, and timely planning ensures that any event is as relaxed for the organizer as for the guests. The following chapters provide guidelines and reminders to ensure that the organizing is easy and the occasion successful. One of the aims of this book is to provide all the advice necessary to make the planning all part of the party fun and satisfying on both informal and formal occasions.

Getting started

The process of deciding on dates, times, venues and occasion style often starts the roller-coaster task of putting

Below *To create a sophisticated look, choose one colour for napkins and table linen, and mix different textures such as linen and organdie.*

Above *Pure linen napkins add style and elegance to any dining table.*

together once-in-a-lifetime gatherings. It can often be a stressful time when you are making decisions such as whether traditional ceremonies take precedence over a relaxed celebration or how to assemble different groups of family and friends. Side-stepping a

frantic start helps to avoid dips in enthusiasm later on. Often the initial problems are not as complicated as they appear. Enthusiasm and energy are the first requirements for overcoming any uncertainties, backed up by making useful lists such as key dates, numbers of guests, types of food and drink. It is important to do this before any celebration, large or small, in advance of getting down to the practicalities of invitation writing, room clearing, cooking and greeting.

Enlisting support

There is no point in playing the party hero and trying to juggle every last item alongside a normal busy life – it is far more sensible and fun to share the load and satisfaction with at least one helper, if not a team of supporters.

Hand-pick a reliable and hard-working friend who shares your aims, ethos and humour to join in the process – most people are flattered to be asked for their support, especially on important occasions. Then be thoughtful about who to add to the team. For children's parties, unless the occasion is a surprise, involve the child whose party it is and allow one special friend to be included in the pre-party organization.

Getting together a round-table of enthusiastic organizers is best avoided unless there are specific, separate tasks that are ideal for distributing among several contributors. Finally, there are times when coordinating a committee of people is an essential part of putting together a group event, such as for a club or school, and adopting the same approach to selecting one or two main helpers while ensuring everyone else is usefully involved is an excellent ploy.

Mix and match
If the occasion is so formal, such as a wedding or christening, or the approach so traditional that there is little room for changing the style and form, it is best to follow the rules of etiquette. For all parties adopt a sensible attitude to all numbers, catering, ambience and entertainment and use tried and tested approaches to ensure success.

Below Add atmosphere to a party with floating candles in a glass bowl.

When the occasion allows for flexibility, do not take yourself too seriously but aim for enjoyment rather than perfection. Mixing and matching can be an inspiring approach to party planning, especially for informal events. Adopt the "do it with a good will or not at all" approach and loosen up on the rules. Concentrate on the aspects you most enjoy. Those who are not keen on cooking for crowds often do best by selecting just one or two practical one-pot dishes and complementing them with well-chosen bought foods. There is plenty of advice on making the most of bought ingredients in the following chapters.

The same goes for party drinks: while all the experts may dictate offering chilled champagne or certain wines and liqueurs to go with individual courses during a meal, or an eclectic array of drinks, if you – or your budget – dictate otherwise, then do so with conviction and without apology. And if you expect guests to make a contribution by bringing a

Above Classic cocktail glasses will impress your guests at drinks parties.

bottle, do not be afraid to make the occasion a "bring a bottle party" by spelling it out on the party invitations.

Enjoy!
Great atmosphere is the most important feature of any party or celebration – and that does not mean ambience alone. Whether you are entertaining in a palace or on a building site, remember to do so with a genuine and warm welcome. Make your guests aware of the type, context and style of the party so that they all come suitably dressed and in the right frame of mind to enjoy themselves. Greet everyone and be sure to encourage them to mingle, making them feel relaxed, at home and with a certain responsibility to participate. At the end of the day, no matter how brilliant the tables, food and decorations, it is the people who make the party.

party
planning

Approach successful entertaining with a clear sense of occasion and a
few concise, practical lists. Once you know what you are doing,
involve others in the fun and share the planning with friends or family.

Grand Design or Simple Style?

A clear picture of the party style and size is the secret of success every time. Before planning venues, invitations, settings, entertainment and food and drink, decide on exactly the right type of party. Energy and enthusiasm are essential for getting things moving, but it is best to sort out guidelines within which to plan before ideas snowball and practicalities are forgotten in an initial wave of excitement.

There are established routines and etiquette for many occasions and utilizing these is often sensible. They range from formal dinner parties, society drinks gatherings or balls to weddings, anniversaries and seasonal gatherings. There are also just as many small or substantially large gatherings that are organized for no particular reason other than meeting up and socializing, for example overcoming winter blues, making the most of the summer sun or catching up with a group of friends.

Below *An attractive buffet table with plates and napkins piled high.*

Who's who?

Start with an outline guest plan: is this a gathering for six or sixty, under-fives or over-fifties, family or friends, best buddies or business associates? If you are inviting a complete mix of family, friends, colleagues and neighbours, a proper plan would be a sensible starting point. Identify the different types and ages; by fitting individuals into groups you will be sure to include something for everyone. This eases the role of host or hostess, which can involve looking after small groups or couples – or worse – individuals drifting about on the fringes of the party.

Time of day

The party may be to celebrate a marriage, baby naming or christening, or it may be a social event. It may not be a particularly jolly occasion, for example a post-funeral wake. Double-check arrangements that cannot be changed later, for example timings for ceremonies, photography or performances and estimated travelling time between event and party venue.

Above *Summer barbecues can be day or early evening social events.*

Consider the different ages of, or relationship between guests before fixing times. A two-phase celebration is popular for very different groups; it would typically comprise a formal meal, low-key lunch or early evening drinks party followed by a lively gathering later for younger guests or close friends. This solution works as well for informal occasions – a house warming, open house for a summer barbecue or an annual family gathering – as for weddings. Plan the transition between day and evening, and decide whether those invited to the first part of the party will also stay late.

Formal gatherings for early evening drinks preceding a late supper for a few friends or pre-lunch gatherings must be well orchestrated. Invitations should indicate the time when guests are expected to leave: "Pre-dinner drinks between 6 p.m. and 7.30 p.m." A verbal or informal note to join family or weekend guests for "a drink before lunch" should include the expected time of arrival and departure. Be clear to avoid any confusion.

Smarten up or dress down?

Once you know whom and when, make a decision on how you want your guests to dress and behave, and follow this through in invitations, food and entertainment. Be clear on invitations if you expect formal dress (white tie and ball gowns; black tie, tuxedo and evening wear; morning wear, or top hats and tails, and hats), lounge suits or smart daywear. You will not need to stipulate dress for an informal occasion. Indicate any special requirements, such as swimming things and towels for poolside parties, sun hats and picnic blankets to sit on, and sweaters or shawls for evenings outdoors.

Before and after

Guests may need accommodation for the night before and/or after the party. After a long journey, house guests will usually want to arrive early enough to freshen up. Include the preparation of guests' rooms in your plans and timings, remembering the little things that make people feel welcome and relaxed – flowers, magazines, drinks, biscuits (cookies) or chocolates, as well as towels, soap, shampoo and tissues. Keeping a few disposable, travel-size miniatures, or spare small toothbrushes, toothpaste, small packs of anti-perspirant and bottles of moisturizer in stock is a good idea for party guests who stay unexpectedly.

Pay attention to detail when entertaining youngsters, especially if they may be too shy to ask for forgotten essentials. For a special occasion sleepover you could prepare fun sleepover packs including novelty toothbrushes, fruit-flavoured toothpaste, wacky toiletries, expanding face cloths, reading material such as comics, mini torches, tasty midnight snacks and fruit, and small packs of drinks or bottles of water.

Above *Add romantic touches to a table dressed in white for a wedding.*

For large gatherings, check the local hotels and provide guests with details of price, location and availability when sending out invitations. Remember breakfast on the morning after the party and make flexible arrangements.

Party price

As each name is added to the guest list and every idea mulled and jotted bear in mind the cost. Decide on the type of party to suit the funds available, then work out a realistic budget in more detail before progressing from idea to plan. This is just as important for small, informal events as for once-in-a-lifetime occasions if you want to avoid overspending.

Sorting an outline budget at this stage is essential and easy: make a list of every aspect of the party, adding a realistic (generous rather than mean) cost and contacting suppliers to check special prices. For extravagant occasions involving hotels, venues, caterers, entertainers and so on, make specific enquiries at this first stage. Divide the costs into fixed amounts for the

occasion and variable prices that increase with the number of guests – refreshments in particular – remember that the venue size may change if the guest list grows too long. Spreading the cost by paying for some items, such as wine, spirits or beer, completely or partly in advance is one way of easing an overstretched budget, especially when planning a party at home.

Below *Simple snacks, drinks and bright decorations are good basics for a party.*

Have List, Will Organize

dinner parties and drinks parties are good Friday affairs, as are after-theatre or post-exhibition suppers.

Weekends are popular for group events for families and for activity club get-togethers or excursions. While weekend brunches are generally great for those without young children, Saturday brunch can also start family activities on a high note and the afternoon is a good choice for children's parties. If Saturday lunch is difficult for working hosts and guests who have to juggle family commitments, the evening is good

Lists are essential when planning for a special occasion. Suggesting that there should be a system for making them may sound like overkill, but even the most super-efficient lists can become so mottled with additions that they become uninterpretable. The answer is to have separate lists with different information. Using a computer or a spiral-bound notepad is brilliant for keeping lists on separate pages but together in one place. Jot the date on each page and include notes of discussions with suppliers, orders placed and ideas, as well as the guest list, special requirements, shopping and so on. Using this system, it is easy to flip through to check detail, and it is a good idea to flag significant pages you refer to frequently, such as the invitation list where you will tick or

Above *Make lists for organizing all aspects of party planning.*

cross off guests' names as replies come in. Start with a list of the usual requirements for different occasions and then personalize it to your style.

Which day?

Work functions are best from midweek onwards. Friday can be a good day for lunch or an evening party if partners are invited; Wednesday or Thursday are more convenient for "colleague only" events (especially if there will be a comparatively early finish).

Weekday dinner parties can be inconvenient, but midweek evenings can be a good choice for drinks gatherings or supper parties designed to end early. Relaxed and informal

Above *Champagne is generally served at weddings and formal occasions.*

Below *One-pot feasts, such as moussaka, are good for supper parties.*

for large and/or formal dinner parties. Saturday is popular for weddings, allowing time for guests to travel; Friday is ideal when the marriage is witnessed by a small number of relations and followed by a party for friends and associates.

Sunday lunch is extremely versatile: it allows plenty of time for preparation and is suitable for informal or smart arrangements for family, couples, singles or a mixture.

Parties and celebrations for clubs and classes are usually planned for the day and time when the meetings are normally held. Annual dinners tend to be organized for Friday or Saturday evenings, depending on the work commitments of members.

Scheduling an important celebration

Lists should include all the details, whereas a schedule will set dates and deadlines for the tasks. Draw up a master schedule of key dates, tasks and reminders with references back to the lists for details where necessary. Lists can then be updated as time passes.

A few months may be enough time for organizing simple weddings but one to two years is usually allowed

Above *A stylishly dressed table for a Thanksgiving celebration.*

for extravagant affairs. Timing often depends on the booking requirements of venues and officials; check these carefully. Find out about caterers, entertainment and transport, and check the availability of all related aspects before booking the main event.

Put dates to the lists and check that they are all possible. Then draw up the outline schedule – the master guide to sourcing, booking, confirming and checking every aspect of the celebration. Schedule key dates for everything. Adding minor aspects may seem picky, particularly when coping with a big party, but they can easily be forgotten later. Use a familiar means of layout, if possible, be that a year planner, kitchen calendar, chart on a noticeboard or computer program.

Scrutinize your schedule for bottlenecks and potential problems. If too many tasks coincide make alternative arrangements by moving jobs to different dates or delegate them to helpers. When you are happy that you have not missed anything, make sure the schedule looks neat, tidy and is easy to follow.

Schedule checks

Below are items to add to the schedule according to the needs of the occasion, placing each against a date when it has to be done.

Formalities: legal/paperwork requirements, booking all officials, confirmation
Venue: viewing, booking, and confirmation, checking facilities, preparation
Entertainment: booking, venue preparation/layout requirements, details of repertoire
Accommodation: source details
Caterers: references/assessing, booking, menu decisions and/or tasting session, confirmation of numbers, caterer's advance visit
Special catering: special diets, finalizing details of presentation
Food preparation: ordering, shopping, key dates for advance cooking, days for final preparation
Bar: delivery/collection of drinks and glasses, return of items
Professional help at home: gardening, cleaning, kitchen help (before or after), butler, waiting staff, bar staff
Flowers: booking, venue visit and design liaison
Guest list: invitations out, give a date for replies back
Gifts: buy, pack

Choosing a Venue

The occasion, type and size of party, budget, convenience and availability all influence the choice of venue.

Home options

Entertaining at home can be stylish if there is suitable space. While clearing furniture to the edges of one or two small rooms and letting everyone spill into the hall or lobby and kitchen may be fine for an informal party, it is not necessarily the answer for a special celebration. Unless there is ample floor and table space, plus kitchen facilities sufficient to cater for a sit-down meal, a buffet is most practical. When serving a fork buffet, remember that some guests may prefer to sit down to eat. When finger buffets or snacks are served, guests do not need so much space, especially if the refreshments are handed around.

Make use of outdoor areas and consider hiring an awning or marquee. Tables, chairs and barbecues can be arranged on firm areas; rugs and cushions can be laid on lawns. Be prepared for poor weather and consider erecting large umbrellas.

Below *With attention to detail, dressing a table at home can be very elegant.*

Hotels and restaurants

Select a venue by recommendation, reputation and personal experience if possible. Visit the restaurant for a meal to assess general quality and ambience. When comparing establishments, prepare a standard checklist and do not be embarrassed to make notes while you are there. The following are points to consider:

• How many guests can be catered for and in which room/bar. Check the maximum number of covers usually catered for; point out, if necessary, that you do not want their capabilities to be overstretched. Will a bar adjoining a function room be exclusively for the use of your party or will it also be open to the public? Check bar closing times.

Above *Put extra tables on patios and in courtyards for home entertaining.*

• What types of menus are offered and at what price per head? What is included in the price per head? Are children's portions provided at reduced cost (prudent when a wedding guest list includes many children)?
• Do the regular kitchen staff prepare special functions, or are outside caterers or temporary chefs employed?
• Check wine lists and bar prices. Ask whether you will be able to supply your own wine or champagne and what corkage charge is applied?
• Check arrangements for overseeing the smooth running of the occasion and whether a master of ceremonies

is available. Ask about the suitability of spaces for speeches or if amplification equipment is available.

• To check accommodation, assess the number and type of rooms, and price per room/person, with or without breakfast. Ask if favourable rates will be offered for a block booking.

• Does the business have existing links with entertainers? At what time in the evening must music end? Are there particular florists who know the hotel/restaurant? Similarly, there may be a useful link with photographers who are familiar with the setting.

• Is the venue easily accessible by car or rail? Is there ample parking?

Hired hall or rooms

Community, sports, arts, social and religious venues often have rooms for hire. Some may have links with caterers, entertainers and dressers to prepare the venue (and you may be obliged to use bar facilities or caterers);

Below Always visit hotel or restaurant venues to check the space and facilities before you book.

accommodation may even be provided in some clubs. Less expensive venues are economical for self-catering. Points to check include:

• Heating (is this included in the cost?).

• Lighting and how it can be adapted to improve the ambience.

• Kitchen facilities for food preparation and storage, heating and clearing up.

• Tables and chairs – check how many there are, the table sizes and make sure they provide enough space for the number of guests.

• Bar facilities and whether alcohol is allowed; entertainment permits.

• Cloakroom facilities.

• Cleaning and preparation of venue – will the space be clear and clean? How far in advance will you have access for setting out tables, decorating the space, laying out food? Clearing up afterwards – will this have to be completed on the evening or next day?

Marquee hire

This may be a practical solution to gaining all-weather space if you have a large, flat garden. Hire companies provide guidance on size, numbers

Above *Brighten up hired tables with table linen and ribbons.*

accommodated and access required for erection. Erected sample marquees or a portfolio of examples should be available. Check the lining is intact, the flooring is solid, and there is provision for power, heating and lighting.

Picnics

These may be informal and fun, or formal social occasions attached to sporting or entertainment events. Follow custom and etiquette for society occasions, such as the serving of stylish car-boot (-trunk) hampers, or candlelit picnics in a country-house garden. When obtaining tickets for events, check details of times and facilities, parking (and distance from picnic area), dress and conduct code.

Parties afloat

Boats range from floating restaurants and bars to those with facilities for extensive parties. Smaller vessels can be hired for small groups with or without professional staff, and entertaining up to a dozen friends with a champagne lunch or early supper is fun. Check that the company rigidly applies safety regulations – if in doubt seek advice from relevant local authorities. Inspect the vessel's facilities thoroughly. Check the duration and route of the trip and access and parking at or transport to the point of departure.

By Invitation Only

Common sense and consideration are vital for informal invitations while rules of etiquette apply to formal invitations. A note can sometimes follow informal verbal invitations or a telephone call of confirmation a couple of days in advance – typically when organizing dinner parties with friends. The timing for sending out informal invitations depends entirely on how busy and flexible everyone is.

Invitation information

It may seem like a statement of the obvious but it is surprisingly easy to miss details or to include incorrect or conflicting dates and days. Invitations need to include the following:
• Guest names, with correct titles.
• Host and/or hostess names.
• Occasion or reason for party.
• Venue.
• Day and date.
• Time: this may be approximate or precise. Before a formal meal, it is usual to indicate a period of about 30 minutes

Below Simple themes work best when making your own invitations.

The right time
• Breakfast may be arranged from early until mid-morning.
• Coffee mornings are usually scheduled for 11 a.m.
• Brunch can be planned for any time from mid-morning to early lunch, between usual breakfast and lunch times.
• Lunch is usually arranged at 12.30 p.m. or 1 p.m. but invitations may be for an early or late lunch.
• Afternoon tea invitations are often scheduled for 3 p.m. or slightly later. Children's tea usually follows the end of afternoon school, usually about 4 p.m.
• Supper is often early or late evening, indicating a light menu rather than dinner.

during which guests are expected (within the first 15 minutes). The time may include the expected duration of the gathering or a time when an evening will end – expressed as "carriages at …" on formal dinner invitations.

• Cocktails and drinks are served from 6 p.m. to 8 p.m.
• Dinner is usually served from 7.30 p.m. until 8.30 p.m., with invitations requesting the arrival of guests about 30 minutes beforehand for pre-dinner drinks.
• "At home" indicates a period of time during which guests may arrive and depart. This is informal and usually includes light nibbles and refreshments rather than a substantial or formal meal.
• "Open house" is the contemporary and particularly informal version of "At home", often extending from lunch (or mid-morning brunch) through to the evening and intended for a mix of families, friends and colleagues of all ages.

• RSVP (*répondez s'il vous plaît* – reply please), sometimes with a date, is a polite way of reminding guests that a reply is required.
• Address, telephone and other contact details for replying.
• Dress code and any other information: white tie indicating wing collars, white ties and tails for men, ball gowns for women; black tie and dinner jacket (tuxedo) is standard evening wear for men, when women may wear long or short dresses. Notes on a party theme or other special dress requirements should be included.

Formal invitations
Written requests for the company of guests at a notable occasion are sent at least a month in advance. This is typical of celebrations, such as weddings, when four to six weeks' notice is practical. (Key guests should be aware of the date well in advance.) Parties organized around public events may be arranged three to six months in advance.

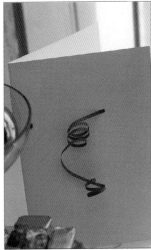

Above Stationery for formal occasions comes in many different styles.

Check the closing date for confirming numbers when booking a venue, confirm with suppliers and make sure invitations are sent out in good time in order for replies to be returned by the required date.

The right title

Addressing guests by an incorrect title may cause offence. Check with the households or offices of those in public or official roles. There are reference books detailing all contemporary and traditionally correct forms of address and greeting, including academic qualifications, religious orders and positions, military ranks, titled persons and those of any office requiring recognition. When in doubt about how acquaintances and relatives prefer to be addressed, check with them, if possible. Otherwise, close family or friends may be able to advise.

Traditionally, a married woman takes the name or initials of her husband when addressed singly or as a couple, for example Mr and Mrs John Smith, Mrs John Smith or Mrs J. Smith. However, some object to this,

preferring to use their first name, and women may retain their own family name after marriage, choosing the title Ms instead of Miss or Mrs. Addressing unmarried couples as "Mr and Mrs" is usually unacceptable to them and both names should be used.

Inventive invitations

Dress the message up according to the type of party. Concentrate on style and quality for all invitations, from heavy flat cards with fine lettering and discreet decorative edging to bright folded cards that may be fun but fall short of becoming garish.

When using professional designers and printers ask to see samples and prices per quantity and remember that selecting from their usual repertoire may be more convenient and more successful than asking them to create something different and complicated. Craft techniques, art skills or calligraphy can be used to make invitations and party stationery. Involve the children when preparing fun invitations for junior events.

A personal computer can be used to design and print stationery to professional standards. If the printer is not likely to deliver the required quality

Above Good quality paper and simple decorations make pretty invitations.

in terms of colour and graphics, ready-printed paper, cards and matching envelopes can be used as a base for plain black printing.

Finally, creative flair and technology are by no means essential, as ready-printed party stationery is available from quality stationers and general stores. Neat handwriting is all that is required to add individual details.

Below For formal occasions, take care to use the correct titles for guests.

Equipment and Materials Lists

Make lists of all equipment needed at the outset to be sure that everything is readily available, budgeted and scheduled. This applies when entertaining at home, particularly for self-catering. When caterers are commissioned they will usually source all equipment related to preparing and serving the food, often including tables and chairs. If you have particular ideas let them be known in advance.

Buying or hiring?

Hiring is often the only practical option for large celebrations. However, if you regularly entertain medium-size gatherings at home, it may be worth buying a basic kit. For example, good quality white china, plain glassware and dishwasher-safe standard cutlery are often available from factory outlets. Plain white flat sheets are an alternative to table linen and perfectly presentable when dressed up for the occasion. For informal, family and children's parties it is worth buying rigid plastic plates and

Above *Table linen, napkins and glassware can all be hired.*

dishes that can be stacked in the dishwasher rather than spending almost as much on disposable ware that will be used just once. Sort out stackable, covered, storage boxes at the same time so that "the kit" can be packed away afterwards for use next time.

Large items

Tables and chairs are usually included in the hire fee for halls. Check numbers and condition when booking, making sure that they all stand securely when opened. For parties at home, it is usually possible to utilize or borrow spare household or garden tables, but chairs can be more of a problem. Hiring folding or stacking plastic chairs may be the answer.

Remember protective floor coverings for pale or precious carpets, especially when planning an indoor-outdoor party with guests of all ages. Specialist non-slip coverings can be useful in hallways or over areas of carpet by the patio or French doors.

When planning a large barbecue party, consider hiring large gas or charcoal barbecues from caterers' suppliers. They will make cooking lots of food easier than coping on the minimum of space on the home barbecue. Outdoor gas heaters can also be hired.

Left *Plain white linen napkins can be decorated with fresh flowers.*

Below *Make sure the barbecue is large enough to cater for all your guests.*

Check availability of entertainment equipment, such as inflatable play centres or bouncy castles, when fixing the party date, to avoid disappointment. Ask if the equipment will be assembled or inflated on delivery or left for you to erect, in which case make sure the necessary tools are also provided.

Food preparation and serving equipment

Catering hire specialists provide everything from disposable items to starched table linen and napkins, china and cutlery and serving equipment, including folding tables and chairs. When making your lists, sort requirements by category and then check outstanding queries with the hire store. Count and check equipment when taking delivery to make sure that it is all clean, present and undamaged. If there is anything dirty, missing or damaged, let the company know immediately otherwise you may be held responsible and charged for the problem at the end of the hire period. Most of the following items can be easily hired:

Below *Check in advance that you have all the cooking equipment you need.*

Above *Champagne flutes, ice buckets and cruets can all be hired for parties.*

• Cooking pans, trays and dishes – make sure your oven and hobs (stovetop) are large enough for them.
• Coffee makers and water boilers.
• Serving bowls, trays and dishes – compare the cost of high-quality disposable items with hire charges.
• Table crockery – make a list from the menu, remembering cruets and sauceboats, if necessary, and cups, pots and spoons for coffee. Water jugs (pitchers) and glasses may be included with table crockery.
• Glassware may be hired or borrowed free of charge from wine suppliers or supermarkets – this may include spirit and beer glasses.
• Table linen, napkins and cutlery, plus serving cutlery.

All the trimmings

List all the decorative trimmings and finishing touches:
• Room decorations and streamers; garden decorations.
• Plants and/or decorations for patio and garden.
• Decorative indoor or outdoor lighting; candles or garden flares.
• Outdoor fireworks.

Above *Bright streamers and party hooters jazz up a birthday party table.*

• Table decorations, separated into fresh or silk flowers and others, such as coloured strings, confetti, candles, party poppers, whistles, bubbles, table crackers, indoor sparklers and other mini indoor fireworks.
• Balloons or balloon decorations.
• Guest gifts or children's goodie bags to take away and party-game prizes.
• Small cake boxes.

Below *Children love brightly coloured goodie bags to take home.*

Table Etiquette, Settings and Style

For formal occasions the host and hostess take their places at the ends of the table, with the most important male and female guests on their right (female to host, male to hostess). The remaining guests are seated in order of rank alternating male and female. When there is a master or top table, the most important guests take centre place. This arrangement is adopted for weddings, with the bride and groom in the middle, flanked by their parents and in-laws, with chief bridesmaid and best man at the ends.

Couples are usually seated opposite each other, the idea being that conversation flows around the table, not across it. When the numbers of men and women are equal, they are seated alternately around the table.

Above *Make sure there is ample elbow-room between each table setting.*

Below *Coloured modern cutlery mixed with elegant antique silver pieces.*

Seat people who are likely to have something in common next to each other. It is considerate to avoid pairing individuals whose opinions clash dramatically. When placing guests among several tables, try to achieve a compatible but interesting mix on each table. When there are children at formal occasions, it is sensible to put them on tables near the entrance, for easy cloakroom access. Guests with babies or small children may need space for prams or high chairs.

Make sure the writing on place cards is large enough to be legible by guests as they walk around the table. Display a seating plan on a board near the entrance to dining areas at large formal gatherings.

Formal table settings

The simple rule for formal settings is to lay cutlery for opening courses on the outside, starting from the right, and work in towards the plate.

• Use a large dinner plate to check the space for each setting and leave plenty of elbow-room between settings.

Above *Use traditional etiquette to avoid confusion: cutlery is placed on either side of the plates in order of courses.*

• Working from the right, lay the bread knife, soup spoon, fish knife or small side knife for the first course, large knife for the main course and dessert-spoon. Working in from the left, lay the fish fork or small fork for first course, fork for main course and dessert fork.

• For slightly less formal arrangements, the dessertspoon and fork may be laid across the top of the setting, spoon at the top (on the outside), with its handle to the right and fork below (on the inside), with its handle to the left.

• Cheese knives and tools, such as a lobster pick or escargot tongs, may be brought in with the appropriate course. The cheese knife may be laid across the top, below the dessertspoon and fork.

• Arrange glasses at the top right above the setting in the order in which they are used. Include a water goblet or glass, white and red wine glasses.

• Distribute serving cutlery, cruets and butter dishes evenly around the table.

Go for graphic lines and clean textures on table decorations, including any flowers and candles.

Base platters that remain in position under plates for first course and main course look attractive. They should be significantly larger than, and comfortably hold, the main-course plate so that it does not rattle. Glass, metal, wood or china in bold colours look especially dramatic under white or black plates. Match napkins to the base platter, arranging them on top as part of the setting.

Above *Chevrons are just one way of folding linen napkins.*

Below *Cutlery can be bound together to add interest to an empty bowl.*

Contemporary style

Flaunt convention to make a design statement. The civilized rule when exploring new table-laying territory is to be practical and avoid confusing diners or causing embarrassment. If the cutlery is not laid in conventional positions it should be clear for which course it is intended. Bread knives can be laid on side plates, cutlery for the first course can be laid on a base platter with a napkin or brought in with the food, leaving the main course cutlery on the table. For a stark effect leave the table bare, laying starched linen napkins at each place and bring out cutlery as courses are served.

Fun and lively

Strew the table with streamers and fun decorations in carefully coordinated colours. Bold flower petals and succulent leaves make a change from the usual floral decorations. Crystals, beads and glass baubles can be used to good effect in centrepieces or corner decorations. Use low or very tall candles to create pools of light. Make sure they do not block the view. Add crackers and indoor table fireworks for lively intervals between courses.

Below *Outdoor entertaining can be formal and stylish.*

Above *A wide selection of novelty items is available for children's parties.*

Mix and match

Ultimately, the best parties and meals are those where good food and entertaining company are shared in a relaxed atmosphere.

Mixing and matching food, table style and room setting can result in a wonderfully eclectic party. There is no reason why all the china, glassware, cutlery and linen should match; picking out one colour to use for decorations will transform a complete muddle of equipment into a lively style.

Presentation and Buffets

Reflect the style in atmosphere and presentation, from the first impression on entering the house to the lingering memories of an enjoyable party.

Formal sit-down meals

Give guests something to dress up for, balancing a sense of occasion and ceremony with a formal, but still pleasantly relaxed atmosphere.

• The home or hired venue should be sparkling clean, sweet smelling and attractive with flowers or appropriate decorations. Aim for understated sophistication. Every area that guests will notice must be pristine.

• The table is the centrepiece of the occasion, so devote time to planning it. Coordinate colour, shape and texture in decorations and presentation. Lay the table well in advance rather than as an afterthought. Lighting should be flattering, rather than bright, but never gloomy. Candlelight is perfect, so use candles around the room and set fairly low on the table or well above eye level of seated diners.

• The dining area should be pleasantly warm rather than uncomfortably hot. Be ready to reduce heating discreetly or provide ventilation as everyone warms

up over a meal, then to warm the room again later, if necessary.

• If possible, allow a beautiful table to be appreciated before everyone sits down. Leave the door to the prepared dining room open so that guests catch a tantalizing glimpse as they arrive. Allow time for seating guests at the table rather than rushing them.

Buffet basics

You can decorate the edge of a buffet table with flowers, garlands, bows or other trimmings. Table coverings and

Above *Highly decorative floral displays look good on buffets.*

edges can be flowing but they must not be so long that they become a hazard as people pass close by.

A fork buffet should include food that is easily eaten with just a fork. Plates should be arranged at one end of the table so that guests move along and help themselves. Displaying forks, napkins and any accompaniments on a small table slightly away from the end of the buffet will encourage guests to move away from the food. Buffet tables are often placed against a wall but moving the table into the room is better, encouraging guests to walk around and serve themselves without having to stretch over dishes.

If the buffet is self-service, all the food should be easy to serve with a spoon, tongs or slice using one hand. Try to arrange food in dishes of different heights, and display one or more large dishes as centrepieces.

Arrange food in a logical order rather than randomly on the table. Moving guests from main dishes on to

Left *A silver and white theme creates a sophisticated dining table.*

accompaniments is logical if the menu takes that form. Replenish or replace dishes as necessary.

When the food takes the form of a main course, rather than a collection of complementary dishes, the savouries are usually cleared away before sweet dishes are brought out. This can be awkward in large gatherings if some guests are ready for dessert before others have finished the main course, so setting out cheese and desserts on a separate table is better.

Fabulously simple

Instead of setting out one large buffet table, you can distribute dishes individually among several occasional tables, adding a stack of small plates, forks and paper or linen napkins in each case. This is a brilliant way of presenting an eclectic collection of dishes, each to be sampled and savoured on its own. Reflect the stylish approach by serving beautifully displayed food on plain white plates and keep decorative room trimmings uncluttered, just one step on from complete minimalism.

For this approach, the trick is to keep "waves" of prepared foods in reserve in the kitchen. Instead of laying them all out at once, replace empty platters as the food is consumed. Moving from one style of food to another is easy – rather like serving different courses of a meal – and it is a good idea to allow a palate-clearing pause between one variety and the next. For example, a range of marinated seafood may be followed

Above *Decorate a table for an autumnal (fall) lunch with fruits of the season.*

by a selection of roasted miniature vegetables and accompanying dips, and finally by the finest home-made chocolate truffles. Remember the rule: less is more.

Informal and fun

It is easy to lose a sense of style when casually decorating a home and displaying an informal buffet. Focus on a limited choice of fun decorations and controlled use of colour to avoid overdoing it with garish clutter.

Presenting just a small number of seriously delicious dishes or one or two types of the finest-quality ingredients is much more sophisticated than laying out an ill-matched mix of home-made and bought bits and pieces. For example, perfect seafood paella, a tureen of superlative soup and glorious platters of charcuterie and cheese will each make a fabulous meal when served with lots of fresh home-made bread and a herb-filled leafy salad.

Left *Bright table linen and plates complemented by colourful utensils add up to informal Mediterranean style.*

organizing your party food

Food with flair is the result of calm
forethought rather than frantic kitchen
activity. Take time out to consider all
options to avoid being overwhelmed by
choice when leafing through recipes or
shopping for ingredients.

Planning Points

last-minute cooking or heating to fit in the oven or for the top of the stove. Some recipes cooked at different temperatures cannot be adapted for cooking in the same oven. Also make sure you have enough crockery and cutlery for the menu.

• Food options are endless, so cost and capabilities are vital. When buying ready-made or commissioning caterers, be aware of prices before dreaming up a menu to blow the budget. When planning to cook, work within your capabilities; being adventurous is fun within reasonable limitations but beyond this it can become a problem. Enlist the help of others or combine bought and home-made to be practical when there is a lot to be done.

Money can evaporate when using expensive ingredients and it is easy to isolate a pricey shopping list and get carried away, forgetting that it all adds up with drinks and other party costs.

The easiest way to make sure a party is successful is by tailoring your requirements to a list of key points. Consider the following planning points:

• The occasion and type of meal are good starting points. Is the celebration formal or informal? Is it for adults or children, or both? Are you serving nibbles and finger food, a fork supper or a sit-down meal? A mixture of dishes can come together successfully as refreshment without fitting into accepted menu courses and this is true for seated eating as well as stand-up situations.

• Numbers and special requirements are important. Thinking up a menu that is over-ambitious to cook for a large number of guests can lead to disaster. An extravagant spread of many courses that is suitable for a dozen guests to sample in small quantities may be difficult to prepare and leave some guests embarrassed not to have done

Above *Lobster Thermidor and fillets of turbot with oysters are stylish dishes for special occasions.*

justice to the food. You should plan to accommodate special diets right from the beginning, for example, include vegetarian, vegan, or low-fat dishes on the menu. If guests have specific needs, such as gluten-free food, it is easier to plan suitable dishes as part of the main menu rather than preparing a set of alternatives at the last minute.

• Facilities should come high on the list of considerations. When finishing or serving food away from home, at a hired venue or a picnic for example, make sure that every dish can be transported, reheated or cooked at the venue as appropriate. Check the facilities available at the venue, if necessary. At home, the danger is overstretching facilities, so avoid planning too many dishes requiring

Match courses or dishes

For formal menus, plan courses that complement each other and balance substantial and light dishes. The same criteria apply to finger or fork buffets, but there is more flexibility when guests don't have to eat dishes in order.

Below *Tarts and quiches are popular choices for a buffet or brunch.*

Selecting recipes

Confident cooks who entertain often and enjoy providing culinary theatre for guests may opt for lots of last-minute cooking, especially when they have kitchen space to accommodate spectators. Otherwise it is sensible to plan the menu around cook-ahead dishes, with last-minute cooking limited according to ability and the occasion. Being with your guests at a dinner party is important, while doing whirling dervish impressions between stove and buffet table can be stressful for both partygoers and you. Consider the following points:

• Balance hot and cold dishes to minimize last-minute work. One or two hot dishes are usually sufficient for a formal, main-meal buffet.

Above *Cut the first slice of cakes so guests can then easily help themselves.*

• Go for recipes that are based on familiar techniques.

• Select dishes that are practical to serve as well as prepare.

• For stand-up buffets, avoid dishes that are difficult to eat with only a fork.

• When arranging a finger buffet, select foods that are bitesize or easy to handle and bite without being messy.

• Leafy salads fill plates and can be difficult to eat when standing up, so guests tend to take less from buffets. Serve dressings separately from salads

that are likely to wilt so that they can be added to taste when served; this prevents the salad from become soggy.

• Creamy salads and dishes that can be piled neatly on plates or in which ingredients cling together are popular.

Increasing quantities

Recipes that can be increased in quantity successfully include soups, casseroles, sauces for pasta and recipes for individual portions (such as a specific number of chicken portions).

• When increasing the volume of stews and casseroles by more than three times, re-assess the volume of liquid as the proportion can be reduced slightly.

• Pies with pre-cooked fillings and a lid can be made in larger portions and cooked in larger dishes without vastly increasing the cooking time.

• Baked pasta dishes (such as lasagne or cannelloni) are excellent candidates for cooking in quantity.

• It is easier to boil large quantities of pasta in separate batches than to try to overfill a pan. Undercook it very slightly, drain and rinse, then toss with a little olive oil and reheat briefly in a suitable covered dish in the microwave.

• When increasing quantities by more than double, do not multiply up the herbs, spices and garlic several times as they may become overpowering.

Above *Baked dishes, such as lasagne, are good choices for supper parties.*

• Accompanying sauces for hot dishes and dressings for salads do not have to be increased by as much as the main ingredients when increasing the recipe by more than two or three times.

Menu cards

Displaying a menu card is an excellent way of letting everyone know what they will be eating or identifying dishes on a buffet. Arrange several menus on a large buffet table and remember to identify those dishes that are suitable for vegetarians or special diets.

Below *Use bought or home-made menu cards to identify buffet dishes.*

Cooking Plans, Shopping and Storage

With the menu organized it is time to get down to practicalities and, yet again, making the right lists eases everything along.

Cooking plan

Make a list of all the cooking. It is a good idea to copy the recipes and keep them together in a plastic folder in the kitchen when preparing them.

Divide the list into those recipes to cook well in advance and freeze, adding notes on when to remove them from the freezer, with likely thawing time and any finishing touches or reheating time. Note down any seasonings or enriching ingredients that have to be added at the last minute and include this on the checklist of things to do.

List the dishes that have to be cooked just before the party, that is the day before or on the same day. Note any advance preparation next to each dish. For example, salad dressings can be made a day or two ahead and chilled; some salad ingredients can be trimmed or peeled and washed the day before, then chilled ready for use – spring onions (scallions), celery sticks and tomatoes are good examples.

When all the dishes are listed, with the days on which they have to be made, it is then easier to draw up a cooking plan. Order the recipes according to the day on which they have to be made, then go through this list to make sure it is all possible. If you have far too much work for any one day, check whether any can be made in advance. If you have chosen too many last-minute dishes, adjust the menu before embarking on a shopping spree.

On your cooking plan, list different items to be prepared separately – this way you are less likely to underestimate the work involved. As well as volume of work, make sure that you have enough containers, work surfaces and note the cooking appliance needed for each dish.

Shopping lists

Working from numbers and menu, check the recipes and increase the quantities if necessary. Then work out

Above *Use good quality meat cuts and poultry from the butcher's.*

Below *Keep fresh fish and shellfish chilled until ready to cook.*

your shopping list, checking store-cupboard (pantry) ingredients. Rather than having one mammoth list, divide it according to types of food, such as items that can be bought in advance and perishable last-minute purchases. Be sure to include any notes, reminders or alternatives on the lists to make shopping as efficient as possible.

Orders and deliveries

Scrutinize the list for items that should or can be ordered: meat cuts from a local butcher; fish to be prepared by the fishmonger; bread to be reserved at the supermarket or ordered from the baker and so on. Take full advantage of the delivery services offered by

Left *Local stores may deliver fresh fruit and vegetables to your door.*

Above *Use temporary containers as colourful ice buckets.*

Below *Thaw frozen items slowly and then keep them cool.*

Above *Some kinds of vegetables can be prepared and chopped in advance.*

supermarkets and organic produce that can be bought over the Internet. Do not be shy about asking for a delivery from local suppliers if you are placing an exceptionally large order.

Seek out mail-order suppliers for specialist or fine-quality ingredients. Virtually all foods are available by this method and it is a particularly good option for specialist items, such as excellent raw or baked hams or high-quality fish and shellfish.

Keeping cool and safe

Check refrigerator and freezer space well in advance. If you are cooking and freezing dishes ahead, make sure you have plenty of storage space. Sort and clean the refrigerator. Assess the amount of storage space you need and sort out practical options – a helpful neighbour

may have refrigerator space or, in cold weather, an unheated utility room or a suitable clean, dry outside area can be useful for less perishable items.

• Chill bottles of wine, beers and soft drinks (sodas) in a large, clean plastic bin or several buckets part-filled with water and ice.

• Use chiller boxes and ice packs when the refrigerator is full – borrow or buy these in advance.

• Make temporary chiller boxes by lining rigid plastic stacking boxes with double-thick, heavy bubble wrap and covering the bottom with ice packs or ice in sealed plastic bags. Place on the floor in a clean, safe and cool area to hold ingredients or less-delicate dishes. Cover the top with more ice packs to keep the cold in.

• Prioritize your refrigerator space for highly perishable food such as fish, meat, poultry and dairy products. Fish should be kept in the coldest section of the refrigerator.

• Cool cooked dishes as quickly as possible. Cover them securely and chill them promptly.

• Leave items to be served cold in the refrigerator until the last minute.

• Thaw frozen items properly, keeping them cool.

Coping with leftovers

There are inevitably leftovers after a large party. Being prepared for coping with them makes clearing up far easier. Buy plenty of large plastic bags and clear film (plastic wrap). Some foods, such as cheese, should be wrapped and chilled promptly. Transfer leftovers to suitably small containers, cover and chill. Leftover cooked vegetables or green salads can be transformed into delicious soup with a minimum of fuss.

Below *Wrap leftovers promptly after a meal and transfer to a refrigerator.*

Cook Ahead, Stay Calm

Meat and poultry sauces and casseroles

Hearty meat and game casseroles freeze well for 3–6 months. Poultry casseroles using portions do not have so good a texture as when they are freshly cooked, but diced poultry casseroles and sauces freeze well. Mushrooms and crisp vegetables are not so good after thawing as when freshly cooked. Add some finely diced vegetables for flavouring the casserole during the cooking, then add more sautéed vegetables when reheating for a good texture. Meat sauces with a fine texture or with minced (ground) meat – bolognese, chilli con carne – are successful when frozen and thawed.

Left *Stocks, sauces and casserole dishes can often be cooked ahead.*

It may be possible to cook the majority of a meal or buffet in advance, spreading the work load over a period of time. You will then have it all ready in the freezer, leaving accompaniments and side dishes for last-minute preparation. Select the right type of dishes for success. Try some of the following ideas, remembering that the freezer life depends on the ingredients used in the dishes more than the type of dish.

Soups

Smooth soups freeze well for up to three months. Do not add cream, yogurt, other dairy products or egg yolks before freezing. Reheat gently, then add the dairy ingredients before serving.

Pâtés

Smooth, rich pâtés freeze well for up to one month. They are best served sliced or scooped, as they can look slightly tired when served from the dishes in which they were frozen. Home-made pâtés and spreads (fish, poultry or meat) are excellent for topping canapés.

Above *Most soups and some types of sauces can be cooked in advance.*

Above *Make stocks and freeze in ice cube trays until ready to use.*

Above *Cook minced (ground) meat sauces in advance and freeze.*

Above *Make curry pastes and sauces ahead of schedule.*

Stuffings

Breadcrumb, meat or fruit stuffings can all be frozen up to 1 month ahead. Rice is not so good, as the grains soften and become slightly granular.

Sauces, gravies and dips

Reduced cooking juices and flour-thickened sauces and gravies freeze well for up to 3 months. However, those based on eggs and oils are not suitable, as they curdle. Finely chopped or puréed vegetable salsas are excellent freezer candidates. Home-made dips also freeze well – try avocado dips (guacamole), chickpeas and pulses (hummus), or roasted vegetables puréed with cream cheese. Light, mayonnaise-based dips do not freeze well as they tend to curdle.

Vegetable dishes

Although the majority should be freshly cooked, there are some useful dishes to freeze ahead. Creamy mashed potatoes and vegetable purées freeze well for up to 6 months – great for decorative gratin edges, pie toppings or reheated in the microwave and stirred before serving. (You will be amazed at how quickly fabulous mash disappears from a buffet – with butter, chopped fresh herbs and a little grated lemon rind mash is a delicious accompaniment and easy to eat.) Grated potato pancakes are also excellent: lay them out on a baking tray ready for rapid reheating and crisping in a hot oven. Firm vegetable terrines also freeze well for up to 1 month.

Pastries

Filled pastries should be frozen raw, then cooked at the last minute. Puff or filo pastries that are time-consuming to prepare but quick to cook are ideal. Buy chilled rather than frozen pastry. Brush shaped filo pastry with a little butter or olive oil (or a mixture) before

Above *Pipe mashed potato into scallop shells for Coquille St. Jacques.*

Above *Make samosas or small pastries in advance and freeze.*

freezing to prevent it from cracking. Cook small pastries from frozen. Large pastry items – pies, tarts and pastry-wrapped fish – should be frozen raw and thawed before cooking. They will keep well for 1–3 months, depending on the ingredients in the filling.

Cooked choux pastries, such as profiteroles, freeze well unfilled. Crisp the pastries very briefly in a hot oven when thawed, then cool and fill. If serving savoury buns hot, fill then reheat them; depending on the filling, they may be filled before freezing and, if small, reheated from frozen.

Batters and baked goods

Pancakes are versatile; interleave them with clear freezer film (plastic wrap), then pack in a freezer bag. They keep well for a few months and are delicious filled with savoury or sweet mixtures, and baked. Baked sponge cakes, meringues, muffins and breads also

Above *Fish cakes can be made in advance and frozen individually.*

Above *Brush small savouries with a little melted butter before freezing.*

freeze well. Protect delicate items by packing them in rigid containers. Fill elaborate cakes and desserts when they are part-thawed.

Ices

You can prepare iced desserts up to a week or two in advance, but any longer and they can become "icy" with ice crystals. Richer mixtures keep better than lighter recipes: cream-rich parfaits frozen in moulds are a good choice.

Safe thawing

Thaw cooked dishes overnight in the refrigerator or a cool place and reheat to their original temperature. This is important for meat and poultry sauces.
• Thaw frozen items to be served chilled (pâtés, sponge cakes, gâteaux) in the refrigerator for up to 24 hours. Transfer delicate items to serving platters while frozen, cover and thaw in the refrigerator.

Simple Presentation

Anticipation of good food is a very enjoyable part of the dining process, so creating a visual feast is as important as making food taste terrific. Getting the look just right for a smart dinner party is less daunting than creating a buffet that does not look messy or ridiculously over-elaborate. Achieving food that is easy to serve as well as appealing and delicious is the ultimate aim and it is not difficult.

Appetizing presentation
Here are a few simple rules for food presentation – they apply to individual or large portions, fork suppers, dinner parties or buffets:
• Drips and drizzles should be wiped off dishes, especially cooking dishes.
• One or more folded clean dishtowels can be wrapped around hot dishes.

Above *Line bread baskets with crisp linen napkins.*

Below *Present hot serving dishes wrapped in clean napkins.*

• The serving dish should be suitable for the food: neither too small nor too large, it should be deep enough to hold liquids without slopping, and large enough for items to be cut, scooped or spooned out without overflowing.
• Select dishes to complement the colour, shape and pattern of the food. Plain foods can be served on patterned crockery but fussy, bitty ingredients look best on plain designs or simple white crockery.

Appropriate garnishes
Any garnish should complement the food in style, flavour, texture, colour and shape. These finishing touches should enhance not mask the dish and they must not clash with the main ingredients.

Herb, vegetable and salad garnishes should complement the flavours of the dish or cooking style. For example, salad garnishes go well with pan-fried main courses and fairly dry baked dishes or pastries, but they are ghastly floating in a delicious hot sauce or

Above *Serve appropriate sauces and accompaniments with each dish.*

gravy, where they do nothing other than become limp and wreck the temperature, flavour and texture.

Crisp croûtons, puff pastry shapes (*fleuron*) and shreds or shapes of pancake or omelette are all excellent for introducing contrasting shapes and textures. Nuts, roasted seeds and crisp-fried noodles or pasta shapes contribute texture. Diced or coarsely shredded potatoes, carrots and beetroot (beet) can be deep-fried to make delicious garnishes.

Divine decorations
Some good-looking sweet dishes are best left to make their own perfect statements with perhaps little more than a dusting of icing (confectioners') sugar – fabulous fruit salads, creamy roulades, whirly meringues, sparkling jellies and feather-light baked soufflés, for example. Others will benefit from a little decoration.

Sweet decorations should complement the main dish in colour, texture, flavour, style and form. The decoration should not overpower or clash with the dessert in any way. Be aware that it is easy to overdo the decoration on desserts, so avoid a cheap-looking concoction.

Many desserts are inherently decorative – set or baked in moulds, using decorative ingredients, topped with swirled cream, or served with colourful fruit sauces. A minimalist hint at decoration is often all that is needed – a single strawberry leaf with a part-sliced fruit; a delicate cluster of perfect redcurrants; the smallest mound of chocolate curls; a simple dusting of dark (unsweetened) cocoa powder or a tiny sprinkling of golden-toasted flaked (sliced) almonds.

Elaborate piped decorations may not make a contemporary fashion statement but they can be lusciously alluring when applied with style. The fatal mistake is adding one swirl too many. Instead of using a decorative nozzle, try a plain one or use a medium-size spoon to apply cream and a fork to swirl it lightly.

Buffet sense

When adding finishing touches to buffet food, keep individual dishes simple, remembering that they will make a mosaic of colour and form when they are together on the buffet. Make the food look approachable and easy to serve when you expect guests to help themselves, otherwise you will find that elaborate or awkward-looking creations will be avoided by all but the most confident.

• So that food is easy to reach, stagger the arrangement of dishes and do not overfill the table. Instead, top up plates or dishes or remove and replace empty dishes occasionally.
• Do not overfill dishes or platters.

• When possible, present individual portions of food that are easier to serve and make them smaller than you would for a sit-down meal as diners usually prefer to sample a range of foods from a buffet than to take a full-size portion of one dish.
• Cut large items into small portions and remove the first piece, resting it on a serving spatula or laying it on the first guest's plate. This applies to items such as quiches, pies, pizzas and cakes.
• When serving whole hams, roasted poultry or large pieces of meat, the best solution is to present the whole item, then make a display of carving the first batch as an invitation to guests to eat. Encourage everyone to cut as much as they require, check occasionally and enlist the help of a friend to check that enough is carved.

Food centrepieces

Buffet tables will benefit from some form of centrepiece, which is usually a large main dish or an elaborate dessert. Alternatively, a fabulous display of fruit

Above *Stunning cakes and tortes make good buffet centrepieces.*

or a superb cheese board arranged on a raised stand, with splendid breads and crackers in a huge basket all look good towards the back of a buffet table. These form a focal point and backdrop, and are ready to bring forward when the main course has been consumed; they also help to keep the buffet looking neat, whole and appealing.

Below *Raised dishes or platters save space on a buffet table.*

Garnishing and Decorating

The possibilities are endless, and much creative use can be made of the main ingredients in the dish, presenting them with a slightly different twist. These classic, simple ideas are versatile, charming and effective.

Herbs

Sturdy sprigs sit well alongside main food, while fine, feathery sprigs can be placed on top. Tiny sprigs are best for small or delicate items.

• Chopped herbs bring fresh colour to soups, casseroles, sauces, rice, pasta and vegetables. As they also add flavour, they should be used with discretion. Neat lines of finely chopped herbs, applied from a large chef's knife, add dimension to large areas of pale and creamy mixtures.

• Fried parsley is delicious with fish and shellfish, and it brings crunchy texture to creamy sauced dishes. Wash and thoroughly dry small tender sprigs of curly parsley, then drop into hot deep oil and deep-fry for a few seconds until bright green and crisp. Drain well on kitchen paper.

Vegetables

Thinly sliced vegetables, such as red (bell) peppers, tomatoes, cucumber or carrots, can be overlapped in threes or arranged in groups.

• Julienne, or fine strips, look good in

Above *Cut four lengths of chives and use another chive to tie them together.*

neat little heaps or criss-cross rows. Root vegetables – carrots, beetroot (beet), potatoes or swede (rutabaga) – are good raw or cooked as appropriate. Other suitable vegetables include celery, courgettes (zucchini), fennel, peppers or cucumber.

• Fine dice of raw or cooked vegetables look good in rows or heaps. Adjacent rows of vegetables with contrasting colours look very smart.

• Ribbons pared using a vegetable peeler can be used raw or cooked, depending on the vegetables. Carrots and courgettes are ideal.

• Grated or shredded raw carrots, white radish or cooked beetroot look good heaped in tiny mounds or other neat arrangements.

• Decorative shapes can be cut from lightly cooked sliced root vegetables,

Above *Chopped fresh parsley sprinkled on savoury dishes is an effective garnish.*

sliced courgettes, blanched peppers, pared cucumber peel or the outer flesh and skin of quartered tomatoes. Use tiny aspic cutters or a small, very sharp knife.

Citrus shapes

Slices and wedges are very easy and effective. Wedges are easier to squeeze if the juice is required to sharpen the food. Slices – whole, halved or cut into sections – are useful for sweet dishes.

• Twists are fine slices with a single cut from centre to edge and the cut edges separated in opposite directions.

• Shreds of citrus rind can be cut using a cannelle knife (zester). Simmer them in boiling water until tender, and then drain. For sweet dishes, quickly roll the shreds in caster (superfine) sugar and set them aside on a board to dry.

Below *Bundles of herbs tied together can be used to garnish savoury dishes.*

Below *Chillies can be arranged as garnishes for hot and spicy dishes.*

Below *Cut vegetables into fine strips to add a splash of colour.*

Above *Cut small chillies with scissors or a sharp knife to make chilli flowers.*

Below *Make cucumber flowers by folding alternate cut slices inwards.*

Salad ingredients

A chiffonade of bright salad leaves makes an extremely fresh garnish. Roll one or two leaves together fairly tightly and use a sharp knife to cut the finest slices, then shake these out into shreds.

• Curls are highly decorative and slightly Asian. Shred spring onions (scallions), leaving the shreds attached at the root end. Pare short, thin, curly strips off carrots using a vegetable peeler. Cut fine julienne of celery. Place the prepared vegetables in a bowl of iced water and leave for at least 30 minutes, or until they curl.

• Tomatoes and red radishes can be decoratively cut to resemble flowers. Use a small, sharp, pointed knife and, starting at the base, make small "V"-shaped cuts with the points at the top. Make sure the flesh is still attached at

the wide base. Make another row of cuts around the base, and then continue making successive neat rows of cuts up to the top of the vegetable. Always curve the knife around the shape of the vegetable to keep the section of cut flesh evenly thin. Place in a bowl of iced water until the cuts open out to create a flower shape.

Vandyke is the name given to a zigzag cut used to divide radishes and tomatoes decoratively in half. Use a small, fine, pointed knife to make zigzag cuts around the middle, cutting in as far as the centre. Carefully pull the two halves apart. This technique is also useful for citrus fruit and apples; eating apples can be sprinkled with lemon juice and sugar and placed under a preheated grill (broiler) until the sugar turns golden and caramelizes.

Above *Individual twists of sliced lemon look good grouped together.*

Above *Tomato flowers are made by peeling back the skin of cut tomatoes.*

Breads

Croûtons, croûtes and croustades are all crisp and browned bread garnishes. Croûtons may be small, neat dice or hearty chunks; croûtes are thin or thick but fairly small slices served on the side or used as a base for serving main ingredients; croustades are small containers that can be filled with a variety of savoury mixtures.

Croûtons and croûtes are fried in a mixture of oil and butter. However, if the slices of bread are brushed with a little oil before being cut up they can be spread out on an ovenproof dish and baked until crisp and golden.

• To make croustades, cut thick slices of bread, then cut them into cubes or rounds and hollow these out neatly. Brush sparingly all over with a little oil and bake until crisp and golden.

Above *Brush croûtons with a little oil before baking.*

Above *Use a sharp knife to make ridges in avocados and then slice thinly.*

Pastries

Puff pastry shapes can be savoury or sweet: glaze savoury shapes with beaten egg before baking or brush sweet ones with a little egg white and sprinkle with sugar. Use aspic cutters or large biscuit (cookie) cutters to stamp out shapes.

• Filo pastry shreds are decorative, crisp and delicious with savoury or sweet dishes that have a soft texture. Roll up the pastry, then cut it into 1cm/½in wide slices. Shake these out on to a greased baking sheet and brush with a little oil before baking until golden. Dust with caster (superfine) sugar for sweet decorations.

The shreds can be sliced more finely and arranged in neat nests to be filled with savoury or sweet ingredients.

Pancakes

Thin crêpes or pancakes make excellent garnishes for clear soups and leafy green salads. To cut shreds, tightly roll up one or two pancakes and, using a sharp knife, slice them into very fine or thin slices, then shake them out. Alternatively, use aspic or biscuit cutters to stamp out shapes.

Below *Toasted coconut is a delicious decoration for many desserts.*

For sweet decorations, melt some unsalted (sweet) butter in a frying pan and cook the shreds or shapes, turning once or twice, for a few minutes, until crisp. Transfer to a board or plate and sprinkle with sugar.

Nuts, seeds and grains

Dry-fry nuts, seeds or grains in a heavy frying pan until they are just lightly browned. Stir them constantly so that they brown evenly. Remove from the pan immediately. Use the nuts, seeds or grains to garnish soups, salads (savoury or sweet) or creamy desserts.

• Lightly toast nuts on a piece of foil under a medium-hot grill (broiler), turning them frequently so that they brown evenly. Use to garnish soups, salads, vegetables or sauced dishes. They are also good on desserts, cakes and ices. For sugary nuts, lightly toast halved blanched almonds, then immediately toss them with sugar and transfer to a plate to cool.

• Praline is made by tossing lightly roasted nuts, usually almonds, in caramel. Toast blanched almonds or hazelnuts under a grill or in a heavy, dry pan. Make a caramel sauce and stir in the nuts, then pour the mixture on to an oiled baking sheet. Leave to cool completely and set. Crush the praline with a rolling pin and use to decorate creamy desserts, cakes or ices.

Jelly garnishes and decorations

Aspic is the savoury jelly used to glaze chilled cold dishes or make attractive garnishes. Available in packet form, for either fish or poultry, or made by adding dissolved gelatine to clarified fish or chicken stock, set the jelly in a thin layer in an oblong container. Use aspic cutters to stamp out tiny shapes or turn the jelly out on to a board and chop it neatly. Aspic can also be set on sliced black or stuffed green olives,

Above *Fresh seasonal fruits look stunning on this Genoese sponge cake.*

herb sprigs or tiny colourful vegetable shapes in ice cube trays.

• Fruit jelly, home-made or from a packet, can be set and cut into shapes or chopped as for aspic. It can also be set over pieces of fruit in ice cube trays.

Creamy finishes

Whipped cream can be swirled or piped over desserts using a decorative or plain nozzle. Small swirls make decorative edging while large and luscious whirls are good toppings for individual desserts. For a slightly looser feel, drop spoonfuls of cream on to the dessert and sprinkle with chopped nuts.

Below *Boston Banoffee pie decorated with piped whipped cream.*

Above *Iced Christmas torte with sugared leaves.*

Use double (heavy) or whipping cream. When whipping cream, make sure it is well chilled and use cold utensils, then whip it until it stands up in soft peaks – slightly softer than you need as it firms when piped or spooned. Swirled cream provides contrast and interest in savoury or sweet dishes, such as smooth soups and fruit or chocolate sauces. Trickle a little single (light) cream into the dish, then drag it slightly with a cocktail stick (toothpick).

Feathered cream is attractive in sauces. Drop small dots of cream into the sauce, then drag them with a cocktail stick into feather shapes.

Sugared decorations
These are effective as decorations on all sorts of sweet dishes. Select tiny bunches of currants, small whole fruit or edible flowers, such as rose petals, and small leaves from mint, scented geraniums or blackcurrants. Make sure the fruit or flowers are clean and dry.

Lightly whisk a little egg white and brush over the fruit or flowers, then dust generously with caster (superfine) sugar. Transfer to a wire rack and leave until crisp and dry.

Chocolate shapes
Melted plain (semisweet), milk or white chocolate can be used to make a variety of shapes. Melt the chocolate in a bowl

over a pan of hot, not boiling, water. Pour the chocolate on to a board covered with baking parchment, then spread it out evenly and thinly using a metal spatula. Leave to cool until just set but not brittle.

Use cutters to stamp out shapes, and use a ruler and sharp knife to cut geometric shapes. Use a large, sharp cook's knife to make chocolate caraque or long curls: hold the knife at an acute angle and scrape off the surface of the chocolate in large curls. Transfer each curl to a separate board and leave until they are firm. To make chocolate leaves, instead of pouring the chocolate on to a board, brush it over the back of washed and dried perfect rose leaves. Apply two or three coats, then set the leaves aside to dry. Ease the leaves away from the chocolate once it has set.

Ice bowls
An ice bowl makes a truly impressive serving dish for ice creams and sorbets (sherbets). Make the bowl well in advance and store it in the freezer. Fill it with scoops of ice cream a few hours before dinner, return to the freezer and dessert is ready to serve at once!

Below *Serve ice cream or sorbets (sherbets) in a spectacular ice bowl.*

Making an ice bowl

1 Select two bowls, one about 5cm/2in smaller than the other. Stand a few ice cubes in the bottom of the larger bowl and place the smaller bowl on top so that the rims of both bowls are level. Tape the bowls at intervals at the edge. Slide slices of fruit or flowers between the bowls and pour in cold water to fill the gap.

2 Freeze the bowls. Use a skewer to push the fruit or flowers down between the bowls if they float during freezing. To release the ice bowl, remove the tape and pour a little hot water into the small bowl and stand the bottom bowl in hot water. As soon as the ice bowl is released place it in the freezer.

party themes

Make the most of every party opportunity by focusing

on a particular approach. Whether the occasion

demands etiquette and sophistication or

relaxation of the rules, there are plenty of

options to consider. Once the style is set,

follow it through with enthusiasm.

Shaken and **Stirred:** the **Drinks Party**

Today's drinks party is a celebration of relaxed sophistication. From easy evenings with friends to an opportunity for semi-formal pre- or post-wedding congratulations, sharing drinks and nibbles is sociable. Plan carefully to make sure the occasion flows smoothly.

Setting the scene

Try the following checklist to help with straightforward drinks party planning. Make lists of all your ideas while you write shopping lists and notes on aspects to organize.

• Define the occasion precisely.
• Focus on the ambience.
• Decide on the type of drinks.
• Select the style of finger food.

Occasion

Drinks party invitations range from "stylishly casual" to "lounge suit and tie" – a balance of relaxed formality in varying proportions. Within this context, define your occasion before making precise plans. For example, a wedding may provide the opportunity for a gathering of friends who are not invited to the ceremony and main meal, or a celebration with colleagues

Below *Colourful drinks add to the thrill of the cocktail hour.*

and business clients, neighbours or other associates who are outside your immediate circle of personal friends.

Whatever the occasion, the number of guests and whether you intend inviting one or more groups of people are important. There is no reason why a drinks party should be connected to any particular event – this is precisely the sort of opportunity to catch up with old friends or meet and greet acquaintances. The party may be short – lunchtime or pre-dinner – or an open-ended evening. So there is plenty of scope for setting subtle differences in ambience once you have clear aims.

Drinks

Decide on the type of drinks: cocktails, champagne, wine or an open bar. Cocktails are classic pre-dinner drinks. Champagne is always acceptable and perfect when there is a special toast to raise. Red and white wines are a popular choice. Providing an open bar (that is, offering a selection of spirits and mixers, wine or beer) is the most difficult and expensive, but this can be successful for a limited number of guests, especially if you know them well. Always provide mineral water and a good selection of soft drinks (sodas) as alternatives to alcohol.

Food style

The food should fit the occasion, ambience and drinks. A plentiful supply of chunky and satisfying finger food is ideal for the sort of relaxed drinks party that drifts into late evening. Dainty canapés and cocktail nibbles are sufficient for a short pre-dinner party. Generous quantities of extra-special, stylish finger food go down well on special occasions. Among the myriad of food options, remember bread and cheese; hot fondues and dips; or international savouries, such as Japanese sushi or Spanish tapas.

Above *Arrange nibbles on platters so that guests can easily help themselves.*

Serving snacks

Distribute plates or bowls of snacks around side tables and surfaces (protect surfaces to avoid damage from spills). Offer nibbles as you mingle, or move them near groups of guests and encourage everyone to dip in. Take platters of hot canapés around or enlist the help of a friend or co-host.

Below *Hire a range of different cocktail glasses for an authentic touch.*

Above *Avocado-filled eggs make excellent little canapés.*

Right *A selection of canapés and light bites suitable for a drinks party.*

Planning finger food

For stylish refreshments, present a modest range of excellent items. Select a number of complementary types of food, including variety in colour, texture and flavour. The following examples show how to match crisp and smooth textures and different ingredients and dishes. Broaden the variety by including a range of sandwich, tart or pastry fillings or toppings. In addition to the main snacks, distribute bowls of good quality bought or even home-made nibbles, such as roasted nuts, pretzels, breadsticks and Chinese rice crackers.

• Mini open sandwiches, crisp short pastry tartlets, fruit and cheese savouries on sticks, and crudités with dips.

• Filo-wrapped savouries, bread-based canapés, filled salad vegetables, and smoked salmon and/or ham rolls.

• Bitesize pizza pieces, Spanish tortilla squares, miniature fish cakes, cheese or meat croquettes, and crudités.

• Miniature kebabs, fish goujons, dried fruit wrapped in prosciutto, walnuts sandwiched with cream cheese.

• Smoked salmon sandwiches, marinated mini-mozzarella cheese skewered with cherry tomatoes.

• Excellent chocolate truffles.

Making canapés

The trick to making impressive canapés without an army of experts is by adopting a conveyor-belt method.

Buy large square sandwich loaves of white, wholemeal (whole-wheat) or rye bread and leave them unwrapped at room temperature for a day. Trim off the crusts, and then cut each loaf lengthways into large, fairly thin slices. Spread with the chosen topping, such as a savoury butter, flavoured soft cheese, pâté or spread. For speed, use a topping that can be piped, rather than spread, such as soft cheese or creamy mixtures. The bases can be prepared to this stage a day ahead; cover with clear film (plastic wrap) and pack in a plastic bag. Cut into squares or fingers.

Arrange the canapés on serving platters and then add the garnishes. For efficiency, prepare a tray that can be added to the topped canapés quickly and easily.

Fuss-free options include: lumpfish roe, peeled cooked tiger prawns (jumbo shrimp), stuffed olives, pecan nut halves, halved cherry tomatoes, halved canned artichoke hearts or peeled and halved cucumber slices.

Portions

The amount guests will eat depends largely on the time of day and length of the party. The following is a rough guide to the number of bitesize canapés or snacks to prepare for comparatively formal occasions. It is as well to be aware that the more relaxed and lively the gathering, the more people are likely to eat.

• Allow 5 items per person as an appetizer with drinks before a meal.

• Allow 10–12 items per person for an early evening drinks party (assuming that guests will be going on to dinner elsewhere).

• Allow 12–14 items per person for evening refreshments following a late lunch party, wedding breakfast or reception. (Remember to increase this when inviting additional guests in the evening that have not shared the main meal.)

• Allow 14–16 small items per person for light lunchtime or supper refreshments.

at a time, keeping the rest of the pastry covered with clear film (plastic wrap) to prevent it from drying and cracking. Brush with a little melted butter or olive oil, or a mixture of both. Cut the sheet widthways into 7.5cm/3in wide strips.

For fingers, place a little full-flavoured filling across one end of a pastry strip. Fold the end and sides of the strip over, and then roll it up. To make triangles, place a little mound of filling in the middle of the strip about 4cm/1½in from the end. Fold the corner of the pastry and filling over into a triangle across one end, then continue folding the triangle of filling over along the length of the strip.

Perfect pastries

These can be prepared in advance; they are easy to eat, satisfying and versatile. Try the following tips for streamlined preparation:

Puff pastries: prepare three different full-flavoured, well-seasoned cooked fillings. For speedy preparation make squares, triangles and oblong shapes.

Brush the rolled-out pastry lightly with beaten egg before cutting it into 6cm/2½in squares. These can be paired to make square pastries or folded in half into triangles or oblongs. Use one filling for each shape and place a small mound in the appropriate place on

Above Little pastries, such as piroshki, are always popular party foods.

each square – centre slightly generous amounts for squares (leave an equal number blank for topping); in one corner for triangles; and to one side for oblongs. Top the squares and fold the others in half. Press the edges together and place on baking sheets. Brush with beaten egg and bake at 220°C/425°F/Gas 7 for 7–10 minutes, until well puffed and golden. Cool on wire racks.

Flaky filo savouries: filo pastry triangles or fingers are extremely easy and quick to make. Work on one sheet

Kebabs and cocktail-stick snacks

For party finger food, make kebabs and snacks on sticks that are super tasty and neat:

• Thread no more than three miniature items on mini-kebabs.

• Cook trays of marinated ingredients, such as chicken or beef, in advance, then cool and thread them on to mini wooden skewers. Reheat on ovenproof serving platters. Try cubes of chicken or gammon (cured ham), mini-meatballs, mini-sausages, slices of spicy sausage, squares of (bell) pepper, small pearl onions, halved baby aubergines (eggplant) or cherry tomatoes.

Below Flaky filo fingers are easy to make for large numbers.

Below Leek, saffron and mussel tartlets are tasty finger food.

Below Little cheese pies with raisins and pine nuts make great nibbles.

Filling ideas for pastries

- Mash a 50g/2oz can of sardines in olive oil with the oil from the can, 1 crushed garlic clove, 2 finely chopped spring onions (scallions), the grated rind of 1 lemon, a squeeze of lemon juice, salt and a pinch of chilli powder.
- Mix finely chopped or minced (ground) cooked ham with a little grated Pecorino cheese, a spoonful of wholegrain mustard and plenty of chopped fresh chives.
- Mix plenty of finely chopped sun-dried tomatoes, pine nuts, a few chopped raisins and a generous pinch of dried oregano into cream cheese.
- Mash feta cheese to fine breadcrumbs and mix with chopped spring onion, a little oregano and enough ricotta cheese to bind the mixture into a paste.
- Mix chopped, well-drained cooked spinach with chopped spring onion, 1 chopped garlic clove (optional), a little freshly grated Parmesan cheese and enough ricotta to make a firm paste. Season with salt, pepper and a little nutmeg.

- Make sure cocktail-stick (toothpick) bites are bitesize rather than too large to pop into the mouth in one go. (Biting savouries off sticks can mean that the piece left on the stick falls off.)
- Strips of tender foods that roll well are good spread with soft cheese or used as wrappers for firm ingredients. Roll smoked halibut or salmon, cured or cooked ham, salami, peeled roasted (bell) peppers or canned pimientos.
- Olives, melon balls, halved cooked baby new potatoes, small cubes of cucumber, pieces of dried fruit (prunes,

Above *Many supermarkets now sell good-quality prepared sushi.*

apricots or dates) and radishes are tasty wrapped in cooked or cured meat.

Simply stylish sushi

Not only is sushi delicious but it is also practical as it can be prepared ahead, arranged on platters, covered and chilled. Ideally, you should make the sushi a few hours in advance; however, it can be prepared the day before if more convenient. Keep it well wrapped to prevent the rice from hardening. Remove from the refrigerator about 30 minutes before serving.

- Rolled sushi: buy mini-sheets of toasted and seasoned nori seaweed to make cocktail-sized rolled sushi rice. Top with dressed cooked sushi rice and add two or three strips of ingredients such as cucumber, spring onion (scallion), cooked carrot or cooked dried shiitake mushrooms marinated in soy sauce and a little sherry. Roll up firmly and neatly. Wrap each roll in clear film (plastic wrap), twisting the ends firmly. Cut into small pieces before serving.

- Mini-moulded sushi: shape mini-sushi squares by pressing the dressed, cooked rice into ice cube trays. Place a small square of smoked salmon, smoked halibut, thin omelette or thinly sliced smoked or marinated tofu in the bottom of each ice cube compartment. Then press in the rice and top each one with another square of the same or a piece of nori. Unmould on to a board and top with a suitable garnish, such as lumpfish or other roe, quartered cucumber slices and/or pieces of pickled ginger. Serve the sushi with small bowls of wasabi or light soy dipping sauce.

Below *Butterfly prawn (shrimp) spiedini with chilli and raspberry dip.*

Fabulous Fork Food

Formal or casual, this type of food is fun to prepare, simple to serve and wonderfully effortless to eat. Make light of the planning by adopting a completely practical approach to this style of buffet instead of stretching it beyond its limits.

Menu options

The fork buffet menu may be for a two- or three-course meal, laid out in stages, or a series of complementary refreshments presented together. Display a menu to let guests know what to expect and to encourage self-service. Although the dishes must be complementary and marry well to form a meal if that is the intention, a party buffet is an occasional treat, so well-balanced nutritional value is not necessarily a priority.

Below *Cut large tarts into slices so that they are easy to eat with just a fork.*

When offering a first course, serve it from a separate side table before placing main dishes on the buffet to avoid any confusion over what should be eaten first. When serving a fairly small number – 10–20 guests – it may be easier to present the first course served on small plates, with suitable accompanying cutlery. These can be arranged on a side table or handed around from trays.

For a stylish main course, focus on one or two main dishes and add easy-to-eat main accompaniments, such as creamy mashed potatoes, rice, pasta or couscous. To avoid overflowing plates, limit the number of vegetable or salad accompaniments to one or two that really make the most of the main dish.

When serving a range of savoury refreshments rather than a traditionally well-balanced main course, select dishes that are contrasting rather than complementary. However, avoid

Above *Tomato and courgette timbale is a light dish and ideal fork food.*

clashing flavours as guests often sample a little of each dish instead of eating just one or two.

Desserts are most unlikely to be confused with the main course, so they can be arranged towards the back of the buffet table to be moved forward when the main dishes have been cleared away.

Cheese can be seen as an alternative to main dishes, so if you want it strictly as a separate course, set the cheese board and accompaniments on a side table away from the main buffet.

Practical fork food

There is nothing worse than doing battle with food that is difficult to eat while balancing a glass and trying to make conversation.

- Serve ingredients in small pieces or that can be broken easily with the side of a fork.
- Select foods and dishes that cling together well and are easily scooped up on a fork.
- While moist dishes are successful, excess thin sauce can be difficult to eat and will drip easily.
- Match dishes or ingredients with complementary sauces or dressings

Above *Stuffed vine leaves can be home-made or bought from the deli.*

rather than serving a main dish and accompaniments in different sauces that clash or are too runny.

Favourite foods

The following dishes are always popular and are easy to serve:
• Baked pasta, such as lasagne and cannelloni. Try fillings with seafood, poultry, vegetable or ricotta cheese as alternatives to meat.
• Dishes full of bitesize chunks in lightly thickened sauces – lamb or chicken curries, boeuf à la bourguignonne, beef casseroles, coq au vin made with boneless chunks of chicken, ratatouille.
• Comforting minced (ground) meat dishes – chilli con carne, moussaka and bitesize meatballs in tomato sauce.
• Moreish rice dishes, such as creamy risotto, slightly spicy kedgeree and rice

salad with a fine yet light, slightly creamy dressing.
• Creamy potato salad, fine-cut coleslaw, tomato and mozzarella salad made with halved cherry tomatoes.

Below *Savoury rice dishes are easily eaten with just a fork.*

Stylish options

Add one or two stylish variations to a fork supper. Try one of the following:
• Savoury moulds and creamy mousses, such as shellfish or vegetable terrines, fish mousses or eggs in aspic.
• Dressed salmon, coquille St. Jacques or other seafood gratins.
• International specialities such as a saffron risotto with shredded prosciutto and basil, seafood paella or a spicy Moroccan-style tagine.

Desserts

These are often overlooked for informal fork buffets: this is unfortunate because there are plenty of options. Individual pots or dishes are easy to eat but they do take up space. Large items that can be cut easily and big bowls that can be spooned out are practical.
• Fruit salads, mousses and fools.
• Filo pastries with soft cheese, nut, fruit or chocolate fillings.
• Superlative trifle, light-as-air meringues, luscious chocolate desserts.
• Miniature portions of desserts, such as cheesecake, individual cakes, bitesize shortcake or tiny fruit tarts.
• Chocolate truffles or mini-meringues.

Below *Fresh feta cheese, good quality olives and bread are excellent party fare.*

Dinner from the **Buffet**

Balance dinner-party formality with self-service simplicity by offering a traditional menu buffet style. This is an excellent way of sharing a special meal with a larger number of guests than you would normally want to invite to dinner. The ambience can be stylish, with attractively garnished food, elegant table settings and all the trimmings that make memorable celebrations, but without the need for close attention from host or hostess during the meal. A buffet is a good way to entertain whether in a hired room or in a marquee erected at home.

Table tips

Lay out a buffet table to one side of the dining room or in a separate area – this may be another adjacent room, hallway or dining area within the kitchen. Prepare a separate side table for dessert, if necessary, and have the cheese course set out ready for self-service or to be taken to the table when appropriate. Allow room for guests to walk past the buffet without disrupting others seated at the table. Plan the "flow" of guests, arranging food to encourage logical movement in one direction. Prepare a discreet table, trolley or area on which to deposit used plates from the first and main courses, remembering to include a suitable container to take cutlery.

Set the dining table or several different dining tables – a conservatory, hallway or patio can be used instead of, or as well as, the usual dining area. When preparing several tables, take care to arrange them so that they are linked without any one being isolated.

Select a cold first course that can be plated and placed on the tables before guests sit down. Have table heaters, if necessary, for hot main-course dishes, so that they can be arranged on the buffet before guests sit down to the appetizer.

Simple dishes guarantee success

The food does not have to be fork friendly – everyone will be sitting down to eat – but it should be approachable for self-service.

• A main course made up of individual portions looks neat and attractive, and

Below Make sure there are plenty of napkins on or near the buffet table.

Above Choose a selection of dishes that are suitable for self-service.

guests will not be intimidated by having to cut or carve. Individual pastries, fish steaks or rolled fillets, or chicken breast portions are typical.

• Casseroles made up of evenly cut ingredients are a good choice.

• Select dishes that can be kept hot successfully without spoiling. Sauced portions or wrapped ingredients that will not dry out easily are the best choices. Pan-fried or freshly grilled items that have to be served freshly cooked are best avoided.

• Instead of plain cooked vegetable accompaniments, select a gratin, purée, casserole or baked dish that will stay hot without spoiling.

• Bowls of refreshing complementary side salad can be placed on the dining table after the first course.

• Cold salsas, sauces or condiments for main dishes can be placed on the dining table.

• Platters of individual desserts look elegant and are easy to serve – try making individual versions of large recipes, such as little fruit tarts, mini cream cakes, meringue pairs, little choux pastries and individual mousses or moulded sweets.

Menu reminders
Remember the usual rules for creating good menus: go for complementary flavours, contrasting textures and appealing colours. In addition, when serving the food buffet-style consider the following ideas:
• Easy appetizers: arrange stylish portions of salads that will not wilt on individual plates at the table. Try marinated roasted vegetables and mini or cubed cheese; cured meats with olives, Parmesan flakes and crusty bread; little cheese or vegetable mousses with crisp savoury biscuits (crackers); home-made fish or meat pâté with tiny dinner rolls; smoked salmon marinated with chopped fresh dill and mustard in olive oil; or pickled herring with shredded cooked beetroot (beet) and horseradish.
• Simple-to-serve main dishes: cubed boneless chicken or turkey breast; venison, beef, lamb or pork all make delicious casseroles enriched with wine and spirits; or cook fillets of chicken, turkey, pheasant or duck in wine sauces reduced to a very thin glaze for coating. Cook boneless portions of fish, poultry or meat in filo or puff pastry, adding herb butter before wrapping. Game, poultry or vegetarian pies are suitable for formal and informal buffet meals, and whole cooked salmon is always popular.
• No-fuss accompaniments: simple leafy salads with dressings served on the side; creamy mashed potatoes flavoured with herbs, garlic, spring onions (scallions) and olives; roasted mixed vegetables dressed with citrus

Above *Whole meat roasts can be carved and served at the buffet.*

rind and herbs after cooking; vegetable gratins; or casseroles of Mediterranean vegetables, such as ratatouille.
• So to dessert: for an elegant statement, make a simple salad of two or three fruits with an intriguing hint of additional flavour – try mango and raspberry dressed with orange juice and a little honey; strawberry and papaya with a hint of lime rind and

Above *Home-made truffles make a wonderful finishing touch to any party.*

juice; chilled pears poached in cider with melon and chopped preserved stem ginger; or pineapple marinated with cardamom and sprinkled with coconut. Classic individual dishes, such as crème caramel or crème brûlée and meringue nests, are all good for a buffet.

Below *Contrasting colours and textures provide an appetizing display.*

Dinner Party Planner

Many dinner parties may be sheer fun, others sedate and some involve a sense of duty but all should be sociable and stylish. Achieving this last ultimate goal does mean putting in a some serious forethought and planning – but do not be daunted, entertaining is the most rewarding part of greeting and meeting. Ultimately, dinner parties should be enjoyable.

Style guide

Hitting the high point means making a few well-calculated plans:
• Scour the guest list for flaws to be sure of surrounding the table with people who will amuse each other (even if they don't entirely agree).
• Adopt a definite approach to ambience: relaxed businesslike, society smart, well-acquainted casual, lively and up-beat, socially sexy, friendly calm, or intimate.

Below *Herb-crusted rack of lamb is a great dinner party dish.*

Above *Home-made rolls add a special touch to a dinner party.*

• Plan the menu, table décor, room trimmings and lighting, background music, pre- and post-dinner nibbles and petits fours to fit in with the required ambience.
• Check out linen, crockery, cutlery and serving dishes in advance.
• Make sure cloakroom and other areas open to guests fit in with the ambience.

Above *Cappuccino soup of Puy lentils, lobster and tarragon.*

• Be sure to allow time for spring cleaning – or organize cleaners to do so for you – a few days beforehand and last-minute tidying up.

Menu impressions

Effortless catering is always the most impressive. As a guest, there is nothing worse than acting as spectator to the host's or hostess's insecurities and kitchen inadequacies. Keep it simple and do not attempt anything out of your league.
• Check guests' diets beforehand if you do not know them well – just call and ask if there is anything they do not eat.
• Plan a practical menu, with the majority of dishes ready in advance and requiring little last-minute attention.
• Buy the best ingredients you can afford and use simple methods.
• Use familiar recipes or try out new ones beforehand.

Planning and timing

From the menu, make a shopping list and then a list of "things to do" in the order in which they have to be done. Make sure you double check that you have included everything:
• Pre-dinner drinks and nibbles.
• Appetizer and bread.

- Fish or soup course.
- Sorbet (sherbet) to cleanse the palate.
- Main course.
- Vegetables and side salads.
- Dessert and biscuits (cookies).
- Cheese board and crackers.
- Coffee and chocolates or petits fours.
- Wine for each course, water and after-dinner drinks.

You may not want to include everything from this definitive list, but make a note of what has to be done and by when. If there is too much to do on the day or at the last minute, change some of the dishes to cook-ahead items or reduce the number of courses. Pre-plan shopping, cooking, serving and clearing up as you go along. Remember to allow time for relaxation and getting yourself in the mood well before guests arrive.

Quantity guide
The following is a rough guide when serving 4–8 people. The quantities vary according to the number of courses and type of dishes, but the amounts give some idea of the portions that "look" generous without being daunting. As numbers increase over about ten, the amounts per person

Below *Prosciutto with potato rémoulade uses fresh seasonal ingredients.*

tend to go down (except for individual items). You may well be preparing a multi-course menu with small portions for each course or you may know that guests have modest appetites.

When inviting people you do not know well, the solution is to opt for pre-portioned foods that you can count out per person and to prepare generous amounts of vegetables and salads rather than risk running out.

Appetizers, per portion:
- 250ml/8fl oz/1 cup soup.
- 75g/3oz shellfish or 115g/4oz prepared fish.
- 25g/1oz salad leaves (such as watercress or lettuce).

Main course:
- 175g/6oz prepared fish, 1 fish steak or 1 small whole fish per portion.
- 175–225g/6–8oz portion of poultry or meat or 1 modest poultry or game fillet per portion.
- 225g/8oz poultry, game or meat for casseroles per portion.
- 1 roast duck serves two to three.
- 1 roast pheasant serves two.
- 1 small game bird per portion.

Above *Medallions of venison with herbed horseradish dumplings.*

Accompaniments, per portion:
- 75g/3oz vegetables such as beans, peas, broccoli and carrots, or salad.
- 1 baked potato.
- 3–5 boiled new potatoes.
- 2–3 roast potatoes.
- 50g/2oz uncooked rice.
- 75–115g/3–4oz uncooked pasta.
- 2–3 thick slices of crusty white or wholemeal (whole-wheat) bread.

Below *Frozen Grand Marnier soufflés are wonderfully easy for a special dinner.*

Fondue Flair

Although the fondue drifts in and out of fashion, it is always enjoyable and definitely a hassle-free option for light-hearted social gatherings. Serving fondue involves the minimum of time-consuming cooking, provides entertaining dining and allows guests to participate in the cooking process and select and sample as much or as little as they wish.

Fondue style

The following styles of fondue are open to interpretation and variation to create a variety of different menus:
• Classic Swiss-style cheese fondue is fabulously creamy with crusty bread and crisp vegetables or fruit.
• Fondue Bourguignonne consists of cubes of lean tender steak cooked in a pot of hot oil, and then eaten with accompanying sauces. Poultry and other meats are also cooked this way.

Fondue etiquette

Long-handled forks with different coloured ends (for identification) are used to dip ingredients into the fondue pot. Forgetting the colour of your fork is greatly frowned upon, as is leaving ingredients to cook in the pot for too long. When someone drops a piece of food off the fork into the pot, they are traditionally expected to kiss the other diners of the opposite sex.

Above *Garlic croûtes make a change from the cubes of bread that are traditionally dipped into a Swiss cheese fondue.*

• Fondue Chinois is an interpretation of the Mongolian firepot method of cooking a mixture of raw ingredients in simmering broth. Seafood, marinated chicken, little Chinese-style dumplings (dim sum) and vegetables are lowered into the broth, and then scooped out in miniature baskets. The wonderful broth is the final treat of the meal, usually with added vegetables, noodles or other ingredients simmered briefly before it is served.
• Dessert fondues are sweet dips served with pieces of fruit, finger biscuits (cookies) or cake for dipping. Chocolate fondues can be dark (bitter-sweet) or luscious with white chocolate and cream. Warm, thick fruit fondues laced with liqueur are perfect with mini-sponge cakes or cubes of brioche.

Dip and dine

Cheese fondue is simple to make and effortless to eat. Depending on the ingredients and accompaniments, it fits well into the simplest or most sophisticated dinner party setting.

Buy good-quality crusty baguette early on the day or a day ahead, so that it is slightly stale, and cut it into bitesize chunks for dipping. Chunks of celery, fennel and apple also go well with cheese fondue. Firm, ripe cherry tomatoes and large juicy seedless grapes are easy to dip and delicious with a robust fondue.

Below *Croûtons make bitesize dippers, but slices of fresh bread are good too.*

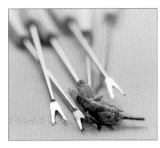

Above *Always use long-handled forks to cook your food.*

Any other accompaniments should be simple – a crisp, refreshing side salad of leaves and herb sprigs clears the palate perfectly. Little new potatoes drizzled with a hint of good olive or walnut oil and sprinkled with chives balance the rich cheese, as does a simple salad of tomato strewn with finely chopped red onion.

Fondue sets

Sets are available that incorporate a pot, stand, forks and a burner. Cheaper sets with just a rack and burner can also be bought, as can individual pots and pans, forks and skewers.

Cutlery

Dinner forks can be used for dipping food into a fondue. However, when cooking food in the fondue, forks with wooden handles are needed, as the metal of a fork or skewer will get hot when left in the fondue. Small wire baskets can be used to fish out food that has been deep-fried or cooked in stock. Chopsticks or wooden tongs are the authentic equipment for cooking sukiyaki and tempura. For dipping, food can also be speared onto skewers.

Simple cheese fondue

For the simplest cheese fondue, the basic proportions to serve four as a main course (with accompaniments) are 500g/1¼lb cheese to 250ml/ 8fl oz/1 cup wine. The finished fondue should have a creamy consistency.

For a fabulous fondue, gently heat 1 halved garlic clove, 1 thin slice of onion, 1 blade of mace and 1 large bay leaf in 150ml/¼ pint/⅔ cup dry or medium-dry white wine until just simmering. Cover and set aside for several hours or overnight. Finely grate 225g/8oz each of Gruyère and Emmenthal cheese and 25g/1oz fresh Parmesan. Place the cheeses in a large bowl and thoroughly but lightly mix in 30ml/2 tbsp plain (all-purpose) flour with a little freshly ground black pepper until the cheese is evenly coated. (Take care not to compact the grated cheese into clumps or it will not melt so easily.)

Strain the wine into a heavy fondue pan and heat until boiling. Reduce the heat to low, so that the wine is kept hot but off the boil, and immediately begin to stir in handfuls of floured cheese. After adding a couple of handfuls, let the cheese melt before adding more. Continue adding the cheese, melting it gently and stirring constantly. Finally, add 45ml/3 tbsp Kirsch and bring to the boil, stirring, until the fondue is smooth and slightly thickened. Add salt and ground black pepper, if required, plus a little freshly grated nutmeg. Transfer the pan to a spirit burner at the table and regulate the flame to keep the fondue hot but not boiling.

Alternative cheeses

Dolcelatte makes a creamy blue cheese fondue when used half and half with Gruyère. For blue cheese fondue that bites back, use Gorgonzola, Bleu d'Auvergne or Roquefort. Pep up blue cheese fondues with brandy instead of Kirsch.

• Other suitable cheeses include Beaufort, mozzarella, Edam, Fontina and Cheddar; try them for their subtle differences of taste and texture.

• For an economical choice, opt for mature (sharp) Cheddar and fruit cider. Add a generous spoon of wholegrain mustard and omit the Kirsch.

Below *Classic Swiss cheese fondue with baby vegetables.*

Fondue Bourguignonne

This dish demands the finest beef and perfect condiments. Complementary side salads and warm crusty bread are the traditional accompaniments. Bring the beef to life with an imaginative mixed green salad, such as lightly dressed fine green beans on a bed of peppery rocket (arugula) and sprinkled with shredded basil, or try finely shredded fennel, celery and (bell) peppers on a generous base of rocket, watercress or salad leaves. Baked potatoes topped with sour cream, or crisp new potatoes roasted in their skins also taste terrific with the beef.

The choice of condiments and sauces can set the style for fondue Bourguignonne: they can be simple to prepare, such as a sophisticated béarnaise sauce or mayonnaise flavoured with garlic, chopped herbs, mustard or tomato. Chutneys, relishes, gherkins, pickled dill cucumbers and finely chopped onion are often served, and barbecue sauce is sometimes

Below Spicy Moroccan meatballs with harissa dip.

offered. Slightly spicy fresh tomato salsa or herb-flavoured green salsa contribute a lighter feel.

Allow 175–225g/6–8oz good quality fillet or rump (round) steak per portion. Trim off all the fat and cut it into 2cm/¾in cubes. Arrange the steak on small individual plates. Individual bowls of condiments and sauces are a good idea or large bowls can be passed around the table. Whatever the choice, the accompaniments can be prepared and chilled in advance.

Heat oil in the fondue pan on the stove, and then place it on the spirit burner at the table to keep it hot for cooking the meat. Remind guests that their forks are hot and the cooked meat should be scraped off for eating.

Fondue Chinois

This is quite different and light. The quality of stock is vital, so make it with 450g/1lb lean pork, 1 chicken leg and thigh quarter, 1 quartered large onion, 4 spring onions (scallions), 2 slices of fresh root ginger, 2 garlic cloves, a few sprigs of fresh coriander (cilantro) and 1 lemon grass stalk or a strip of pared

Above Crunchy vegetables perfectly complement a savoury fondue.

lemon rind. Place in a large pan, cover with cold water and bring to the boil. Skim the stock, then reduce the heat and cover the pan. Leave the stock to simmer very gently for 1½ hours. Strain and season lightly.

To serve the broth: when all the ingredients have been cooked, taste the broth, which will be concentrated by this stage. Dilute the broth to taste with boiling water or adjust the seasoning and add some shredded spring onions and greens. Simmer the soup for a few minutes before ladling it into bowls.

Safety notes

- If oil is overheated it could burst into flames. If it catches light, carefully place a lid or a large plate over the top of the pan to cut off the air supply. Never pour water on to burning oil.
- Make sure that the food for dipping is dry, as wet food will cause the oil to spit.
- Protect your hands when moving a hot pan.
- Check that the fondue pot is secure on its stand on the table and that it cannot be knocked over accidentally.
- Never leave a lighted burner or candle unattended.

Above *Biscotti, small fruits and cakes are wonderful with sweet fondues.*

Right *Crab cakes cooked in oil with a chunky, spicy cucumber relish.*

Ingredients to cook
Prepare a selection of ingredients to cook in oil or stock – remember that dumplings for simmering can be bought from specialist stores. Try peeled raw tiger prawns (jumbo shrimp), scallops, cubes of chicken fillet or pork, pork meatballs flavoured with sesame, ginger and garlic, dim sum, tofu and

Below *Crème Anglaise with raspberry meringue and summer fruits.*

vegetables such as mustard greens or Chinese leaves (Chinese cabbage). The ingredients can be marinated with aromatics or seasonings, such as soy sauce, Chinese five-spice powder, ginger, spring onions (scallions) or garlic.

Dipping sauces and accompaniments
Whether plain or marinated, the cooked ingredients are dipped in a little sauce before they are eaten. Provide individual dishes of dipping sauce for each diner. A mixture of soy sauce and dry sherry, with a drop of sesame oil, a little finely shredded spring onion and finely chopped garlic is powerful and delicious. Plain soy sauce, hoisin sauce or plum sauce also make good dips.

Shredded vegetables, such as cucumber, spring onions and Chinese leaves, are refreshing accompaniments, and plain boiled or steamed rice will complete the meal.

Sweet fondues
• Some fruits, such as grapes and apples, are suitable for dipping into savoury as well as sweet fondues. Take advantage of fruits in season for sweet fondues: strawberries, cherries, plums, peaches, apricots and nectarines are all suitable, as well as exotic fruits, such as figs, pineapple, papaya, mangoes, star fruit and lychees. Fruits available all year, such as bananas and the citrus fruits, also dip well. Underripe fruit can be lightly poached in sugar syrup, fruit juice or a fruity wine.
• Cakes, biscuits and cookies: slices of dense-textured cake and sweet biscuits or cookies make excellent dippers for sweet fondues. Try Madeira cake, meringues, biscotti or Danish pastries.

Brunches and Lunches

Parties between mid-morning and mid-afternoon range from laid-back indulgence time to really lively and invigorating gatherings, and from sophisticated low-key relaxation to fun with friends.

Dining and sharing

Brunch or lunch is often closely linked to shared activities, such as family excursions, sport or shopping; they may be part of a weekend house party; or a follow-on with overnight dinner or party guests. Food should be inconspicuously successful rather than dominating on these occasions, which calls for well-planned and completely practical menus. Prepare ahead or serve the easiest cook-and-share dishes; creative deli shopping is the clever choice.

Cook-ahead options include large or individual quiches, such as classic quiche Lorraine; set omelettes, such as Italian-style frittata or Spanish tortilla that can be served hot or cold; and chunky soups. Sweet breads, muffins and fruit compotes or salads are all good cook-ahead items. Refresh baked goods briefly in the oven before serving. Cook-and-share dishes are ideal for kitchen gatherings, when

Below *Keep family and informal entertaining relaxed by using simple napery, crockery and cutlery.*

guests congregate to help cook and serve and then eat in an informal atmosphere. Pancakes or waffles are ideal for eating over a long, relaxed shared cooking session. Egg dishes, such as fluffy omelettes or scrambled eggs, are also good options for sociable cook-together brunches.

Self-assembly open sandwiches are ideal for kitchen lunches – just lay out all the prepared ingredients and breads for guests to help themselves. For relaxed success, have all breads, ingredients and accompaniments prepared and laid out in platters, bowls and baskets.

Creative deli shopping makes a superbly simple meal. For menu sense and stylish presentation, focus on one type of food or, for larger gatherings, keep different types of ingredients separate. Display a selection of different salami and cured raw meats, such as prosciutto and bresaola, on a large platter. Arrange cooked or smoked poultry and meat on another tray, and shellfish and smoked fish together. Present cheeses on a board. Garnish each platter lightly with herbs and wedges of citrus fruit. Provide olive oil for drizzling.

Include dried and fresh fruit, pickles and breads to complement the savoury platters. Croissants, bagels and mixed breads can be served with savoury as well as sweet foods; brioches, sweet breads and fruit buns go with fruit conserves, marmalade, honey or maple syrup. Sour cream or cream cheese go well with savoury or sweet ingredients, including smoked salmon or croissants with fruit conserve.

Summertime chill-out

Light foods are ideal for relaxed brunches or lunches in the sun. Offer warm crusty bread, light rye bread, mini-rolls, croissants or thinly sliced bread and butter as accompaniments.

Above *Fish chowders are excellent for winter lunches and brunches.*

Below *American pancakes with crisp bacon make a tasty brunch dish.*

Below *Chive scrambled eggs in brioches are the ultimate brunch treat.*

Above *Iced melon soup with mint sorbet is a refreshing summer dish.*

Include one, two or more courses, or just set out an array of foods in a cool kitchen for everyone to wander and sample as they please, such as:

• Chilled fruit soups, lively citrus sorbets (sherbets) or fresh fruit salads are stylish and refreshing. Alternatively, serve prepared exotic fruit, melons and berries on a bed of ice.

• Muesli (granola) ingredients are satisfying with fruit – oat, barley and rye flakes, nuts, seeds and dried fruit can be mixed or served in separate bowls. Offer honey, maple syrup, yogurt and milk as accompaniments.

• Offer grilled (broiled) seafood – lobster, large prawns (shrimp), scallops or oysters – dressed with butter and served with lemon.

• Summer dishes, such as dressed salmon, chicken salads or baked ham, are good cook-ahead main dishes.

• Asparagus or globe artichokes are a treat with melted butter and lemon.

Winter indulgence

Cold weather is the time for lingering over several courses.

• Serve warm compotes of dried fruit lightly spiced with cinnamon and cloves.

• Simmer porridge slowly, then serve it with brown sugar and extra cream.

• Opt for an indulgent cooked breakfast, with gloriously aromatic grilled bacon, sausages, kidneys, tomatoes and crisp fried bread. Fried potatoes or potato pancakes and poached or fried eggs are essential.

• Poached kippers or smoked haddock are delicious with poached eggs, and buttered, lightly cooked spinach.

• Serve pats of butter creamed with chopped parsley and grated lemon rind to dress plain cooked eggs – baked, poached or boiled. Creamy scrambled eggs are special when served with smoked salmon.

• Remember to round off winter breakfasts with warm fresh American muffins or toasted English muffins with butter and marmalade.

House-guest breakfasts and brunches

A take-it-or-leave-it kitchen buffet of fresh fruits, yogurt, cereals and warm breakfast breads provides an informal and successful start to the day. This can be extended to include sophisticated cold platters or cooked dishes.

• Wake-up trays of tea or coffee and biscuits or cookies in the bedroom provide welcome refreshment.

• Prepare cook-ahead dishes to avoid early morning work before guests rise.

• Set the breakfast table or prepare everything last thing the night before, after guests have retired, if possible, so that you can relax in the morning.

Lingering over a roast lunch

The great British tradition of Sunday roast lunch with all the trimmings is still comforting in cool weather. Start by serving a tray of little canapés or nibbles with pre-lunch drinks – offer small quantities of tiny smoked salmon sandwiches, salted nuts and pretzels. Serve a small portion of smooth, light soup as a first course.

Then cleanse the palate with a melon or citrus fruit cocktail or a small portion of sorbet (sherbet). For the main course, you could try the following traditional combinations:

• Rib of beef with Yorkshire pudding, roast and boiled potatoes, roast parsnips, buttered carrots, crisp, lightly cooked cabbage, rich port-reduced cooking jus, horseradish sauce and wholegrain mustard.

• Leg of lamb with new potatoes, baby carrots in tarragon butter, fine green beans, red-wine cooking jus, mint sauce and redcurrant jelly.

• Shoulder of pork with crisp crackling, roast potatoes, sage and onion stuffing, stir-fried red cabbage with raisins, creamy mashed swede (rutabaga), apple sauce and gravy.

• Chicken with parsley and thyme stuffing, salad or new potatoes roasted in their skins, roasted carrot wedges, crunchy broccoli, lightly cooked spinach and bread sauce.

• Desserts can be traditional favourites, such as fruit pies or crumbles and custard, or baked rice pudding with a poached fruit compote, or lighter alternatives, including crème caramel, fruit salad or a light mousse, chilled soufflé or creamy cheesecake.

Below *Succulent roast rib of beef cooked to perfection, served with horseradish, is a Sunday lunch treat.*

Children's Parties

Setting the scene for children's parties is enormous fun. Selecting a favourite character and using bought stationery and decorations is comparatively quick but it can be expensive. Picking an individual theme is more flexible and it can be based on anything from a popular figure to a favourite subject.

Below *Young guests will feel special with individual place name cards.*

Fun themes

The following are a few ideas to use as the basis for designing – or buying – invitations, goodie bags, decorations and games. They can be used as a theme for fancy dress or making masks, as well as on stationery and decorations. Draw simple images in bold black pen (or use a computer) and copy or print to make cut-out decorations to hang on the wall or stick on the corners of the table. Paint splashes of colour on the copies and add glitter. The birthday cake and novelty foods, such as cut-out cookies and sandwiches, should also match.
• Clowns – you could also hire a juggler to teach the young clowns.
• Pirates – a good theme for a treasure hunt; make sure everyone has a loot bag to take home.
• Witches and wizards – enlist a conjuror to add a little magic.

Above *A children's party is an ideal opportunity to create a bright table.*

• Dragons and monsters – friendly or fierce, hire a musician for musical participation and entertainment on the theme or set up a monster karaoke session.

Below *Sugar mice in bright colours will go down a treat with youngsters.*

Above *Decorate home-made letter cookies with pretty ribbon.*

Above *Bright plastic cups and plates are practical for children's parties.*

• Wild animals – a great theme for hiring a face-painting entertainers.
• Balloons – use the balloon theme for decoration and fancy dress, and hire a balloon modeller to keep the youngsters entertained.
• Puppet party – have a hand puppet-making party and hire a puppet show.
• Girls' makeover – for little girls or teenagers, put together fun make-up kits and demonstrate a few beauty tips or persuade a gifted friend to help.

For a simpler party, these themes would work equally well combined with traditional party games, such as musical statues, musical bumps, pass the parcel, pin the tail on the donkey, sardines and hunt the thimble.

Below *Make simple place cards from coloured card cut-outs.*

Table magic

Use disposable or wipe-clean table covers and disposable or shatterproof plates and tumblers with colourful drinking straws. Make a centrepiece of sweets (candies) or floating balloons. Decorate plain paper tablecloths with colourful cut-outs on the party theme, sticking them firmly in place. Keep decorations towards the middle of the table so that they do not get in the way and cause more spills than necessary. Secure the table cover in place with sticky tape or ties so that it cannot be pulled to one side.

It is better to have lots of small plates of food within easy reach than a few large platters. Follow with little dishes of ice cream. Try a neat pyramid of fun little cakes instead of a big cake.

Small sweets

Children love desserts, so opt for small portions of simple sweet dishes. Buy colourful dessert containers.
• Fruit set in jelly is still a winner, especially with ice cream. Canned fruit is easy and halved fresh strawberries or whole raspberries work well.
• Start ice cream sundaes in advance. Pile scoops of chocolate, strawberry and vanilla ice cream in dishes and keep them in the freezer.

Add spoonfuls of prepared fruit and drizzle with chocolate or strawberry flavour sauce just before serving. Top with a whirl of whipped cream and a little iced cookie or jellied sweet.
• For ice cream chocolates on sticks, use a melon scoop to make balls of ice cream, placing them on a tray to go back in the freezer. Stick a cocktail stick (toothpick) in each one and freeze until firm. Melt some chocolate, leave it to cool, then dip in the ice cream balls. Roll them in sugar strands or chopped nuts and return to the freezer. Stick the chocolates in a halved orange to serve.

Below *Individual cup cakes can replace a large birthday or celebration cake.*

Barbecue Entertaining

Above *Serve small snacks that guests can nibble while the food is cooking.*

Below *Chargrilled pineapple with pineapple and chilli granita.*

Achieving a relaxed atmosphere is the most important key to success for outdoor entertaining. The ultimate compliment guests can pay is being so at ease that they spontaneously become involved in cooking and serving at a barbecue. This *al fresco* impression of super-easy, impromptu entertaining is, in fact, usually the result of careful planning.

Barbecue food basics

The whole barbecue ambience is geared towards savouring the cooking process as well as the eating, so the menu should provide a relaxed first course that allows everyone to nibble while the main-course food items sizzle to perfection. For some occasions the idea of a main course of grilled food plus side dishes can be abandoned to a glorified sampling session. However, for the majority of occasions the following is a safe approach.

• An appetizer of dips, Italian-style antipasti or Greek-style meze works well. This may be finger food to nibble while standing around with drinks or trays of salads or marinated savouries to eat with bread at the table.

Above *Long, hot days herald the start of the barbecue season.*

• The main course can be grilled selected ingredients with planned accompaniments or a wider choice of "main" items and a range of side dishes. The latter can turn the whole barbecue into a relaxed and lengthy multi-course tasting session.
• It is a good idea to include fruit that can be grilled on the remains of the barbecue for dessert – bananas are terrific grilled in their skins and served with maple syrup and ice cream or cream; halved and stoned (pitted) peaches sprinkled with brown sugar and wrapped in foil can be cooked on the rack above dying embers; sliced fresh pineapple can be grilled on the barbecue or cooked in foil with rum and brown sugar; or marshmallows can be toasted on long forks.

Moreish morsels

Serve little dishes of the following to keep everyone happy while the barbecue heats and cooks the main course. Offer crusty bread and breadsticks with the savouries.

Below *Sweet romano peppers stuffed with mozzarella cheese and olives.*

Above *Grilled bananas and ice cream are a classic barbecue dessert.*

• Mix thinly sliced garlic and chopped black olives with chopped fresh oregano and olive oil as a marinade for cubes of feta or mozzarella cheese.
• Halve baby plum tomatoes and toss with a little sugar, chopped red onion and plenty of chopped fresh mint. Drizzle with walnut oil.
• Buy plain canned rice-stuffed vine (grape) leaves and cut each one in half. Heat a crushed garlic clove with some dry white wine, plenty of olive oil, 2–4 bay leaves, a handful of pine nuts and a few fresh sage leaves. Bring to the boil, then remove from the heat and leave to cool before pouring over the halved stuffed vine leaves. Cover and chill for several hours or overnight. Sprinkle with chopped fresh parsley and grated lemon rind before serving.
• Roast a mixture of pickling (pearl) onions, baby carrots, turnips, radishes and chunks of red (bell) pepper in olive oil in the oven until tender. Transfer to a serving dish, sprinkle with a dressing made from lemon juice, sugar, seasoning, a little mustard, capers and olive oil. Leave to cool and serve sprinkled with shredded fresh basil.
• Heat a few bay leaves and a handful of fennel seeds in olive oil in a large pan. Add button (white) or closed-cap mushrooms and season lightly.

Cover and cook, stirring often, until the mushrooms have given up their liquid and are greatly reduced in size. Uncover and continue cooking until the liquor has evaporated, stirring occasionally. The mushrooms should be virtually dry and just beginning to sizzle in the remains of the olive oil. Transfer to a serving dish and drizzle with more olive oil. Leave to cool, then sprinkle with chopped parsley, a little chopped garlic and grated lemon rind. Serve with lemon wedges.

Bastes and glazes

Marinating is not essential but food should be brushed with oil, butter or another basting mixture to prevent it from drying out during grilling. The following can be brushed on foods during and after cooking.
• Olive oil flavoured with herbs, garlic, citrus rind or chillies.
• Dijon or wholegrain mustard diluted to a thin paste with sunflower or olive oil and sweetened with a little sugar.
• Equal quantities of tomato ketchup and wholegrain mustard mixed and thinned with a little sunflower oil.
• Sunflower oil flavoured and sweetened with clear honey and lemon or orange juice for a sharp contrast.
• A little tahini (sesame seed paste) stirred into natural (plain) yogurt

Above *Serve a selection of side dishes to accompany the cooked food.*

with a crushed garlic clove and finely chopped spring onion (scallion).
• Tomato purée (paste), a good pinch of sugar and a crushed garlic clove stirred into olive oil.
• The grated rind and juice of 1 lime mixed with natural yogurt with a pinch of dried red chillies, chopped fresh root ginger and chopped spring onion.

Below *Tongs are invaluable for turning and moving food over the hot coals.*

Marinating food

The point of marinating is to add flavour and moisten the food before grilling. Marinating also helps to tenderize meat. As a guide, a good marinade includes ingredients to keep the food moist during cooking – typically oil mixed with other liquid – aromatics and seasoning. Salt encourages moisture to seep from the food during marinating, so it is best to salt the food after marinating and just before grilling or part way through the cooking time.

• Always cool a hot marinade before pouring it over the food.

Grilling times

Cooking times are influenced by many factors, including the type of barbecue, heat of the coals, closeness of the cooking rack to the coals and thickness of food. All poultry, pork, sausages and burgers should be thoroughly cooked through. The following is a guide:

Total cooking time (turn items halfway through):
Fish steaks: 6–10 minutes
Small whole fish (sardines or small mackerel): 5–7 minutes
Large prawns (shrimp) in shells: 6–8 minutes
Chicken quarters: 30–35 minutes
Chicken drumsticks: 25–30 minutes
Boneless chicken or turkey breast portion: 10–15 minutes
Beef steaks (about 2.5cm/1in thick): 5–12 minutes (depending on required extent of cooking)
Burgers: 6–8 minutes
Lamb chops: 10–15 minutes
Pork chops: 15–18 minutes
Sausages: 8–10 minutes
Halved and seeded (bell) peppers: 5–8 minutes

• Keep food covered and cool during marinating – in the refrigerator if it is left for any more than an hour.
• Drain the food well before cooking and heat the marinade to boiling point in a small pan. Use this for basting food during cooking, then bring any leftover marinade to the boil and use it to glaze the food before serving. (Do not serve any remaining marinade from fish, meat or poultry without first boiling it as it will contain bacteria from the uncooked ingredients.)

Simple marinades

Lemon, thyme and caper marinade: for fish, shellfish, poultry, gammon (cured ham) or game. Gently heat several sprigs of thyme in a little olive oil until they are just beginning to sizzle, then remove from the heat and add the grated rind and juice of 1 lemon. Whisk in freshly ground black pepper and some more oil, so that there is about twice the quantity of oil to lemon juice. Add 15ml/1 tbsp chopped capers and whisk well.
Orange, garlic and red wine marinade: this is good for all meats, game and red or green (bell) peppers. Peel a whole head of garlic and place the cloves in a small pan. Add 2 bay

Above *Fish brochettes with lime, lemon, garlic and olive oil marinade.*

leaves and 60ml/4 tbsp olive oil and cook gently for 5 minutes, stirring occasionally. Add the grated rind and juice of 1 orange, 5ml/1 tsp sugar, freshly ground black pepper and 300ml/½ pint/1¼ cups robust red wine. Bring to the boil and cook for about a minute, then remove from the heat and leave to cool before pouring over the ingredients to be marinated.
Mustard and rosemary marinade: a versatile marinade for oily fish, especially mackerel, and for poultry,

Below *Brush fish or meat frequently with a marinade during cooking to keep it moist.*

Above Home-made beef or lamb
burgers are popular dishes.

meat, peppers, onions or mushrooms.
Whisk 30ml/2 tbsp wholegrain mustard
with 60ml/4 tbsp olive oil, 5ml/1 tsp
sugar and black pepper to taste. Gently
heat 250ml/8fl oz/1 cup dry white
wine or dry (hard) cider with 3–4 fresh
rosemary sprigs until boiling. Whisk
into the mustard mixture and leave to
cool before using.

Shortcuts for success

• Chicken pieces, such as quarters and
drumsticks, require lengthy cooking.
For safety and speed when entertaining
a crowd, pre-cook the portions in a
covered roasting pan in the oven until
just cooked but not well browned. Pour
over a marinade or add seasoning.
Cool and chill. Brown and thoroughly
reheat the chicken on the barbecue.
• Potatoes take up lots of space, so
pre-bake them in the oven until tender,
then brush with oil and finish on the
barbecue for crisp, well-flavoured skins.
• Boil small new potatoes in their skins
until just tender, then toss with olive
oil, a pinch of sugar, seasoning and a
little mustard. Thread on metal skewers
and grill until crisp and well browned.
• Grated potato pancakes are terrific
on the barbecue. Make them in
advance, cooking them until they are
set but only very lightly browned. Cool,
cover and chill. Grill on the barbecue
until crisp and well browned.

Vegetarian barbecues

When cooking a mixed barbecue,
organize a separate cooking area for
vegetarian foods.
• Vegetables for marinating and grilling
include halved and seeded peppers;
slices or wedges of aubergine
(eggplant); whole mushrooms; halved
small beetroot (beet); par-boiled
carrots; slices of butternut squash;
halved courgettes (zucchini); blanched
asparagus; and blanched fennel.
• For easy vegetable burgers, mix
cooked and mashed carrots and
potatoes, finely shredded white
cabbage, chopped spring onions
(scallions), finely chopped celery and
chopped red pepper. Season, flavour
with crushed garlic and shredded basil,
then add enough fresh wholemeal
(whole-wheat) breadcrumbs to bind
the mixture firmly. Shape into burgers
and brush with oil before grilling.
• Grill halved peppers, cut sides down,
remove them and fill with chopped
fresh tomato, garlic and finely
chopped fresh oregano, then grill, skin
sides down, until well browned and
tender. Serve topped with thin shavings
of Parmesan cheese.

Food safety

• Keep food chilled until just
before cooking.
• When serving food outside or
keeping it ready for cooking, shade
the table from the sun and cover
food to keep insects off.
• Keep separate utensils for
removing cooked fish, meat or
poultry from the grill so as not to
contaminate them with juices from
raw or part-cooked items.
• Grill poultry and meat, and their
products, high above the coals,
or over medium heat, so that they
cook through before becoming
too brown outside.

• Marinate firm tofu with garlic and
herbs in oil, then wrap in vine leaves
and brush with oil for grilling.
• Marinate slices of firm halloumi
cheese in olive oil with garlic and herbs,
then grill until crisp and golden on both
sides. Serve immediately.

Below Lobsters are excellent barbecue
food. Serve with good mayonnaise.

Packing up a **Picnic**

Above A day beside the sea is an ideal opportunity for a summer picnic.

Individual adult hampers can be just as exciting and inventive as children's versions, especially when stylishly packed in extra-large linen napkins and tied into neat bundles. Try out a sample bundle, checking the amount and type of food it will hold and the number that can be stored in an insulated bag. Bundle contents can include portions of tasty cheese and charcuterie; small seeded rolls or baguettes, a small bowl of salad or marinated baby vegetables; and a little pot of condiment, salsa or dip. Individual bottles of champagne or wine can be included for a special touch.

Plan all the practical aspects of packing, transporting and consuming a picnic on separate lists compiled from menu requirements alongside the choice of food.

Picnic baskets are attractive and, while they are not the most practical choice for transporting food and equipment on large or informal family picnics, they are stylish for carrying china, cutlery and glassware for grand picnic meals. Lightweight crates that fit neatly into the storage area of a car are ideal for holding equipment. Wrap dishtowels and table linen around and between fragile items. Rigid plastic or disposable dishes, plastic cutlery and drinking containers can be stacked without fear of damage. Open baskets are light to carry and useful for bread.

Insulated bags keep food cool and in good condition. Soft bags are easy to carry and insulated backpacks are particularly practical when packing modest picnics. Although more awkward to carry, rigid chiller boxes protect delicate foods and bottles from damage as well as keeping food cool. Sort out or buy storage containers that stack neatly in chiller boxes to avoid tedious searching and shuffling when assembling the prepared picnic.

Hi-tech storage boxes (designed for camping expeditions) can be plugged into the electrical supply of a car to act as a mini-refrigerator or as a modest oven for reheating food.

Relaxing in comfort

Folding chairs and tables may be *de rigueur* for flamboyant evening picnics, but they are also comfortable for relaxed and informal meals. Proper chairs are far better than tiny, uncomfortable stools.

Rugs and cushions are a good choice. Damp-proof groundsheets or rugs with plastic backing are ideal. Pack umbrellas, sunshades and spare sun hats. Remember insect-repellent and storm candles.

Individual hampers

Children and adults alike love personal food packs and they are easy to prepare, distribute and eat. Colourful boxes that stack in a chiller bag can be filled with a selection of fun food packs. Drink packs can be packed separately and snack bags can contain fruit for a sweet course.

Above Filled baguettes, fruit and snacks form the basics of a tasty picnic.

Below Individual picnic packs are especially popular with children.

Above *A wicker basket is practical when transporting bottles of wine.*

Safe carrying

Wicker baskets are good for carrying cutlery, crockery, loaves of bread, crackers, biscuits (cookies) and cakes. Perishable foods that deteriorate in quality should be carried on chiller packs in insulated bags. Lightweight insulated bags and insulated boxes are practical for out-and-about snacks. Stacking rings that are used to separate plates of food for microwave heating are useful for stacking plated items in a chiller box. Sturdy foods in plastic containers are easier to transport and more successful than delicate items with the potential for disaster.

Supermarket dash

Simple or special, it is easy to buy a complete picnic menu from a good supermarket or deli without having to compromise on quality. There is more to discover than the usual baguettes, cheese and fruit, so try adding some of the following to the shopping list:
• Breads: select interesting breads, wraps or flour tortillas for scooping up or holding salads, cooked meats or cheese. Try bagels, Italian-style crusty breads or ciabatta, rye breads, naan, mini pitta breads, chappatis, pancakes or crêpes.

Buy a full-flavoured extra virgin olive oil, walnut, macadamia or pumpkin seed oil to go with breads or rolls. Pour a little oil on to saucers and serve chunks of bread to mop it up.
• Salads and vegetables: select washed, ready-to-eat produce that does not have to be cut up but can simply be emptied into bowls and eaten by the sprig without cutlery or as crudités with sour cream, garlic and herb soft cheese, soft goat's cheese or garlic mayonnaise. Among the leaves try watercress, rocket (arugula) and lamb's lettuce; and select from cherry tomatoes or baby plum tomatoes, trimmed sugar snap peas or mangetouts (snow peas), cauliflower and broccoli florets, baby carrots, baby corn or radishes. Washed parsley, coriander (cilantro) leaves, fennel and basil are also brilliant.

Plain cooked beetroot (beet), vacuum packed without vinegar, is excellent drizzled with walnut oil and sprinkled with ground black pepper; it is also irresistible with soft goat's cheese or mascarpone and a trickle of raspberry vinegar. Canned artichoke hearts are good drained.
• From the deli: smoked salmon or mackerel, pickled herring (packed in oil if possible) and peeled, cooked prawns (shrimp) are versatile with sour cream and lemon wedges. Cured and cooked meats, fish or meat pâtés and terrines are all ideal for picnics. Choose good-quality olives and marinated (bell) peppers instead of the mixed salads.

Below *A stylish hamper for carrying china, cutlery and glassware for grand picnic meals.*

Simply different

These are just a few ideas for dishes that are easy to carry and simple to eat.

• Cut a large loaf into horizontal slices and sandwich them back together with complementary fillings. Wrap tightly in clear film (plastic wrap). Cut the loaf into vertical slices to make attractive-looking ribbon sandwiches.

• Slit a large baguette lengthways, scoop out the crumb and fill with layers of mozzarella cheese and roasted spring onions (scallions) and (bell) peppers. Drizzle the layers lightly with good olive oil and sprinkle with shredded basil. Replace the top of the baguette, press firmly together and wrap tightly in clear film. Leave overnight in the refrigerator. Cut into wide chunks to serve.

• Sandwich soft wheat tortillas together into a neat stack with a filling of ricotta cheese, salami, cooked chicken and spring onions. Shred the salami and cooked chicken and chop the spring onions. Spread each tortilla with ricotta and sprinkle with salami, chicken and spring onions before adding the next. Press the stack firmly together and wrap in clear film. Make a spicy tomato salsa to serve with wedges of the tortilla stack.

• Cut short fine strips of spring onion, carrot, cucumber and cooked ham. Thin smooth peanut butter with a little tahini (sesame paste) and olive oil, then add a crushed garlic clove and a few drops of sesame oil. Add a dash of chilli sauce, if you like. Spread this paste thinly over Chinese pancakes and place a little of the shredded vegetables and ham on each. Roll up each pancake tightly and wrap in clear film.

Above *Filled baguettes in colourful napkins are practical and fun.*

Stepping out

The grand picnic party, so popular with gentility of previous generations, is still a fabulous way of celebrating at a special event. Summer season events, such as a day at the races, sailing regattas or country-house operas, typify picnic grandeur. The picnic may be served with ceremony and silver at a table (with chauffeur-cum-butler) or for stylish lounging on rugs and large cushions but always with linen napkins, proper cutlery, china and glassware.

• First courses: arrange smoked salmon sandwiches on a serving platter or plates and offer a separate bowl of lemon wedges.

Prepare individual pots of pâté, spread or mousse, sealed with clarified butter and garnished with herb sprigs.

Below *Select alcoholic and non-alcoholic drinks to suit your guests.*

Serve curly Melba toast, rye crisp breads or small shaped dinner rolls as an accompaniment.

Pack chilled soup, such as classic vichyssoise, gazpacho or a fruit soup, in a vacuum flask and take separate containers of cream or a selection of chilled garnishing ingredients to add to individual portions.

• The main dish: poached salmon steaks can be dressed at the last minute with a slightly thinned herb or lemon mayonnaise.

An impressive pie or pastry dish, such as game pie or pork pie in large or mini versions, travels well.

Cold roast whole or stuffed boned chicken, turkey, duck or pheasant can be served with a mayonnaise-based sauce or lighter salsa; alternatively, individual boned breast portions can be coated with mayonnaise and aspic.

Baked glazed ham can be accompanied by pickled peaches poached in spiced syrup made with cider vinegar instead of water.

• Desserts: for exciting fruit salads combine a limited number of complementary fruits, such as

Above *Coleslaw, gherkins and creamy potato salad are all picnic favourites.*

strawberries with papaya and lime, pineapple with mango and toasted shreds of fresh coconut, or physalis with cherries. Whole tropical fruits, such as passion fruits, rambutans and mangoes, are delicious on their own.

Fruit tarts and flans filled with confectioner's custard, vanilla custard or a sweetened cream and topped with summer berries are practical when the pastry case is baked in a serving dish.

Set custards baked in individual pots are easy to carry ready for turning out on to serving plates at the last minute.

• And finally, serve two or three perfect cheeses with finger oatcakes, classic Bath Olivers or plain crackers.

Pack home-made chocolate truffles or high-quality after-dinner mints in a cool box to serve with coffee. (Take a vacuum flask full of boiling water and instant coffee granules separately rather than keeping the coffee hot for several hours.)

Simple picnic feasts

Try these food combinations for escaping into simple indulgence or to excite the palate as part of an impressive menu:

• Creamy ripe goat's cheese with sweet fresh figs, and take a small pepper mill full of black peppercorns for freshly ground pepper.

• Fine slices of prosciutto, Smithfield or Serrano ham with little bunches of sweet seedless grapes and lime or lemon wedges.

• Ruffles of finely sliced smoked venison with halved strawberries and cucumber slices.

• Smoked loin of pork and succulent ready-to-eat dried apricots drizzled with walnut oil, and lemon wedges.

• Mozzarella cheese slices layered with finely shredded fresh basil and chopped fresh coriander (cilantro) leaves, drizzled with good olive oil and served with lemon wedges.

Above *A quick trip to the local deli can provide you with all the picnic basics.*

Outdoor escapes

Summer excursions and picnics may be the main focus for outdoor feasts, but there are other occasions when food goes down well in the fresh air:

• On Halloween or bonfire nights cook turkey burgers on the barbecue; wrap potatoes in foil to cook them on the barbecue or pre-bake them in the oven and then finish them on the barbecue. Finish with your favourite muffins, served warm with lots of whipped cream and chocolate sauce.

• The seaside can be exhilarating for winter walks, especially when seafood – tiger prawns (jumbo shrimp) in their shells, prepared squid and skewered swordfish or tuna – is served straight from a portable barbecue and accompanied by pats of garlic and parsley butter with lots of crusty bread. A vacuum flask of light, clear vegetable or seafood broth with chopped herbs and finely diced vegetables goes well with grilled seafood.

• When the winter snow provides the opportunity for outdoor fun and sport, assemble an impromptu afternoon party with toasted chestnuts, crumpets and English muffins on a barbecue. Mulled wine is a warming drinks option.

party basics

You do not have to be a five-star chef to throw

a good party bash but having a few smart

food and drink ideas to hand is a real help.

From exciting deli-selections to confidence

with basic recipes, inspiration and essential

information are the ingredients for

planning the perfect menu.

Just Nibbles

Tune in the party by serving the right type and quantity of snacks with drinks when guests first arrive. Too few or poor-quality nibbles look mean and awkward; too many or filling snacks overfill guests before the meal. Flavours should preview the courses to follow; for example, it is not good form to serve powerful, spicy snacks before a delicate meal.

Off-the-shelf selection
The array makes it difficult to resist trying some of the amazing commercial creations, but it is best to do this in your non-entertaining time. Select plain snacks and classic products rather than bizarre concoctions. Many bought savouries are wildly over-seasoned and they completely dull the palate for a delicate meal. Plain salted nuts, Chinese-style rice crackers, simple breadsticks, lightly flavoured croûtons, and good quality crisps (US potato chips) and cocktail crackers complement home-made snacks.

Roasted nuts
Place blanched almonds and plain, shelled pistachio and macadamia nuts in a large, shallow ovenproof dish. Sprinkle with a little salt and cook at 200°C/400°F/Gas 6 for about

6–10 minutes, until pale golden. Shake the dish well to coat the nuts with the salt and leave to cool. For a deliciously elusive hint of spice, sprinkle the nuts with two or three pinches each of grated nutmeg and ground mace.

Above *Good-quality bread, cheese, olives and wine are essential party basics.*

Marinated olives
Lightly crumble 4 bay leaves and place in a small pan with 15ml/1 tbsp fennel seeds, the grated rind of 1 lemon and 2 peeled and sliced garlic cloves. Pour in a little olive oil and cook gently for 15 minutes so that the ingredients barely sizzle. Remove from the heat and whisk in the juice of 1 lemon, 5ml/1 tsp caster (superfine) sugar and a little salt and pepper. Stir in 250ml/8fl oz/1 cup olive oil. Drain a 250g/9oz can pitted black olives in brine, then add them to the oil and mix well. Transfer to a covered container and leave to marinate in the refrigerator for 2–7 days. Drain the olives before serving. (The oil is fabulous for dressing cured meats, vegetables and salads.)

Below *Feta cheese with roast pepper dip with chillies on toast.*

Below *Pistachio nuts, almonds and macadamia nuts are good party snacks.*

Marinated cheese

Prepare the marinade used for olives to flavour bitesize cubes of feta cheese or mini-mozzarella cheeses. The fennel seeds are good with the cheese but they can be omitted and replaced by several sprigs of fresh oregano instead. Alternatively, instead of fennel and oregano, sprinkle the drained cheese with finely shredded basil when serving. Gouda or Jarlsberg cheese is excellent soaked in the same marinade with fennel, cumin or caraway seeds.

Vegetable crisps

Home-made potato crisps (US chips) are special when combined with other vegetables, such as beetroot (beet), sweet potatoes, celeriac and carrots.

Peel and thinly slice the potatoes and/or vegetables using a hand peeler, food processor or mandolin. Rinse well in cold water, drain and dry thoroughly on clean dishtowels. Make sure all the slices are separate before deep-frying, a handful at a time, in hot oil until they

Below Lemon and herb marinated olives are tasty party nibbles.

are crisp and golden brown. Drain thoroughly on kitchen paper and season lightly with salt.

Roasted cardamom cauliflower florets

Split 8 green cardamom pods and heat gently in a large pan with 60ml/4 tbsp sunflower oil until the pods are just sizzling, then cook for 2 minutes. Break a trimmed cauliflower into bitesize florets. Add the florets to the pan and toss to coat thoroughly in the oil, then turn them out into a shallow ovenproof dish, scraping all the oil over them. Roast at 220°C/425°F/Gas 7 for

Above Spiced plantain chips with hot chilli sauce.

10 minutes, turning once, until lightly browned. Season lightly with salt and pepper and cool. Remove and discard the cardamoms when transferring the cauliflower florets to serving bowls.

Baguette croûtons

Cut a good baguette with good, soft centre crumb into quarters lengthways. Cut the quarters across into large bitesize chunks. Spread the chunks out in a large roasting pan and bake at 160°C/325°F/Gas 3 for about 40 minutes, turning occasionally, until crisp, dry and lightly browned. Finely chop 1 garlic clove and cook lightly in 30ml/2 tbsp olive oil for 1 minute. Add 5ml/1 tsp each of dried oregano and thyme, then pour in a further 60ml/4 tbsp olive oil. Heat gently for a few minutes, then drizzle evenly and thinly over the croûtons. Season lightly with salt and toss well, then return to the oven for a further 5 minutes. Toss with plenty of finely chopped fresh parsley and finely grated lemon rind, if you like, just before serving.

For lightly flavoured croûtons, heat 2 bay leaves, a blade of mace and the pared rind of 1 lemon with the oil instead of the garlic, oregano and thyme. Leave to stand for several hours before pouring over the croûtons.

Salsas, Dips and Dippers

A few good salsas and dips go a long way, and a repertoire of basic recipes can be varied to create exciting snacks. Try them as fillings for hollowed vegetables or halved hard-boiled eggs; spread them on soft tortillas, wraps or pancakes and roll up into tasty picnic snacks or slice them into stylish canapés.

Matching dippers to dips

Vegetable crudités, breadsticks, croûtes and crackers taste good with most dips. For a juicy dip, select dippers to scoop up and hold juice or absorb a little – thick, curly crisps (US potato chips) and tortilla chips work well.

Below *Crunchy tacos are perfect with tomato salsa and guacamole.*

Do's and don'ts for dips and dippers

Do …
• Make smooth, fairly soft, but not sloppy, dips for easy eating.
• Select sturdy and fairly short nibbles to dunk – chunky lengths of celery, carrot, (bell) pepper and fennel; mini breadsticks; pitta bread fingers and crackers.
• Use cocktail sticks (toothpicks) for small, firm bits to dunk.
• Match dippers to dips.
• Serve dips in small bowls on platters, surrounded by enough dippers for the entire bowlful of dip.

Don't …
• Make the dip too thick to scoop easily.
• Prepare dips that separate or become watery on standing.
• Serve fragile dippers that break or bend; avoid fine crisps (US potato chips), fine puff pastries and flopping wedges of pitta.
• Offer nibbles that are too small to dunk without putting your fingers into the dip.
• Serve a huge bowl of dip that does the rounds for 30 minutes only to become messy.
• Offer dressed or sauced dunks that discolour and flavour the dip.

• For crisp potato wedges cut medium to large potatoes into quarters lengthways and place in a plastic bag. Add a little sunflower oil and salt, and then shake well. (Add a generous pinch of dried oregano or rosemary if appropriate for the dip.) Turn out into a roasting pan and cook at 240°C/475°F/Gas 9 for about 40 minutes, turning two or three times, until crisp and browned. Serve freshly cooked.

These can be three-quarters cooked in advance, then finished in the oven at the last minute. Sweet potatoes and new potatoes also work well.
• For crisp skins, halve baked potatoes and scoop out the middle, leaving a fairly thick shell. Brush all over with oil, place in a greased roasting pan and season lightly with salt. Roast at 200°C/400°F/Gas 6 for about 30 minutes, or until crisp and browned.

Red salsa

Play with this basic mixture to impress your personality on it and excite your palate – add a little extra sugar or chilli, perhaps, and increase the paprika for a deeper, warmer flavour. To lighten the salsa and add a lively zing, omit the tomato purée (paste) and stir in a little lemon juice. The salsa complements fish, poultry, meat or cheese; it makes a terrific dip with fingers of pitta bread or cheese cubes on sticks; and it is delicious on bitesize croûtes, topped with halved, hard-boiled quails' eggs.

Mix 60ml/4 tbsp tomato purée, 1 finely chopped red onion, 1 seeded and finely chopped red (bell) pepper, 1 seeded and finely chopped mild red chilli, 1 crushed garlic clove, 10ml/2 tsp caster (superfine) sugar, 2.5ml/½ tsp paprika and 30ml/2 tbsp balsamic vinegar until thoroughly combined. Peel and chop 450g/1lb ripe tomatoes, then stir them into the mixture. Add salt and pepper to taste. Cover and chill for 1–3 days in the refrigerator.

Cucumber and avocado salsa

This lively salsa complements fish and shellfish, salami and cured meats, and grilled (broiled) meats and burgers and barbecue meats. It enlivens creamy cheeses. As a dip, it is wonderful with potato wedges or skins, and chunky cheese straws.

Peel and finely chop 1 cucumber, then place it in a sieve. Sprinkle with

Below *Tomato-based salsas are very versatile: add chillies, coriander or garlic.*

salt and leave over a bowl to drain for 30 minutes. Meanwhile, finely chop 1 large seeded green (bell) pepper, 1 seeded mild green chilli, 1 bunch of spring onions (scallions) and mix with 15ml/1 tbsp caster sugar, 45ml/3 tbsp good olive oil and the grated rind and juice of 1 lime. Squeeze the cucumber and then dry it on kitchen paper before adding it to the salsa. Peel, halve, stone (pit) and finely chop 2 avocados, then mix them into the salsa. Chop a big bunch of coriander (cilantro) leaves and stir them into the salsa.

Cover and chill for several hours or up to 1 day. Before serving, finely shred a handful of tender basil sprigs and stir them in.

Below *Pitta bread makes excellent dippers for creamy dips.*

Above *Spicy pumpkin dip served with cucumber crudités.*

Onion and chive dip

This is delicious as a filling for baked potatoes or with crispy new potatoes cooked on the barbecue; it is a good accompaniment for gammon (cured ham) or a filling for cherry tomatoes.

Peel and quarter 6 onions. Mix 15ml/1 tbsp sugar, 15ml/1 tbsp wholegrain mustard, 30ml/2 tbsp sunflower oil and 30ml/2 tbsp cider vinegar in a shallow ovenproof dish just large enough to hold the onions. Turn the onions in this mixture, then roast at 200°C/400°F/Gas 6 for about 45 minutes, turning once or twice, until tender. Cover and cool.

Purée the onions with their juices. Gradually stir the onion purée into 450g/1lb curd (farmer's) cheese. Finely snip a handful of chives into the dip, add a little freshly grated nutmeg and mix well. Taste for seasoning, then chill.

Gorgonzola and parsley dip

Mash 225g/8oz Gorgonzola cheese and mix in 225g/8oz/1 cup ricotta cheese. Finely chop 50g/2oz flat leaf parsley and mix it into the dip with freshly ground black pepper. Stir in 250ml/8fl oz/1 cup crème fraîche and season to taste. Chill before serving.

Salad Talk

In a flurry of curly leaves or a frisée of fine shreds, every salad should make a stunning statement. Move on from making irrelevant "side salads" to presenting classy creations by marrying vegetables with taste-bud-tingling dressings and well-textured toppings.

Salad reminders

Harmonize all aspects of a salad; the base, main ingredients, dressing and topping or garnish should contrast and blend to perfection.

• Include a limited selection of complementary flavours and textures rather than a mishmash of ingredients – this is especially relevant with rice or pasta salads.

• Dress leafy salads at the last minute, otherwise they become limp. For buffets, serve the dressing separately.

• Sprinkle crisp or crunchy toppings over when serving, or offer them separately for buffets.

• Have a generous taste of the dressing to check the seasoning and balance of

Below *Classic Caesar salad is a popular party dish.*

sweet to sour. The dressing must complement not mask the salad.

• There should be enough dressing to coat but not drown the ingredients.

• Light-textured and thin dressings complement soft and crisp ingredients; crunchy and firm ingredients support creamy coatings.

• Unless they should be served chilled, remove salads from the refrigerator about 30 minutes before serving.

Full-of-flavour leaves

The palate-cleansing properties of fresh leaves are welcome with firm, substantial main dishes, such as grilled (broiled) poultry or meat and hearty raised pies or pastries. They are also an excellent base for sautéed or grilled fish and shellfish, thinly sliced cured meats or crumbly or creamy cheeses.

For exciting leafy ensembles mix green flavours with subtly different textures. Crisp iceberg, cos or romaine lettuces contrast with lamb's lettuce, lollo rosso or Little Gem (Bibb) leaves.

Baby spinach brings a firm, rather than crisp, texture and a subtle, slightly musty flavour. Peppery watercress and savoury rocket (arugula) bring positive textures as well as lively flavour.

Above *Olive oil and ripe black olives add plenty of flavour.*

Herb sprigs are excellent in leafy salads, either singly or in a burst of mixed flavours. Chopping the herbs changes the result completely, distributing their flavour rather than providing the occasional interesting mouthful; so include small sprig ends with their tender edible stems.

Salad portions

Estimating salad portions for large gatherings is not easy; simply multiplying portion sizes for a meal for four or six by a larger number for a buffet does not work. Portion sizes are smaller for buffet salads. As a rough guide for gatherings of over 20, 1 large lettuce (lollo rosso, iceberg, cos or romaine) will provide eight portions, 500g/1¼lb tomatoes will be enough for six, 1 small white cabbage will serve 12 when finely shredded, 500g/1¼lb new potatoes will serve four and 500g/1¼lb shredded carrots will serve six to eight.

The crunch factor

The greater resistance of crunch is different from crisp and it is a texture that supports substantial ingredients and flavours or creamy dressings very well. Fennel, celery, radishes, cucumber, carrots, celeriac, red or white cabbage, courgettes (zucchini), (bell) peppers, beansprouts and onions are packed with crunch. For super-crunchy salads, add drained and thinly sliced canned water chestnuts.

Tender not soft

Cooked root vegetables, tomatoes, mushrooms, canned bamboo shoots and olives are examples of tender ingredients that can be marinated in dressings to impart or absorb flavours. A suitable marinade should not spoil their textures but it will enrich the salad and give it depth.

Tip-top finishes

The decorative garnishes or toppings for salad add essential flavour and introduce interesting textures.

• Chopped, slivered or whole nuts can complement main ingredients or be a focal point. Walnuts, pecans, pistachios, macadamia nuts and hazelnuts are all excellent on salads.

• Lightly roasted seeds bring strength of flavour and texture. Linseeds, pumpkin, sesame, sunflower, mustard and poppy seeds are all delicious individually or together. Pine nuts are delicious, tender and nutty and go especially well with spinach.

• Lightly roasted grains bring texture and flavour, and they go well with seeds and/or bacon. Barley, rye and/or oat flakes can all be roasted in a dry, heavy pan until lightly browned and crisp.

• Croûtons bring crunch and they can be tasty with herbs and/or garlic.

• Crisp sautéed diced bacon, pancetta or gammon (cured ham), salami or chorizo are full of flavour and texture.

Above *White beans with green peppers in a spicy dressing.*

Asides to centrepieces

Salads make appealing first courses or light main courses and many are just a twist away from becoming impressive centrepieces for either picnics or buffets. The trick is to marry punchy main ingredients with a salad base full of character, then link them with a sympathetic dressing. Experiment with the following examples:

• A substantial full-flavoured leaf and herb base is brilliant for pan-fried fish, poultry, cheese or tofu. Sliced scallops, peeled raw tiger prawns (jumbo shrimp), chunks of salmon, strips of chicken or turkey breast fillet, cubes of halloumi cheese or firm tofu can all be marinated with a little olive oil, garlic and lemon rind, then pan-fried and tossed into the salad while hot. Deglaze the pan with lemon juice or balsamic vinegar, a sprinkling of sugar, seasoning and a final drizzle of olive oil to make a delicious dressing. To serve the salad cold, transfer the pan-fried ingredients to a container, pour over the deglazed dressing and cool, then mix with the leaves before serving.

• Use shredded crunchy salad in a light oil-based dressing as a base for ruffles of thinly sliced cured meats; julienne of cooked meats; quartered hard-boiled eggs and diced smoked salmon or ham; or diced firm cheese. Add a creamy dressing and crunchy topping.

• A mixture of soft and crisp, lightly flavoured leaves (for example lollo biondo, lamb's lettuce and shredded iceberg) is a good base for fresh fruit, rich dried fruit and creamy cheese. Crisp and juicy green grapes, sliced dried apricots and sliced ripe Brie combine well. Add a topping of coarsely chopped walnuts and dress with a drizzle of walnut oil. Add lemon wedges as a little zest to taste.

Below *Refreshing tabbouleh with masses of chopped fresh herbs.*

Sauces, Dressings and Relishes

A good home-made sauce elevates plain cooked foods to a stylish dish. Here are a few classic recipes:

Tomato sauce

This good basic sauce freezes well. Thaw it for several hours at room temperature or in the microwave. Apart from the myriad of uses in compound dishes, the sauce goes well with plain cooked fish, poultry or meat.

For the simplest informal supper party, serve fresh pasta with tomato sauce, topped with lots of finely shredded fresh basil and coriander (cilantro), and shavings of Parmesan cheese. Add a punchy, crunchy salad of shredded fennel and white cabbage with chopped spring onion (scallion) and toasted pine nuts.

Chop 1 onion, 1 celery stick, 1 carrot and 1 garlic clove, then cook in 30ml/2 tbsp olive oil with 2 bay leaves and 1 large sprig each of thyme and oregano for 15 minutes. Cover the pan to keep the moisture in and prevent the vegetables from browning. Add 1kg/2lb chopped ripe tomatoes, 30ml/2 tbsp tomato purée (paste),

Below Pickles add full flavour to accompaniments and condiments.

15ml/1 tbsp sugar, 2.5ml/½ tsp paprika and a little seasoning. Heat, stirring, until the tomatoes give up some of their juice, then cover the pan and cook gently for 40–45 minutes, until the vegetables are tender and the tomatoes reduced. Discard the bay leaves and herb sprigs, then purée the sauce. Use the sauce as it is (slightly coarse) or press it through a fine sieve for a smooth texture.

Mayonnaise

Home-made mayonnaise is superb, and the flavour can be fine-tuned to your personal taste by adjusting the balance of sunflower and olive oils (or using different types of oil) and the quantity of lemon juice.

Home-made mayonnaise contains raw egg; pregnant women, the very young and the elderly are generally advised not to eat raw eggs.

Commercial mayonnaise, however, is pasteurized to destroy any micro-organisms in the egg and it can be a safer option for buffet dishes that are likely to be left sitting for several hours in a warm room.

Below Home-made garlic mayonnaise with crudités.

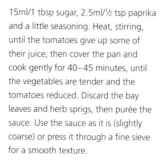

Above Home-made mayonnaise is quick to make and so delicious.

Use an electric beater to whisk 1 large (US extra large) egg with a little salt and pepper, 2.5ml/½ tsp Dijon mustard and the juice of ½ small lemon, until thoroughly combined. Mix 150ml/¼ pint/⅔ cup each of sunflower and olive oil. Whisking constantly, gradually add the oils to the egg in a very thin trickle, broken at first, then more constantly as the mixture thickens and becomes creamy. The finished mayonnaise should be thick, pale and glossy. Add salt, pepper and lemon juice to taste if required.

• The mayonnaise can be made in a food processor by processing the egg mixture first, then gradually dropping and trickling in the oil with the motor running. Scrape the mixture down frequently. A large food processor bowl may be too large for a single quantity.

• For a rich mayonnaise, use egg yolks rather than whole egg and allow 2 egg yolks to 250ml/8 fl oz/1 cup oil.

Flavouring mayonnaise

A well-flavoured mayonnaise can be served as a filling for baked potatoes or a dip with potato wedges.

• Add 1 crushed garlic clove to the egg. For a mellow flavour, first cook 1 garlic clove in a little olive oil until lightly browned.

• Stir in 60ml/4 tbsp chopped fresh chives, parsley, tarragon, dill or fennel, or a handful of shredded basil leaves.

• Stir in the grated rind of 1 lemon, lime or orange. Use the juice of 1 lime instead of the lemon juice. (Orange juice is not sharp enough to balance the oil and egg mixture.)

• To make a spicy rouille, add 1 crushed garlic clove, 5ml/1 tsp paprika and a good pinch of cayenne pepper to the egg. Taste the prepared mayonnaise for seasoning and add a little extra cayenne if you like. Rouille is a traditional accompaniment for fish soups, served with slices of warm baguette, but it also goes with a wide variety of other foods or it makes a delicious dip for plain breadsticks.

Excellent salad dressing

This is a good basic oil and vinegar salad dressing, which can be varied to suit all sorts of salads. Different types of oil (sunflower, grapeseed, walnut, hazelnut or pumpkin seed) or vinegar (remember all the flavoured vinegars) can be used, and there are many types of mustard that will vary the flavour. Strong nut oils should be used in modest amounts with light grapeseed or sunflower oil.

Below *Herbs, garlic or lemon rind can enliven a plain salad dressing.*

Above *Quail's eggs served with mayonnaise dip and olive oil.*

Whisk 5ml/1 tsp sugar, salt and ground black pepper, and 7.5ml/ 1½ tsp mustard (wholegrain or Dijon, mild or strong to taste) with 30ml/ 2 tbsp balsamic or cider vinegar until the sugar and salt have dissolved. Whisking hard and constantly, slowly pour in 150ml/¼ pint/⅔ cup olive oil. The dressing will emulsify and thicken slightly. Store in an airtight jar in the refrigerator and shake before serving.

Flavouring dressings

Try some of the following additions.
• Add 1 chopped garlic clove.
• Add 30ml/2 tbsp chopped fresh parsley, mint, tarragon or chives.
• Add the grated rind of ½–1 lemon.
• To make a spicy peanut dressing, omit the mustard and use 30ml/2 tbsp crunchy peanut butter. Add the juice of 1 lime and a pinch of dried red chillies.

Beetroot relish

This sweet and sour preserve is terrific with hot or cold meats or with cheese. Serve it with a Christmas buffet or a summer barbecue.

Peel and coarsely grate 450g/1lb raw beetroot (beet). Peel, core and coarsely grate 450g/1lb cooking apples.

Finely chop 450g/1lb onions. Peel and chop 25g/1oz fresh root ginger. Mix all the ingredients in a pan and add 2 crushed garlic cloves, 5ml/1 tsp each of ground cinnamon and nutmeg, 225g/8oz/1 cup soft brown sugar and 450ml/¾ pint/scant 2 cups cider vinegar. Bring to the boil, stirring occasionally. Reduce the heat and cover the pan. Simmer for about 1½ hours. Pot the relish in warmed sterilized jars immediately the pan is removed from the heat. Cover with airtight lids and store for at least 2 weeks before eating. It makes about 1.3kg/3lb.

Below *Beetroot relish.*

Making the Best of Bread

The advantage of baking your own bread is that you can create individual rolls or loaves to complement the menu or to become a real feature on their own, especially for breakfast, brunch, lunch or late suppers. Breads can be baked or bought well in advance and frozen. The following are variations on the basic dough (far right).

• Wholemeal bread: use wholemeal (whole-wheat) flour and add an extra 50ml/2fl oz/¼ cup water.

• Seeded breads: use all wholemeal or half and half wholemeal and white. Add 15ml/1 tbsp each of caraway and cumin seeds, and 30ml/2 tbsp each of poppy and sesame seeds.

• Rye bread: use half rye flour and half white flour. Add 30ml/2 tbsp caraway seeds and an extra 50ml/2fl oz/¼ cup water to the mixture.

Below *For a party, buy interesting bread flavoured with seeds and herbs.*

• Milk bread: use hand-hot milk instead of water for richer bread. Rub 50g/2oz/¼ cup butter into the flour before adding the yeast, salt and sugar then omit the olive oil. Do not glaze the bread before baking.

• Herb bread: add 10ml/2 tsp dried sage, 10ml/2 tsp dried thyme and 60ml/4 tbsp chopped fresh chives to the flour. Also try oregano, dill, fennel, coriander (cilantro) and parsley.

Shaping dough

Make interestingly shaped loaves for a special occasion.

• Braid: cut the dough into thirds and roll these into long, thin strips. Pinch the ends of the strips together, and then braid them. Leave to rise, brush with beaten egg and sprinkle with poppy seeds before baking. Use milk bread for a richer dough.

• Oval loaves: cut the dough in half and shape each piece into a roll about

Basic bread dough

Mix 450g/1lb strong white bread flour with 1 sachet (envelope) easy-blend (rapid-rise) yeast, 5ml/1 tsp salt and 5ml/1 tsp sugar. Make a well in the middle and add 250ml/8fl oz/1 cup hand-hot water and 30ml/2 tbsp olive oil. Gradually work the liquid into the flour to make a stiff dough. Turn the dough out on to a lightly floured surface and knead it for about 10 minutes, or until very smooth and elastic. Shape the dough as required and place on a greased baking tray. Cover with oiled clear film (plastic wrap) and leave in a warm place until doubled in size before baking. Bake large loaves at 220°C/425°F/Gas 7 for about 40 minutes, or until well risen and browned. Bake rolls at the same temperature for 20–25 minutes. Turn the bread over and tap the base: the loaf should sound hollow. If it sounds damp and solid, it is not properly cooked through, so return it to the oven for a further 5 minutes and check again.

20cm/8in long. Leave to rise, then use a sharp knife to cut shallow diagonal slits across the top before brushing with a little warm water and baking.

• Rolls: cut the dough into 12 equal portions and shape these into round or oval rolls. To make a knot, roll a portion into a thin strip and twist it into a knot. For twists, divide each portion in half, roll into strips and twist these together. Transfer the rolls to a greased baking tray and leave to rise. Brush with beaten egg or milk, then sprinkle with sesame or poppy seeds before baking.

• Swirl: make up two batches of dough: one plain white and one

Above *Warm, fresh home-baked bread can be a real feature at parties.*

seeded half and half wholemeal and white. Cut each type in half. Roll out a portion of white into an oval, and then roll a portion of seeded into a equal-size oval. Lay the seeded dough on the white and roll up both into an oval loaf. Repeat with the remaining dough to make a second loaf. Leave to rise, brush with warm water and sprinkle with seeds before baking.

Buying guide

Buy bread on the day it is to be eaten or buy and freeze it in advance, then thaw it early on the day or overnight.

• Crusty breads, such as baguettes, French and Italian country breads, and the British bloomer, are good for mopping up dressings and sauces, and they go well with cheese. Cut them into chunks to make crusty croûtons.

• Rich breads, such as milk bread, brioche or challah/cholla, are a good choice for brunch or to accompany marinated vegetables and salads for lunch. They are excellent for picnics.

• Flat breads, such as pitta, naan or soft wheat tortillas, can be used more widely than in their traditional roles. They go well with dips or pâtés, and are good filled with salads, roasted vegetables, grilled (broiled) or cured meat.

• Individual breads are perfect for buffets, picnics, breakfast or brunch. Croissants, bagels, English muffins and crumpets, teacakes or currant buns are real treat breads, as good packed with fabulous fillings as they are served in traditional style.

• Close-textured or coarse breads bring out the best in smoked fish, shellfish, cured meats, fine pâtés and cheese. While firm dark or light rye bread can be thinly sliced, the coarser grainy breads tend to be more crumbly and are good served in thick chunks.

Serving bread

Warm bread has a better flavour and texture than cold.

• Present a whole loaf on a cutting board, with knife. For a large party, when guests are less likely to slice their own bread, the loaf may be part or completely sliced and presented with the slices re-assembled to prevent them from drying out.

• Pile warm flat or individual breads in a linen-lined basket and fold the cloth over to keep the bread warm.

• Sliced baguette and thinly cut breads complement light first courses; chunks, wedges and hearty lengths of baguette are more filling with main dishes and substantial salads.

Hot savoury breads

Slice a baguette, bloomer or crusty French country bread ring, leaving the slices attached at the base. Spread one of the following fillings on the slices and press them back together. Spread a little extra filling over the top. Wrap the loaf securely in foil and heat in the oven at 200°C/400°F/Gas 6 for about 15 minutes. Serve hot.

• Garlic butter: cream 115g/4oz/½ cup butter with 1 crushed garlic clove.

• Herb butter: cream 60ml/4 tbsp chopped fresh herbs into 115g/4oz/ ½ cup butter.

Above *Serve garlic or herb buttered baguettes warm and with napkins.*

• Anchovy and olive butter: finely chop a 50g/2oz can anchovies in olive oil, and cream with 115g/4oz/½ cup butter, gradually working in the oil from the can. Add 115g/4oz chopped black olives, a squeeze of lemon juice and freshly ground black pepper.

• Spring onion, lime and coriander butter: finely chop 4 spring onions (scallions) and a good handful of fresh coriander (cilantro) leaves, then cream with 115g/4oz/½ cup butter, adding the grated rind of 1 lime and a squeeze of lime juice. Add a chopped garlic clove, if you like.

Croûtons and croûtes

These can be cut into small cubes or chunks to match any dishes. Sauté them in olive oil and butter or bake until crisp and lightly browned, then drizzle with a little oil. Alternatively, lightly brush slices of bread with oil and grill (broil) until golden, then cut into cubes.

• Croûtes are bread slices, brushed with melted butter or oil, and baked, grilled or fried until golden on both sides. They may be small and thin, or thick and crusty slices. Croûtes complement soft foods or make a good base to absorb juices.

Stunning Cheese Boards

Whether the cheese board is an international extravaganza or a celebration of one or two good cheeses depends on the occasion and the role of the cheese in the menu.

Dinner-party cheese course

When the cheese board is served as a dinner-party course among many there may be just one or two cheeses or a small selection of different types. Offering one fine example is quite acceptable, typically Brie or a similar universally popular type of cheese. It is fun to focus on something special you know your guests will appreciate, such as a good blue or tangy goat's cheese.

The more usual approach to the basic dinner-party cheese board is to include an example each of hard, blue and semi-soft cheese. One or two other cheeses are often added according to what is good at the deli. Availability and quality are important and it is better to limit the cheeses to a few good-quality examples than to offer many second-rate selections.

Above *Keep to a few fresh, good-quality cheeses for the cheese board.*

• Vary the sizes, shapes and textures of pieces of cheese.
• Make sure that there is enough of each cheese for every guest to have a modest sample; buy more than one of a small cheese if necessary.
• Cheese may be served after the main course and before dessert, in the French style, or after the dessert and before coffee. If it is practical, the cheese can be brought to the table and offered at the same time as the dessert, allowing individuals to decide which they would prefer to eat first.

Cheese on the buffet

The selection of cheeses may be one of many courses of food or it may be the main focus for a buffet. The modern cheese and wine party is way beyond squares of hard cheese on sticks: it is a celebration of cheese.

• When serving a wide variety, keep the different types of cheese separate. Large pieces can be given their own

platters or stands. If there is more than one type of hard white, semi-soft or blue cheese, group them by type on separate boards or platters.
• Contrasting colours and shapes are important, so include cheeses with different rinds, and display logs, pyramids, squares, domes or rounds as well as wedges and wheels.
• One or more whole cheeses in perfect condition are a real delight. Order from a good supplier well in advance, requesting that the cheese be in peak condition for the party. A whole Brie and a half or whole Stilton are a good classic combination.

Presentation tips

Wooden or marble boards are traditional but china platters and glass or china cake stands work extremely well. Baskets lined with heavy linen napkins, topped with fresh vine (grape) leaves make an attractive backdrop.

• Remove cheese from the refrigerator several hours beforehand and leave it in a cool room. Unwrap any pre-packed cheeses and cover them loosely.
• Always have separate knives for hard, soft, blue and goat's cheeses.
• Allow enough space on the board or base for cutting.
• Do not clutter a board with grapes if it already contains several cheeses; it is better to serve the fruit separately.

Below *Remove cheese from the refrigerator shortly before serving.*

Accompaniments

Crackers should be plain. Oatcakes, water biscuits, Bath Oliver biscuits and Melba toast are excellent. Flavoured and salted biscuits ruin good cheese.

• Crusty bread with plenty of substantial, soft crumb should be offered as well as biscuits (crackers). When offering cheese as the main food for a meal or buffet, choose a good selection of breads that are light in flavour but substantial in texture.

• Serve bowls of watercress or rocket (arugula) sprigs with the cheese. A light green salad can clear the palate.

• Celery sticks and pieces of fennel.

• Fresh figs, apples, pears, grapes, physalis, fresh dates and apricots go well with all cheeses. Dried fruits to serve with cheese include apricots, dates, peaches, pears and figs.

• Nuts in the shell or shelled.

• When serving cheese as a main course, black or green olives, or sweet ripe tomatoes may be offered.

• Chutneys, pickles, relishes and salsas are all delicious with a main-course cheese board. Sweet-sour flavours are particularly successful.

Below *Chopped egg and onions with white cheese and olives.*

Above *Edible flowers, such as scented geraniums, add flavour and interest.*

• Offer an excellent oil with the cheese – walnut, hazelnut, macadamia or olive oils may be trickled on a plate as a condiment for cheese.

Lower-fat options

Watching everyone else indulge in a lavish cheese course is dismal for guests who have to limit their intake of saturated fat. Fortunately, it is possible to offer lower-fat options without compromising on quality.

• Ricotta cheese is available in low-fat versions and is delicious with fresh or dried fruit. Slit and stone (pit) fresh dates, separate the halves leaving them joined underneath, fill with ricotta and top with a fine shaving of Parmesan.

• Creamy medium-fat soft goat's cheese is delicious with fresh figs. Slit each fig almost down into quarters, leaving them joined at the base. Fill with soft goat's cheese and serve with freshly ground black pepper.

• Sandwich walnut halves together with low-fat soft cheese.

• Slit ready-to-eat dried apricots and fill them with a little low-fat soft cheese, then add a young mint leaf to each.

• Ready-to-eat dried apricots are delicious with feta cheese. Place small cubes of feta in slit apricots.

• Make delicious potted cheese with nuts by mixing very finely chopped walnuts with low-fat soft cheese. Add a little walnut oil to intensify the flavour, if you like. Pistachio nuts and pistachio nut oil can also be used – do not chop the nuts so finely as the walnuts and use the pistachio nut oil sparingly as it is very strong. Serve with celery and fennel.

Cheese savouries

Hot savouries can be served instead of a cheese board. The important point is to keep everything small to add a final burst of flavour at the end of the meal or before the dessert rather than to introduce another filling course.

A small pot of cheese fondue, neat fingers of cheese on toast or Welsh rarebit are all suitable. Little croûtes topped with goat's cheese and grilled (broiled) can be served with peppery watercress or rocket. Miniature tartlets made with cheese pastry can be filled with warm Stilton topped with a grape.

Below *A small pot of cheese fondue can be served as the final course.*

Wine for All Occasions

The variety of drinks available, as well as attitudes to entertaining and drinking have changed significantly in the last couple of decades such that providing liquid refreshment involves more than buying a few anonymous bottles of red and white wine. There is better information in supermarkets, and wine merchants who provide reliable, practical advice are no longer limited to élite outlets. Parties offering an "open bar" are not common but it is usual to offer a mixed selection of pre-dinner drinks. Cocktail parties are fun occasions and can be combined with dressing up in 1920s style.

Whatever the occasion or refreshment, non-alcoholic drinks are important, as most people prefer to avoid alcohol completely when they are driving and many also prefer to drink small amounts. Generous quantities of table water are essential at every meal to complement wine, and a selection of sophisticated alcohol-free aperitifs should be offered on every occasion.

Below *Choose a selection of red and white wines to suit different tastes.*

Above *There is a choice of several wine glasses from your wine merchant.*

Party wines

For the majority of parties it is still usual to provide white or red wine. Offering a choice of dry to medium-dry white is a good idea, especially when the menu is finger food rather than a main meal. Medium-bodied and soft reds are more flexible than their robust counterparts. Take advantage of wine-tasting opportunities at supermarkets, wine merchants or warehouses, particularly the latter where there is always a selection of wines for tasting.

Sparkling white wine is fun for parties, but always offer still wine as an alternative. Champagne is the choice for special celebrations. If you are planning a large gathering and want to serve expensive wines, it is worth taking expert and practical advice from a reputable wine merchant. You may well find expensive wines and sparkling wines offered there on a sale-or-return basis for whole cases.

Wine with food
The tradition of serving white wine with fish or poultry, and red with meat or cheese is still a good rule of thumb, but the vastly increased choice and changing cooking styles have widened the goalposts dramatically. Personal wine preference is just as important as bowing to expert opinion, so if you want to share your favourite wines with friends, do not feel inhibited even if they do not feature in wine guides or fashionable columns.

As a general rule, match light foods with light wines; crisp textures with crisp wines; and robust foods with characterful or full-bodied wines. Never

Below *Sparkling wine or champagne is popular for a special occasion.*

Above *Crisp, dry white wines complement fish, shellfish and poultry.*

make the mistake of using cheap and nasty wine in special cooking but use a good wine and complement it by serving the same or similar at the table. For example, when cooking fish, poultry or meat in wine or serving a wine sauce buy enough wine for cooking and serving with the meal.

First courses
When champagne or sparkling wine is offered as an aperitif it is often served with the first course. Light and crisp white wines complement salad-style appetizers and fine soups, while slightly more complex or fuller whites support fish or vegetables, pâté and egg dishes.

Fish, poultry and meat
• Fish and shellfish take crisp, dry white wines, including Sauvignon Blanc, Chablis, Muscadet sur lie or Chardonnay from Alto Adige. Firm-fleshed fish, shellfish and richer fish dishes or pâtés take the more robust whites, such as white Rioja, Australian Sémillon, oaked Chardonnays, and Californian Fumé Blanc.
• Chicken takes a soft red, such as mature burgundy, Crianza, Reserva Rioja or Californian Merlot. Light cooking methods, such as poaching in white wine, call for lighter wine but

Above *Choose full-bodied reds to accompany beef or pork.*

this could well be a rich white to match a creamy sauce.
• Turkey is slightly more powerful than chicken. An impressive red is essential for serving with Thanksgiving or Christmas dinner. St-Emilion, Pomerol claret, Châteauneuf-du-Pape, Australian Cabernet-Merlot or Cabernet Shiraz blends are all suitable.
• Duck benefits from a young red with some acidity, such as Crozes-Hermitage, Chianti Classico or Californian or New Zealand Pinot.
• Game birds take a fully aged Pinot Noir from the Côte d'Or, Carneros or Oregon while powerful venison is matched by concentrated red Bordeaux or northern Rhône wines, or Cabernet Shiraz and Zinfandel.
• Beef takes medium- to full-bodied reds. Serve reds from lighter Bordeaux wines or a medium Châteauneuf-du-Pape to the most powerful Zinfandels, Barolo, Barbaresco or Coonawarra Shiraz. Syrah or Grenache match mustard and horseradish condiments.
• Cabernet Sauvignon complements lamb, especially ripe examples from any of the producing countries.
• Pork takes full-bodied, slightly spicy reds, such as southern Rhône blends, Australian Shiraz, California Syrah or Tuscan Vino Nobile or Brunello.

Pasta

Match the wine to the sauce or type of pasta dish, for example the dominant flavours may be fish, poultry or meat. Light to medium reds go well with tomato-based sauces. Good Soave complements creamy pasta dishes, especially those containing seafood.

Desserts

Sauternes, Barsac and Monbazillac are classic wines for creamy desserts and custards. Rich Sauternes and high-alcohol dessert wines complement chocolate desserts. German or Austrian Rieslings or late-harvest Muscat from North America are great with baked fruit desserts and tarts. Slightly sweeter sparkling wines, such as Asti or Moscato d'Asti, are light and wash down Christmas pudding, cakes and meringues. Rich desserts, fruit cakes and nut-based specialities, such as pecan pie, will take a liqueur Muscat, sweet oloroso sherry or Madeira.

Cheese

Traditionally, cheese was always served with red wine, and although the combination of full rich and powerful

Below *High-alcohol dessert wines go especially well with chocolate desserts.*

cheese with a full red is an enjoyable one, the very heavy, tannic wines tend to mask the subtle nuttiness and lingering slight sweetness that comes with good ripe cheese.

Happily, the picture is now a little more varied. Any red wine or substantial white served with the main course can be finished off with cheese. Selecting wine to complement cheese is different and the idea of matching flavours and fullness is a good one to consider. Fresh, crisp and slightly acidic and dry cheeses are best matched by crisp, fruity wines. Mellow, richer and creamy cheese takes a more rounded white, such as a full Chardonnay, or a light red. Blue cheeses are well matched by sweet wines.

• As a general rule, offer a choice of a substantial white and a soft red.
• Light whites, such as Sauvignon or Chenin Blanc, go well with light

Above *Whatever type you select, always go for a good-quality corkscrew.*

cheeses, such as the crumbly mild whites and fresh light goat's cheese.
• Chianti, Merlot or Rioja support the more substantial, ripe and well-flavoured semi-soft cheeses.
• New Zealand Cabernet Sauvignon or Côte du Rhône marry well with the medium-strong hard cheeses.
• Save Australian Shiraz and Californian Cabernet Sauvignon for well-matured hard cheese.
• Fruity wines, such as Vouvray, Chenin Blanc or rosé, match mild and creamy blue cheese while the stronger blues with a piquant flavour take the more robust reds.
• Sweet wines, such as Monbazillac, complement the stronger blue cheeses. Classic combinations include port with Stilton and Sauternes with Roquefort.

Serving wine

Much of the ceremony and elaborate paraphernalia of wine opening is conspicuous rather than practical.

Temperature

White wines should be chilled and reds served at room temperature. Over-chilling whites dulls their flavour – light whites should be served at 10°C/50°F, or just below, while the fuller Chardonnays, dry Sémillons and Alsace wines can be slightly less cool. The chilling time depends on the starting temperature of the bottle, but as a general rule allow a couple of hours in the refrigerator.

Leave red wines in a warm room for a couple of hours before serving. Heating them on a radiator is a bad idea as this clouds the flavours and aromas. Some light reds, such as young Beaujolais, can be served lightly chilled.

Allowing wine to breathe

Opening red wine in advance and allowing it to breathe before drinking is intended to take the tannic or acidic edge off the flavour of young reds. However, as the amount of air that

Below *Sniff lightly and long, with the nose slightly below the rim of the glass.*

Above *When opening sparkling wines, control the release of the cork.*

gets at the wine through the top of the bottle is minimal, unless the wine is decanted into a jug (pitcher) or carafe, merely opening the bottle normally has very little effect.

Decanting

This involves pouring wine off the sediment that has formed in the bottle. Leave the bottle to stand upright undisturbed overnight so that all the sediment sinks to the bottom. Open the bottle gently and pour the wine into the decanter in a slow steady

Below *A foil cutter removes a neat circle from the seal over the cork.*

Above *This type of corkscrew requires the minimum of effort.*

stream, keeping the bottle at a minimum angle the whole time to retain the sediment in the bottom. Keep your eye on the sediment and stop pouring as soon as it reaches the neck of the bottle. If there is more than half a glass of wine left, strain it through muslin (cheesecloth).

Opening

Sparkling wine or chilled champagne will not go off like a cannon if properly opened, providing it has not been vigorously moved or shaken.

Have the glasses ready. Remove the foil and wire, holding the cork firmly in place. Hold the cork with one hand and the bottom part of the bottle with the other. Keep a firm hold on the cork. Concentrate on twisting the bottle, not the cork, until you feel the cork beginning to yield. Once it begins to go, the cork will push itself out, so the aim is to control its exit rather than leaving go and letting it pop out. The cork often needs a slight twist to help it on its way – just help it to move gently in the opposite direction to the bottle.

Pour a third to half a glass first to prevent the sparkling wine or champagne from overflowing, then go around again topping up the glasses when the first foam has subsided.

Organizing Drinks, Glasses and Quantities

If you intend making an open offer of drinks, make sure guests know what is available. Tell them or display the bottles on a table or set up a bar.

As a rule, include gin, vodka, whisky, sherry and dry white vermouth as a basic selection. Rum, Campari, red vermouth and sweet white vermouth are other options. Pimm's is a favourite summer drink. Tonic, American dry ginger ale, lemonade, cola and soda water (club soda) are the usual mixers; Russian is a pomegranate-flavoured mixer that goes well with vodka. Have ice cubes and sliced lemons to hand.

After-dinner drinks may include a selection of liqueurs, Cognac, brandy and port.

Alcohol-free drinks

Have a plentiful supply of non-alcoholic drinks chilled. Still and sparkling mineral waters and jugs (pitchers) of tap water with ice and lemon are essential. Orange or tomato juice are

Below *Offer a selection of spirits for pre-dinner drinks.*

basic options, while apple, pineapple, exotic fruit and cranberry juices are popular. Alcohol-free beer is an acceptable alternative to beer.
• Add a generous dash of bitters to sparkling mineral water.
• Serve a squeeze of lime juice, lime slices and mint sprigs in tonic.

Beer

While beer is traditionally associated with informal barbecues and student parties, it is also an excellent drink to offer as an alternative to wine at drinks parties or as a pre-dinner drink on more formal occasions.

There is a vast choice of bottled beers available in most supermarkets. Coming from all over the world, they range from some light in colour and flavour to others that are dark, malty with a rich deep flavour. Fruit-flavoured beers are also popular. Colour and flavour are not necessarily related to strength – something to be especially aware of at parties – and some of the paler, light and fizzy beers are actually extremely strong.

Make the most of any specialist local breweries that offer particularly good or unusual beers not readily available outside the area. As well as selling live beer on its yeasty sediment, in casks or by the bottle, or bottled "bright" beer without the same level of active yeast (and therefore to be consumed within a couple of days), specialist breweries usually prepare seasonal beers. For example, for a limited period they may offer refreshing summer brews or warming winter ales. When buying a cask, always take advice from the brewery on the delivery and setting up of the barrel or storing the beer before the party, if appropriate.

When beer is offered as an alternative to wine, a light, lager-type brew that is thirst quenching and not too strong usually appeals to most tastes. This type of beer is good for barbecues, informal cooking (such as pasta dishes and meat sauces) and spicy meals (Mexican or Indian dishes, for example).

Fruit-flavoured beers are a good choice for drinks parties. The rich ales and very dark beers – such as British stout or the famous Irish Guinness – are a good alternative to red wine with robust, hard cheeses, such as mature (sharp) Cheddar. They are also excellent with meaty stews and casseroles and are a popular substitute for wine for informal lunches and suppers.

Light beers should be served well chilled. Darker beers are usually served cool – at cellar or cool room temperature – rather than chilled. However, this is a matter for personal preference and many prefer dark beers lightly chilled. Tall, slim lager glasses or large, stemmed balloon glasses are ideal for light beers. Larger tankards are traditional for the darker beers but they are not necessarily ideal for parties, when tall glasses are much more practical.

Glasses

Disposable cups may be cheap and good for avoiding hours at the sink but they do absolutely nothing for any drink, wine, spirits or otherwise. Even the most humble wine tastes better from a decent glass, and a pleasing glass is one that is well balanced to hold, sturdy enough to feel safe but not chunky, and with a fine rim from which to sip. The bowl should be big and it should taper in towards the mouth to capture the aromas given off by the wine.

Conventionally, white wine glasses are smaller than red, which was thought to have more aroma and body to occupy a part-filled glass, but there is no good reason for this as whites are just as pleasing to swirl and sniff before sipping. The best solution for dinner parties is to have large white wine glasses and extra-large glasses for red.

Champagne and sparkling wines should be served in tall, slim, straight-sided flutes. These are designed to hold the bubbles, or mousse, of the wine for as long as possible, keeping it sparkling down to the last sip. The champagne saucers of the 1960s – wide and shallow glasses – allow all the bubbles to escape from the large surface area of the wine.

Fortified wines are served in smaller quantities, so smaller glasses are used, but they should still be large enough for the aroma and substance of the wine to be appreciated. Old-fashioned sherry glasses and even smaller liqueur glasses are sad receptacles.

Tall glasses and tankards

In addition to wine glasses, medium to large plain glasses (250ml/8fl oz/ 1 cup to 300ml/½ pint/1¼ cups) are basic, ideally the smaller ones for spirits and mixed drinks and the larger for water, soft drinks (sodas), juices, cider or beer. Large-bowled wine glasses

Above *Wine glasses are a preferable option to disposable cups.*

with sturdy stems are excellent for light beers, cider and substantial soft drinks. Tall, larger glasses are good for light beers, retaining the fizz and being well balanced to hold. Straight-sided glasses holding 600ml/1 pint/2½ cups are preferred for larger quantities of beer; jugs (pitchers) with handles or tankards are also satisfying for large amounts.

Quantities

A bottle of wine yields six average glasses. The amount consumed at a dinner party depends entirely on the company, ambience and attitude. It is always better to have more wine than needed and more than one bottle of each type than too little. When serving a selection of wines, remember that some guests may prefer to drink all white or all red rather than change with the courses. On average, allow one bottle for two non-drivers.

When catering for a large gathering, calculate the number of glasses based on six from a bottle. When serving sparkling wine as an introductory drink, allow extra unless the wine will not be served until everyone is gathered, as those who arrive first will probably

Above *Serve beer in tall glasses, pint glasses or tankards.*

consume slightly more. When selecting special wines, such as good champagne for a large special-occasion party, it can be worth buying from a supplier offering a special deal. Guests will often bring a bottle to informal parties.

Below *One bottle of wine will provide around six average glasses.*

Classic Cocktails

The cocktail party can be a fun occasion for a Twenties or Thirties theme or a sophisticated contemporary gathering. If you are planning a fancy dress party, write fun invitations and ask guests to dress in style. Go to town on decorative, colourful cocktails, with novelty cocktail sticks, swizzle sticks and straws. Follow the theme through with music from the era and encourage guests to dance. Conversely, adopt a stylishly understated approach to a contemporary cocktail party, with smart drinks, canapés and nibbles. Keep the music low and lighting discreet, and concentrate on circulating and instigating stimulating conversation.

The cocktail bar
Invite guests to join in the mixing and shaking at a fun party, with the bar working from the kitchen. For more sophisticated gatherings, arrange a trolley or small table from which to shake, stir and pour, then use the kitchen as back-up. Hiring a good bartender will be worth every penny as long as the cocktail list, numbers and shopping list are discussed and agreed in advance.

Below *Cool and refreshing cocktails are ideal on a hot day.*

Whether the party is fun or formal, focus on a few cocktails based on a limited number of drinks, and stick to that list. Have a recipe sheet and all decorations or accessories ready. Include a number of alcohol-free drinks.

Cocktail equipment
Bar measures and a small measuring jug (cup) are useful. The traditional single measure is 25ml/¾fl oz/1½ tbsp and the double is 45ml/1½fl oz/3 tbsp. If you do not have specialist measures, use a small sherry glass or similar. A set of measuring spoons is also essential.
Shaker: you will need several cocktail shakers for a party. Look out for those that have integral strainers. Make sure the shakers have tight-fitting tops and that they pour well.

Above *The choice of equipment is vast but you only need a few essentials.*

Mixing jug (pitcher): use for drinks that are stirred not shaken – look for one with a good pouring spout.
Blender: a goblet blender is useful for frothy cocktails. Do not crush ice in the blender, as this will blunt the blade.
Strainer: for straining mixed drinks into glasses.
Muddler: a long stirring stick with a bulbous end, which is used for crushing sugar or mint leaves.
Mini-whisk: a long-handled balloon whisk with a small balloon for whisking and frothing drinks.
Citrus squeezer: look for one with a deep container underneath and a good strainer to keep out the pips (seeds).

Cannelle knife (zester): Use for paring
fine shreds of rind from citrus fruit. It
can also be used for cutting individual,
slightly larger but thin strips and to
mark a pattern in the fruit rind. When
sliced the rind forms a decorative edge
– add the slices to drinks or place over
the edge of glasses.
Nutmeg grater: a small, fine grater
for grating whole nutmeg.
**Straws, swizzle sticks and decorative
cocktail sticks**: just some of the
finishing touches for decorating drinks.

Glasses
Cocktail or martini glass: the classic
V-shaped cocktail glass keeps warm
hands away from cool drinks. This
holds about 100ml/3½fl oz/½ cup.
Collins glass: the tallest of glasses with
narrow, straight sides, this holds about
250ml/8fl oz/1 cup.
Old-fashioned glass: the classic
whisky glass, this is wide and short
and it is referred to as a 175ml/6oz/
¾ cup glass.
Highball glass: this is a 250ml/8fl oz/
1 cup glass.
Liqueur glass: the smallest of glasses,
this holds about 50ml/2fl oz/¼ cup.

Below *A wide variety of different
shaped glasses are suitable for cocktails.*

Above *Small whole fruit, such as
cherries or strawberries, can be used
as decorations.*

Brandy balloon or snifter: the
rounded shape is designed to be
cupped in the hands to warm the
contents while the narrow rim traps
the aroma of the drink.
Large cocktail goblets: these vary in
size and shape. Designed for serving
longer or frothy drinks, these glasses
have wide rims.
Champagne glasses: either saucers or
tall narrow flutes. The flute is the best
for sparkling wine and champagne
cocktails; the saucer can be used for a
variety of cocktails or drinks.
Red wine balloon: holding 250ml/
8fl oz/1 cup, this should be filled about
half-full to allow room for swirling the
wine and releasing its aroma.
White wine glass: a long-stemmed
glass held by the stem, so that warm

hands keep away from chilled wine.
Pousse-café: a thin and narrow glass
with a short stem, this is used for
layered and floating cocktails.

Below *Slices of lemon or lime add
colour and flavour to many cocktails
such as a Moscow Mule.*

Drinks Checklist

Familiarize yourself with the flavours before writing your cocktail menu. The following is a basic guide:

Brandy: Cognac and Armagnac are the two French brandies. Fruit brandies or eaux-de-vie include peach, cherry and apricot brandy.

Champagne: dry (brut) champagne features in many cocktails. Champagne has the best mousse for making excellent fizzy cocktails, but less expensive sparkling wines, such as Spanish Cava, can be used instead.

Gin: familiar as an aperitif with tonic, gin is used in a variety of cocktails. It is flavoured with juniper berries.

Rum: dark rum is punchy but light rum is clear; both can be used for cocktails.

Tequila: a powerful Mexican spirit distilled from the juice of the agave cactus. Used in a variety of cocktails.

Vermouth: dry white, sweet white or red, or bittersweet rosé, there are many brands of these herb-flavoured aperitifs. The more expensive brands are generally better quality.

Vodka: as well as the basic, slightly peppery strong spirit, there are many varieties of flavoured vodkas, some subtle with herbs or spices, others distinct with fruit. A good quality plain vodka is useful for most cocktails.

Whisky: basic whisky is good enough for cocktails rather than masking the flavour of a long-matured single malt.

Liqueur flavours

Amaretto di Saronno: a sweet almond-flavoured liqueur.

Anisette: aniseed-flavoured liqueurs include French Pernod, Italian sambuca and Spanish anis.

Bénédictine: made by Benedictine monks of Fécamp in Normandy, this golden liqueur is flavoured with myrrh, honey and herbs.

Chartreuse: originally made by Carthusian monks at La Grande

Chartreuse monastery. This brandy-based liqueur is available as a green or yellow drink. Herbs, honey and spices flavour the liqueur. Yellow Chartreuse is flavoured with orange and myrtle.

Cointreau: orange liqueur.

Crème de cacao: French cocoa-flavoured liqueur.

Crème de cassis: blackcurrant-flavoured liqueur – add a little to chilled dry white wine to make kir or use it to flavour champagne for kir royale.

Crème de menthe: mint liqueur.

Curaçao: orange-flavoured, rum-based liqueur that is available coloured blue, clear or orange-brown.

Drambuie: malt whisky liqueur with herbs, honey and spices.

Galliano: golden liqueur flavoured with herbs, liquorice and aniseed.

Grand Marnier: French Cognac-based liqueur, flavoured with bitter bergamot and orange.

Kahlúa: Mexican coffee-based liqueur with a rich flavour.

Southern Comfort: sweet fruity liqueur based on bourbon whiskey.

Above *Strawberry and banana daiquiris are popular cocktails.*

Crushing ice

In the absence of an ice-crushing machine, lay out a clean dishtowel and cover half with ice cubes. Fold the other half of the cloth over, and then use a rolling pin or mallet to crush the ice fairly coarsely. Store in plastic bags in the freezer. If necessary, crush the ice finely just before using it.

Below *Crushed ice can be prepared in advance and frozen until ready to use.*

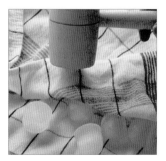

Making decorative ice cubes

These are particularly good for enlivening simple cocktails and mixed soft drinks.

1 Half-fill ice cube trays with water and freeze until firm.

2 Dip pieces of fruit, olives, citrus rind, edible flowers or mint leaves in cold water, then place in the ice cube trays.

3 Top up the trays with water and freeze until hard.

Below *Ice cubes with edible flowers.*

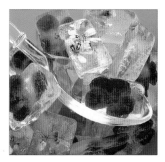

Frosting glasses

This simple technique adds a decorative and/or flavoured edge to the glass. Instead of sugar, the rim can be dipped into celery salt, grated coconut, grated chocolate, coloured sugar or cocoa powder. The flavouring depends on the type of drink you intend to serve. Place the frosted glass in the refrigerator until it is required.

1 Hold the glass upside down so that the juice does not run down the outside when you wet it. Rub the rim of the glass with the cut surface of a lemon, lime or orange.

2 Keep the glass upside down, then lightly dip it in a shallow dish of sugar, coconut, salt or celery salt. Re-dip the glass, if necessary, so that the rim is well coated.

3 Turn the glass the right way up and leave to stand for a while until the rim has dried. Chill in the refrigerator before pouring the drink into the middle of the glass.

Basic sugar syrup

Some cocktails include sugar syrup. This can be made in advance and stored in a sterilized airtight bottle in the refrigerator for up to 1 month.

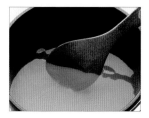

1 Mix 175g/6oz/scant 1 cup sugar and 600ml/1 pint/2½ cups water in a heavy pan. Heat gently, stirring, until the sugar has dissolved.

2 Brush the inside of the pan with cold water to clean any splashes of sugar that may crystallize.

3 Stop stirring and boil for 3–5 minutes. Skim off any scum and, when it stops forming, remove the pan from the heat. Pour the cooled syrup into sterilized bottles.

Traditional Cocktails

Knowledge of a good selection of classic cocktails is essential, and some favourites are given here, but you may also enjoy creating your own.

Black Velvet: combine equal parts Guinness and champagne.

Bloody Mary: mix 1 part vodka with 2 parts tomato juice. Stir in a dash of Worcestershire sauce or Tabasco and add a squeeze of lemon.

Brandy Alexander: shake together 1 part brandy, 1 part crème de cacao and 1 part double (heavy) cream. Serve dusted with freshly grated nutmeg.

Buck's Fizz: serve 1 part freshly squeezed orange juice topped up with 1 part champagne.

Daiquiri: shake 15ml/1 tbsp lime juice with 45ml/3 tbsp white rum and 5ml/

Below Bloody Mary served with celery, olives and cherry tomatoes.

1 tsp sugar on crushed ice. Pour into a sugar-frosted glass. Add fruit, such as banana or strawberry, if you like.

Dry Martini: shake 2 parts gin with 1 part dry white vermouth. Pour into a glass and add a stuffed green olive. Some prefer to reverse the quantities, with 1 part gin to 2 parts vermouth.

Harvey Wallbanger: place some ice in a tall glass and add 2 parts vodka and 6 parts orange juice, then float 1 part Galliano on the surface.

Long Island Iced Tea: Mix equal parts vodka, gin, light rum, and tequila (optional) and lemon. Sweeten with a little sugar syrup and top up with cola. Serve on ice.

Manhattan: Mix 1 part each of dry and sweet vermouth with 4 parts rye whisky.

Margarita: shake 1 part Curaçao, 4 parts tequila and 1 part lime juice. Serve in a salt-frosted glass.

Above *Brandy Alexander.*

Above *Martini with olives and chillies.*

Below *Strawberry Daiquiri.*

Above *Harvey Wallbanger with orange.*

Above *Long Island Iced Tea with mint.*

Below *Perfect Manhattan.*

Above *Margarita with lime.*

Below *Blushing Piña Colada.*

Piña Colada: shake 3 parts white rum with 4 parts pineapple juice, 2 parts coconut cream, 30ml/2 tbsp grenadine and 15ml/1 tbsp sugar syrup. Serve decorated with pineapple and a maraschino cherry.

Pink Gin: add a dash of Angostura bitters to a gin.

Rusty Nail: stir 2 parts whisky with 1 part Drambuie and serve on ice.

Tequila Sunrise: mix 1 part tequila with 2 parts orange juice. Pour 5ml/ 1 tsp grenadine into a glass and add ice, then carefully pour in the orange mix.

Whisky Sour: shake 1 measure whisky with the juice of ½ lemon and 5ml/ 1 tsp sugar on crushed ice. Pour into a glass.

Punches and **Cups**

Warming mulled wine, heady punches or delicate fruit cups are excellent welcome drinks for medium to large parties. Most well-seasoned party givers have their favourite recipes for a summer punch and a warming winter wine cup. The following are basic recipes to tempt you into experimenting further.

Mulled Wine: the classic Christmas drink for complementing melt-in-the-mouth mince pies. Stud 1 orange with 8 cloves and place it in a pan. Add 1 cinnamon stick and 60ml/4 tbsp sugar. Pour in a bottle of red wine and add 150ml/¼ pint/⅔ cup brandy or rum. Cover and place over very gentle heat for 30 minutes. The wine should be just hot and aromatic. Taste and add more sugar if required. Serve hot.

Honey Glühwein: mix a handful each of raisins and blanched almonds with 1 lemon studded with 4 cloves, 1 cinnamon stick, 150ml/¼ pint/⅔ cup rum, 30ml/2 tbsp honey and 1 bottle red wine in a pan. Cover and heat very gently for about 30 minutes, or until the wine is just hot. Taste for sweetness and add more honey as required.

White Wine Cup: place 150ml/ ¼ pint/⅔ cup brandy in a bowl. Add ½ sliced orange, ¼ sliced cucumber and some mint sprigs. Cover and leave to macerate for several hours – this can

Below *Warming mulled wine.*

be left overnight. Add 1 well-chilled bottle dry white wine and top up with 900ml/1½ pints/3¾ cups chilled tonic water or lemonade.

Elderflower Strawberry Cup: rinse 4 elderflower heads and place in a bowl with 50g/2oz/½ cup halved strawberries. Add 750ml/1¼ pints/ 3 cups sparkling mineral water and 60ml/4 tbsp sugar. Stir well, crushing the elderflowers slightly and pressing

Below *Cider punch with lemon rind.*

Above *Serve refreshing white wine cup with ice and garnish with borage.*

the strawberries without crushing them. Cover and leave to stand overnight, then chill well. Strain the mineral water into a bowl. Add 175g/6oz/1½ cups sliced strawberries and a bottle of chilled sparkling white wine. Taste for sweetness and decorate the bowl with washed elderflowers before serving.

Cider Punch: place 1 sliced lemon, 1 sliced orange, 1 quartered, cored and sliced apple and several mint sprigs in a bowl. Pour in 300ml/½ pint/1¼ cups medium-dry sherry. Cover and leave to macerate for several hours or overnight. Add 1 litre/1¾ pints/4 cups well-chilled dry (hard) cider and top up with 1 litre/ 1¾ pints/4 cups sparkling mineral water.

Sangria: slice 2 oranges and 2 lemons and place in a jug (pitcher) with 150ml/ ¼ pint/⅔ cup brandy or Grand Marnier. Add 1 bottle red wine, cover and leave to macerate for several hours. Add 2 cored and sliced apples and top up with 1 litre/1⅓ pints/4 cups lemonade and 600ml/1 pint/2½ cups orange juice, soda water (club soda), or sparkling mineral water.

Alcohol-free drinks

Although there is a wide choice of commercial soft drinks (sodas), there are many home-made cold drinks that are a real summer's treat for picnics or garden parties. Here is a selection:

Lemonade: grate the rind of 4 lemons and squeeze their juice. Place the rind and juice in a bowl and add 175g/6oz/scant 1 cup sugar. Add 600ml/1 pint/2½ cups boiling water, stir well and cover. Leave to stand overnight. Stir in a further 600ml/ 1 pint/2½ cups water, add 1 lemon cut into slices and some ice cubes. For picnics, carry the chilled lemonade in a bottle in a chiller bag.

Above *Sangria is a cool summer drink.*

Ice Cream Soda: place a scoop of good-quality vanilla ice cream in a tall glass. Slowly add lemonade or soda water (lemonade is sweeter and tastes

Above *Thirst-quenching St. Clements.*

better even though soda water is correct), allowing the ice cream to froth up before filling the glass more than half-full. Decorate with berries, add a straw and long spoon and serve.

Strawberry Banana Shake: purée 115g/4oz/1 cup hulled strawberries and 1 banana with 50g/2oz/¼ cup caster (superfine) sugar in a blender. Gradually add 600ml/1 pint/2½ cups chilled milk with the motor running. Pour into four glasses, add a large scoop of vanilla ice cream to each and decorate with fresh strawberries. For picnics, carry the chilled shake in a vacuum flask and omit the ice cream.

Mango and Lime Smoothie: peel, stone (pit) and dice 1 ripe mango, then purée it with the grated rind and juice of 1 lime. Add 600ml/1 pint/2½ cups chilled natural (plain) yogurt and process for a few seconds. Sweeten with honey and serve immediately. For picnics, carry the chilled drink in a vacuum flask.

St. Clements: top up orange juice with an equal quantity of lemonade and serve with ice.

Left *Old-fashioned lemonade is great at summer barbecues and picnics.*

welcome nibbles

Stylish snacks and little bites set every gathering

off to the right start. Choose a variety of different tastes

and textures to complement the drinks you serve.

Tortilla Chips

A useful and quick-to-prepare appetizer, tortilla chips or *totopos* as they are also known are excellent for scooping up a salsa or dip. They can also be sprinkled with a little grated cheese and grilled until golden, then served with a selection of other nibbles. Use corn tortillas that are a few days old; fresh tortillas will not crisp up so well.

Makes 48

8 corn tortillas
oil, for frying
salt

COOK'S TIP
The oil needs to be very hot for cooking the tortillas chips – test it first by carefully adding one of the wedges to the frying pan. It should float and begin to bubble in the oil immediately.

1 Cut each corn tortilla into six triangular wedges. Pour oil into a large, heavy frying pan to a depth of about 1cm/½ in, place the frying pan over a medium heat and heat until very hot (see Cook's Tip).

VARIATION
To give a spicy flavour to the chips, prepare a mixture of garlic salt, paprika and a pinch of mace. Sprinkle over the freshly drained tortilla chips while they are still hot.

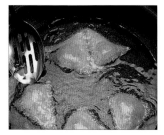

2 Fry the tortilla wedges in the hot oil in small batches until they turn golden and are crisp. This will only take a few moments. Remove with a slotted spoon and drain on kitchen paper. Sprinkle with salt.

3 The tortillas should be served warm. They can be cooled completely and stored in an airtight container for a few days, but will need to be reheated in a microwave or a warm oven before being served.

Pepitas

These crunchy, spicy and slightly sweet pumpkin seeds are absolutely irresistible, especially if you use hot and tasty chipotle chillies to spice them up. Their smoky flavour is the perfect foil for the nutty taste of the pumpkin seeds and the hint of sweetness provided by the sugar. Serve bowls of pepitas with pre-dinner drinks and cocktails as an alternative to nuts.

Makes 2 bowls

250g/9oz/2 cups pumpkin seeds
8 garlic cloves, crushed
2.5ml/½ tsp salt
20ml/4 tsp crushed dried chillies
10ml/2 tsp caster (superfine) sugar
2 wedges of lime

1 Heat a small, heavy frying pan, add the pumpkin seeds and dry-fry for a few minutes, stirring constantly as they swell.

COOK'S TIPS
• It is important to keep the pumpkin seeds moving as they cook. Watch them carefully and do not let them burn, or they will taste bitter.
• Chipotle chillies are smoke-dried jalapeño chillies.

2 When all the seeds have swollen, add the garlic and cook for a few minutes more, stirring constantly. Add the salt and the crushed chillies and stir to mix. Turn off the heat, but keep the pan on the stove. Sprinkle the sugar over the seeds and shake the pan to make sure that they are all coated.

3 Tip the pepitas into a bowl and serve with the wedge of lime for squeezing over the seeds. If the lime is omitted, the seeds can be cooled and stored in an airtight container for serving cold or reheating later, but they are best served fresh and warm.

VARIATION
If you are using the pepitas cold, they can be mixed with cashew nuts and dried cranberries to make a spicy and fruity bowl of nibbles.

Marinated Feta Cheese with Capers

Marinating cubes of feta cheese with herbs and spices gives it a really marvellous flavour.

Serves 6

350g/12oz feta cheese
2 garlic cloves
2.5ml/¹/₂ tsp mixed peppercorns
8 coriander seeds
1 bay leaf
15–30ml/1–2 tbsp drained capers
fresh oregano or thyme sprigs
olive oil, to cover
hot toast and chopped tomatoes,
  to serve

1 Cut the feta cheese into cubes. Thickly slice the garlic. Put the mixed peppercorns and coriander seeds in a mortar and crush lightly with a pestle.

2 Pack the feta cubes into a large preserving jar with the bay leaf, interspersing layers of cheese with garlic, crushed peppercorns and coriander, capers and the fresh oregano or thyme sprigs.

3 Pour in enough olive oil to cover the cubes of cheese. Close tightly and leave to marinate for 2 weeks in the refrigerator.

4 Lift out the feta cubes and serve on hot toast, with some chopped tomatoes and a little of the flavoured oil from the jar drizzled over.

COOK'S TIP
Add 50–75g/2–3oz/¹/₂–³/₄ cup pitted black or green olives to the feta cheese in the marinade if you like.

Tapas of **Almonds**, **Olives** and **Cheese**

These three simple ingredients are lightly flavoured to create a Spanish tapas medley that is perfect to serve with pre-dinner drinks.

Serves 6–8

For the marinated olives
2.5ml/½ tsp coriander seeds
2.5ml/½ tsp fennel seeds
5ml/1 tsp chopped fresh rosemary
10ml/2 tsp chopped fresh parsley
2 garlic cloves, crushed
15ml/1 tbsp sherry vinegar
30ml/2 tbsp olive oil
225g/8oz/1⅓ cup black and green
    pitted or stuffed olives

For the marinated cheese
150g/5oz goat's cheese
90ml/6 tbsp olive oil
15ml/1 tbsp white wine vinegar
5ml/1 tsp black peppercorns
1 garlic clove, sliced
3 fresh tarragon or thyme sprigs
fresh tarragon sprigs, to garnish

For the salted almonds
1.5ml/¼ tsp cayenne pepper
30ml/2 tbsp sea salt
25g/1oz/2 tbsp butter
60ml/4 tbsp olive oil
200g/7oz/1¾ cups blanched almonds

1 To marinate the olives, crush the coriander and fennel seeds. Mix with the rosemary, parsley, garlic, vinegar and oil and pour over the olives in a bowl. Cover and chill for up to 1 week.

2 To make the marinated cheese, cut the cheese into bitesize pieces, leaving the rind on. Mix together the oil, vinegar, peppercorns, garlic and herb sprigs and pour over the cheese in a bowl. Cover and chill for up to 3 days. Use a spoon and fork to turn the cheese cubes in the marinade.

3 To make the salted almonds, mix together the cayenne pepper and salt in a bowl. Melt the butter with the olive oil in a frying pan. Add the almonds and cook, stirring constantly, for 5 minutes, or until the almonds are golden.

4 Tip the almonds out of the frying pan, into the salt mixture and toss together until the almonds are coated. Leave to cool, then store them in a jar or airtight container for up to 1 week.

5 To serve the tapas, arrange in small, shallow serving dishes. Use fresh sprigs of tarragon to garnish the cheese and sprinkle the almonds with a little more salt, if you like.

Dates Stuffed with Chorizo

This is a delicious combination from Spain, using fresh dates and spicy chorizo sausage. Serve as a hot snack at a drinks party or before a robust meal.

Serves 4–6

50g/2oz chorizo sausage
12 fresh dates, stoned (pitted)
6 streaky (fatty) bacon
  rashers (strips)
oil, for frying
plain (all-purpose) flour,
  for dusting
1 egg, beaten
50g/2oz/1 cup fresh breadcrumbs

1 Using a sharp knife, trim the ends of the chorizo sausage and then peel off the skin with your fingers and discard. Cut the sausage into three 2cm/¾in slices. Cut the slices in half lengthways, then cut them into quarters, giving 12 pieces in total.

2 Stuff the cavity of each date with a piece of chorizo, closing the date around it. Stretch the bacon, by running the back of a knife along the rasher. Cut each rasher in half, widthways. Wrap a piece of bacon around each date and secure with a wooden cocktail stick (toothpick).

3 In a deep pan, heat 1cm/½in of oil. Dust the dates with flour, dip them in the beaten egg, then coat in breadcrumbs. Cook the dates in the hot oil, turning them, frequently until golden. Remove the dates with a slotted spoon, and drain on kitchen paper. Serve immediately.

Spicy Peanut Balls

Tasty rice balls, rolled in chopped peanuts and deep-fried, make a delicious party snack. Serve them as they are, or with a sweet chilli sauce for dipping.

Makes 16

1 garlic clove, crushed
1cm/¹/₂ in piece fresh root ginger,
* peeled and finely chopped*
1.5ml/¹/₄ tsp ground turmeric
5ml/1 tsp granulated sugar
2.5ml/¹/₂ tsp salt
5ml/1 tsp chilli sauce
10ml/2 tsp Thai fish sauce or soy sauce
30ml/2 tbsp chopped fresh
* coriander (cilantro)*
juice of ¹/₂ lime
225g/8oz/2 cups cooked white long
* grain rice*
115g/4oz/1 cup peanuts, chopped
vegetable oil, for deep-frying
lime wedges and chilli dipping sauce,
* to serve (optional)*

1 Put the garlic, ginger and turmeric in a food processor or blender and process until the mixture forms a paste. Add the sugar, salt, chilli sauce and fish sauce or soy sauce, with the chopped coriander and lime juice. Process briefly to mix the ingredients.

COOK'S TIP

Be sure to include a variety of nibbles so that guests with a nut allergy will have plenty to eat too.

2 Add three-quarters of the cooked rice to the paste in the food processor and process until smooth and sticky. Scrape into a mixing bowl and stir in the remainder of the rice. Wet your hands and shape the mixture into thumb-size balls.

3 Place the chopped peanut in a dish and roll the balls in them, making sure they are evenly coated.

4 Heat the oil in a deep-fryer or wok. Add the peanut balls and cook until crisp. Drain well on kitchen paper and then pile on to a warmed platter. Serve hot with lime wedges and chilli dipping sauce, if you like.

Potato and Onion Tortilla with Broad Beans

This Spanish omelette, which includes herbs and broad beans, is ideal for a summer party when cut into pieces and served as a tapa.

Serves 8–10

45ml/3 tbsp olive oil
2 Spanish onions, thinly sliced
300g/11oz waxy potatoes, cut into
*   1cm/½in dice*
250g/9oz/1½ cups shelled broad
*   (fava) beans*
5ml/1 tsp chopped fresh thyme or
*   summer savory*
6 large (US extra large) eggs
45ml/3 tbsp mixed chopped chives
*   and chopped flat leaf parsley*
salt and ground black pepper

1 Heat 30ml/2 tbsp of the oil in a 23cm/9in deep non-stick frying pan. Add the onions and potatoes and stir to coat. Cover and cook gently, stirring frequently, for 20–25 minutes, until the potatoes are cooked and the onions collapsed. Do not let the vegetables turn brown.

2 Meanwhile, cook the beans in salted, boiling water for 5 minutes. Drain well and set aside to cool.

3 When the beans are cool enough to handle, peel off the grey outer skins. Add the beans to the frying pan, together with the thyme or savory and season with salt and pepper to taste. Stir well and cook for 2–3 minutes.

4 Beat the eggs with salt and pepper to taste, add the mixed herbs, then pour over the potatoes and onions and increase the heat slightly. Cook gently until the egg on the bottom sets and browns, gently pulling the omelette away from the sides of the pan and tilting it to allow the uncooked egg to run underneath.

5 Invert the tortilla on to a plate. Add the remaining oil to the pan and heat until hot. Slip the tortilla back into the pan, uncooked side down, and cook for another 3–5 minutes to allow the underneath to brown.

6 Slide the tortilla out on to a clean plate. Use a sharp knife to cut the tortilla into eight to ten pieces or small squares and serve warm.

COOK'S TIP
Cook the tortilla very gently once the eggs have been added to the pan – trying to speed up the cooking process by raising the temperature browns the underneath much too soon, before the egg has had time to set.

Little Onions Cooked with **Wine, Coriander** and **Olive Oil**

If you can find the small, flat Italian cipolla or borettane onions, they are excellent in this recipe – otherwise use pickling onions, small red onions or shallots.

Serves 6

105ml/7 tbsp olive oil
675g/1½ lb small onions, peeled
150ml/¼ pint/⅔ cup dry white wine
2 bay leaves
2 garlic cloves, bruised
1–2 small dried red chillies
15ml/1 tbsp coriander seeds, toasted
   and lightly crushed
2.5ml/½ tsp sugar
a few fresh thyme sprigs
30ml/2 tbsp currants
10ml/2 tsp chopped fresh oregano
5ml/1 tsp grated lemon rind
15ml/1 tbsp chopped fresh flat
   leaf parsley
30–45ml/2–3 tbsp pine nuts, toasted
salt and ground black pepper

1 Place 30ml/2 tbsp olive oil in a wide pan. Add the onions and cook gently over a medium heat for about 5 minutes, or until they begin to colour. Remove from the pan and set aside.

2 Add the remaining oil, the wine, bay leaves, garlic, chillies, coriander seeds, sugar and thyme to the pan. Bring to the boil and cook briskly for 5 minutes. Return the onions to the pan.

3 Add the currants, reduce the heat and cook gently for 15–20 minutes, or until the onions are tender but not falling apart. Use a slotted spoon to transfer the onions to a serving dish.

4 Boil the liquid over a high heat until it reduces considerably. Taste and adjust the seasoning, if necessary, then pour the reduced liquid over the onions. Sprinkle the oregano over the onions, set aside to cool and then chill.

5 Just before serving stir in the grated lemon rind, chopped flat leaf parsley and toasted pine nuts.

COOK'S TIP
Serve this dish with other small dishes such as an antipasto, or with some thinly sliced prosciutto or other air-dried ham.

Party Eggs

Hard-boiled eggs make perfect party food. Use a variety of fillings for a stunning centrepiece. Double the quantities if you are making larger batches.

Each variation fills 6 eggs

EGGS WITH CAVIAR

6 eggs, hard-boiled
4 spring onions (scallions), trimmed
   and very thinly sliced
30ml/2 tbsp sour cream
5ml/1 tsp lemon juice
25g/1oz/2 tbsp caviar
salt and ground black pepper
lemon rind and caviar, to garnish

Mix all the ingredients with the egg yolks, spoon back into the egg whites and garnish with lemon rind and caviar.

PRAWN AND CUCUMBER EGGS

6 eggs, hard-boiled
75g/3oz/scant 1 cup cooked peeled
   prawns (shrimp), reserving 12 for
   garnish and the rest chopped
25g/1oz cucumber, peeled and diced
5ml/1 tsp tomato ketchup
15ml/1 tbsp lemon mayonnaise
salt and ground black pepper
fennel sprigs, to garnish

Mix all the ingredients with the egg yolks, spoon back into the egg whites and garnish with the reserved prawns and fennel sprigs.

NUTTY DEVILLED EGGS

6 eggs, hard-boiled
40g/1½oz cooked ham, chopped
4 walnut halves, very finely chopped
15ml/1 tbsp Dijon mustard
15ml/1 tbsp mayonnaise
5ml/1 tsp white wine vinegar
few large pinches of cayenne pepper
salt and ground black pepper
paprika and gherkins, to garnish

Mix together all the ingredients with the egg yolks, spoon into the whites and garnish with paprika and gherkin slices.

GARLIC AND GREEN PEPPERCORN EGGS

5ml/1 tsp garlic purée or 1 large garlic
   clove, crushed
45ml/3 tbsp crème fraîche
6 eggs, hard-boiled
salt and ground black pepper
2.5ml/½ tsp green peppercorns,
   crushed, to garnish

Mix the garlic, crème fraîche, egg yolks and seasoning. Place in a piping (pastry) bag and pipe into the egg whites. Sprinkle with the peppercorns.

Stuffed Devilled Eggs

These eggs are so simple to make yet guests will always be impressed by them. They have a wonderful flavour and can be given quite a spicy "kick" too by including the cayenne pepper.

Serves 6

6 eggs, hard-boiled
40g/1¹/₂oz/¹/₄ cup minced (ground)
    cooked ham
6 walnut halves, minced
15ml/1 tbsp minced spring
    onion (scallion)
15ml/1 tbsp Dijon mustard
15ml/1 tbsp mayonnaise
10ml/2 tsp vinegar
1.5ml/¹/₄ tsp salt
1.5ml/¹/₄ tsp ground black pepper
1.5ml/¹/₄ tsp cayenne pepper (optional)
paprika and gherkin slices, to garnish

1 Cut each hard-boiled egg in half lengthways. Put the yolks in a bowl and set the whites aside.

2 Mash the egg yolks well with a fork, or push them through a sieve with a wooden spoon. Add the ham, nuts, spring onion, mustard, mayonnaise, vinegar, salt, black pepper and cayenne pepper, if using, and mix well with the yolks. Taste and add more salt and pepper if necessary.

3 Spoon the filling into the egg white halves, or pipe it in with a piping (pastry) bag and nozzle. Garnish the top of each stuffed egg with a little paprika and a small star or other shape cut from the pickle slices. Serve the stuffed eggs at room temperature.

Stuffed Celery Sticks

The creamy filling contrasts well with the crunchy celery, and the walnuts add a wonderful flavour. These tasty nibbles go well with pre-dinner drinks.

Serves 4–6

12 crisp, tender celery sticks
25g/1oz/¹/₄ cup crumbled blue cheese,
    such as Roquefort or Gorgonzola
115g/4oz/¹/₂ cup cream cheese
45ml/3 tbsp sour cream
50g/2oz/¹/₂ cup chopped walnuts

1 Trim the celery sticks. Wash them, if necessary, and dry well on kitchen paper. Cut into 10cm/4in lengths.

2 In a small bowl, combine the crumbled blue cheese, cream cheese and sour cream. Stir together with a wooden spoon until smoothly blended. Fold in all but 15ml/1 tbsp of the walnuts.

3 Fill the celery pieces with the cheese and nut mixture. Chill before serving, garnished with the reserved walnuts.

COOK'S TIP
Use the same filling to stuff cherry tomatoes. Cut off a slice at the top of each tomato, scoop out the seeds with a small spoon and fill. You could also fill chicory (Belgian endive) leaves in the same way as the celery. Serve all the stuffed vegetables together if you like.

Pickled Quail's Eggs

These Chinese eggs are pickled in alcohol and can be stored in a preserving jar in a cool, dark place for several months. They will make delicious bitesize snacks at a drinks party and are sure to delight guests.

Serves 12

12 quail's eggs
15ml/1 tbsp salt
750ml/1¼ pints/3 cups distilled or
   previously boiled water
15ml/1 tsp Sichuan peppercorns
150ml/¼ pint/²⁄₃ cup spirit such as
   Mou-tal (Chinese brandy), brandy,
   whisky, rum or vodka
dipping sauce (see Cook's Tip) and
   toasted sesame seeds, to serve

1 Boil the eggs for about 4 minutes until the yolks are soft but not runny.

2 Place the salt and the distilled or previously boiled water in a large pan and heat gently until the salt has dissolved. Add the peppercorns, then remove the pan from the heat, leave the water to cool, then add the spirit.

3 Gently tap the eggs all over to crack the shells, but do not peel them. Place in a large, airtight, sterilized jar and fill up with the liquid, totally covering the eggs. Seal the jar and leave the eggs to stand in a cool, dark place for about 7–8 days.

4 To serve, remove the eggs from the liquid and peel off the shells carefully. Serve whole with a dipping sauce and a bowl of toasted sesame seeds.

COOK'S TIPS
• Although you can buy Chinese dipping sauces in the supermarket, it is very easy to make your own at home. To make a quick dipping sauce, mix equal quantities of soy sauce and hoisin sauce.
• Be sure to use only boiled water or distilled water for the eggs, as the water must be completely free of bacteria or it will enter the porous shells.
• You can also pickle hard-boiled hen's eggs in the same way. Shell, then cut in half or quarters to serve. You will need to increase the quantity of liquid.

Eggs Mimosa

The use of the word mimosa describes the fine yellow and white grated egg which looks not unlike the flower of the same name. It can be used to finish any dish.

Serves 20

12 eggs, hard-boiled
2 ripe avocados, halved and
stoned (pitted)
1 garlic clove, crushed
Tabasco sauce, to taste
15ml/1 tbsp virgin olive oil
salt and ground black pepper
20 chicory (Belgian endive) leaves or
small crisp lettuce leaves, to serve
basil leaves, to garnish

1 Reserve 2 eggs, halve the remaining eggs and put the yolks in a mixing bowl. Blend or beat the yolks with the avocados, garlic, Tabasco sauce, oil and salt and pepper. Check the seasoning. Pipe or spoon this mixture back into the halved egg whites.

2 Sieve the two remaining egg whites and sprinkle over the filled eggs. Sieve the yolks on top. Arrange each half egg on a chicory or lettuce leaf and place them on a serving platter. Sprinkle the shredded basil over the filled egg halves before serving.

Mozzarella and Tomato Skewers

There's stacks of flavour in these layers of oven-baked mozzarella, tomatoes, basil and bread. These colourful kebabs will be popular with children and adults alike, so make plenty for everyone to enjoy.

Serves 10–12

24 slices white country bread, each
 about 1cm/½ in thick
90ml/6 tbsp olive oil
250g/9oz mozzarella cheese, cut into
 5mm/¼ in slices
6 ripe plum tomatoes, cut into
 5mm/¼ in slices
25g/1oz/1 cup fresh basil leaves,
 plus extra to garnish
salt and ground black pepper
60ml/4 tbsp chopped fresh flat leaf
 parsley, to garnish

1 Preheat the oven to 220°C/425°F/ Gas 7. Trim the crusts from the bread and cut each slice into four equal squares. Arrange on baking sheets and brush with half the olive oil. Bake for 3–5 minutes, until the squares are a pale golden colour.

2 Remove the bread squares from the oven and place them on a chopping board with the other ingredients.

3 Make 32 stacks, each starting with a square of bread, then a slice of the mozzarella topped with a slice of tomato and a basil leaf. Sprinkle with salt and pepper, then repeat, ending with a piece of bread. Push a skewer through each stack and place on the baking sheets. Drizzle with the remaining oil and bake for 10–15 minutes, until the cheese begins to melt. Garnish with basil and parsley.

Cherry Tomatoes with **Pesto**

These make a colourful and tasty appetizer to go with drinks before you move to the table. Make the pesto when fresh basil is plentiful, and freeze it in batches.

Serves 8–10

450g/1lb small cherry tomatoes

For the pesto
90g/3½ oz/3½ cups fresh basil leaves
3–4 garlic cloves
60ml/4 tbsp pine nuts
5ml/1 tsp salt, plus extra to taste
120ml/4fl oz/½ cup olive oil
45ml/3 tbsp freshly grated
   Parmesan cheese
90ml/6 tbsp freshly grated
   Pecorino cheese
ground black pepper

1 Wash the tomatoes. Slice off the top of each tomato and carefully scoop out the seeds with a melon baller or small spoon.

2 To make the pesto, place the basil, garlic, pine nuts, salt and olive oil in a blender or food processor and process until smooth. Remove the contents to a bowl with a rubber spatula. If you like, the pesto may be frozen at this point, before the cheeses are added.

3 If you have frozen the pesto, allow it to thaw completely before use.

4 Fold in the grated Parmesan and Pecorino cheeses. Season with pepper, and more salt if necessary.

5 Use a small spoon to fill each tomato with a little pesto. This dish is at its best if chilled in the refrigerator for about an hour before serving.

Stilton Croquettes

These are perfect little party bites, which you can make in advance and reheat at the last minute. For a really crisp result, double coat the croquettes in breadcrumbs.

Makes about 20

350g/12oz floury (mealy)
    potatoes, cooked
75g/3oz/¾ cup creamy Stilton
    cheese, crumbled
3 eggs, hard-boiled, peeled
    and chopped
few drops of Worcestershire sauce
plain (all-purpose) flour, for coating
1 egg, beaten
45–60ml/3–4 tbsp fine,
    dry breadcrumbs
vegetable oil, for deep-frying
salt and ground black pepper
dipping sauce or salsa, to serve

1 Mash the potatoes with a potato masher or fork until they are quite smooth. Work in the crumbled Stilton, chopped egg and Worcestershire sauce. Season with salt and ground black pepper to taste.

2 Divide the potato and cheese mixture into about 20 equal portions. Dust your hands lightly with flour and shape the pieces into small sausage shapes, no longer than about 2.5cm/1in in length.

3 Coat in flour, shaking off the excess, then dip into the beaten egg and, finally, coat evenly in breadcrumbs. Reshape, if necessary. Chill for about 30 minutes then deep-fry, seven to eight at a time, in hot oil turning frequently until they are golden brown all over. Drain well on kitchen paper, transfer to a serving dish and keep warm for up to 30 minutes. Serve with a dipping sauce, such as soy sauce or a tomato salsa.

Cheese Aigrettes

Choux pastry is often associated with sweet pastries, such as profiteroles, but these little savoury buns, flavoured with Gruyère and dusted with grated Parmesan, are just delicious. They are best made ahead and deep-fried to serve.

Makes 30

90g/3¹/₂ oz/scant 1 cup strong plain (all-purpose) flour
2.5ml/¹/₂ tsp paprika
2.5ml/¹/₂ tsp salt
75g/3oz/6 tbsp cold butter, diced
200ml/7fl oz/scant 1 cup water
3 eggs, beaten
75g/3oz/³/₄ cup mature (sharp) coarsely grated Gruyère cheese
corn or vegetable oil, for deep-frying
50g/2oz/²/₃ cup freshly grated Parmesan cheese
ground black pepper

1 Mix the flour, paprika and salt together by sifting them on to a large sheet of baking parchment. Add a generous amount of ground black pepper.

2 Put the diced butter and water into a medium pan and heat gently. As soon as the butter has melted and the liquid starts to boil, quickly tip in all the seasoned flour at once and beat very hard with a wooden spoon. Continue beating vigorously over a low heat until the paste comes away cleanly from the sides of the pan.

3 Remove the pan from the heat and leave the paste to cool for 5 minutes. Gradually beat in enough of the beaten egg to give a stiff dropping consistency that still holds a shape on the spoon. Mix in the Gruyère.

4 Heat the oil for deep-frying to 180°C/350°F or until a cube of bread, added to it, browns in 45 seconds. Take a teaspoonful of the choux paste and use a second spoon to slide it into the oil. Make more aigrettes in the same way. Deep-fry for 3–4 minutes, then drain on kitchen paper and keep warm while you are cooking successive batches. To serve, pile the aigrettes on a warmed serving dish and sprinkle with Parmesan.

COOK'S TIP

Filling these aigrettes gives a delightful surprise as you bite through their crisp shell. Make slightly larger aigrettes by dropping a slightly larger spoonful of paste into the hot oil. Slit them open and scoop out any soft paste. Fill the centres with taramasalata, hummus or crumbled Roquefort mixed with a little fromage frais (farmer's cheese).

Aromatic Tiger Prawns

There is no elegant way to eat these delicious aromatic prawns – just hold them by the tails, pull them off the sticks with your fingers and pop them into your mouth.

Serves 4

16 raw tiger prawns (jumbo shrimp)
2.5ml/½ tsp chilli powder
5ml/1 tsp fennel seeds
5 Sichuan or black peppercorns
1 star anise, broken into segments
1 cinnamon stick, broken into pieces
30ml/2 tbsp groundnut (peanut) oil
2 garlic cloves, chopped
2cm/¾in piece fresh root ginger,
    peeled and finely chopped
1 shallot, chopped
30ml/2 tbsp water
30ml/2 tbsp rice vinegar
30ml/2 tbsp soft brown or palm sugar
salt and ground black pepper
lime slices and chopped spring onion
    (scallion), to garnish

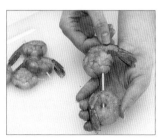

1 Peel the prawns, but leave the tails intact. Cut along the back of each prawn and remove the dark vein. Thread the prawns in pairs on to 8 wooden cocktail sticks (toothpicks) or small skewers. Set aside.

2 Heat a heavy frying pan, add the chilli powder, fennel seeds, Sichuan or black peppercorns, star anise and cinnamon stick and dry-fry for 1–2 minutes to release the flavours. Leave to cool, then grind coarsely in a grinder or tip into a mortar and crush with a pestle.

3 Heat the groundnut oil in a shallow pan, add the garlic, ginger and chopped shallot and cook over a low heat, stirring occasionally, until very lightly coloured. Add the crushed spices, season with salt and pepper and cook the mixture gently for 2 minutes. Pour in the water and simmer gently, stirring constantly, for about 5 minutes.

4 Add the rice vinegar and soft brown or palm sugar, stir until dissolved, then add the prawns. Cook for about 3–5 minutes, until the prawns have turned pink, but are still very juicy. Serve hot, garnished with lime slices and spring onion.

COOK'S TIP
You can use whole prawns for this recipe, but remove the heads before cooking the prawns.

Deep-fried Whitebait

A spicy coating on these fish gives this favourite dish a crunchy bite.

Serves 6

115g/4oz/1 cup plain (all-purpose) flour
2.5ml/$\frac{1}{2}$ tsp curry powder
2.5ml/$\frac{1}{2}$ tsp ground ginger
2.5ml/$\frac{1}{2}$ tsp cayenne pepper
1.2kg/2$\frac{1}{2}$ lb whitebait, thawed if frozen
vegetable oil, for deep-frying
salt
lemon wedges, to garnish

1 Mix together the flour, curry powder, ginger, cayenne pepper and a little salt in a large bowl or shallow dish.

2 Coat the fish in the seasoned flour, covering them evenly. Shake off any excess.

COOK'S TIP
To coat the fish evenly, place the seasoned flour in a clean plastic bag, add a few fish at a time and shake well.

3 Heat the oil in a large, heavy pan to 190°C/375°F or until a cube of bread, added to the oil, browns in about 30 seconds. Fry the whitebait, in batches, for 2–3 minutes, until the fish is golden and crispy.

4 Drain the whitebait well on kitchen paper. Transfer to a dish and keep warm in a low oven until you have cooked all the fish. Serve immediately garnished with lemon wedges for squeezing over.

Mini Sausage Rolls

These miniature versions of old-fashioned sausage rolls are always popular – the Parmesan cheese gives them an extra special flavour.

Makes about 48

15g/¹/₂oz/1 tbsp butter
1 onion, finely chopped
350g/12oz good quality sausage meat
  (bulk sausage)
15ml/1 tbsp dried mixed herbs, such as
  oregano, thyme, sage, tarragon or dill
25g/1oz finely chopped pistachio
  nuts (optional)
350g/12oz puff pastry, thawed if frozen
60–90ml/4–6 tbsp freshly grated
  Parmesan cheese
salt and ground black pepper
1 egg, lightly beaten, for glazing
poppy seeds, sesame seeds, fennel
  seeds and aniseeds, for sprinkling

1 Melt the butter in a small frying pan over a medium heat. Add the onion and cook, stirring occasionally, for about 5 minutes, until softened. Remove the pan from the heat and leave to cool. Put the softened onion, sausage meat, herbs and nuts (if using) in a mixing bowl. Season with a little salt and pepper and stir together until completely blended.

2 Divide the sausage mixture into four equal portions and roll into thin sausages measuring about 25cm/10in long. Set aside.

3 On a lightly floured surface, roll out the pastry to about 3mm/¹/₈in thick. Cut the pastry into four strips measuring 25 × 7.5cm/10 × 3in. Place a long sausage on each pastry strip and sprinkle each with a little grated Parmesan cheese.

VARIATION
Filo pastry can be used instead of puff pastry for a very light effect. Depending on the size of the filo sheets, cut into eight pieces 25 × 7.5cm/10 × 3in. Brush four of the sheets with a little melted butter or vegetable oil and place a second pastry sheet on top. Place one sausage log on each of the four layered sheets and roll up and bake as above.

4 Brush one long edge of each of the pastry strips with a little of the egg glaze and roll up to enclose each sausage. Set them seam side down and press gently to seal. Brush each one with the egg glaze and sprinkle with one type of seeds. Repeat with remaining pastry strips, sprinkling each with different seeds.

5 Preheat the oven to 220°C/425°F/Gas 7. Lightly grease a large baking sheet. Cut each of the pastry logs into 2.5cm/1in lengths and arrange them on the baking sheet. Bake for about 15 minutes, until the pastry is crisp and brown. Serve warm or leave to cool before serving.

COOK'S TIP
For best results, handle pastry dough as little as possible and keep it cool. Although frozen pastry needs to be thawed before use, keep it chilled until required. Rinse your hands in cold water and use a marble or glass rolling pin. Alternatively, use a rolling pin that can be filled with cold water. This helps to make sure that the pastry is crisp when cooked.

Tuna in Rolled Red Peppers

This lovely savoury combination originated in southern Italy. Grilled peppers have a sweet, smoky taste that combines particularly well with a robust fish like tuna. You could try canned mackerel instead.

Serves 8–10

3 large red (bell) peppers
200g/7oz can tuna, drained
30ml/2 tbsp lemon juice
45ml/3 tbsp olive oil
6 green or black olives, pitted
   and chopped
30ml/2 tbsp chopped fresh parsley
1 garlic clove, finely chopped
1 celery stick, very finely chopped
salt and ground black pepper

1 Arrange the peppers on a baking sheet and place under a hot grill (broiler). Cook, turning them occasionally, until they are charred and blistered on all sides. Remove from the heat with tongs and place them in a plastic bag. Tie the top.

2 Leave for 5 minutes until cool enough to handle. then remove from the bag and peel. Cut the peppers into quarters and remove and discard the stems, seeds and membranes.

3 Meanwhile, flake the tuna and combine with the lemon juice and oil. Stir in the olives, parsley, garlic and celery. Season with salt and plenty of ground black pepper.

4 Lay the pepper segments out flat, skinned side down. Divide the tuna mixture equally among them. Spread it out, pressing it into an even layer. Roll the peppers up. Place the pepper rolls in the refrigerator for at least 1 hour. Just before serving, cut each roll in half with a sharp knife, then arrange on a large serving platter.

Smoked Trout Mousse in Cucumber Cups

This delicious creamy mousse can be made in advance and chilled for 2–3 days in the refrigerator. Serve it in crunchy cucumber cups or simply with crudités if you like.

Makes about 24

115g/4oz/¹/₂ cup cream cheese, softened
2 spring onions (scallions), chopped
15–30ml/1–2 tbsp, chopped fresh dill or parsley
5ml/1 tsp horseradish sauce
225g/8oz smoked trout fillets, flaked and any fine bones removed
30–60ml/2–4 tbsp double (heavy) cream
salt and cayenne pepper
2 cucumbers
fresh dill sprigs, to garnish

1 Start by making the trout mouse. Put the cream cheese, spring onions, dill or parsley and horseradish sauce into a blender or the bowl of a food processor and process until well blended. Add the trout and process until smooth, scraping down the sides of the bowl once. With the machine running, pour in the cream through the feeder tube until a soft mousse-like mixture forms. Season with salt and cayenne pepper to taste, turn into a bowl and chill for 15 minutes.

2 To make the cucumber cups, using a cannelle knife (zester) or vegetable peeler, score the length of each cucumber to create a striped effect. Cut each cucumber into 2cm/³⁄₄in thick rounds. Using a small spoon or melon baller, scoop out the seeds from the centre of each round.

3 Spoon the smoked trout mousse into a piping (pastry) bag fitted with a medium-sized star nozzle and pipe swirls of the mousse mixture into the prepared cucumber rounds. Arrange the cucumber cups on a serving platter and chill until ready to serve. Garnish the cucumber cups with small sprigs of dill.

COOK'S TIP
The easiest way to remove any fine bones remaining in the fish fillets is to pull them out with a small pair of tweezers.

Cheese and Potato Bread Twists

These individual "ploughman's lunch" twists have the cheese cooked in the bread. They can be filled with smoked salmon seasoned with lemon juice after cooking to make them extra special.

Makes 12

225g/8oz potatoes, diced
225g/8oz/2 cups strong white bread
    flour, plus extra for dusting
5ml/1 tsp easy-blend (rapid-rise)
    dried yeast
150ml/¼ pint/⅔ cup lukewarm water
175g/6oz/1½ cups finely grated red
    Leicester cheese
10ml/2 tsp olive oil, for greasing
salt

1 Cook the potatoes in a large pan in plenty of lightly salted boiling water for 20 minutes, or until tender. Drain through a colander and return to the pan. Mash with a potato masher or fork until smooth and set aside to cool.

2 Meanwhile, sift the flour into a large bowl and add the yeast and a good pinch of salt. Stir in the mashed potatoes and rub with your fingers to form a crumb consistency.

VARIATION
Any hard, well-flavoured cheese can be used. Mature (sharp) Cheddar is the traditional choice for a ploughman's lunch, or you could try a smoked cheese or a variety with added herbs.

3 Make a well in the centre of the mixture and pour in the lukewarm water. Start by bringing the mixture together with a round-bladed knife, then use your hands. Turn out on to a well-floured surface and knead for 5 minutes. Return the dough to the bowl. Cover with a damp dishtowel and leave to rise in a warm place for 1 hour, or until doubled in size.

4 Turn the dough out and knock back (punch down) the air bubbles. Knead again for a few seconds.

5 Divide the dough into 12 even pieces and shape into rounds.

6 Sprinkle the cheese over a baking sheet. Take each ball of dough and roll it in the cheese.

7 Roll each cheese-covered roll on a dry surface to form a long sausage shape. Fold the two ends together and twist the bread. Lay the bread twists on an oiled baking sheet.

8 Cover with a damp cloth and leave the bread to rise in a warm place for 30 minutes. Preheat the oven to 220°C/425°F/Gas 7. Bake the bread for 10–15 minutes. These bread twists stay moist and fresh for up to 3 days if stored in airtight food bags.

Bitesize Cheese Brioches

These mouthfuls of golden, buttery dough have a surprise in the middle: a nugget of melting cheese, so be sure to serve them warm to enjoy them at their best.

Makes about 40

450g/1lb/4 cups plain (all-purpose) or strong white bread flour, plus extra for dusting
5ml/1 tsp salt
5ml/1 tsp ground turmeric
1 sachet (envelope) easy-blend (rapid-rise) dried yeast
150ml/¼ pint/⅔ cup warm milk
2 eggs, plus 2 egg yolks
75g/3oz/6 tbsp butter, melted and slightly cooled
50g/2oz/½ cup grated Cheddar cheese
oil, for greasing
50g/2oz/½ cup cubed cheese, such as Cheshire, Gouda or Port Salut

1 Sift the dry ingredients into a large bowl with the yeast and make a hollow in the middle. Mix the milk, eggs and one yolk with the butter and Cheddar.

2 Pour the liquid into the well in the dry ingredients and blend with a fork to bring the mixture together. Continue mixing in the bowl or in a food processor with a dough blade, until it is evenly mixed. Turn out the mixture on to a lightly floured surface and knead, working in as little flour as possible, until the surface of the mixture becomes smooth and dry.

3 Place the dough in a lightly oiled bowl. Lightly oil the top of the dough, cover with a clean dishtowel and leave in a warm place for at least 1 hour, until the dough has doubled in bulk.

4 Turn out on to a floured surface and knead the dough until it becomes firm and elastic again.

5 Divide the dough into four batches, then divide each batch into eight to ten pieces. Knead each piece until smooth.

COOK'S TIP
For a special party, use gold petits fours cases; they are firmer and give more support, and they look smart and elegant.

6 Press a cube of cheese into the middle of each piece of dough, then shape into a round and place in paper sweet (candy) cases. Place the paper cases in mini muffin trays to support the soft dough during baking or, alternatively, put the dough in doubled paper cases. Set the brioches aside in a warm place until they are well risen and have almost doubled in size.

7 Preheat the oven to 200°C/400°F/ Gas 6. Mix the remaining yolk with 15ml/1 tbsp water and glaze the brioches with the mixture, using a pastry brush. Bake for 15 minutes, or until golden brown, well-risen and firm underneath if tapped.

Pretzels

Pretzels or brezeln, as they are known in Germany, are said to be derived from the Latin *bracellae* or arms, referring to the crossed "arms" of dough inside the oval. In Alsace the pretzel shape is part of the emblem of quality that bakers display outside their shops.

Makes 12 pretzels

For the yeast sponge
10g/¼ oz fresh yeast
75ml/5 tbsp water
15ml/1 tbsp unbleached plain
  (all-purpose) white flour

For the dough
10g/¼ oz fresh yeast
150ml/¼ pint/⅔ cup lukewarm water
75ml/5 tbsp lukewarm milk
400g/14oz/3½ cups unbleached strong
  white bread flour
7.5ml/1½ tsp salt
25g/1oz/2 tbsp butter, melted

For the topping
1 egg yolk
15ml/1 tbsp milk
sea salt or caraway seeds, for sprinkling

1 Flour a baking sheet and grease two baking sheets. Cream the yeast for the yeast sponge with the water. Mix in the flour, cover and leave to stand at room temperature for 2 hours.

2 Mix the yeast for the dough with the water, then stir in the milk. Sift 350g/12oz/3 cups of the flour and the salt into a bowl. Add the yeast sponge and the butter and mix for 3–4 minutes. Turn out on to a lightly floured surface and knead in the remaining flour. Place in a lightly oiled bowl, cover with lightly oiled clear film (plastic wrap) and leave to rise in a warm place for 30 minutes.

3 Turn out on to a floured surface and knock back (punch down) the dough. Knead into a ball, return to the bowl, cover and leave to rise for 30 minutes.

4 Turn out the dough on to a floured surface, divide into 12 pieces and form into balls. Take one ball of dough and cover the remainder with a dishtowel.

5 Roll the dough into a stick 46cm/18in long and about 1cm/½in thick in the middle and thinner at the ends. Bend each end of the dough stick into a horseshoe. Cross over and place the ends on top of the thick part of the pretzel. Repeat with the remaining dough balls.

6 Place on the floured baking sheet to rest for 10 minutes. Preheat the oven to 190°C/375°F/Gas 5. Bring a large pan of water to the boil, then reduce to a simmer. Add the pretzels, in batches of 2–3 at a time, and poach for about 1 minute. Drain on a dishtowel and place on the greased baking sheets, spaced well apart.

7 Mix the egg yolk and milk and brush over the pretzels. Sprinkle with sea salt or caraway seeds and bake the pretzels for 25 minutes.

Parmesan Thins

These thin, crisp, savoury biscuits will melt in the mouth, so make plenty for guests. They are a great snack at any time of the day, so don't just keep them for parties.

Makes 16–20

50g/2oz/½ cup plain
  (all-purpose) flour
40g/1½ oz/3 tbsp butter, softened
1 egg yolk
40g/1½oz/⅔ cup freshly grated
  Parmesan cheese
pinch of salt
pinch of mustard powder

1 Rub together the flour and the butter in a bowl using your fingertips, then work in the egg yolk, Parmesan cheese, salt and mustard powder. Mix to bring the dough together into a ball. Shape the mixture into a log, wrap in foil or clear film (plastic wrap) and chill for 10 minutes.

2 Preheat the oven to 200°C/400°F/ Gas 6. Cut the Parmesan log into very thin slices, 3–5mm/⅛–¼in maximum, and arrange on a baking sheet. Flatten with a fork to give a pretty ridged pattern. Bake for 10 minutes, or until the Parmesan thins are crisp but not changing colour.

dips and dippers

Smooth or slightly chunky, luscious or refreshing, dips and dippers are ideal for large gatherings or instead of a formal appetizer for supper with friends.

Walnut and Garlic Dip, Salsa Verde and Yogurt with Garlic, Cucumber and Mint

Full-flavoured classic sauces and salsas make terrific dips.

WALNUT AND GARLIC DIP

Makes 1 bowl

2 x 1cm/½in slices white bread
60ml/4 tbsp milk
150g/5oz/1¼ cups shelled walnuts
4 garlic cloves, chopped
120ml/4fl oz/½ cup mild olive oil
15–30ml/1–2 tbsp walnut
    oil (optional)
juice of 1 lemon
salt and ground black pepper
walnut or olive oil, for drizzling
paprika, for dusting (optional)

1 Remove the crusts from the bread, and soak the slices in the milk for 5 minutes, then process with the walnuts and chopped garlic in a food processor or blender to a coarse paste.

2 Gradually add the olive oil to the paste with the motor still running, until the mixture forms a smooth thick sauce. Blend in the walnut oil, if using.

3 Scoop the sauce into a bowl and add lemon juice to taste, season with salt and pepper and beat well.

4 Transfer the dip to a serving bowl, drizzle over a little more walnut or olive oil, then dust lightly with paprika, if using.

SALSA VERDE

Makes 1 bowl

1–2 garlic cloves, finely chopped
25g/1oz/1 cup flat leaf parsley leaves
15g/½oz/½ cup fresh basil, mint
    or coriander (cilantro) or a mixture
    of fresh herbs
15ml/1 tbsp chopped fresh chives
15ml/1 tbsp salted capers, rinsed
5 anchovy fillets in olive oil, drained
    and rinsed
10ml/2 tsp French mustard (tarragon or
    fines herbes mustard are both good)
120ml/4fl oz/½ cup extra virgin olive oil
grated lemon rind and juice (optional)
ground black pepper

1 Process the garlic, parsley, basil, mint or coriander, chives, capers, anchovies, mustard and 15ml/1 tbsp of the oil in a blender or food processor.

2 Gradually add the remaining oil in a thin stream with the motor running.

3 Transfer to a bowl and adjust the seasoning to taste – there should be enough salt from the capers and anchovies. Add a little lemon juice and rind if you like. Serve immediately.

VARIATIONS

If dipping prawns (shrimp), substitute fresh chervil, tarragon, dill or fennel, for the basil, mint or coriander (cilantro).

YOGURT WITH GARLIC, CUCUMBER AND MINT

Makes 1 bowl

15cm/6in piece cucumber
5ml/1 tsp sea salt
300ml/½ pint/1¼ cups Greek
    (US strained plain) yogurt
3–4 garlic cloves, crushed
45ml/3 tbsp chopped fresh mint
ground black pepper
chopped fresh mint and/or ground
    toasted cumin seeds, to garnish

1 Slice the cucumber, place in a sieve and sprinkle with half the salt. Leave over a bowl for 30 minutes to drip.

2 Rinse the cucumber in cold water, pat dry and mix with the yogurt, garlic and mint. Season to taste. Leave for 30 minutes, stir and sprinkle with fresh mint and/or toasted cumin seeds.

COOK'S TIP

To make a yogurt and garlic dressing, spoon 150ml/¼ pint/⅔ cup Greek (US strained plain) yogurt into a bowl. Beat in 1 chopped garlic clove, 5ml/1 tsp French mustard and a pinch of sugar. Season. Beat in 15–30ml/1–2 tbsp olive oil and 15–30ml/1–2 tbsp chopped herbs.

Right, from top to bottom:
Walnut and Garlic Dip, Yogurt with Garlic, Cucumber and Mint, and Salsa Verde.

Avocado Salsa

A popular chunky dip that is
excellent with tortilla chips.

Makes 1 bowl

2 large ripe avocados
1 small red onion, very finely chopped
1 fresh red or green chilli, seeded and
very finely chopped
½–1 garlic clove, crushed (optional)
finely shredded rind of ½ lime and
juice of 1–1½ limes
pinch of caster (superfine) sugar
225g/8oz tomatoes, seeded
and chopped
30ml/2 tbsp coarsely chopped fresh
coriander (cilantro)
2.5–5ml/½–1 tsp ground cumin seeds
15ml/1 tbsp olive oil
15–30ml/1–2 tbsp sour cream (optional)
salt and ground black pepper
lime wedges dipped in sea salt, and
coriander (cilantro) sprigs, to garnish

1 Halve, stone (pit) and peel the
avocados. Set half the flesh aside and
coarsely mash the remainder in a bowl
using a fork.

COOK'S TIPS
• Leaving some of the avocado in chunks
adds a slightly different texture, but if you
like a smoother salsa, mash all the
avocado together.
• Hard avocados will soften in a few
seconds in a microwave. Check frequently
until you get the softness that you like.

2 Add the onion, chilli, garlic, if using,
lime rind, juice of 1 lime, sugar,
tomatoes and coriander. Add the
ground cumin, seasoning and more
lime juice to taste. Stir in the olive oil.

3 Dice the remaining avocado and stir
into the avocado salsa, then cover and
leave to stand for 15 minutes so that
the flavour develops. Stir in the sour
cream, if using. Serve immediately with
lime wedges dipped in sea salt and
fresh coriander sprigs.

Guacamole

Avocados discolour quickly so make this dip just before serving. If you do need to keep it for any length of time, cover the surface of the sauce with clear film and chill in the refrigerator.

Makes 1 bowl

2 large ripe avocados
2 fresh red chillies, seeded
1 garlic clove
1 shallot
20ml/2 tbsp olive oil,
  plus extra to serve
juice of 1 lemon
salt and ground black pepper
fresh flat leaf parsley leaves, to garnish

1 Halve the avocados, remove the stones (pits) and scoop out the flesh into a large bowl.

2 Using a fork or potato masher, mash the avocado flesh until smooth.

3 Finely chop the chillies, garlic and shallot, then stir into the mashed avocado with the olive oil and lemon juice. Season to taste with salt and pepper and stir again.

4 Spoon the mixture into a small serving bowl. Drizzle over a little olive oil and sprinkle with a few flat leaf parsley leaves. Serve immediately.

VARIATION
Substitute lime juice for the lemon juice and fresh coriander (cilantro) leaves for the flat leaf parsley.

Basil and Lemon Dip

This lovely dip is based on fresh mayonnaise flavoured with lemon juice and two types of basil. Serve with crispy potato wedges for a delicious appetizer.

Makes 1 bowl

2 large (US extra large) egg yolks
15ml/1 tbsp lemon juice
150ml/¼ pint/²⁄₃ cup olive oil
150ml/¼ pint/²⁄₃ cup sunflower oil
4 garlic cloves
handful of fresh green basil
handful of fresh opal basil
salt and ground black pepper

1 Place the egg yolks and lemon juice in a blender or food processor and process them briefly until they are just lightly blended.

2 Pour the olive oil and sunflower oil into a jug (pitcher) and stir them together. With the motor running, very gradually pour the oil into the blender or food processor, a little at a time.

3 Once half of the oil has been added, the remaining oil can be incorporated more quickly in a steady stream. Continue processing to form a thick, creamy mayonnaise.

4 Peel and crush the garlic cloves. Alternatively, place them on a chopping board and sprinkle with salt, then flatten them with the heel of a heavy-bladed knife and chop the flesh. Flatten the garlic again to make a coarse purée.

COOK'S TIPS
• Make sure all the ingredients are at room temperature before you start to help prevent the mixture from curdling.
• To make a really quick and easy version of this dip, use good quality bottled mayonnaise and simply stir in the garlic and chopped herbs.

5 Tear both types of basil into small pieces and then stir them into the mayonnaise along with the crushed garlic purée.

6 Add salt and pepper to taste, then transfer the dip to a serving dish. Cover with clear film (plastic wrap) and chill until ready to serve.

Hummus Bi Tahina

Blending chickpeas with garlic and oil creates a surprisingly creamy purée that is delicious as part of a Turkish-style mezze, or as a dip with vegetables. Leftovers make a good sandwich filler.

Makes 1 bowl

150g/5oz/³⁄₄ cup dried chickpeas
juice of 2 lemons
2 garlic cloves, sliced
30ml/2 tbsp olive oil
pinch of cayenne pepper
150ml/¹⁄₄ pint/²⁄₃ cup tahini paste
salt and ground black pepper
extra olive oil and cayenne pepper,
    for sprinkling
fresh flat leaf parsley sprigs, to garnish

1 Put the chickpeas in a bowl and add cold water to cover. Leave to soak for 8 hours or overnight.

2 Drain the chickpeas, place in a pan and add fresh water to cover. Bring to the boil over a high heat and boil rapidly for 10 minutes. Reduce the heat and simmer gently for about 2 hours, until soft. (The cooking time depends on how long the chickpeas have been stored.) Drain in a colander.

3 Process the chickpeas in a food processor to a smooth purée. Add the lemon juice, garlic, olive oil, cayenne pepper and tahini paste and blend until creamy, scraping the mixture down from the sides of the bowl.

4 Season the purée with plenty of salt and ground black pepper and transfer to a serving dish. Sprinkle with a little olive oil and cayenne pepper, and serve garnished with a few parsley sprigs.

COOK'S TIPS
• For convenience, canned chickpeas can be used instead. Allow two 400g/14oz cans and drain them thoroughly.
• Tahini paste can now be purchased from most good supermarkets or health-food stores.
• The cooking time for chickpeas will vary, depending on how long they've been allowed to soak.

Baba Ganoush with Lebanese Flatbread

Baba Ganoush is a delectable aubergine dip from the Middle East. Tahini, a sesame seed paste with cumin, is the main flavouring, giving a subtle hint of spice.

Makes 1 bowl

2 small aubergines (eggplant)
1 garlic clove, crushed
60ml/4 tbsp tahini
25g/1oz/¹/₄ cup ground almonds
juice of ¹/₂ lemon
2.5ml/¹/₂ tsp ground cumin
30ml/2 tbsp fresh mint leaves
30ml/2 tbsp olive oil
salt and ground black pepper

For the flatbread
4 pitta breads
45ml/3 tbsp sesame seeds
45ml/3 tbsp fresh thyme leaves
45ml/3 tbsp poppy seeds
150ml/¹/₄ pint/²/₃ cup olive oil

1 Start by making the Lebanese flatbread. Split the pitta breads through the middle and carefully open them out. Mix the sesame seeds, chopped thyme and poppy seeds in a mortar. Grind them lightly with a pestle to release the flavour.

2 Stir in the olive oil. Spread the mixture over the cut sides of the pitta bread. Grill (broil) until golden brown and crisp. Leave to cool, then break into pieces and set aside in an airtight container until required.

3 Grill the aubergines, turning them frequently, until the skin is blackened and blistered. Peel off the skins, chop the flesh coarsely and leave to drain in a colander.

4 Squeeze out as much liquid from the aubergines as possible. Place the flesh in a blender or food processor, then add the garlic, tahini, ground almonds, lemon juice and cumin, with salt to taste. Process to a smooth paste, then coarsely chop half the mint and stir it into the dip.

5 Spoon the aubergine paste into a serving bowl, sprinkle the remaining mint leaves on top of the dip and drizzle with the olive oil. Serve with the Lebanese flatbread.

Taramasalata

This smoked roe speciality is one of the most famous Greek dips. It is ideal for a buffet or for handing round with drinks. Fingers of warm pitta bread, breadsticks or crispy crackers all make good dippers.

Makes 1 bowl

115g/4oz smoked grey mullet roe (see
  Cook's Tip)
2 garlic cloves, crushed
30ml/2 tbsp grated onion
60ml/4 tbsp olive oil
4 slices white bread, crusts removed
juice of 2 lemons
30ml/2 tbsp milk or water
ground black pepper
warm pitta bread, breadsticks or
  crackers, to serve

1 Place the smoked roe, garlic, onion, oil, bread and lemon juice in a blender or food processor and process briefly until just smooth.

COOK'S TIP

Since the roe of grey mullet is expensive, smoked cod's roe is often used instead for this dish. It is paler than the burnt-orange colour of mullet roe but is still very good.

2 Add the milk or water and process again for a few seconds. (This will give the taramasalata a creamier texture.)

3 Pour the taramasalata into a serving bowl, cover with clear film (plastic wrap) and chill for 1–2 hours in the refrigerator before serving. Sprinkle the dip with freshly ground black pepper just before serving.

Tzatziki

Serve this classic Greek dip with toasted small pitta breads.

Makes 1 bowl

1 mini cucumber
4 spring onions (scallions)
1 garlic clove
200ml/7fl oz/scant 1 cup Greek
 (US strained plain) yogurt
45ml/3 tbsp chopped fresh mint
fresh mint sprigs, to garnish (optional)
salt and ground black pepper

1 Trim the ends from the mini cucumber, then cut it into 5mm/¼in dice, using a sharp knife.

2 Trim the spring onions and garlic, then chop both very finely.

COOK'S TIP
Choose Greek (US strained plain) yogurt for this dip – it has a higher fat content than most yogurts, which gives it a deliciously rich, creamy texture.

3 Spoon the yogurt into a bowl and beat until it is completely smooth, if necessary, then gently stir in the diced cucumber, spring onions, garlic and chopped mint.

4 Add salt and plenty of freshly ground black pepper to taste. Transfer the mixture to a serving bowl. Cover and chill until ready to serve; garnish with mint if you like.

Lemon and Coconut Dhal Dip

A warm spicy dish, this can be served either as a dip or as an accompaniment to cold meats.

Makes 2 bowls

5cm/2in piece fresh root ginger
1 onion
2 garlic cloves
2 small fresh red chillies, seeded
30ml/2 tbsp sunflower oil
5ml/1 tsp cumin seeds
150g/5oz/²⁄₃ cup red lentils
250ml/8fl oz/1 cup water
15ml/1 tbsp hot curry paste
200ml/7fl oz/scant 1 cup coconut cream
juice of 1 lemon
handful of fresh coriander
*   (cilantro) leaves*
25g/1oz/¹⁄₄ cup flaked (sliced) almonds
salt and ground black pepper

1 Use a vegetable peeler to peel the ginger, then chop it finely with the onion, garlic and chillies.

VARIATION
Try making this dhal with yellow split peas: they take longer to cook and a little extra water has to be added but the result is equally tasty.

2 Heat the sunflower oil in a large, shallow pan. Add the ginger, onion, garlic, chillies and cumin. Cook over a medium heat, stirring occasionally, for about 5 minutes, until the onion is softened but not coloured.

3 Stir the lentils, measured water and curry paste into the pan. Bring to the boil, then reduce the heat to low, cover and simmer gently, stirring occasionally, for 15–20 minutes, until the lentils are just tender but have not yet broken up.

4 Stir in all but 30ml/2 tbsp of the coconut cream. Bring to the boil and cook, uncovered, for 15–20 minutes, until the mixture is thick and pulpy. Remove the pan from the heat, stir in the lemon juice and coriander leaves. Season to taste.

5 Heat a large, heavy frying pan and dry-fry the flaked almonds for about 1–2 minutes on each side, until golden brown. Stir about three-quarters of the toasted almonds into the dhal. Reserve the remainder for the garnish.

6 Transfer the dhal to a serving bowl; swirl in the remaining coconut cream. Sprinkle the reserved almonds on top and serve warm.

Chilli Bean Dip

This deliciously spicy and creamy bean dip is best served warm with triangles of grilled pitta bread or a bowl of crunchy tortilla chips.

Makes 1 bowl

2 garlic cloves
1 onion
2 fresh green chillies
30ml/2 tbsp vegetable oil
5–10ml/1–2 tsp hot chilli powder
400g/14oz can kidney beans
75g/3oz/³⁄₄ cup grated Cheddar cheese
1 fresh red chilli
salt and ground black pepper

1 Finely chop the garlic and onion. Slit the green chillies and remove and discard the seeds, then chop finely.

2 Heat the vegetable oil in a large sauté pan or deep frying pan and add the garlic, onion, green chillies and chilli powder. Cook over a low heat, stirring frequently, for about 5–8 minutes, until the onion has softened and become translucent, but is not browned.

3 Drain the kidney beans, reserving the can juice. Process all but 30ml/2 tbsp of the beans to a purée in a food processor.

4 Add the puréed beans to the pan with 30–45ml/2–3 tbsp of the reserved can juice and stir well. Cook over a low heat, stirring occasionally.

5 Stir in the reserved whole beans and the grated Cheddar cheese. Cook gently for a further 2–3 minutes, stirring until the cheese has melted. Season with salt and pepper to taste.

6 Slit the red chilli and remove and discard the seeds, then cut the flesh into tiny strips.

7 Spoon the dip into a serving bowl or into several small bowls and sprinkle the chilli strips over the top to garnish. Serve warm.

COOK'S TIP

To make a dip with a coarser texture, do not purée the beans; instead mash them roughly with a potato masher.

Potato Skins with Cajun Dip

Divinely crisp, these potato skins
are great on their own or served
with this piquant dip as a garnish
or on the side.

Serves 4

2 large baking potatoes
vegetable or groundnut (peanut) oil,
*   for deep-frying*

For the dip
120ml/4fl oz/¹/₂ cup natural
*   (plain) yogurt*
1 garlic clove, crushed
5ml/1 tsp tomato purée (paste) or
*   2.5ml/¹/₂ tsp green chilli purée*
*   (paste) or ¹/₂ small fresh green chilli,*
*   seeded and chopped*
1.5ml/¹/₄ tsp celery salt
salt and ground black pepper

1 Preheat the oven to 180°C/350°F/
Gas 4. Prick the potatoes with a fork
and bake, for 45–50 minutes until
tender. Cut them in half and scoop out
the flesh, leaving a thin layer on the
skins. Keep the flesh for another
recipe. Cut the potato skins in half
once more.

2 To make the dip, mix together all the
ingredients and chill.

3 Heat a 1cm/¹/₂in layer of oil in a large
pan or deep-fat fryer. Deep-fry the
potato skins until crisp and golden on
both sides. Drain well on kitchen
paper, then sprinkle with salt and black
pepper. Serve the potato skins
immediately with a bowl of dip or a
spoonful of dip in each skin.

Spicy Potato Wedges with Chilli Dip

These dry-roasted potato wedges with crisp spicy crusts are delicious with the chilli dip. They make a tasty appetizer or can be served with other dishes as part of a barbecue or informal buffet supper.

Serves 6

4 baking potatoes, about 225g/
*   8oz each*
60ml/4 tbsp olive oil
4 garlic cloves, crushed
10ml/2 tsp ground allspice
10ml/2 tsp ground coriander
30ml/2 tbsp paprika
salt and ground black pepper

For the dip
30ml/2 tbsp olive oil
2 small onions, finely chopped
2 garlic clove, crushed
400g/14oz can chopped tomatoes
2 fresh red chillies, seeded and
*   finely chopped*
30ml/2 tbsp balsamic vinegar
30ml/2 tbsp chopped fresh coriander
*   (cilantro), plus extra to garnish*

1 Preheat the oven to 200°C/400°F/ Gas 6. Cut the potatoes in half, then into eight wedges.

2 Add the wedges to a large pan of cold water. Bring to the boil, reduce the heat and simmer for 10 minutes, or until the wedges have softened but the flesh has not started to disintegrate. Drain well and pat dry on kitchen paper.

3 Mix the olive oil, garlic, allspice, coriander and paprika in a roasting pan. Add salt and pepper to taste. Add the potatoes to the pan and shake to coat them thoroughly. Roast for 20–25 minutes, until the wedges are browned, crisp and fully cooked. Turn the potato wedges occasionally during the roasting time.

4 Meanwhile, make the chilli dip. Heat the oil in a small pan, add the onion and garlic, and cook for 5–10 minutes, until softened.

5 Tip in the chopped tomatoes, with any juice. Stir in the chilli and vinegar. Cook gently for 10 minutes, until the mixture has reduced and thickened, then taste and check the seasoning. Stir in the chopped fresh coriander.

6 Pile the spicy potato wedges on a plate, garnish with the extra coriander and serve with the chilli dip.

VARIATION
Instead of balsamic vinegar, try brown rice vinegar, which has a mellow flavour.

Stilton-stuffed Mushrooms Baked with Garlic Breadcrumbs

Serve these succulent stuffed mushrooms with warm bread.

Serves 8

900g/2lb chestnut mushrooms
6 garlic cloves, finely chopped
200g/7oz/scant 1 cup butter, melted
juice of 1 lemon
225g/8oz Stilton cheese, crumbled
115g/4oz/1 cup walnuts, chopped
200g/7oz/3 cups white breadcrumbs
50g/2oz/²⁄₃ cup freshly grated
   Parmesan cheese
60ml/4 tbsp chopped fresh parsley
salt and ground black pepper

For the sauce
225g/8oz/1 cup fromage frais or
   Greek (US strained plain) yogurt
1 bunch chopped fresh herbs
15ml/1 tbsp Dijon mustard

1 Preheat the oven to 200°C/400°F/Gas 6. Place the mushrooms in an ovenproof dish and sprinkle half the garlic over them. Drizzle with 50g/2oz/¼ cup of the butter and the lemon juice. Season with salt and pepper, and bake for 15–20 minutes. Remove from the oven and leave to cool.

2 Cream the crumbled Stilton with the chopped walnuts and mix in 30ml/2 tbsp of the breadcrumbs.

3 Divide the Stilton mixture among the chestnut mushrooms.

4 To make the sauce, mix the fromage frais or Greek yogurt with the chopped fresh herbs and the Dijon mustard until thoroughly combined.

5 Preheat the grill (broiler). Mix the remaining garlic, breadcrumbs and melted butter together. Stir in the grated Parmesan and chopped, fresh parsley and season with plenty of ground black pepper. Cover the mushrooms with the breadcrumb mixture and grill (broil) for about 5 minutes, or until crisp and browned. Serve immediately with the sauce.

VARIATION
Use other types of mushrooms such as large flat mushrooms or ceps.

Vegetable Tempura

Tempura is a Japanese type of savoury fritter. Originally prawns were used, but vegetables can be cooked in the egg batter successfully too. The secret of making the incredibly light batter is to use really cold water, and to have the oil at the right temperature before you start cooking the fritters.

Serves 4

2 courgettes (zucchini)
1/2 aubergine (eggplant)
1 large carrot
1/2 small Spanish onion
1 egg
120ml/4fl oz/1/2 cup iced water
115g/4oz/1 cup plain
    (all-purpose) flour
salt and ground black pepper
vegetable oil, for deep-frying
sea salt flakes, lemon slices and
    Japanese soy sauce (shoyu), to serve

1 Pare strips of peel from the courgettes and aubergine.

2 Using a chef's knife, cut the courgettes, aubergine and carrot into strips measuring about 7.5–10cm/ 3–4in long and 3mm/⅛in wide. Place in a colander and sprinkle with salt. Put a small plate over and weigh it down. Leave for 30 minutes, then rinse under cold running water to remove all traces of salt. Drain well, then dry with kitchen paper.

3 Thinly slice the onion from top to base, discarding the plump pieces in the middle. Separate the layers so that there are lots of fine, long strips. Mix all the vegetables together and season with salt and pepper.

4 Make the batter immediately before frying, as it should not be left to stand. Mix the egg and iced water in a bowl, then sift in the flour. Mix briefly with a fork or chopsticks. Do not overmix: the batter should remain fairly lumpy. Add the vegetables to the batter and mix to combine and coat.

COOK'S TIP
Other suitable vegetables for tempura include mushrooms, cauliflower florets and slices of red, green, yellow or orange (bell) peppers.

5 Half-fill a wok with oil and heat to 180°C/350°F or until a cube of bread, added to it, browns in about 45 seconds. Scoop up a generous tablespoonful of the mixture at a time and carefully lower it into the oil. Deep-fry in batches for about 3 minutes, until golden brown and crisp. Remove with a slotted spoon and drain well on kitchen paper. Keep warm while you cook the remaining batches.

6 Serve each portion with sea salt, slices of lemon and a tiny bowl of Japanese soy sauce for dipping.

Quail's **Eggs** with **Herbs** and **Dips**

For *al fresco* eating or informal entertaining this platter of contrasting tastes and textures is delicious and certainly encourages a relaxed atmosphere. Choose the best seasonal vegetables and substitute for what is available.

Serves 6

1 large Italian focaccia or 2–3 Indian
    parathas or other flatbread
extra virgin olive oil, plus extra to serve
1 large garlic clove, finely chopped
small handful chopped fresh mixed
    herbs, such as coriander (cilantro),
    mint, parsley and oregano
18–24 quail's eggs
30ml/2 tbsp home-made mayonnaise
30ml/2 tbsp thick sour cream
5ml/1 tsp chopped capers
5ml/1 tsp finely chopped shallot
225g/8oz fresh beetroot (beet),
    cooked, peeled and sliced
1/2 bunch spring onions (scallions),
    trimmed and coarsely chopped
60ml/4 tbsp red onion or tamarind and
    date chutney
salt and ground black pepper
coarse sea salt and mixed ground
    peppercorns, to serve

1 Preheat the oven to 190°C/375°F/ Gas 5. Brush the focaccia or flatbread liberally with olive oil, sprinkle with garlic and your choice of herbs and season with salt and pepper. Bake for 10–15 minutes, or until golden. Keep warm until ready to serve.

2 Put the quail's eggs into a pan of cold water, bring to the boil over a medium heat and boil for 5 minutes. Arrange in a serving dish. Peel the eggs, if you like, or leave guests to do their own.

3 To make the dip, combine the mayonnaise, sour cream, capers, shallot and seasoning.

4 To serve, cut the bread into wedges and serve with dishes of the quail's eggs, mayonnaise dip, beetroot, spring onion and chutney. Serve with tiny bowls of the coarse salt, ground peppercorns and olive oil for dipping.

VARIATION

For a truly impressive dish for a special occasion, use guinea fowl eggs, which are slightly larger than quail's eggs and have attractive brown shells. They have a rich flavour and are delicious hard-boiled. However, they are difficult to obtain.

COOK'S TIP

If you don't have time to make your own mayonnaise use the best commercial variety available. You will probably find that you need to add less seasoning to it.

Sesame Seed-coated Falafel with **Tahini dip**

Sesame seeds are used to give a delightfully crunchy coating to these spicy chickpea patties.

Serves 6

250g/9oz/1 1/3 cups dried chickpeas
2 garlic cloves, crushed
1 fresh red chilli, seeded and sliced
5ml/1 tsp ground coriander
5ml/1 tsp ground cumin
15ml/1 tbsp chopped fresh mint
15ml/1 tbsp chopped fresh parsley
2 spring onions (scallions),
* finely chopped*
1 large (US extra large) egg, beaten
sesame seeds, for coating
sunflower oil, for frying
salt and ground black pepper

For the tahini yogurt dip
30ml/2 tbsp light tahini
200g/7oz/scant 1 cup natural (plain)
* live yogurt*
5ml/1 tsp cayenne pepper, plus extra
* for sprinkling*
15ml/1 tbsp chopped fresh mint
1 spring onion (scallion), thinly sliced
fresh herbs, to garnish

1 Place the chickpeas in a bowl, cover with cold water and leave to soak overnight. Drain and rinse the chickpeas, then place in a pan and cover with fresh cold water. Bring to the boil over a medium heat and boil rapidly for 10 minutes. Reduce the heat to low and simmer gently for 1½–2 hours, until tender.

2 Meanwhile, make the tahini yogurt dip. Mix together the tahini, yogurt, cayenne pepper and mint in a small bowl. Sprinkle the spring onion and extra cayenne pepper on top, cover with clear film (plastic wrap) and chill in the refrigerator until required.

3 Drain the chickpeas and combine with the garlic, chilli, coriander, cumin, mint, parsley, spring onions and seasoning, then mix in the egg. Place in a food processor and process until the mixture forms a coarse paste. If the paste seems too soft, chill it for about 30 minutes.

4 Spread out the sesame seeds on a plate. Form the chilled chickpea paste into 12 patties with your hands, then roll each one in the sesame seeds to coat thoroughly.

5 Heat enough oil to cover the base of a large frying pan. Add the falafel, in batches if necessary, and cook for 6 minutes, turning once. Serve with the tahini yogurt dip garnished with fresh herbs.

Celeriac Fritters with Mustard Dip

The combination of the hot, crispy fritters and cold mustard dip is extremely good.

Serves 4

1 egg
115g/4oz/1 1/2 cups ground almonds
45ml/3 tbsp freshly grated
  Parmesan cheese
45ml/3 tbsp chopped fresh parsley
1 celeriac, about 450g/1lb
lemon juice
vegetable or sunflower oil, for
  deep-frying
salt and ground black pepper
sea salt flakes, to garnish

For the dip
150ml/1/4 pint/2/3 cup sour cream
15–30ml/1–2 tbsp wholegrain mustard

1 Beat the egg well and pour into a shallow dish. Mix together the ground almonds, grated Parmesan and parsley in a separate dish. Season with salt and plenty of ground black pepper. Set aside.

2 Peel and slice the celeriac, then cut into batons about 1cm/1/2in wide and 5cm/2in long. Drop them immediately into a bowl of water with a little lemon juice added to prevent discoloration.

VARIATION
For a spicier dip, use chilli mustard. Herb mustard, such as tarragon, or garlic mustard may also be used.

3 Heat the vegetable or sunflower oil to 180°C/350°F or until a cube of bread, added to it, browns in about 45 seconds. Drain about half the celeriac batons and pat dry with kitchen paper. Dip them first into the beaten egg, then into the ground almond mixture, making sure that the pieces are coated completely and evenly. Shake off any excess.

4 Deep-fry the fritters, in batches, for 2–3 minutes, until golden. Drain on kitchen paper. Keep warm while you cook the remaining fritters.

5 Make the dip. Mix the sour cream and mustard in a small bowl and season with salt to taste. Spoon into a serving bowl. Sprinkle the fritters with sea salt and serve with the dip.

Charred Artichokes with Lemon Oil Dip

Here is a lip-smacking change from traditional fare.

Serves 4

15ml/1 tbsp lemon juice or white
   wine vinegar
2 artichokes, trimmed
12 garlic cloves, unpeeled
90ml/6 tbsp olive oil
1 lemon
sea salt
fresh flat leaf parsley sprigs, to garnish

1 Preheat the oven to 200°C/400°F/ Gas 6. Add the lemon juice or vinegar to a bowl of cold water. Cut each artichoke into wedges. Pull the hairy choke out from the centre of each wedge and discard, then drop the wedges into the acidulated water to prevent discoloration.

2 Drain the wedges and place in a roasting pan with the garlic and 45ml/ 3 tbsp of the oil. Toss well to coat. Sprinkle with a little salt and roast for about 40 minutes, until tender and slightly charred.

COOK'S TIP
Artichokes are usually boiled, but dry-heat cooking also works very well. If you can get young artichokes, try roasting them over a barbecue.

3 Meanwhile, make the lemon oil dip. Using a small, sharp knife thinly pare away two strips of rind from the lemon. Lay the strips of rind on a board and carefully scrape away any remaining pith. Place the rind in a small pan and add just enough cold water to cover. Bring to the boil over a medium heat, then lower the heat and simmer for 5 minutes. Drain the rind, refresh in cold water, then chop coarsely. Set aside. Meanwhile, cut the lemon in half and squeeze out the juice. Set aside with the blanched rind.

4 Arrange the cooked artichokes on a large serving plate and leave to cool for 5 minutes.

5 Using the back of a fork gently flatten the garlic cloves so that the flesh squeezes out of the skins. Transfer the garlic flesh to a bowl, mash to a paste, then add the lemon rind and juice. Using the fork, whisk the remaining olive oil into the garlic mixture. Garnish with the parsley. Serve the artichokes still warm with the lemon oil dip.

Cheese-crusted Party Eggs

Similar to the popular Scotch egg, these whole small eggs are wrapped in a tasty herb-flavoured coating, then deep-fried. Tiny bantam or quail's eggs will look dainty and are ideal for dipping into mayonnaise.

Makes 12–20

225g/8oz/4 cups stale
  white breadcrumbs
1 small leek, very finely chopped
225g/8oz mild but tasty cheese, grated
10ml/2 tsp garlic and herb seasoning
60ml/4 tbsp chopped fresh parsley
10ml/2 tsp mild mustard
4 eggs, separated
60–90ml/4–6 tbsp milk
12–20 small spinach or sorrel leaves,
  stalks removed
12 very small eggs, such as bantam,
  guinea fowl, or 16–20 quail's eggs,
  hard-boiled and peeled
50–75g/2–3oz/½–⅔ cup plain
  (all-purpose) flour, for coating,
  plus extra for dusting
50g/2oz/4 tbsp sesame seeds
vegetable oil, for deep-frying
salt and ground black pepper
mayonnaise, for dipping

1 Mix the breadcrumbs, leek, cheese, seasoning, parsley and mustard. Beat the egg yolks with the milk and blend into the mixture. Whisk two egg whites until stiff and gradually work sufficient stiff egg white into the breadcrumb mixture to give a firm, dropping (pourable) consistency. Chill for 1 hour.

2 Divide the mixture into 12 portions (or 16–20 if using the smaller eggs). Mould one portion in the palm of your hand, place a spinach leaf inside and then an egg and carefully shape the mixture around the egg to enclose it completely within a thin crust. Seal well and dust lightly with flour. Repeat with the remaining portions.

3 Beat the remaining egg white with 30ml/2 tbsp water, then pour into a shallow dish. Mix the flour with salt and pepper and the sesame seeds and place in another shallow dish. Dip the eggs first in the beaten egg white, then in the sesame flour. Cover and chill for at least 20 minutes.

4 Heat the oil in a pan until a crust of bread turns golden in about 1¼ minutes. Deep-fry the eggs in the hot oil, turning frequently, until they are golden brown all over. Remove the eggs with a slotted spoon, drain on kitchen paper and leave to cool completely. Serve the cooked eggs whole or sliced in half, with a bowl of good mayonnaise for dipping.

Crisp-fried Crab Claws

Crab claws are readily available in the freezer cabinet in many Asian stores and supermarkets. Thaw out thoroughly and dry on kitchen paper before dipping in the batter. They are just the right size to munch on for a burst of flavour.

Makes 12

50g/2oz/½ cup rice flour
15ml/1 tbsp cornflour (cornstarch)
2.5ml/½ tsp sugar
1 egg
60ml/4 tbsp cold water
1 lemon grass stalk, root trimmed
2 garlic cloves, finely chopped
15ml/1 tbsp chopped fresh
  coriander (cilantro)
1–2 fresh red chillies, seeded and
  finely chopped
5ml/1 tsp Thai fish sauce
vegetable oil, for frying
12 half-shelled crab claws
ground black pepper

For the chilli vinegar dip
45ml/3 tbsp sugar
120ml/4fl oz/½ cup water
120ml/4fl oz/½ cup red wine vinegar
15ml/1 tbsp Thai fish sauce
2–4 fresh red chillies, seeded
  and chopped

1 Combine the rice flour, cornflour and sugar in a bowl. Beat the egg with the cold water, then stir the egg and water mixture into the flour mixture and mix well until it forms a light batter.

2 Cut off the lower 5cm/2in of the lemon grass stalk and chop it finely. Add the lemon grass to the batter, with the garlic, coriander, red chillies and fish sauce. Stir in pepper to taste.

3 Make the chilli dip. Mix the sugar and water in a pan, stirring until the sugar has dissolved, then bring to the boil. Lower the heat and simmer for 5–7 minutes. Stir in the rest of the dip ingredients and set aside.

4 Heat the vegetable oil in a wok or deep-fryer. Pat the crab claws dry and dip into the batter. Drop the battered claws into the hot oil, a few at a time. Deep-fry until golden brown. Drain on kitchen paper and keep hot. Pour the chilli vinegar dip into a serving bowl and serve with the hot crab claws.

VARIATION
This Asian-style batter can also be used to coat king prawns (jumbo shrimp).

Parmesan Fish Goujons

The batter used here is light and crisp, making it the perfect choice for these moreish strips of fish. Serve as an appetizer or as part of a fork buffet.

Serves 4

375g/13oz plaice, flounder or sole fillets, or thicker fish such as cod, haddock or hoki
plain (all-purpose) flour, for dusting
vegetable oil, for deep-frying
salt and ground black pepper
fresh dill sprigs, to garnish

For the cream sauce
60ml/4 tbsp sour cream
60ml/4 tbsp mayonnaise
2.5ml/¹/₂ tsp grated lemon rind
30ml/2 tbsp chopped gherkins or capers
15ml/1 tbsp chopped mixed fresh herbs, or 5ml/1 tsp dried

For the batter
75g/3oz/³/₄ cup plain (all-purpose) flour
25g/1oz/¹/₄ cup freshly grated Parmesan cheese
5ml/1 tsp bicarbonate of soda (baking soda)
1 egg, separated
150ml/¹/₄ pint/²/₃ cup milk

1 To make the cream sauce, mix the sour cream, mayonnaise, lemon rind, gherkins or capers, fresh or dried herbs and seasoning together, then place in the refrigerator to chill.

2 To make the batter, sift the flour into a bowl. Mix in the cheese, soda and a pinch of salt, then whisk in the egg yolk and milk to give a thick yet smooth batter. Then gradually whisk in 90ml/6 tbsp water. Season, cover with clear film (plastic wrap) and place in the refrigerator to chill.

3 Skin the fish and cut into thin strips of similar length. Season the flour and then dip the fish strips lightly in the flour, shaking off any excess.

4 Heat at least 5cm/2in oil in a large pan with a lid. Whisk the egg white until stiff and gently fold it into the batter until just blended.

5 Dip the floured fish into the batter, drain off any excess and then drop gently into the hot oil.

6 Cook the fish for only 3–4 minutes, turning once. You may need to cook the goujons in batches to prevent them from sticking to each other. When the batter is golden and crisp, remove the fish with a slotted spoon. Place on kitchen paper on a plate and keep warm in a low oven while you are cooking the remaining goujons.

7 Serve the goujons hot garnished with sprigs of dill and accompanied by the cream sauce.

Thai Tempeh Cakes with **Dipping Sauce**

Made from soya beans, tempeh is similar to tofu but has a nuttier taste. Here, it is combined with a fragrant blend of lemon grass, coriander and ginger, and formed into small patties, then served with a spicy dipping sauce.

Makes 8 cakes

1 lemon grass stalk, outer leaves
   removed, finely chopped
2 garlic cloves, finely chopped
2 spring onions (scallions),
   finely chopped
2 shallots, finely chopped
2 fresh red or green chillies, seeded
   and finely chopped
2.5cm/1in piece fresh root ginger,
   peeled and finely chopped
60ml/4 tbsp chopped fresh coriander
   (cilantro), plus extra to garnish
250g/9oz/2¼ cups tempeh, thawed if
   frozen, sliced
15ml/1 tbsp lime juice
5ml/1 tsp caster (superfine) sugar
45ml/3 tbsp plain (all-
   purpose) flour
1 large (US extra large) egg,
   lightly beaten
vegetable oil, for frying
salt and ground black pepper

For the dipping sauce
45ml/3 tbsp mirin
45ml/3 tbsp white wine vinegar
2 spring onions (scallions),
   thinly sliced
15ml/1 tbsp sugar
2 fresh red or green chillies,
   finely chopped
30ml/2 tbsp chopped fresh
   coriander (cilantro)
large pinch of salt

1 To make the dipping sauce, mix together the mirin, vinegar, spring onions, sugar, chillies, coriander and salt in a small bowl and set aside.

2 To make the tempeh cakes, place the lemon grass, garlic, spring onions, shallots, chillies, ginger and coriander in a food processor or blender, then process to a coarse paste. Add the tempeh, lime juice and sugar, then process until combined.

3 Add the flour and beaten egg to the food processor or blender and season well with salt and pepper. Process again until the mixture forms a coarse, sticky paste.

4 Take a generous tablespoonful of the tempeh paste mixture at a time and form into rounds with your hands. The mixture will be quite sticky.

5 Heat enough oil to cover the base of a large, heavy frying pan. Add the tempeh cakes, in batches if necessary, and cook over a medium heat, turning once, for 5–6 minutes, until golden. Drain well on kitchen paper and serve warm with the dipping sauce, and garnished with chopped coriander.

Butterfly Prawn Spiedini with Chilli and Raspberry Dip

The success of this dish depends upon the quality of the prawns, so it is worthwhile getting really good ones, which have a fine flavour and firm texture. A fruity, slightly spicy dip is an astonishingly easy, but fabulous accompaniment.

Makes 30

30 raw king prawns (jumbo shrimp), peeled
15ml/1 tbsp sunflower oil
sea salt

For the chilli and raspberry dip
30ml/2 tbsp raspberry vinegar
15ml/1 tbsp sugar
115g/4oz/²⁄₃ cup raspberries
1 large fresh red chilli, seeded and finely chopped

1 Soak 30 wooden skewers in cold water for about 30 minutes. Make the dip by mixing the vinegar and sugar in a small pan. Heat gently until the sugar has dissolved, stirring constantly, then add the raspberries.

2 When the raspberry juices start to flow, tip the mixture into a sieve set over a bowl. Push the raspberries through the sieve using the back of a ladle. Discard the seeds. Stir the chilli into the purée. When the dip is cold, cover and place in a cool place until it is needed.

COOK'S TIP

These mini kebabs also taste really delicious with a vibrant chilli and mango dip. Use 1 large, ripe mango in place of the raspberries.

3 Preheat the grill (broiler) or barbecue. Remove the dark spinal vein from the prawns using a small, sharp knife.

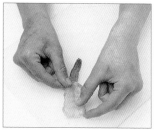

4 Make an incision down the curved back and butterfly each prawn.

5 Mix the sunflower oil with a little sea salt in a bowl. Add the prawns and toss to coat them completely.

6 Thread the prawns on to the drained skewers, spearing them head first.

7 Grill (broil) the prawns for about 5 minutes, depending on their size, turning them over once. Serve hot, with the chilli and raspberry dip.

VARIATIONS
• Thin strips of chicken or turkey escalope (scallop) can be seasoned and threaded on to the skewers and grilled (broiled) instead of the prawns. They are delicious with the fruity dip.
• For a vegetarian version, use chunks of halloumi cheese or firm tofu.

Seafood Spring Onion Skewers
with **Tartare Sauce**

Make these skewers quite small to
serve as a canapé at a drinks party
or before dinner, with the tartare
sauce offered as a dip.

Makes 9

*675g/1½lb monkfish, filleted, skinned
    and membrane removed
1 bunch thick spring onions (scallions)
75ml/5 tbsp olive oil
1 garlic clove, finely chopped
15ml/1 tbsp lemon juice
5ml/1 tsp dried oregano
30ml/2 tbsp chopped fresh flat
    leaf parsley
12–18 small scallops or raw king
    prawns (jumbo shrimp)
75g/3oz/1½ cups fine
    fresh breadcrumbs
salt and ground black pepper*

For the tartare sauce
*2 egg yolks
300ml/½ pint/1¼ cups olive oil, or
    vegetable oil and olive oil mixed
15–30ml/1–2 tbsp lemon juice
5ml/1 tsp French mustard, preferably
    tarragon mustard
15ml/1 tbsp chopped gherkin or
    pickled cucumber
15ml/1 tbsp chopped capers
30ml/2 tbsp chopped fresh flat
    leaf parsley
30ml/2 tbsp chopped fresh chives
5ml/1 tsp chopped fresh tarragon*

1 Soak nine wooden skewers in water
for 30 minutes to prevent them from
scorching under the grill (broiler).

2 To make the tartare sauce, whisk the
egg yolks and a pinch of salt. Whisk in
the oil, a drop at a time at first. When
about half the oil is incorporated, add it
in a thin stream, whisking constantly.
Stop when the mayonnaise is thick.

3 Whisk in 15ml/1 tbsp of the lemon
juice, then a little more oil. Stir in the
mustard, gherkin or cucumber, capers,
parsley, chives and tarragon. Add more
lemon juice and seasoning to taste.

4 Cut the monkfish into 18 even-size
pieces. Cut the spring onions into
18 pieces about 5cm/2in long. In a bowl,
mix the oil, garlic, lemon juice, oregano
and half the parsley with seasoning.
Add the seafood and the spring onions,
then marinate for 15 minutes.

5 Mix the breadcrumbs and remaining
parsley together. Toss the seafood and
spring onions in the mixture to coat.

6 Preheat the grill. Drain the wooden
skewers and thread the monkfish,
scallops or prawns and spring onions
on to them. Drizzle with a little of the
marinade, then grill (broil), turning
once and drizzling with the marinade,
for 5–6 minutes, until the seafood is
just cooked. Serve immediately with
the tartare sauce.

King Prawns with Spicy Dip

The tasty dip served with this dish is equally good made from peanuts instead of cashew nuts.

Serves 4–6

24 raw king prawns (jumbo shrimp)
juice of 1/2 lemon
5ml/1 tsp paprika
1 bay leaf
1 thyme sprig
vegetable oil, for brushing
salt and ground black pepper

For the spicy dip
1 onion, chopped
4 canned plum tomatoes, plus 60ml/
   4 tbsp of the juice
1/2 green (bell) pepper, seeded
   and chopped
1 garlic clove, crushed
15ml/1 tbsp cashew nuts
15ml/1 tbsp soy sauce
15ml/1 tbsp desiccated (dry
   unsweetened shredded) coconut

1 Peel the prawns, leaving the tails intact and reserving the shells. Place in a shallow dish and sprinkle with the lemon juice, paprika and seasoning. Cover and chill in the refrigerator.

2 Put the shells in a pan with the bay leaf and thyme, add cold water to cover and bring to the boil. Simmer gently for 30 minutes, then strain the stock into a measuring jug (cup). Top up with water, if necessary, to 300ml/ 1/2 pint/1 1/4 cups.

3 To make the spicy dip, place all the ingredients in a blender or food processor and process until the mixture is smooth.

4 Pour the mixture into a pan, add the measured prawn stock and simmer gently over a medium heat for 30 minutes, until the sauce is fairly thick.

5 Preheat the grill (broiler). Thread the prawns on to small skewers, then brush the prawns on both sides with a little oil and grill (broil) under a low heat until cooked, turning once. Serve immediately with the dip.

VARIATION
For a vegetarian version of this dish, use tofu cubes or vegetables, such as baby corn, mushrooms or (bell) peppers. Substitute vegetable stock for the prawn (shrimp) stock in the dip.

COOK'S TIP
If unshelled raw prawns are not available, use cooked king prawns instead. Just grill them for a short time, until they are completely heated through.

King Prawns in Crispy Batter

Serve these delightfully crispy prawns
with this simple Chinese-style
dipping sauce.

Serves 4

120ml/4fl oz/¹/₂ cup water
1 egg
115g/4oz/1 cup plain
  (all-purpose) flour
5ml/1 tsp cayenne pepper
12 raw king prawns (jumbo shrimp)
vegetable oil, for deep-frying
fresh flat leaf parsley, to garnish
lemon wedges, to serve

For the dipping sauce
30ml/2 tbsp soy sauce
30ml/2 tbsp dry sherry
10ml/2 tsp clear honey

3 To make the dipping sauce, stir
together the soy sauce, dry sherry and
honey in a small bowl until thoroughly
combined. Set aside.

4 Heat the vegetable oil in a large pan
or deep-fryer until a cube of stale
bread tossed into it browns in about
1 minute.

5 Holding the prawns by their tails, dip
them into the batter, one at a time,
shaking off any excess. Drop the
prawns carefully into the oil and deep-
fry for 2–3 minutes, until crisp and
golden brown. Drain well on kitchen
paper and serve immediately with the
dipping sauce and lemon wedges,
garnished with parsley.

1 In a large bowl, whisk the water with
the egg. Add the flour and cayenne,
and whisk until smooth.

2 Carefully peel the prawns, leaving just
the tail sections intact. Make a shallow
cut down the back of each prawn with
a sharp knife, then pull out and discard
the dark intestinal vein.

COOK'S TIP
Use leftover batter to coat thin strips of
other vegetables, such as sweet potato,
beetroot (beet), carrot or (bell) pepper,
then deep-fry until golden.

Chicken Satay with Peanut Sauce

A great choice for parties, these skewers of marinated chicken can be prepared in advance and served at room temperature. Beef, pork or even lamb fillet can be used instead of chicken if you prefer.

Makes about 24

450g/1lb boneless, skinless chicken
*   breast portions*
groundnut (peanut) oil,
*   for brushing*
sesame seeds, for sprinkling
red (bell) pepper strips,
*   to garnish*

For the marinade
90ml/6 tbsp vegetable oil
60ml/4 tbsp tamari or light soy sauce
60ml/4 tbsp fresh lime juice
2.5cm/1in piece fresh root ginger,
*   peeled and chopped*
3–4 garlic cloves
30ml/2 tbsp light brown sugar
5ml/1 tsp Chinese-style chilli sauce or
*   1 small fresh red chilli, seeded*
*   and chopped*
30ml/2 tbsp chopped fresh
*   coriander (cilantro)*

For the peanut sauce
30ml/2 tbsp smooth peanut butter
30ml/2 tbsp soy sauce
15ml/1 tbsp sesame or vegetable oil
2 spring onions (scallions),
*   finely chopped*
2 garlic cloves
15–30ml/1–2 tbsp fresh lime or
*   lemon juice*
15ml/1 tbsp brown sugar

COOK'S TIP
When using metal skewers, look for flat ones which prevent the food from spinning around. If using wooden skewers, be sure to soak them in cold water for at least 30 minutes to prevent them from burning.

1 Prepare the marinade. Place all the marinade ingredients in a food processor or blender and process until smooth and well blended, scraping down the sides of the bowl once or twice. Pour the marinade into a shallow, non-metallic dish and set aside.

2 Put all the peanut sauce ingredients into the same food processor bowl or blender goblet and process until well blended. If the sauce is too thick, add a little water and process again. Pour into a small bowl, cover and set aside until ready to serve.

3 Slice the chicken breast portions into thin strips, then cut the strips into 2cm/¾in pieces.

4 Add the chicken pieces to the marinade. Toss well to coat, cover with clear film (plastic wrap) and marinate for about 3–4 hours in a cool place, or overnight in the refrigerator.

5 Preheat the grill (broiler). Line a baking sheet with foil and brush lightly with oil. Thread 2–3 pieces of the marinated chicken on to skewers and sprinkle with the sesame seeds. Grill (broil) for 4–5 minutes until golden, turning once. Serve hot or cold with the peanut sauce and a garnish of red pepper strips.

Yakitori Chicken

These Japanese-style kebabs
are easy to eat and ideal for
barbecues or parties.

Makes 12

6 boneless, skinless chicken thighs
1 bunch of spring onions (scallions)
shichimi (seven-flavour spice),
to serve (optional)

For the yakitori sauce
150ml/¼ pint/⅔ cup Japanese
soy sauce
90g/3½oz/½ cup sugar
25ml/1½ tbsp sake or dry white wine
15ml/1 tbsp plain (all-purpose) flour

1 Soak 12 wooden skewers in water
for at least 30 minutes. Make the
sauce. Stir the soy sauce, sugar and
sake or wine into the flour in a small
pan and bring to the boil, stirring.
Lower the heat and simmer the mixture
for 10 minutes, or until the sauce is
reduced by one-third. Set aside.

2 Cut each chicken thigh into bitesize
pieces and set aside.

3 Cut the spring onions into 3cm/1¼in
pieces. Preheat the grill (broiler) or
prepare the barbecue.

COOK'S TIP
If shichimi is difficult to obtain, paprika
can be used instead.

4 Thread the chicken and spring onions
alternately on to the drained skewers.
Grill (broil) under a medium heat or
cook on the barbecue, brushing
generously several times with the
sauce. Allow 5–10 minutes, or until
the chicken is cooked but still moist.

5 Serve with yakitori sauce, offering
shichimi with the kebabs if available.

VARIATION
Bitesize chunks of turkey breast fillet, lean
boneless pork or lamb fillet can be used
instead of chicken. Small, whole button
(white) mushrooms are also delicious for
a vegetarian alternative.

Tandoori Chicken Sticks

This aromatic chicken dish is a sure-fire success at any party.

Makes about 25

450g/1lb boneless, skinless chicken breast portions

For the coriander yogurt
250ml/8fl oz/1 cup natural (plain) yogurt
30ml/2 tbsp whipping cream
1/2 cucumber, peeled, seeded and finely chopped
15–30ml/1–2 tbsp fresh chopped mint or coriander (cilantro)
salt and ground black pepper

For the marinade
175ml/6fl oz/3/4 cup natural yogurt
5ml/1 tsp garam masala or curry powder
1.5ml/1/4 tsp ground cumin
1.5ml/1/4 tsp ground coriander
1.5ml/1/4 tsp cayenne pepper (or to taste)
5ml/1 tsp tomato purée (paste)
1–2 garlic cloves, finely chopped
2.5cm/1in piece fresh root ginger, peeled and finely chopped
grated rind and juice of 1/2 lemon
15–30ml/1–2 tbsp chopped fresh mint or coriander

1 Prepare the coriander yogurt. Combine all the ingredients in a bowl and season with salt and ground black pepper to taste. Cover with clear film (plastic wrap) and chill until you are ready to serve.

2 Prepare the marinade. Place all the ingredients in the bowl of a food processor and process until the mixture is smooth. Pour the marinade into a shallow, non-metallic dish.

3 Place the chicken breast portions in the freezer for 5 minutes to firm, then slice in half horizontally. Cut the slices into 2cm/3/4in strips and add them to the marinade. Toss to coat all over. Cover and chill in the refrigerator for 6–8 hours or overnight.

4 Preheat the grill (broiler) and line a baking sheet with foil. Using a slotted spoon, remove the chicken from the marinade and arrange the pieces in a single layer on the baking sheet. Scrunch up the chicken strips slightly so that they make wavy shapes. Grill (broil) for 4–5 minutes, until golden brown and just cooked, turning once. When cool enough to handle, thread 1–2 pieces on to cocktail sticks (toothpicks) or short skewers and serve with the coriander yogurt dip.

Duck Wontons with Spicy Mango Sauce

These Chinese-style wontons are easy to make using ready-cooked smoked duck or chicken, or even leftovers from the Sunday roast.

Makes about 40

15ml/1 tbsp light soy sauce
5ml/1 tsp sesame oil
2 spring onions (scallions), chopped
grated rind of ¹/₂ orange
5ml/1 tsp brown sugar
275g/10oz/1¹/₂ cups chopped
  smoked duck
about 40 small wonton wrappers
15ml/1 tbsp vegetable oil
whole fresh chives, to garnish (optional)

For the mango sauce
30ml/2 tbsp vegetable oil
5ml/1 tsp ground cumin
2.5ml/¹/₂ tsp ground cardamom
1.5ml/¹/₄ tsp ground cinnamon
250ml/8fl oz/1 cup mango purée
  (about 1 large mango)
15ml/1 tbsp clear honey
2.5ml/¹/₂ tsp Chinese chilli sauce (or
  to taste)
15ml/1 tbsp cider vinegar
chopped fresh chives, to garnish

1 First, prepare the sauce. Heat the oil in a medium-sized pan over a medium-low heat. Add the ground cumin, cardamom and cinnamon and cook for about 3 minutes, stirring constantly.

2 Stir in the mango purée, honey, chilli sauce and vinegar. Remove the pan from the heat and leave to cool. Pour the sauce into a bowl and cover until ready to serve.

3 Prepare the wonton filling. Mix together the soy sauce, sesame oil, spring onions, orange rind and brown sugar in a large bowl until thoroughly blended. Add the chopped duck and toss to coat well.

4 Place a teaspoonful of the duck mixture in the centre of each wonton wrapper. Brush the edges of the wrappers with water and then draw them up to the centre, twisting to seal and forming a pouch shape.

5 Preheat the oven to 190°F/375°C/ Gas 5. Line a large baking sheet with foil and brush lightly with oil. Arrange the wontons on the baking sheet and bake for 10–12 minutes, until crisp and golden.

6 Transfer the wontons to a warm platter and serve with the mango sauce garnished with chopped fresh chives. If you like, tie each wonton with a fresh chive.

COOK'S TIP
Wonton wrappers, available in some large supermarkets and Asian food shops, are usually sold in 450g/1lb packets and can be stored in the freezer almost indefinitely. Remove as many as you need, keeping the rest frozen.

Pork and Peanut Wontons with Plum Sauce

These crispy filled wontons are delicious served with a sweet plum sauce. They can be filled for up to 8 hours before they are cooked.

Makes 40–50 wontons

175g/6oz/1½ cups minced (ground) pork
2 spring onions (scallions), chopped
30ml/2 tbsp peanut butter
10ml/2 tsp oyster sauce (optional)
40–50 wonton wrappers
30ml/2 tbsp flour paste (see Cook's Tip)
vegetable oil, for deep-frying
salt and ground black pepper
lettuces and radishes, to garnish

For the plum sauce
225g/8oz/generous ¾ cup dark plum jam
15ml/1 tbsp rice or white wine vinegar
15ml/1 tbsp dark soy sauce
2.5ml/½ tsp chilli sauce

1 Combine the minced pork, spring onions, peanut butter, oyster sauce, if using, in a bowl and season with salt and pepper, then set aside.

2 For the plum sauce, combine the plum jam, vinegar, soy and chilli sauces in a serving bowl and set aside.

COOK'S TIP
To make the flour paste, mix 4 parts cornflour (cornstarch) with 5 parts cold water in a small bowl, stirring well to make a smooth paste.

3 To fill the wonton wrappers, place eight wrappers at a time on a work surface, moisten the edges with the flour paste and place 2.5ml/½ tsp of the filling on each one. Fold them in half, corner to corner, and twist.

4 Fill a large wok or deep frying pan one-third full with vegetable oil and heat to 190°C/375°F or until a cube of bread, added to the oil, browns in 30 seconds. Have ready a wire strainer or frying basket and a tray lined with kitchen paper. Drop the wontons, eight at a time, into the hot oil and deep-fry for 1–2 minutes, until golden all over. Lift the wontons out on to the paper-lined tray and sprinkle with fine salt. Serve hot with the plum sauce, and garnished with lettuce and radishes.

Pork Balls with a **Minted Peanut Sauce**

This recipe is equally delicious
when made with chicken.

Serves 4–6

275g/10oz leg of pork, trimmed and diced
1cm/¹/₂in piece fresh root ginger,
  peeled and grated
1 garlic clove, crushed
10ml/2 tsp sesame oil
15ml/1 tbsp medium-dry sherry
15ml/1 tbsp soy sauce
5ml/1 tsp sugar
1 egg white
2.5ml/¹/₂ tsp salt
pinch of white pepper
350g/12oz/scant 1³/₄ cups long grain rice,
  washed and cooked for 15 minutes
50g/2oz ham, diced
1 iceberg or Bibb lettuce, to serve

For the peanut sauce
90ml/6 tbsp coconut cream
30ml/2 tbsp smooth peanut butter
juice of 1 lime
1 fresh red chilli, seeded and chopped
1 garlic clove, crushed
15ml/1 tbsp chopped fresh mint
15ml/1 tbsp chopped fresh
  coriander (cilantro)
15ml/1 tbsp Thai fish sauce (optional)

1 Place the diced pork, ginger and
garlic in a food processor and process
for 2–3 minutes, until smooth. Add the
sesame oil, sherry, soy sauce and sugar
and blend with the pork mixture.
Finally, add the egg white, salt and
white pepper.

2 Spread the cooked rice and ham in a
shallow dish. Using wet hands, shape
the pork mixture into thumb-size balls.
Roll in the rice to coat and pierce each
ball with a bamboo skewer.

3 To make the peanut sauce, heat the
coconut cream in a small pan over a
medium heat. Meanwhile, place the
peanut butter, lime juice, chilli, garlic,
mint and coriander in a bowl. Stir until
thoroughly combined, then add the
creamed coconut and season with the
fish sauce if using. Stir well to mix,
cover with clear film (plastic wrap) and
set aside until ready to serve.

4 Place the pork balls in a bamboo
steamer, then steam over a pan of
boiling water for about 8–10 minutes.
Arrange the pork balls on a bed of
lettuce leaves on a plate with the
sauce to one side and serve.

Nonya Pork Satay

These skewers of tender pork with a spicy nut coating make tasty snacks for a drinks party.

Makes 8–12

450g/1lb pork fillet (tenderloin)
15ml/1 tbsp light muscovado (brown) sugar
1cm/½ in cube shrimp paste
1–2 lemon grass stalks
30ml/2 tbsp coriander seeds, dry-fried
6 macadamia nuts or blanched almonds
2 onions, coarsely chopped
3–6 fresh red chillies, seeded and coarsely chopped
2.5ml/½ tsp ground turmeric
300ml/½ pint/1¼ cups canned coconut milk
30ml/2 tbsp groundnut (peanut) oil or sunflower oil
salt

1 Soak 8–12 bamboo skewers in water for at least 30 minutes to prevent them from scorching when they are placed under the grill (broiler).

2 Cut the pork into small, bitesize chunks, then spread it out in a single layer in a shallow dish. Sprinkle with the sugar, to help release the juices, and set aside.

3 Fry the shrimp paste briefly in a foil parcel in a dry frying pan. Alternatively, warm the foil parcel on a skewer held over the gas flame.

COOK'S TIP

Nonya Pork Satay can be served either as part of a buffet or as a light party snack – in which case serve it with cubes of cooling cucumber, which contrast well with the spicy meat.

4 Cut off the lower 5cm/2in of the lemon grass stalks and chop finely. Process the dry-fried coriander seeds to a powder in a food processor. Add the nuts and chopped lemon grass, process briefly, then add the onions, chillies, shrimp paste, turmeric and a little salt and process to a fine paste.

5 Pour in the coconut milk and oil. Switch the machine on very briefly to mix. Pour the mixture over the pork and leave to marinate for 1–2 hours.

6 Preheat the grill or prepare the barbecue. Thread three or four pieces of marinated pork on to each bamboo skewer and grill (broil) or cook on the barbecue for 8–10 minutes, or until tender, basting frequently with the remaining marinade. Serve the skewers immediately while hot.

Beef Satay with a Hot Mango Dip

Strips of tender beef are flavoured with a delicious spicy marinade before being grilled then served with a fruit dip.

Makes 12 skewers

450g/1lb sirloin steak, trimmed

For the marinade
15ml/1 tbsp coriander seeds
5ml/1 tsp cumin seeds
50g/2oz/¹⁄₃ cup cashew nuts
15ml/1 tbsp vegetable oil
2 shallots, or 1 small onion, finely chopped
1cm/¹⁄₂in piece fresh root ginger,
  peeled and finely chopped
1 garlic clove, crushed
30ml/2 tbsp tamarind sauce
30ml/2 tbsp dark soy sauce
10ml/2 tsp sugar
5ml/1 tsp rice or white wine vinegar

For the mango dip
1 ripe mango
1–2 small fresh red chillies, seeded and
  finely chopped
15ml/1 tbsp Thai fish sauce
juice of 1 lime
10ml/2 tsp sugar
1.5ml/¹⁄₄ tsp salt
30ml/2 tbsp chopped fresh
  coriander (cilantro)

1 Soak 12 bamboo skewers in cold water for 30 minutes. Slice the beef into long narrow strips and thread, zigzag-style, on to the skewers. Place on a flat plate and set aside.

2 For the marinade, dry-fry the coriander and cumin seeds and cashews in a large wok over a low heat until evenly brown. Transfer to a mortar with a rough surface and crush finely with the pestle. Add the oil, shallots or onion, ginger, garlic, tamarind and soy sauces, sugar and rice or white wine vinegar.

3 Spread this marinade over the beef, cover and leave to marinate for up to 8 hours. Cook the beef skewers under a moderate grill (broiler) or over a barbecue for 6–8 minutes, turning to make sure that they are evenly cooked. Meanwhile, make the mango dip.

4 Cut away the skin and remove the stone (pit) from the mango. Put the mango flesh, chillies, fish sauce, lime juice, sugar and salt into a food processor or blender and process until smooth, then add the coriander. Serve the skewers with the dip.

finger food and light bites

Standing-and-eating food has to be easy to eat

and sufficiently satisfying to keep everyone

munching through hours of chatting.

Grilled Polenta with Gorgonzola

This delicious, hot Italian-style snack can be served with any creamy cheese, but a richly flavoured blue cheese looks attractive and tastes fabulous. Here the polenta is cut into triangles but you could make different shapes if you like.

Serves 6–8

1.5 litres/2¹/₂ pints/6¹/₄ cups water
15ml/1 tbsp salt
350g/12oz/2¹/₂ cups polenta
*   (corn) flour*
225g/8oz Gorgonzola or other creamy
*   blue cheese, at room temperature*

1 Bring the water to the boil in a large heavy pan over a medium heat. Add the salt. Reduce the heat so that the water is simmering and begin to add the polenta flour in a steady stream. Stir constantly with a whisk until the polenta has all been incorporated.

2 Switch to a long-handled wooden spoon and continue to stir the polenta over a low to medium heat until it is a thick mass and pulls away from the sides of the pan. This may take from 25–50 minutes, depending on the type of flour used. For best results, never stop stirring the polenta until you remove it from the heat. However, note that if you are using quick-cook polenta, it will take far less time to thicken – about 5 minutes.

3 When the polenta is cooked, sprinkle a work surface or large board with a little water. Spread the polenta out on the surface in a layer 2cm/³/₄in thick. Leave to cool completely. Preheat the grill (broiler).

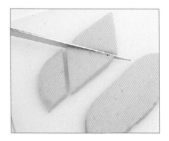

4 Cut the polenta into triangles. Grill (broil) until hot and speckled with brown on both sides. Spread the triangles with the Gorgonzola or other cheese. Serve immediately.

Buckwheat Blinis with Mushroom Caviar

These little Russian pancakes are traditionally served with fish roe, caviar and sour cream. Here is a vegetarian alternative that uses a selection of delicious wild mushrooms in place of the fish roe. The blinis can be made ahead of time and warmed in the oven just before topping.

Serves 4

115g/4oz/1 cup strong white
   bread flour
50g/2oz/¹/₂ cup buckwheat flour
2.5ml/¹/₂ tsp salt
300ml/¹/₂ pint/1¹/₄ cups milk
5ml/1 tsp easy-blend (rapid-rise)
   dried yeast
2 eggs, separated
200ml/7fl oz/scant 1 cup sour cream or
   crème fraîche

For the caviar
350g/12oz mixed wild mushrooms
   such as field (portabello)
   mushrooms, orange birch bolete,
   bay boletus and oyster
5ml/1 tsp celery salt
30ml/2 tbsp walnut oil
15ml/1 tbsp lemon juice
45ml/3 tbsp chopped fresh parsley
ground black pepper

1 To make the caviar, trim and chop the mushrooms, then place them in a glass bowl, toss with the celery salt and cover with a weighted plate.

2 Leave the mushrooms for about 2 hours, until the juices have run out into the base of the bowl. Rinse the mushrooms thoroughly to remove the salt, drain and press out as much liquid as you can with the back of a spoon. Return them to the bowl and toss with walnut oil, lemon juice, parsley and a twist of pepper. Chill in the refrigerator until ready to serve.

3 Sift the white bread flour and buckwheat flour together with the salt into a large mixing bowl. Gently warm the milk to approximately blood temperature. Add the yeast, stirring until dissolved, then pour into the flour, add the egg yolks and stir to make a smooth batter. Cover with a clean damp dishtowel and leave in a warm place for 1 hour.

4 Whisk the egg whites in a clean grease-free bowl until stiff, then fold them into the risen batter.

COOK'S TIP
It is important that there are no traces of grease in the bowl or yolk in the egg whites when they are whisked. Otherwise, they will not foam up and become stiff.

5 Heat an iron pan or griddle to a moderate temperature. Moisten with oil, then drop spoonfuls of the batter on to the surface. When bubbles rise to the top, turn them over and cook briefly on the other side.

6 Transfer to a serving plate. Spoon on the mushroom caviar top with the sour cream or crème fraîche, and serve.

Potato Pancakes

These light pancakes originate from Russia, where they are served with caviar. Here they are topped with an equally luxurious mixture of sour cream and smoked salmon.

Serves 6

115g/4oz floury (mealy) potatoes,
    boiled and mashed
15ml/1 tbsp easy-blend (rapid-rise)
    dried yeast
175g/6oz/1½ cups plain (all-
    purpose) flour
oil, for frying
90ml/6 tbsp sour cream
6 slices smoked salmon
salt and ground black pepper
lemon slices, to garnish

COOK'S TIP

These small pancakes can easily be prepared in advance and stored in the refrigerator until ready for use. Simply warm them through in a low oven.

1 Place the mashed potatoes, dried yeast and flour in a large bowl and pour in 300ml/½ pint/1¼ cups lukewarm water. Mix together well.

2 Leave to rise in a warm place for about 30 minutes, until the mixture has doubled in size.

VARIATIONS

• Substitute salmon roe for the smoked salmon and garnish with fresh dill.
• For a vegetarian version, top the pancakes with sour cream or tapenade and halved, hard-boiled quail's eggs or cherry tomatoes.

3 Heat a non-stick frying pan and add a little oil. Drop spoonfuls of the mixture on to the preheated pan. Cook the potato pancakes over a medium heat for about 2 minutes, until lightly golden on the underside, turn with a spatula and cook on the second side for about 1 minute.

4 Season the pancakes with some salt and pepper and transfer them to a warm platter. Top with a little sour cream and a small slice of smoked salmon folded on top. Garnish with a final grind of black pepper and slices of lemon and serve immediately.

Cannellini Bean and Rosemary Bruschetta

This sophisticated, Italian variation on the theme of beans on toast makes an unusual party snack.

Serves 6

150g/5oz/²/₃ cup dried cannellini beans
5 tomatoes
45ml/3 tbsp olive oil, plus extra
for drizzling
2 sun-dried tomatoes in oil, drained
and finely chopped
1 garlic clove, crushed
30ml/2 tbsp chopped fresh rosemary
12 slices Italian-style bread, such
as ciabatta
1 large garlic clove
salt and ground black pepper
handful of fresh basil leaves, to garnish

1 Put the beans in a bowl, add sufficient cold water to cover and leave to soak overnight.

2 Drain and rinse the beans, then place in a pan and cover with fresh water. Bring to the boil and boil rapidly for 10 minutes. Then simmer for 50–60 minutes, or until tender. Drain, return to the pan and keep warm.

3 Meanwhile, place the tomatoes in a bowl, cover with boiling water; leave for 30 seconds, then peel, seed and chop the flesh. Heat the oil in a frying pan, add the fresh and sun-dried tomatoes, garlic and rosemary. Cook for 2 minutes until the tomatoes begin to break down and soften.

4 Add the tomato mixture to the cannellini beans and season to taste with salt and pepper. Mix together well. Keep the bean mixture warm.

5 Rub the cut sides of the bread slices with the garlic clove, then toast them lightly on both sides. Spoon the cannellini bean mixture evenly on top of the toast. Sprinkle with basil leaves and drizzle with a little extra olive oil before serving.

Deep-fried New Potatoes with Saffron Aioli

Serve these crispy golden potatoes dipped into a garlicky mayonnaise – and watch them disappear.

Serves 4

20 baby, new or salad potatoes
vegetable oil, for deep-frying
salt and ground black pepper

For the aioli
1 egg yolk
2.5ml/¹/₂ tsp Dijon mustard
300ml/¹/₂ pint/1¹/₄ cups extra virgin olive oil
15–30ml/1–2 tbsp lemon juice
1 garlic clove, crushed
2.5ml/¹/₂ tsp saffron threads

1 To make the aioli put the egg yolk in a bowl with the Dijon mustard and a pinch of salt. Stir to mix together well. Using a balloon whisk or an electric mixer, beat in the olive oil very gradually, drop by drop at first and then in a very thin stream. Stir in the lemon juice.

2 Season the mayonnaise with salt and pepper to taste, then add the crushed garlic and beat the mixture thoroughly to combine.

3 Place the saffron in a small bowl and add 10ml/2 tsp hot water. Press the saffron with the back of a teaspoon to extract the colour and flavour, then leave to infuse (steep) for 5 minutes. Beat the saffron and the soaking liquid into the aioli.

4 Cook the potatoes in their skins in a large pan of lightly salted, boiling water for 5 minutes, then turn off the heat. Cover the pan and leave to stand for 15 minutes. Drain the potatoes well, then dry them thoroughly in a clean dishtowel.

5 Heat a 1cm/¹/₂in layer of vegetable oil in a deep pan. When the oil is very hot, add the potatoes and cook quickly, turning them constantly, until crisp and golden all over. Drain well on kitchen paper, transfer to a warm platter and serve immediately with the saffron aioli.

Fried Rice Balls Stuffed with Mozzarella

These deep-fried balls of risotto go by the name of *Suppli al Telefono* in their native Italy because the strings of melted mozzarella resemble telephone wires. Stuffed with mozzarella cheese, they are very popular snacks, which is hardly surprising as they are quite delicious. They make wonderful party bites or a great start to any dinner party meal.

Serves 4

1 quantity Risotto alla Milanese
3 eggs
breadcrumbs and plain (all-purpose) flour, for dusting
115g/4oz mozzarella cheese, cut into small cubes
vegetable oil, for deep-frying
dressed frisée lettuce leaves and cherry tomatoes, to serve (optional)

1 Put the risotto in a bowl and leave it to cool completely. Beat two of the eggs and stir them into the cooled risotto until well mixed.

2 Use your hands to form the rice mixture into balls the size of a large egg. If the mixture is too moist to hold its shape well, stir in a few spoonfuls of breadcrumbs.

3 Poke a hole in the centre of each ball with your finger, then fill it with small cubes of mozzarella and close the hole over again with the rice mixture.

4 Heat the oil for deep-frying until a small piece of bread sizzles as soon as it is dropped in.

5 Spread out some flour on a plate. Beat the remaining egg in a shallow bowl. Sprinkle another plate with breadcrumbs. Roll the risotto balls in the flour, then in the egg and, finally, in the breadcrumbs.

6 Deep-fry the rice balls, a few at a time, in the hot oil until golden and crisp. Drain on kitchen paper while the remaining balls are being fried, and keep warm. Transfer to warm plates and serve immediately, with dressed frisée leaves and cherry tomatoes if serving as an appetizer. For finger food, transfer to a warm platter and serve plain.

COOK'S TIP
These provide the perfect solution for the problem of to what to do with leftover risotto, as they are best made with a cold mixture, cooked the day before. This also makes them a perfect choice for parties as much of the preparation is done ahead.

Mini Baked Potatoes with Blue Cheese

These miniature potatoes can be eaten with the fingers. They provide a great way of starting off an informal supper party.

Makes 20

20 small new or salad potatoes
60ml/4 tbsp vegetable oil
coarse salt
120ml/4fl oz/¹/₂ cup sour cream
25g/1oz/¹/₄ cup crumbled blue cheese, such as Dolcelatte
30ml/2 tbsp chopped fresh chives, to garnish

VARIATION

Use a strong-flavoured cheddar in place of the blue cheese.

1 Preheat the oven to 180°C/350°F/ Gas 4. Wash and dry the potatoes. Toss with the oil in a bowl to coat.

2 Dip the potatoes in the coarse salt to coat lightly, then spread them out on a baking sheet. Bake for 45–50 minutes, until the potatoes are tender.

3 In a small bowl, combine the sour cream and blue cheese, mixing them together well.

COOK'S TIP

This dish works just as well as a light snack; if you don't want to be bothered with lots of fiddly small potatoes, simply bake an ordinary baking potato.

4 Cut a cross in the top of each potato. Press gently with your fingers to open the potatoes.

5 Top each potato with a generous spoonful of the blue cheese mixture. Place on a serving dish and garnish with the chives. Serve hot or leave to cool to room temperature.

Glamorgan Sausages

These tasty, traditional "sausages" are ideal for vegetarians.

Makes 8

150g/5oz/2$\frac{1}{2}$ cups fresh breadcrumbs
150g/5oz/1$\frac{1}{4}$ cups grated
   Caerphilly cheese
1 small leek, very finely chopped
15ml/1 tbsp chopped fresh parsley
leaves from 1 thyme sprig, chopped
2 eggs
7.5ml/1$\frac{1}{2}$ tsp English (hot)
   mustard powder
about 45ml/3 tbsp milk
plain (all-purpose) flour, for coating
15ml/1 tbsp oil
15g/$\frac{1}{2}$oz/1 tbsp butter, melted
salt and ground black pepper
salad leaves and tomato halves, to serve

1 Mix the breadcrumbs, cheese, leek, herbs and seasoning. Whisk the eggs with the mustard and reserve 30ml/ 2 tbsp. Stir the rest into the cheese mixture with enough milk to bind.

2 Divide the cheese mixture into eight portions and form into sausage shapes with your hands.

3 Dip the sausages into the reserved egg and mustard mixture to coat. Spread out the flour on a plate and season with a little salt and pepper, then roll the sausages in it to give a light, even coating. Transfer to a plate, cover with clear film (plastic wrap) and chill in the refrigerator for about 30 minutes, until firm.

4 Preheat the grill (broiler) and oil the grill rack. Mix the oil and melted butter together and brush the mixture all over the sausages. Grill (broil) the sausages for 5–10 minutes, turning them carefully every now and then, until they are golden brown all over. Serve hot or cold, with salad leaves and tomato halves.

COOK'S TIPS
• You can make these sausages well in advance of the party and open freeze them, then transfer to a bag and seal. To serve, thaw for about 1 hour and reheat in a moderately hot oven for 10–15 minutes.
• Make 16 smaller sausages to serve as finger food. Grill (broil) for 5–6 minutes and serve on cocktail sticks (toothpicks).

Son-in-law Eggs

This fascinating name comes from a delightful story about a prospective bridegroom who was anxious to impress his future mother-in-law and devised a recipe from the only other dish he knew how to make – boiled eggs. The hard-boiled eggs are deep-fried and then drenched with a sweet piquant tamarind sauce before serving.

Serves 4–6

75g/3oz/generous 1/3 cup palm sugar
60ml/4 tbsp light soy sauce
105ml/7 tbsp tamarind juice
vegetable oil, for frying
6 shallots, thinly sliced
6 garlic cloves, thinly sliced
6 fresh red chillies, sliced
6 hard-boiled eggs, shelled
coriander (cilantro) sprigs, to garnish
lettuce, to serve

1 Combine the palm sugar, soy sauce and tamarind juice in a small pan. Bring to the boil over a low heat, stirring until the sugar dissolves, then simmer the sauce, without stirring, for about 5 minutes.

2 Taste the sauce and add more palm sugar, soy sauce or tamarind juice, if necessary. It should be a balanced combination of sweet, salty and slightly sour. Transfer the sauce to a bowl and set aside until needed.

3 Heat a couple of spoonfuls of the oil in a frying pan. Add the shallots, garlic and chillies and cook over a low heat, until golden brown. Transfer the mixture to a bowl and set aside.

4 Deep-fry the eggs in hot oil for 3–5 minutes, until golden brown. Drain on kitchen paper, cut into quarters and arrange on a bed of lettuce. Sprinkle the shallot mixture over them, drizzle with the sauce and garnish with coriander.

Birds' Nests

These are also known as Welsh Eggs because they resemble Scotch Eggs, but have leek in the filling.

Serves 6

6 eggs, hard-boiled
plain (all-purpose) flour, seasoned with
    salt and paprika, for dusting
10ml/2 tsp sunflower oil
1 leek, chopped
115g/4oz/2 cups fresh
    white breadcrumbs
grated rind and juice of 1 lemon
50g/2oz/$\frac{1}{2}$ cup vegetarian shredded suet
60ml/4 tbsp chopped fresh parsley
5ml/1 tsp dried thyme
salt and ground black pepper
1 egg, beaten
75g/3oz/$\frac{1}{2}$ cup dried breadcrumbs
vegetable oil, for deep-frying
lettuce and tomato wedges, to garnish

1 Shell the hard-boiled eggs and toss them in the seasoned flour. Set aside until needed.

2 Heat the sunflower oil in a small frying pan. Add the leek and cook for about 3 minutes, until softened but not browned. Remove from the heat and leave to cool, then mix with the fresh breadcrumbs, lemon rind and juice, suet, parsley, thyme and salt and pepper. If the mixture is a bit too dry, add a little water.

3 Shape the leek and breadcrumb mixture around the eggs, moulding it firmly with your hands, then toss the coated eggs first into the beaten egg and then into the dried breadcrumbs. Place the eggs on a plate and chill for 30 minutes. This will firm them up before cooking.

4 Pour enough oil to fill a deep-fat fryer one-third full and heat to 190°C/ 375°F or until a cube of bread browns in 45 seconds. Deep-fry the eggs for about 3 minutes in two batches. Remove and drain on kitchen paper.

5 Serve cool, cut in half to reveal the "birds' nests", garnished with lettuce and tomato wedges.

Crispy Spring Rolls

These small and dainty spring rolls are ideal served as appetizers or as cocktail snacks.

Makes 40 rolls

115g/4oz small leeks or spring
* onions (scallions)*
115g/4oz carrots
115g/4oz bamboo shoots
115g/4oz mushrooms
225g/8oz fresh beansprouts
45–60ml/3–4 tbsp vegetable oil
5ml/1 tsp salt
5ml/1 tsp light brown sugar
15ml/1 tbsp light soy sauce
15ml/1 tbsp Chinese rice wine or
* dry sherry*
20 frozen spring roll wrappers, thawed
15ml/1 tbsp cornflour (cornstarch)
* paste (see Cook's Tip)*
plain (all-purpose) flour,
* for dusting*
vegetable oil, for deep-frying

1 With a sharp knife, cut the leeks or spring onions, carrots, bamboo shoots and mushrooms into thin shreds, about the same size and shape as the beansprouts.

2 Heat the oil in a wok. Add the vegetables and stir-fry for about 1 minute. Add the salt, sugar, soy sauce and rice wine or sherry, and continue stirring and tossing the vegetables for 1½–2 minutes. Remove from the heat and drain away the excess liquid, then leave to cool.

3 To make the spring rolls, cut each spring roll wrapper in half diagonally, then place about a tablespoonful of the cooled vegetable mixture one-third of the way down on the wrapper, with the triangle pointing away from you.

4 Lift the lower edge of the spring roll wrapper over the filling and roll once. Fold in both ends and roll once more, then brush the upper pointed edge with a little cornflour paste and roll into a neat package, pressing lightly to seal. Lightly dust a tray with flour and place the spring rolls on the tray with the flapside underneath.

5 To cook, heat the oil in a wok or deep-fryer to 180°C/350°F or until a cube of bread added to it browns in about 30 seconds. Reduce the heat to low. Deep-fry the spring rolls in batches – about 8–10 at a time – for 2–3 minutes, or until golden and crispy, then remove and drain on kitchen paper. Serve the spring rolls hot with a dipping sauce, such as soy sauce, or mixed salt and pepper.

COOK'S TIPS

• To make cornflour (cornstarch) paste, put 4 parts cornflour and 5 parts cold water into a small bowl and stir well until smooth.

• Classic Chinese salt and pepper sauce is made with Sichuan peppercorns and sea salt. Dry-fry 30ml/2 tbsp Sichuan peppercorns and 60ml/4 tbsp sea salt in a heavy frying pan, stirring frequently, until the mixture begins to brown. Remove the pan from the heat and leave to cool, then grind in a mortar with a pestle or in a spice grinder.

Samosas

Crisp and spicy, these tasty party snacks are enjoyed the world over. Throughout the East, they are sold by street vendors, and eaten at any time of day. Filo pastry can be used if you like a lighter, flakier texture.

Makes about 20

1 packet 25cm/10in square spring roll
    wrappers, thawed if frozen
30ml/2 tbsp plain (all-purpose) flour,
    mixed to a paste with water
vegetable oil, for deep-frying
fresh coriander (cilantro) leaves,
    to garnish

For the filling
25g/1oz/2 tbsp ghee or unsalted
    (sweet) butter
1 small onion, finely chopped
1cm/½in piece fresh root ginger,
    peeled and chopped
1 garlic clove, crushed
2.5ml/½ tsp chilli powder
1 large potato, about 225g/8oz
    cooked until just tender and
    finely diced
50g/2oz/½ cup cauliflower florets,
    lightly cooked, chopped into
    small pieces
50g/2oz/½ cup frozen peas, thawed
5–10ml/1–2 tsp garam masala
15ml/1 tbsp chopped fresh coriander
    (cilantro) leaves and stems
squeeze of lemon juice
salt

1 Heat the ghee or butter in a large frying pan. Add the onion, ginger and garlic and cook over a low heat, stirring occasionally, for 5 minutes, until the onion has softened but not browned. Add the chilli powder and cook for 1 minute, then stir in the potato, cauliflower and peas. Sprinkle with garam masala and set aside to cool. Stir in the chopped coriander, lemon juice and salt.

2 Cut the spring roll wrappers into three strips (or two for larger samosas). Brush the edges with a little of the flour paste. Place a small spoonful of filling about 2cm/¾in in from the edge of one strip. Fold one corner over the filling to make a triangle and continue this folding until the entire strip has been used and a triangular pastry has been formed. Seal any open edges with more flour and water paste, if necessary adding more water if the paste is very thick.

3 Heat the vegetable oil in a large pan or a deep-fryer to 190°C/375°F or until a cube of bread added to it browns in about 45 seconds. Add the samosas, a few at a time, and deep-fry until golden and crisp. Drain well on kitchen paper and serve hot garnished with chopped coriander leaves.

COOK'S TIP
You can prepare samosas in advance of the party by deep-frying them until they are just cooked through, then drain well. Cook in hot oil for a few minutes to brown and heat through, then drain again before serving.

Thai Fish Cakes with Cucumber Relish

These wonderful little nibbles are a very familiar and popular appetizer. They are usually accompanied with Thai beer or choose a robust oaked Chardonnay instead.

Makes about 12

300g/11oz white fish fillet, such as
    cod, cut into chunks
30ml/2 tbsp Thai red curry paste
1 egg
30ml/2 tbsp Thai fish sauce
5ml/1 tsp granulated sugar
30ml/2 tbsp cornflour (cornstarch)
3 kaffir lime leaves, shredded
15ml/1 tbsp chopped fresh
    coriander (cilantro)
50g/2oz green beans, thinly sliced
vegetable oil, for frying
Chinese mustard cress, to garnish

For the cucumber relish
60ml/4 tbsp rice vinegar
60ml/4 tbsp water
50g/2oz/¼ cup granulated sugar
1 whole bulb pickled garlic
1 cucumber, quartered and sliced
4 shallots, thinly sliced
15ml/1 tbsp chopped fresh root ginger

1 To make the cucumber relish, bring the vinegar, water and sugar to the boil. Stir until the sugar dissolves, then remove from the heat and leave to cool.

2 Combine the rest of the relish ingredients together in a bowl and pour the vinegar mixture over.

3 Combine the fish, curry paste and egg in a food processor and process until combined. Transfer the mixture to a bowl, add the Thai fish sauce, sugar, cornflour, lime leaves, coriander and green beans and mix well.

4 Mould and shape the mixture into patties about 5cm/2in in diameter and 5mm/¼in thick.

5 Heat the oil in a wok or deep-fryer. Add the fish cakes, in small batches, and deep-fry for about 4–5 minutes, or until golden brown. Remove and drain well on kitchen paper. Keep the cooked fish cakes warm in a low oven while you cook the remainder. Garnish with Chinese mustard cress and serve immediately with a little cucumber relish spooned on the side.

Thai Fish and Egg Cakes

These tangy little mouthfuls, with a kick of Eastern spice, make great party food or appetizers.

Makes about 20

225g/8oz smoked cod or haddock
    fillet (undyed)
225g/8oz fresh cod or haddock fillet
1 small fresh red chilli, seeded and
    finely chopped
2 garlic cloves, grated
1 lemon grass stalk, very finely chopped
2 large spring onions (scallions), very
    finely chopped
30ml/2 tbsp Thai fish sauce or
    30ml/2 tbsp soy sauce and a few
    drops anchovy essence (extract)
60ml/4 tbsp thick coconut milk
2 large (US extra large) eggs, beaten
15ml/1 tbsp chopped fresh
    coriander (cilantro)
15ml/1 tbsp cornflour (cornstarch),
    plus extra for moulding
vegetable oil, for frying
soy sauce, rice vinegar or Thai fish
    sauce, for dipping

2 Add the chilli, garlic, lemon grass, spring onions, fish or soy sauce and the coconut milk and process until the fish is well blended with the spices. Add the eggs and coriander and process for a further few seconds. Cover with clear film (plastic wrap) and chill in the refrigerator for 1 hour.

3 To make the fish cakes, flour your hands with cornflour and shape large teaspoonfuls of the fish mixture into neat balls, coating them with the flour.

4 Heat 5–7.5cm/2–3in oil in a medium pan until a crust of bread turns golden in about 1 minute. Add the fish balls, 5–6 at a time, turning them carefully with a slotted spoon for 2–3 minutes, until they turn golden all over. Remove with a slotted spoon and drain on kitchen paper. Keep the fish cakes warm in the oven until they are all cooked. Serve immediately with a small dish of soy sauce, rice vinegar or Thai fish sauce or a combination of sauces for dipping.

1 Place the smoked fish in a bowl of cold water and leave to soak for 10 minutes. Dry well on kitchen paper. Remove and discard the skin and any stray bones from the smoked and fresh fish, chop the flesh coarsely and place in a food processor.

Futo-Maki

Thick-rolled sushi, such as futo-maki, is a fashionable and attractive food to serve as canapés with drinks.

Makes 16

2 nori seaweed sheets

For the su-meshi (vinegared rice)
200g/7oz/1 cup short grain rice
275ml/9fl oz/scant 1¼ cups water
45ml/3 tbsp rice vinegar
37.5ml/7½ tsp sugar
10ml/2 tsp salt

For the omelette
2 eggs, beaten
25ml/1½ tbsp dashi stock
10ml/2 tsp sake
2.5ml/½ tsp salt
vegetable oil, for frying

For the fillings
4 dried shiitake mushrooms,
*   soaked in water overnight*
120ml/4fl oz/½ cup dashi stock
15ml/1 tbsp shoyu
7.5ml/1½ tsp sugar
5ml/1 tsp mirin
6 raw king prawns (jumbo shrimp),
*   heads and shells removed*
4 asparagus spears, boiled and cooled
10 fresh chives, about 23cm/9in long
salt
wasabi, gari and soy sauce, to serve

1 To make the su-meshi, wash the rice in cold water, drain and set aside for one hour. Put the rice into a pan and add the water. Cover and boil for 5 minutes, then simmer until the water has been absorbed. Remove from the heat and set aside for 10 minutes.

2 Mix the rice vinegar with the sugar and salt. Tip the rice into a bowl and sprinkle with the vinegar mixture. Fold into the rice with a spatula, but do not stir. Cool the su-meshi before shaping.

3 To make the omelette, mix the beaten eggs, dashi stock, sake and salt in a bowl. Heat a little oil in a frying pan on a medium-low heat. Pour in just enough egg mixture to cover the base of the pan. As soon as the mixture sets, fold the omelette in half towards you and wipe the space left with a little oil. With the first omelette still in the pan, repeat until all the mixture is used.

4 Each new omelette is laid on to the first to form a multi-layered omelette. Slide the layered omelette on to a chopping board. When cool, cut lengthways into 1cm/½in wide strips.

5 Put the shiitake mushrooms and the water, stock, shoyu, sugar and mirin in a small pan. Bring to the boil, then reduce the heat to low. Cook for 20 minutes, or until half of the liquid has evaporated. Drain the shiitake mushrooms, remove and discard the stalks, and slice the caps thinly. Squeeze out any excess liquid, then dry on kitchen paper. Discard the liquid.

6 Make three cuts in the belly of each of the prawns to stop them curling up, and boil in salted water for 1 minute, or until they turn bright pink. Drain and cool, then remove the vein using a cocktail stick (toothpick).

COOK'S TIP
If you make the rolled sushi ahead, wrap each roll in clear film (plastic wrap) until ready to slice and serve the rolls.

7 Place a nori sheet, rough side up, at the front edge of a sushi rolling mat. Scoop up half of the su-meshi and spread it on the nori. Leave a 1cm/½in margin at the side nearest you, and 2cm/¾in at the side furthest from you. Make a shallow depression lengthways across the centre of the rice. Fill this with half the omelette strips and half the asparagus. Place half the prawns along the egg and asparagus. Top with five chives and half the shiitake slices.

8 Lift the mat with your thumbs while pressing the filling with your fingers. Roll the mat up gently. When completed, gently roll the mat to firm it up. Unwrap and set the futo-maki aside. Repeat to make another roll.

9 Cut each futo-maki into eight pieces, using a very sharp knife. Wipe the knife with a clean dishtowel dampened with rice vinegar after each cut.

10 Line up all the pieces on a large tray or serving platter. Serve with small dishes of wasabi, gari and soy sauce for dipping.

Sushi-style Tuna Cubes

These tasty tuna cubes are easier to prepare than classic Japanese sushi but retain the same fresh taste.

Makes about 24

675g/1½ lb fresh tuna steak, about
2cm/¾in thick
1 large red (bell) pepper, seeded and
cut into 2cm/¾in pieces
sesame seeds, for sprinkling

For the marinade

15–30ml/1–2 tbsp lemon juice
2.5ml/½ tsp salt
2.5ml/½ tsp sugar
2.5ml/½ tsp wasabi paste
120ml/4 fl oz/½ cup vegetable oil
30ml/2 tbsp chopped fresh
coriander (cilantro)

For the soy dipping sauce

105ml/7 tbsp soy sauce
15ml/1 tbsp rice wine vinegar
5ml/1 tsp lemon juice
1–2 spring onions (scallions), chopped
5ml/1 tsp sugar
2–3 dashes Asian hot chilli oil

1 Cut the tuna into 2.5cm/1in pieces and then arrange them in a single layer in a large non-metallic ovenproof dish.

2 Prepare the marinade. In a small bowl, stir the lemon juice with the salt, sugar and wasabi paste. Slowly whisk in the oil until thoroughly blended and slightly creamy. Stir in the coriander. Pour the marinade over the tuna cubes and toss to coat. Cover with clear film (plastic wrap) and marinate for about 40 minutes in a cool place.

3 Meanwhile, prepare the soy dipping sauce. Put the soy sauce, vinegar, lemon juice, spring onions, sugar and chilli oil to taste in a small bowl and stir until thoroughly blended. Cover with clear film and set aside until ready to serve.

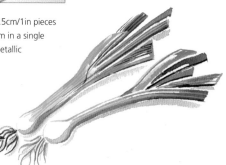

4 Preheat the grill (broiler) and line a baking sheet with foil. Thread a cube of tuna, then a piece of pepper on to each skewer and arrange on the baking sheet.

5 Sprinkle with sesame seeds and grill (broil) for 3–5 minutes, turning once or twice, until just beginning to colour but still pink inside. Serve immediately with the soy dipping sauce.

COOK'S TIP

Wasabi is a hot, pungent Japanese horseradish available in powder form and as paste in a tube from gourmet and Japanese food stores. The powdered form needs to be reconstituted with water in the same way as mustard powder.

VARIATIONS

• Substitute spring onions (scallions) for the (bell) pepper. Cut them into short lengths, about 2.5cm/1in long and thread them on to the skewers in the same way.
• Use another firm-fleshed fish, such as swordfish instead of the tuna.

Rice Triangles

These rice shapes – *Onigiri* – are very popular in Japan. You can put anything you like in the rice, so you could invent your own *Onigiri*.

Makes 8

1 salmon steak
15ml/1 tbsp salt
450g/1lb/4 cups freshly cooked
*   sushi rice*
¼ cucumber, seeded and cut
*   into thin batons*
½ sheet yaki-nori seaweed, cut into
*   four equal strips*
white and black sesame seeds,
*   for sprinkling*

1 Grill (broil) the salmon steak on each side until the flesh flakes easily when tested with a sharp knife. Set aside to cool while you make the cucumber *onigiri*. When the salmon is cold, flake it, discarding any skin and bones.

2 Put the salt in a bowl. Spoon an eighth of the warm, cooked rice into a small rice bowl. Make a hole in the middle of the rice and put in a few cucumber batons. Smooth the rice over to cover.

3 Wet the palms of both hands with cold water, then rub the salt evenly on to your palms.

4 Empty the rice and cucumbers from the bowl on to one hand. Use both hands to shape the rice into a triangular shape, using firm but not heavy pressure, and making sure that the cucumber is encased by the rice. Make three more rice triangles the same way, dampening your palms and sprinkling with salt as before.

5 Mix the flaked salmon into the remaining rice, then shape it into triangles as before.

6 Wrap a strip of yaki-nori around each of the cucumber triangles. Sprinkle sesame seeds on the salmon triangles. Set aside to cool completely before serving.

COOK'S TIP
Always use warm rice to make the triangles. Leave them to cool completely, then wrap each in foil or clear film (plastic wrap) and store in a cool place.

Paella Croquettes

Paella is probably Spain's most famous dish, and here it is used for a tasty fried tapas.

Serves 4

pinch of saffron threads
150ml/¹/₄ pint/²/₃ cup white wine
30ml/2 tbsp olive oil
1 small onion, finely chopped
1 garlic clove, finely chopped
150g/5oz/²/₃ cup risotto rice
300ml/¹/₂ pint/1¹/₄ cups hot
*   chicken stock*
50g/2oz /¹/₂ cup cooked prawns
*   (shrimp), peeled, deveined and*
*   coarsely chopped*
50g/2oz cooked chicken,
*   coarsely chopped*
75g/3oz/²/₃ cup petits pois (baby peas),
*   thawed if frozen*
30ml/2 tbsp freshly grated
*   Parmesan cheese*
1 egg, beaten
30ml/2 tbsp milk
75g/3oz/1¹/₂ cups fresh white
*   breadcrumbs*
vegetable or olive oil, for shallow frying
salt and ground black pepper
fresh flat leaf parsley, to garnish

1 Stir the saffron into the wine in a small bowl; set aside.

2 Heat the measured olive oil in a pan and gently cook the onion and garlic for 5 minutes, until softened. Stir in the risotto rice and cook, stirring, for 1 minute.

3 Keeping the heat fairly high, add the wine and saffron mixture to the pan, stirring until it is completely absorbed. Gradually add the stock, a little at a time, stirring until all the liquid has been absorbed and the rice is cooked – this should take about 20 minutes.

COOK'S TIP

If you can find Valencia rice, use that instead as it is more authentic.

4 Stir in the prawns, chicken, petits pois and freshly grated Parmesan. Season to taste with salt and pepper. Remove the pan from the heat and leave to cool slightly, then use two tablespoons to shape the mixture into 16 small lozenges.

5 Mix the egg and milk in a shallow bowl. Spread out the breadcrumbs on a sheet of foil. Dip the croquettes in the egg mixture, then coat them evenly in the breadcrumbs.

6 Heat the oil for shallow frying in a large, heavy frying pan. Then add the croquettes and cook for 4–5 minutes, until crisp and golden brown. Work in batches. Drain on kitchen paper and keep hot. Serve garnished with a sprig of flat leaf parsley.

Spinach Empanadillas

These are little Spanish pastry turnovers, filled with ingredients that have a strong Moorish influence – pine nuts and raisins. Serve with pre-dinner drinks at an informal supper party, allowing two to three per person.

Makes 20

25g/1oz/2 tbsp raisins
25ml/1¹/₂ tbsp olive oil
450g/1lb fresh spinach, washed
 and chopped
6 drained canned anchovies, chopped
2 garlic cloves, finely chopped
25g/1oz/¹/₃ cup pine nuts, chopped
1 egg, beaten
350g/12oz puff pastry
salt and ground black pepper

1 To make the filling, soak the raisins in a little warm water for 10 minutes. Drain, then chop coarsely.

2 Heat the oil in a large sauté pan or wok, add the spinach, stir, then cover and cook over a low heat for about 2 minutes. Uncover, increase the heat to medium and cook until any liquid has evaporated. Add the anchovies, garlic and seasoning, then cook, stirring, for a further minute. Remove from the heat, add the raisins and pine nuts and leave to cool.

3 Preheat the oven to 180°C/350°F/ Gas 4. Roll out the pastry to a 3mm/ ¹/₈in thickness.

4 Using a 7.5cm/3in pastry (cookie) cutter, stamp out 20 rounds, re-rolling the dough if necessary. Place about two teaspoonfuls of the filling in the middle of each round, then brush the edges with a little water. Bring up the sides of the pastry and press together gently to seal.

5 Press the edges of the pastry together with the back of a fork. Brush the turnovers, with a little beaten egg, then place them on a lightly greased baking sheet and bake for about 15 minutes, until well rised and golden brown. Serve the empanadillas warm.

COOK'S TIP

If using frozen pastry, make sure that it is completely thawed before you try to roll it out. Once the pastry has thawed, store in the refrigerator until required. It is essential to keep it chilled so that it puffs up when cooked.

Thai-style Seafood Turnovers

These elegant appetizer-size turnovers are filled with fish, prawns and fragrant Thai rice.

Makes 18

plain (all-purpose) flour, for dusting
500g/1¼lb puff pastry, thawed
if frozen
1 egg, beaten with 30ml/2 tbsp water
lime twists, to garnish

For the filling
275g/10oz skinned white fish fillets
seasoned plain (all-purpose) flour
8–10 large raw prawns (shrimp)
15ml/1 tbsp sunflower oil
about 75g/3oz/6 tbsp butter
6 spring onions (scallions), finely sliced
1 garlic clove, crushed
225g/8oz/2 cups cooked jasmine rice
4cm/1½in piece fresh root
ginger, grated
10ml/2 tsp finely chopped fresh
coriander (cilantro)
5ml/1 tsp finely grated lime rind

1 Preheat the oven to 190°C/375°F/ Gas 5. Make the filling. Cut the fish into 2cm/¾in cubes and dust with seasoned flour, shaking off any excess. Peel and devein the prawns and cut each one into four pieces.

2 Heat half of the oil and 15g/½oz/ 1 tbsp of the butter in a large frying pan. Add the spring onions and cook gently for 2 minutes.

3 Add the garlic and cook for a further 5 minutes, until the spring onions are very soft. Transfer to a large bowl.

4 Heat the remaining oil and a further 25g/1oz/2 tbsp of the butter in a clean pan. Add the fish pieces and cook briefly. As soon as they begin to turn opaque, use a slotted spoon to transfer them to the bowl with the spring onions.

5 Cook the prawns in the oil mixture remaining in the pan. When they begin to change colour, lift them out with a slotted spoon and add them to the bowl.

6 Add the cooked rice to the bowl, with the fresh root ginger, coriander and grated lime rind. Mix gently, taking care not to break up the fish.

7 Dust the work surface with a little flour. Roll out the pastry and cut into 10cm/4in rounds. Place spoonfuls of filling just off centre on the pastry rounds. Dot with a little of the remaining butter. Dampen the edges of the pastry with a little of the beaten egg mixture, fold one side of the pastry over the filling and press the edges together firmly.

8 Place the turnovers on two lightly greased baking sheets. Decorate them with the pastry trimmings, if you like, and brush them with remaining beaten egg to glaze. Bake the turnovers for 12–15 minutes, or until golden brown all over.

9 Transfer the turnovers to a warm platter and garnish with lime twists, then serve immediately.

Herbed Fish Fritters

Serve these mini fritters with a tartare sauce if you like. Simply chop some capers and gherkins, and stir into home-made or good quality ready-made mayonnaise.

Makes 20

450g/1lb plaice or flounder fillets
300ml/¹/₂ pint/1¹/₄ cups milk
450g/1lb cooked potatoes
1 fennel bulb, finely chopped
45ml/ 3 tbsp chopped fresh parsley
2 eggs
15g/¹/₂oz/1 tbsp unsalted
*   (sweet) butter*
250g/9oz/2 cups white breadcrumbs
25g/1oz/2 tbsp sesame seeds
vegetable oil, for deep-frying
salt and ground black pepper

1 Gently poach the fish fillets in the milk for about 15 minutes, until the flesh flakes easily. Drain and reserve the milk.

2 Peel the skin off the fish and remove any stray bones. In a food processor fitted with a metal blade, process the fish, potatoes, fennel, parsley, eggs and butter.

3 Transfer the mixture to a bowl, add 30ml/2 tbsp of the reserved cooking milk and season with salt and plenty of ground black pepper. Mix well. Cover with clear film (plastic wrap) and chill for 30 minutes, then shape into twenty even-size fritters with your hands.

4 Mix together the breadcrumbs and sesame seeds in a shallow dish, then roll the croquettes in this mixture to form a good coating.

5 Heat the oil in a large, heavy pan until it is hot enough to brown a cube of stale bread in 30 seconds. Deep-fry the croquettes, in small batches, for about 4 minutes, until they are golden brown all over. Drain well on kitchen paper and serve the fritters hot.

Breaded Sole Batons

Goujons of lemon sole are coated in seasoned flour and breadcrumbs, and fried until deliciously crispy.

Serves 4

275g/10oz lemon sole fillets, skinned
2 eggs
115g/4oz/1¹/₂ cups fine
*   fresh breadcrumbs*
75g/3oz/6 tbsp plain (all-purpose) flour
salt and ground black pepper
vegetable oil, for frying
tartare sauce and lemon wedges,
*   to serve*

1 Cut the fish fillets into long diagonal strips about 2cm/³⁄₄in wide, using a sharp knife.

2 Break the eggs into a shallow dish and beat well with a fork. Place the breadcrumbs in another shallow dish. Put the flour in a large plastic bag and season with salt and plenty of ground black pepper.

3 Dip the fish strips into the egg, turning to coat well. Place on a plate and then, taking a few at a time, place them in the bag of flour and shake well to coat. Dip the fish strips in the egg again, then in the breadcrumbs, turning to coat well. Place on a tray in a single layer, not touching. Leave to stand for at least 10 minutes to let the coating set.

4 Heat 1cm/¹⁄₂in oil in a large, heavy frying pan over a medium-high heat. When the oil is hot – a cube of bread will sizzle – add the coated fish strips, in batches, and cook for about 2–2¹⁄₂ minutes, turning once, taking care not to overcrowd the pan. Drain on kitchen paper and keep warm. Serve the fish with tartare sauce and lemon wedges.

Prawn Toasts

These crunchy sesame-topped toasts are simple to prepare using a food processor for the prawn paste.

Makes 64

225g/8oz cooked prawns (shrimp)
1 egg white
2 spring onions (scallions), chopped
5ml/1 tsp chopped fresh root ginger
1 garlic clove, chopped
5ml/1 tsp cornflour (cornstarch)
2.5ml/$^{1}/_{2}$ tsp salt
2.5ml/$^{1}/_{2}$ tsp sugar
2–3 dashes hot pepper sauce
8 slices firm-textured white bread
60–75ml/4–5 tbsp sesame seeds
vegetable oil, for frying
spring onion tassel,
    to garnish

1 Peel the prawns, if necessary, devein them, then drain well and pat dry on kitchen paper. Put the prawns, egg white, spring onions, ginger, garlic, cornflour, salt, sugar and pepper sauce into a food processor and process until the mixture forms a smooth paste, scraping down the side of the bowl from time to time.

COOK'S TIP

To make your party preparations easier, you can prepare these prawn toasts in advance and heat them through in a hot oven just before serving. Make sure they are really crisp and hot though, because they won't be nearly so enjoyable if there's no crunch when you bite them.

2 Spread the prawn paste evenly over the bread slices, then sprinkle over the sesame seeds, pressing gently to make them stick. Cut off the crusts and discard, then cut each slice of bread diagonally into four triangles. Cut each triangle in half again to make 64 triangles in total.

3 Heat 5cm/2in vegetable oil in a large, heavy pan or wok, until it is hot but not smoking. Cook the triangles, in batches, for about 30–60 seconds, turning the toasts once. Drain on kitchen paper and keep hot in the oven while you cook the rest. Serve hot with the garnish.

Mussels in Black Bean Sauce

The large green-shelled mussels from New Zealand are perfect for this delicious dish. Buy the cooked mussels on the half-shell – it is an elegant way to serve them.

Makes 20

15ml/1 tbsp vegetable oil
2.5cm/1in piece fresh root ginger,
    finely chopped
2 garlic cloves, finely chopped
1 fresh red chilli, seeded
    and chopped
15ml/1 tbsp black bean sauce
15ml/1 tbsp dry sherry
5ml/1 tsp granulated sugar
5ml/1 tsp sesame oil
10ml/2 tsp dark soy sauce
20 cooked New Zealand
    green-shelled mussels
2 spring onions (scallions), 1 shredded
    and 1 cut into fine rings

1 Heat the vegetable oil in a frying pan or wok. Cook the ginger, garlic and chilli with the black bean sauce for a few seconds, then add the sherry and sugar and cook for 30 seconds more, stirring with chopsticks or a wooden spoon until the sugar is dissolved.

2 Remove from the heat, stir in the oil and soy sauce. Mix thoroughly.

COOK'S TIP
Provide cocktail sticks (toothpicks) for spearing the mussels and removing them from their half-shells.

3 Have ready a bamboo steamer or a medium pan holding 5cm/2in of simmering water and fitted with a metal trivet. Place the mussels in layers on a heatproof plate that will fit inside the steamer or pan. Spoon the prepared sauce evenly over the half-shell mussels.

4 Sprinkle all the spring onions over the mussels. Place in the steamer or cover the plate tightly with foil and place it on the trivet in the pan. It should be just above the level of the water. Cover and steam over a high heat for about 10 minutes, or until the mussels have heated through. Serve immediately.

Marinated Mussels

This is an ideal recipe to prepare
and arrange well in advance.
Remove from the refrigerator
15 minutes before serving to allow
the flavours to develop fully.

Makes about 48

1kg/2¹/₄lb mussels, large if possible
(about 48)
175ml/6fl oz/³/₄ cup dry white wine
1 garlic clove, finely crushed
120ml/4fl oz/¹/₂ cup olive oil
50ml/2fl oz/¹/₄ cup lemon juice
5ml/1 tsp hot chilli flakes
2.5ml/¹/₂ tsp mixed (apple pie) spice
15ml/1 tbsp Dijon mustard
10ml/2 tsp sugar
5ml/1 tsp salt
15–30ml/1–2 tbsp chopped fresh dill
or coriander (cilantro)
15ml/1 tbsp capers, drained and
chopped if large
ground black pepper

1 With a stiff kitchen brush, under
cold running water, scrub the mussels
to remove any sand and barnacles; pull
out and remove the beards. Discard
any open shells that will not shut when
they are tapped.

2 In a large, flameproof casserole or
pan set over a high heat, bring the
white wine to the boil with the garlic
and ground black pepper. Add the
mussels and cover tightly. Reduce the
heat to medium and simmer for 2–4
minutes, until the shells open, shaking
the pan occasionally.

3 In a large bowl combine the olive oil,
lemon juice, chilli flakes, mixed spice,
Dijon mustard, sugar, salt, chopped dill
or coriander and capers. Stir well, then
set aside.

4 Discard any mussels with closed
shells. With a small sharp knife,
carefully remove the remaining
mussels from their shells, reserving the
half shells for serving. Add the mussels
to the marinade. Toss the mussels to
coat thoroughly, then cover with clear
film (plastic wrap) and chill in the
refrigerator for 6–8 hours or overnight,
stirring gently from time to time.

5 With a teaspoon, place one mussel
with a little marinade in each shell.
Arrange on a platter and cover until
ready to serve.

VARIATION
You can prepare other shellfish in the
same way. Venus, Amandes and other
medium-size clams would work well and,
if you can find them, razor clams would
look very impressive. This would also be
an unusual way to serve scallops.

COOK'S TIP
Mussels can be prepared ahead of time
and marinated for up to 24 hours. To
serve, arrange the mussel shells on a bed
of crushed ice, well-washed seaweed or
even coarse salt to prevent them from
wobbling on the plate.

Crab Egg Rolls

These wonderful crab rolls are similar to authentic Chinese spring rolls. They are made with wafer-thin pancakes, which provide the very crisp case for the filling. If you prefer a softer version the rolls can be steamed – they are equally delicious and quite light. These are ideal for buffets, children's parties and summer picnics.

Makes about 12

3 eggs
450ml/¾ pint/scant 2 cups water
175g/6oz/1½ cups plain
    (all-purpose) flour
2.5ml/½ tsp salt
vegetable oil, for deep-frying
45ml/3 tbsp light soy sauce mixed with
    5ml/1 tsp sesame oil, for dipping
lime wedges, to serve

For the filling

225g/8oz/1⅓ cups white crab meat
    or small prawns (shrimp)
3 large spring onions
    (scallions), shredded
2.5cm/1in piece fresh root
    ginger, grated
2 large garlic cloves, chopped
115g/4oz bamboo shoots, chopped,
    or beansprouts
15ml/1 tbsp soy sauce
10–15ml/2–3 tsp cornflour (cornstarch)
    blended with 15ml/1 tbsp water
1 egg, separated
salt and ground black pepper

1 Lightly beat the eggs and gradually stir in the water. Sift the flour and salt into another bowl and work in the egg mixture. Blend to a smooth batter, then remove any lumps if necessary. Leave to rest for 20 minutes.

2 When ready to use, lightly whisk the batter and stir in 15ml/1 tbsp cold water to thin it slightly if necessary.

3 Lightly grease a 25cm/10in non-stick frying pan and heat gently. To make smooth, pale wrappers for the egg rolls, the frying pan must be hot enough to set the batter, but should not be hot enough for the batter to brown, bubble or develop holes. Pour in about 45ml/3 tbsp batter and swirl around the pan to spread evenly and very thinly. Cook for 2 minutes, or until loose underneath. There is no need to cook the pancake on the other side.

4 Make a further 11 pancakes. Stack the pancakes, cooked side upwards, between sheets of baking parchment. Set aside until ready to use.

5 To make the filling, combine the crab or prawns, spring onions, ginger, garlic, bamboo shoots or beansprouts, soy sauce, cornflour and water, egg yolk and seasoning.

6 Lightly beat the egg white. Place a spoonful of filling in the middle of each pancake, brush the edges with egg white and fold into neat parcels, tucking in the ends well.

7 Heat the oil in a deep-frying pan and when a cube of bread turns light golden in 1 minute, carefully add four of the parcels, fold side downwards. Cook for 1–2 minutes, or until golden and crisp. Remove with a slotted spoon and place on kitchen paper. Keep warm in the oven while you cook the remaining egg rolls. Alternatively, using a stacking bamboo steamer, arrange four parcels in each layer, cover with a lid and steam for 30 minutes.

8 Serve with the soy sauce and sesame oil dipping sauce and wedges of lime.

Crab and Ricotta Tartlets

Use the meat from a freshly cooked crab, weighing about 450g/1lb, if you can. Otherwise, look out for frozen brown and white crab meat.

Serves 4

225g/8oz/2 cups plain
   (all-purpose) flour
pinch of salt
115g/4oz/½ cup butter, diced
225g/8oz/1 cup ricotta cheese
15ml/1 tbsp grated onion
30ml/2 tbsp freshly grated
   Parmesan cheese
2.5ml/½ tsp mustard powder
2 eggs, plus 1 egg yolk
225g/8oz crab meat
30ml/2 tbsp chopped fresh parsley
2.5–5ml/½–1 tsp anchovy
   essence (extract)
5–10ml/1–2 tsp lemon juice
salt and cayenne pepper
salad leaves, to garnish

1 Sift the flour and salt into a bowl, add the butter and rub it in until the mixture resembles fine breadcrumbs. Stir in about 60ml/4 tbsp cold water to make a firm dough.

2 Turn the dough on to a lightly-floured surface and knead lightly. Roll out the pastry and use to line four 10cm/4in tartlet tins (muffin pans). Prick the bases all over with a fork, then chill in the refrigerator for about 30 minutes. Preheat the oven to 200°C/400°F/Gas 6.

3 Line the pastry cases (pie shells) with baking parchment or foil and fill with baking beans. Bake them for 10 minutes, then remove the paper or foil and beans. Return to the oven and bake for a further 10 minutes.

4 Place the ricotta, grated onion, Parmesan and mustard powder in a bowl and beat until soft and well combined. Gradually beat in the eggs and egg yolk.

5 Gently stir in the crab meat and chopped parsley, then add the anchovy essence and lemon juice and season with salt and cayenne pepper, to taste.

6 Remove the tartlet cases from the oven and reduce the temperature to 180°C/350°F/Gas 4. Spoon the filling evenly into the cases and bake for 20 minutes, until set and golden brown. Serve hot with a garnish of salad leaves.

Foie Gras Pâté in Filo Cups

This is an extravagantly rich hors d'oeuvre – so save it for a special anniversary or celebration.

Makes 24

3–6 sheets fresh or thawed filo pastry
40g/1½oz/3 tbsp butter, melted
225g/8oz canned foie gras pâté
*   or other fine liver pâté, at*
*   room temperature*
50g/2oz/4 tbsp butter, softened
30–45ml/2–3 tbsp Cognac (optional)
chopped pistachio nuts, to garnish

1 Preheat the oven to 200°C/400°F/ Gas 6. Grease a bun tray (muffin pan) with 24 × 4cm/1½in cups. Stack the filo sheets on a work surface and cut into 6cm/2½in squares. Cover with a damp dishtowel to prevent them from drying out.

COOK'S TIPS

• The pâté and pastry are best eaten soon after preparation. If preparing ahead of time and then chilling in the refrigerator, be sure to bring the cups back to room temperature before serving.

• Pâté de foie gras is made from the liver of specially fattened geese or ducks. Duck liver – foie gras de canard – is more delicate in texture, but stronger in flavour than goose liver – foie gras d'oie. Both are regarded as a great delicacy and are very expensive. However, some people object to the method used to produce the enlarged livers of these birds and so prefer to buy more conventional pâté.

2 Keeping the rest of the filo squares covered until required, place one square on a work surface and brush lightly with melted butter, then turn and brush the other side.

3 Butter a second square and place it over the first at an angle. Butter a third filo square and place it at an angle over the first two sheets to form an uneven edge.

4 Press the stacked layers into one cup of the bun tray. Continue with the remaining filo pastry and melted butter until all the cups in the bun tray have been filled.

5 Bake the filo cups for about 4–6 minutes, until they are crisp and golden, then remove and cool in the tray for 5 minutes. Carefully transfer each filo cup to a wire rack and leave to cool completely.

6 In a small bowl, beat the pâté with the softened butter until smooth and well blended. Add the Cognac to taste, if using.

7 Spoon the filling into a piping (pastry) bag fitted with a medium star nozzle and pipe a swirl into each filo cup. Sprinkle with pistachio nuts and chill until you are ready to serve.

Chicken Bitki

This is a popular Polish dish and makes an attractive appetizer when offset by deep red beetroot.

Makes 12

15g/¹/₂oz/1 tbsp butter, melted
115g/4oz flat mushrooms,
   finely chopped
50g/2oz/1 cup fresh white breadcrumbs
350g/12oz skinless chicken breast
   portions or guinea fowl, minced
   (ground) or finely chopped
2 eggs, separated
1.5ml/¹/₄ tsp grated nutmeg
30ml/2 tbsp plain (all-purpose) flour
45ml/3 tbsp vegetable oil
salt and ground black pepper
salad leaves and grated pickled
   beetroot (beet), to serve

1 Melt the butter in a pan and cook the mushrooms for about 5 minutes, until softened and the juices have evaporated. Leave to cool.

2 Mix together the mushrooms, breadcrumbs, minced or chopped chicken or guinea fowl, egg yolks and nutmeg in a bowl and season to taste with salt and pepper.

3 Whisk the egg whites until stiff in a clean, grease-free bowl. Gently stir half the whites into the chicken or guinea fowl mixture to slacken it, then fold in the remainder with a rubber spatula or metal spoon.

4 Shape the mixture into 12 even-size meatballs, about 7.5cm/3in long and 2.5cm/1in wide. Spread out the flour on a shallow plate. Roll the meatballs in the flour to coat.

5 Heat the oil in a large, heavy frying pan, add the bitki and cook over a medium heat for about 10 minutes, turning occasionally until evenly golden brown and cooked through. Serve hot with salad leaves and grated pickled beetroot.

Chicken Parcels

These home-made chicken parcels look splendid piled high and golden brown.

Makes 35

225g/8oz/2 cups strong white bread
　flour, plus extra for dusting
2.5ml/¹/₂ tsp salt
2.5ml/¹/₂ tsp caster (superfine) sugar
5ml/1 tsp easy-blend (rapid-rise)
　dried yeast
25g/1oz/2 tbsp butter, softened
1 egg, beaten, plus a little extra
90ml/6 tbsp warm milk
lemon wedges, to serve

For the filling
15ml/1 tbsp sunflower oil
1 small onion, finely chopped
175g/6oz/1¹/₂ cups minced
　(ground) chicken
75ml/5 tbsp chicken stock
30ml/2 tbsp chopped fresh parsley
pinch of grated nutmeg
salt and ground black pepper

1 Sift the flour, salt and sugar into a large bowl. Stir in the dried yeast, then make a well in the centre of the flour.

2 Add the butter, egg and milk and mix to a soft dough. Turn on to a lightly-floured surface and knead for 10 minutes, until smooth and elastic.

3 Put the dough in a clean bowl, cover with clear film (plastic wrap) and leave in a warm place to rise for 1 hour, or until the dough has doubled in size.

4 Meanwhile, heat the oil in a frying pan. Add the onion and chicken and cook over a low heat, stirring occasionally, for about 10 minutes, until the onion has softened and the chicken is beginning to colour. Add the stock and simmer for 5 minutes. Stir in the parsley, grated nutmeg and salt and ground black pepper. Then leave to cool.

5 Preheat the oven to 220°C/425°F/ Gas 7. Knead the dough, then roll it out on a lightly floured surface until it is 3mm/¹/₈in thick. Stamp out rounds with a 7.5cm/3in cutter.

6 Brush the edges with beaten egg. Put a little filling in the middle, then press the edges together. Place on oiled baking sheets, cover with oiled clear film, leave in a warm place to rise for 15 minutes.

7 Brush the parcels with a little more egg, then bake for 5 minutes. Lower the oven temperature to 190°C/375°F/ Gas 5, and bake for about 10 minutes more, until well risen and golden. Serve with lemon wedges.

Tunisian Brik

You can make these little parcels into any shape you like, but the most important thing is to encase the egg white quickly before it starts to escape.

Makes 6

45ml/3 tbsp butter, melted
1 small red onion, finely chopped
150g/5oz skinless chicken or turkey
    fillet, minced (ground)
1 large garlic clove, crushed
juice of ½ lemon
30ml/2 tbsp chopped fresh parsley
12 sheets of filo pastry, each about
    15 × 25cm/6 × 10in, thawed
    if frozen
6 small (US medium) eggs, such as
    bantam, pheasant or guinea fowl
vegetable oil, for deep-frying
salt and ground black pepper

1 Heat half the butter in a pan and cook the onion for 3 minutes. Add the chicken or turkey, garlic, lemon juice, parsley and seasoning, and cook, stirring, for 2–3 minutes, or until the meat is just cooked. Set aside to cool.

COOK'S TIP
If you prefer to cook these pastries in the oven, preheat it to 220°C/425°F/Gas 7. Brush the pastries with butter or beaten egg and cook for 8–10 minutes.

2 Place one sheet of pastry lengthways on the work surface and brush with melted butter; top with a second sheet. Brush the edges with butter and place one-sixth of the filling about 2.5cm/1in from the bottom left-hand side of the pastry sheet. Flatten the filling, making a slight hollow in it.

3 Carefully crack an egg into the hollow and fold up the pastry immediately so the egg white does not run out. Lift the right-hand edge and fold it over to the left edge to enclose the filling and seal quickly. Fold the bottom left-hand corner straight up and then fold the bottom left corner up to the right edge, forming a triangle.

4 Use the remaining pastry sheets and filling to make another five parcels, then heat the oil in a frying pan until a cube of bread turns golden in about 1½ minutes. Cook the pastries, two or three at a time, until golden. Lift them out of the pan with a slotted spoon and drain on kitchen paper. Serve hot or cold.

Golden Parmesan Chicken

Served cold with the garlicky
mayonnaise, these morsels of
chicken make great finger food.

Serves 4

4 skinless chicken breast fillets
75g/3oz/1 1/2 cups fresh
  white breadcrumbs
40g/1 1/2 oz/1/2 cup finely grated
  Parmesan cheese
30ml/2 tbsp chopped fresh parsley
2 eggs, beaten
120ml/4fl oz/1/2 cup mayonnaise
120ml/4fl oz/1/2 cup fromage frais
  (farmer's cheese)
1–2 garlic cloves, crushed
50g/2oz/4 tbsp butter, melted
salt and ground black pepper

1 Cut each fillet into four or five
chunks. Mix together the breadcrumbs,
Parmesan, parsley and salt and pepper
in a shallow dish.

2 Dip the chicken pieces in the egg,
then into the breadcrumb mixture.
Place in a single layer on a baking sheet
and chill for 30 minutes.

3 Meanwhile, to make the
garlic mayonnaise, mix together the
mayonnaise, fromage frais and garlic,
and season to taste with ground black
pepper. Spoon the mayonnaise into
a small serving bowl, cover with clear
film (plastic wrap) and chill in the
refrigerator until required.

4 Preheat the oven to 180°C/350°F/
Gas 4. Drizzle the melted butter over
the chicken pieces and cook them for
about 20 minutes, until crisp and
golden. Transfer to a warm platter
and serve the chicken immediately,
accompanied by the garlic mayonnaise
for dipping.

Chicken Croquettes

This recipe comes from Rebato's, a tapas bar in London. The chef there makes croquettes with a number of different flavourings.

Makes 8

25g/1oz/2 tbsp butter
25g/1oz/¼ cup plain
*   (all-purpose) flour*
150ml/¼ pint/⅔ cup milk
15ml/1 tbsp olive oil
1 boneless chicken breast portion with
*   skin, about 75g/3oz, diced*
1 garlic clove, finely chopped
1 small (US medium) egg, beaten
50g/2oz/1 cup fresh white breadcrumbs
vegetable oil, for deep-frying
salt and ground black pepper
fresh flat leaf parsley, to garnish
lemon wedges, to serve

1 Melt the butter in a small pan over a low heat. Add the flour and cook gently, stirring constantly, for 1 minute. Gradually add the milk, whisking constantly to make a smooth, very thick sauce. Cover with a lid and remove from the pan from the heat.

2 Heat the oil in a heavy frying pan. Add the chicken and garlic and cook over a low heat, stirring frequently, for 5 minutes, until the chicken is lightly browned and cooked through.

3 Turn the contents of the frying pan into a food processor or blender and process until finely chopped. Do not over-process to a paste. Stir the chicken into the sauce, mixing it well. Season with salt and pepper to taste. Leave to cool completely.

4 Shape the mixture into eight even-sized sausages, then dip each in egg and then breadcrumbs. Deep-fry in hot oil for 4 minutes, until crisp and golden. Drain on kitchen paper and serve garnished with parsley and lemon wedges for squeezing.

Chicken with Lemon and Garlic

Extremely easy to cook and delicious to eat, serve this succulent tapas dish with home-made aioli if you like.

Serves 4

225g/8oz skinless chicken breast fillets
30ml/2 tbsp olive oil
1 shallot, finely chopped
4 garlic cloves, finely chopped
5ml/1 tsp paprika
juice of 1 lemon
30ml/2 tbsp chopped fresh parsley
salt and ground black pepper
fresh flat leaf parsley, to garnish
lemon wedges, to serve

1 Sandwich the chicken breast fillets between two sheets of clear film (plastic wrap) or baking parchment. Bat out with a rolling pin or meat mallet until the fillets are about 5mm/¼in thick.

2 Using a sharp knife, cut the chicken into strips about 1cm/½ in wide.

3 Heat the oil in a large, heavy frying pan or wok until it is very hot but not smoking. Add the chicken strips, shallot, garlic and paprika and stir-fry over a high heat for about 3 minutes, until the chicken is lightly browned and cooked through.

4 Stir in the lemon juice and parsley and season with salt and pepper to taste. Transfer to a warm platter and serve immediately with lemon wedges, garnished with flat leaf parsley.

Prosciutto and Mozzarella Parcels on Frisée Salad

Italian prosciutto crudo is a delicious raw smoked ham. Here it is baked with melting mozzarella in a light, crisp pastry case, making it an ideal finger food.

Serves 6

a little hot chilli sauce
6 prosciutto crudo slices
200g/7oz mozzarella cheese, cut into
* 6 slices*
6 sheets filo pastry, each measuring
* 45 × 28cm/18 × 11in, thawed*
* if frozen*
50g/2oz/¹⁄₄ cup butter, melted
150g/5oz frisée lettuce, to serve

1 Preheat the oven to 200°C/400°F/ Gas 6. Sprinkle a little of the chilli sauce over each slice of prosciutto crudo. Place a slice of mozzarella on each slice of prosciutto, then fold it around the cheese. The cheese should be enclosed by the ham.

2 Brush a sheet of filo pastry with melted butter and fold it in half to give a double-thick piece measuring 23 × 14cm/9 × 5½in. Place a ham and mozzarella parcel in the middle of the pastry and brush the remaining pastry with a little butter, then fold it over to enclose the prosciutto and mozzarella in a neat parcel. Place on a baking sheet with the edges of the pastry underneath and brush with a little butter. Repeat with the remaining parcels and sheets.

3 Bake the filo parcels for 15 minutes, or until the pastry is crisp and evenly golden. Arrange the salad on six plates and add the parcels. Serve immediately.

Smoked Chicken with Peach Mayonnaise in Filo Tartlets

These tartlets require the minimum of culinary effort because smoked chicken is widely available ready cooked. The filling can be prepared a day in advance and chilled overnight but do not fill the pastry cases until you are ready to serve.

Makes 12

25g/1oz/2 tbsp butter, melted
3 sheets filo pastry, each measuring
* 45 × 28cm/18 × 11in, thawed*
* if frozen*
2 skinless cooked smoked chicken
* breast fillets, thinly sliced*
150ml/¹⁄₄ pint/²⁄₃ cup mayonnaise
grated rind of 1 lime
30ml/2 tbsp lime juice
2 ripe peaches, peeled, stoned (pitted)
* and chopped*
salt and ground black pepper
fresh tarragon sprigs, lime slices and
* salad leaves, to garnish*

1 Preheat the oven to 200°C/400°F/ Gas 6. Brush 12 small individual tartlet tins (muffin pans) with a little of the melted butter. Cut each sheet of filo pastry into 12 equal rounds large enough to line the tins, allowing just enough to stand up above the tops of the tins.

2 Place a round of pastry in each tin and brush with a little butter, then add another round of pastry. Brush each with more butter and add a third round of pastry.

COOK'S TIP
To peel peaches, place them in a bowl and pour in freshly boiled water to cover. Leave to stand for 30–60 seconds (the riper the peaches, the quicker their skins loosen). Use a slotted spoon to remove a peach from the water. Working quickly, slit the skin with the point of a knife, then slip it off. Repeat with the remaining peaches.

3 Bake the tartlets for 5 minutes, or until the pastry is golden brown. Leave in the tins for a few moments before transferring to a wire rack to cool.

4 In a mixing bowl combine the chicken, mayonnaise, lime rind and juice, peaches and salt and pepper. Chill the mixture for at least 30 minutes, or up to 12 hours overnight. When you are ready to serve the tartlets, spoon the chicken mixture into the filo tartlets. Garnish with the fresh tarragon sprigs, lime slices and salad leaves.

Savoury Pork Pies

These little pies come from Spain and are really delicious.

Makes 12 pastries

350g/12oz shortcrust pastry, thawed
*   if frozen*

For the filling
15ml/1 tbsp vegetable oil
1 onion, chopped
1 garlic clove, crushed
5ml/1 tsp fresh thyme
115g/4oz/1 cup minced (ground) pork
5ml/1 tsp paprika
1 hard-boiled egg, chopped
1 gherkin, chopped
30ml/2 tbsp chopped
*   fresh parsley*
vegetable oil, for deep-frying
salt and ground black pepper

1 To make the filling, heat the oil in a large, heavy frying pan or wok. Add the onion, garlic and thyme and cook over a medium heat, stirring occasionally, for about 3–4 minutes, until softened but not browned. Add the pork and paprika, then brown evenly for 6–8 minutes. Season well, turn out into a bowl and cool. When the mixture is cool, add the hard-boiled egg, gherkin and parsley.

2 Turn the pastry out on to a lightly floured work surface and roll out to a 38cm/15in square. Cut out 12 rounds 13cm/5in in diameter. Place 15ml/ 1 tbsp of the filling on each round, moisten the edges with a little water, fold over and seal.

3 Heat the vegetable oil in a deep-fryer fitted with a basket, to 196°C/ 385°F. Place three pies at a time in the basket and deep-fry until golden brown. Frying should take at least 1 minute or the inside filling will not be heated through. Serve warm in a basket covered with a napkin.

COOK'S TIP
For the best flavour and texture, buy lean pork and mince (grind) it yourself.

Chorizo Pastry Puffs

These flaky pastry puffs, filled with spicy chorizo sausage and grated cheese, make a really superb accompaniment to a glass of cold sherry or beer. You can use any type of hard cheese for the puffs, but for best results, choose a mild variety, as the chorizo has plenty of flavour.

Makes 16

225g/8oz puff pastry, thawed if frozen
115g/4oz cured chorizo sausage,
   finely chopped
50g/2oz/¹/₂ cup grated cheese
1 small (US medium) egg, beaten
5ml/1 tsp paprika

1 Roll out the pastry thinly on a lightly floured work surface. Using a 7.5cm/ 3in cutter, stamp out as many rounds as possible, then re-roll the trimmings, if necessary, and stamp out more rounds to make 16 in all.

2 Preheat the oven to 230°C/450°F/ Gas 8. Put the chorizo sausage and grated cheese in a bowl and toss together lightly.

3 Lay one of the pastry rounds in the palm of your hand and place a little of the chorizo mixture across the centre.

COOK'S TIP
There are many varieties of chorizo sausages, but they are all made from pork and are flavoured and coloured with paprika. Some are spicier than others.

4 Using your other hand, pinch the edges of the pastry together along the top to seal, as when making a miniature turnover. Repeat the process with the remaining rounds to make 16 puffs in all.

5 Place the pastries on a non-stick baking sheet and brush lightly with the beaten egg to glaze. Using a small sifter or strainer, dust the tops lightly with a little of the paprika.

6 Bake the pastries for 10–12 minutes, until they are puffed and golden brown. Transfer the pastries to a wire rack. Leave to cool slightly for about 5 minutes, then transfer to a warm platter and serve the chorizo pastry puffs warm, lightly dusted with the remaining paprika.

Mini Ham, Roasted Pepper and Mozzarella Ciabatta Pizzas

These quick ciabatta pizzas are eye-catching with their bright pepper topping and great for children.

Makes 8

2 red (bell) peppers
2 yellow (bell) peppers
1 loaf ciabatta bread
8 slices prosciutto or other thinly-sliced
    ham, cut into thick strips
150g/5oz mozzarella cheese
ground black pepper
tiny basil leaves, to garnish

1 Preheat a grill (broiler), Grill (broil) the peppers, skin sides up, until they are black. Place them in a bowl, cover and leave for 10 minutes. Peel off the skins.

2 Cut the bread into eight thick slices and toast both sides until golden.

3 Cut the roasted peppers into thick strips and arrange them on the toasted bread with the strips of prosciutto or other ham.

4 Thinly slice the mozzarella cheese and arrange on top. Grind over plenty of black pepper. Place under a hot grill for 2–3 minutes, until the cheese is bubbling.

5 Arrange the fresh basil leaves on top and to serve, transfer to a serving dish or platter. Leave the cheese to cool for a few minutes, if serving the mini-pizzas to children.

Monte Cristo Triangles

These opulent little sandwiches are stuffed with ham, cheese and turkey, dipped in egg, then fried in butter and oil. They are rich, very filling – and very popular too.

Makes 64

16 slices firm-textured thin-sliced
   white bread
120g/4oz/¹/₂ cup butter, softened
8 slices oak-smoked ham
45–60ml/3–4 tbsp wholegrain mustard
8 slices Gruyère or Emmenthal cheese
45–60ml/3–4 tbsp mayonnaise
8 slices turkey or chicken breast
5 eggs
50ml/2 fl oz/¹/₄ cup milk
5ml/1 tsp Dijon mustard
vegetable oil, for frying
butter, for frying
salt and ground white pepper
64 pimiento-stuffed green olives and
   fresh parsley leaves, to garnish

1 Arrange eight of the bread slices on a work surface and spread with half the softened butter. Lay a slice of ham on each slice of bread and spread with a little mustard. Cover with a slice of Gruyère or Emmenthal cheese and spread with a little of the mayonnaise, then cover with a slice of turkey or chicken breast.

2 Butter the rest of the bread slices and use to top the sandwiches. Cut off and discard the crusts, trimming to an even square.

3 Place the eggs, milk and Dijon mustard in a large, shallow dish and beat until thoroughly combined. Season with a little salt and pepper. Add the sandwiches in a single layer and leave them in the egg mixture to soak, turning them once, until all the egg has been absorbed.

4 Heat about 1cm/¹/₂in of the oil with a little butter in a large heavy frying pan until hot but not smoking. Add the sandwiches, in batches, and cook for about 4–5 minutes, until crisp and golden, turning once. Add more oil and butter as necessary. Drain well on kitchen paper.

5 Transfer the sandwiches to a bread board or chopping board and cut each into four triangles, then cut each triangle in half to make 64 triangles in total. Thread an olive and parsley leaf on to a cocktail stick (toothpick), then stick into each triangle. Arrange on a platter and serve immediately, while the triangles are still warm.

Deep-fried Lamb Patties

These patties are a tasty North African speciality – called kibbeh – of minced meat and bulgur wheat. They are sometimes stuffed with additional meat and deep fried. Moderately spiced, they're good served with yogurt.

Serves 6

450g/1lb lean lamb or lean minced (ground) lamb or beef
salt and ground black pepper
vegetable oil, for deep-frying
avocado slices and fresh coriander (cilantro) sprigs, to serve

For the patties
225g/8oz/1¹⁄₃ cups bulgur wheat
1 red chilli, seeded and coarsely chopped
1 onion, coarsely chopped

For the stuffing
1 onion, finely chopped
50g/2oz/²⁄₃ cup pine nuts
30ml/2 tbsp olive oil
7.5ml/1¹⁄₂ tsp ground allspice
60ml/4 tbsp chopped fresh coriander (cilantro)

1 If necessary, coarsely cut up the lamb and process the pieces in a blender or food processor until minced. Divide the minced meat into two equal portions.

2 For the patties, soak the bulgur wheat for 15 minutes in cold water. Drain then process in a blender or a food processor with the chilli, onion, half the meat and salt and pepper.

3 For the stuffing, cook the onion and pine nuts in the oil for 5 minutes. Add the allspice and remaining meat and cook gently, breaking up the meat with a wooden spoon, until browned. Stir in the coriander and seasoning.

4 Turn the patty mixture out on to a work surface and shape into a cake. Cut into 12 wedges.

5 Flatten one piece and spoon some of the stuffing into the centre. Bring the edges of the patty up over the stuffing, making sure that the filling is completely encased.

6 Pour the oil into a large pan to a depth of 5cm/2in and heat until a few patty crumbs sizzle on the surface.

7 Gently lower half of the filled patties into the oil and deep-fry for about 5 minutes, until golden. Drain well on kitchen paper and keep hot while you are cooking the remainder. Serve immediately, with avocado slices and coriander sprigs.

COOK'S TIPS
• When you are filling the kibbeh, it helps to dampen your hands with cold water to prevent the mixture from sticking to them.
• You can prepare the kibbeh a day in advance and store them, covered, in the refrigerator until ready to cook.

Spicy Koftas

These koftas will need to be cooked in batches. Keep them hot when they are cooked while you cook the rest.

Makes 20–25

450g/1lb minced (ground) lamb
30ml/2 tbsp ground ginger
30ml/2 tbsp finely chopped garlic
4 green chillies, finely chopped
1 small onion, finely chopped
1 egg
2.5ml/½ tsp ground turmeric
5ml/1 tsp garam masala
50g/2oz/2 cups coriander (cilantro)
   leaves, chopped
4–6 mint leaves, chopped
175g/6oz potato
salt, to taste
vegetable oil, for deep-frying

1 Place the meat in a large bowl with the ginger, garlic, chillies, onion, egg, turmeric, garam masala, coriander and mint. Grate the potato into the bowl, and season with salt. Knead together to blend well and form a soft dough.

VARIATION
Although lamb is traditionally used for making koftas, they are also delicious made with lean minced (ground) beef.

COOK'S TIP
Leftover koftas can be coarsely chopped and packed into pitta bread spread with chutney or relish for a quick, easy and delicious snack.

2 Using your fingers, shape the kofta mixture into portions about the size of golf balls. You should be able to make 20–25 koftas. Place the balls in a single layer on a baking sheet or large tray, cover with a clean dishtowel and leave to rest at room temperature for about 25 minutes.

3 Heat the oil in a large, heavy frying pan or wok to medium-hot. Add the koftas, in small batches, and deep-fry until they are golden brown in colour. Drain the koftas well on kitchen paper and keep hot in a low oven while you are cooking the remaining batches. Transfer to a platter and serve.

brunches, lunches and fork suppers

Stylish dishes that are understated and easy to eat, go down well for these light meal occasions, bringing a sophisticated touch to informal entertaining.

Griddled Tomatoes on Soda Bread

Nothing could be simpler than this appetizing snack, yet a drizzle of olive oil and balsamic vinegar and shavings of Parmesan cheese transform it into something really rather special. It's the perfect choice for a brunch party that includes children.

Serves 4

*extra virgin olive oil, for brushing
  and drizzling
6 tomatoes, thickly sliced
4 thick slices soda bread
balsamic vinegar, for drizzling
salt and ground black pepper
thin shavings of Parmesan cheese,
  to serve*

1 Brush a griddle pan with olive oil and heat. Add the tomato slices and cook, turning them once, for about 4 minutes, until softened and slightly blackened. Alternatively, heat the grill (broiler) to high and line the rack with foil. Brush the tomato slices with oil and grill (broil), turning them once, for 4–6 minutes, until softened.

2 Meanwhile, lightly toast the soda bread. Place the tomatoes on top of the toast and drizzle each portion with a little olive oil and balsamic vinegar. Season to taste with salt and pepper and serve immediately with the shavings of Parmesan cheese.

COOK'S TIP

Using a griddle pan reduces the amount of oil required for cooking the tomatoes, which is useful for those guests who are watching their weight. It also gives the tomatoes a delicious flavour as if they have been cooked on a barbecue.

VARIATION

Substitute sherry vinegar for the balsamic if you like.

Baked Mediterranean Vegetables

Crisp and golden crunchy batter surrounds these vegetables, turning them into a substantial vegetarian dish. Use other vegetables instead if you prefer.

Serves 10–12

1 small aubergine (eggplant), trimmed,
    halved and thickly sliced
1 egg
115g/4oz/1 cup plain
    (all-purpose) flour
300ml/^{1}/$_2$ pint/1^1/$_4$ cups milk
30ml/2 tbsp fresh thyme leaves
1 red onion
2 large courgettes (zucchini)
1 red (bell) pepper
1 yellow (bell) pepper
60–75ml/4–5 tbsp sunflower oil
salt and ground black pepper
30ml/2 tbsp freshly grated
    Parmesan cheese and fresh herbs,
    to garnish

1 Place the aubergine in a colander or sieve, sprinkle generously with salt and leave for 10 minutes. Drain, rinse and pat dry on kitchen paper.

2 Meanwhile, to make the batter, beat the egg in a large bowl, then gradually beat in the flour and a little milk to make a smooth, thick paste. Blend in the rest of the milk, add the thyme leaves and season to taste with salt and pepper, blend until smooth. Cover with clear film (plastic wrap) and leave in a cool place until required.

3 Cut the onion into quarters and slice the courgettes. Seed and quarter the peppers. Put the oil in a roasting pan and place in the oven. Preheat the oven to 220°C/425°F/Gas 7. Add all the vegetables to the roasting pan, turn in the oil to coat them well and return to the oven for 20 minutes, until they start to cook.

4 Whisk the batter again, then pour it over the vegetables and return the roasting pan to the oven for a further 30 minutes, until the batter is well puffed up and golden.

5 Reduce the oven temperature to 190°C/375°F/Gas 5 and cook for a further 10–15 minutes, until the batter is crisp around the edges. Sprinkle with Parmesan and herbs and serve.

COOK'S TIP

It is essential to get the oil in the roasting pan really hot before adding the batter, or it will not rise well. Use a roasting pan or ovenproof dish that is not too deep.

Scrambled Eggs with Smoked Salmon

For a luxury brunch, you cannot beat this special combination. Try it with a glass of champagne or sparkling wine mixed with freshly squeezed orange juice.

Serves 8

8 slices of pumpernickel or wholemeal (whole-wheat) bread, crusts trimmed
115g/4oz/½ cup butter
250g/9oz thinly sliced smoked salmon
12 eggs
90–120ml/6–8 tbsp double (heavy) cream
120ml/8 tbsp crème fraîche
salt and ground black pepper
generous 120ml/8 tbsp lumpfish roe or salmon caviar and fresh dill sprigs, to garnish

VARIATION
Another real treat is to grate a little fresh truffle into the scrambled eggs.

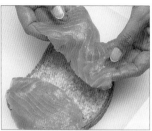

1 Spread the slices of bread with half of the butter and place them on eight individual plates. Arrange the smoked salmon on top and cut each slice in half. Set aside while you make the scrambled eggs.

2 Lightly beat the eggs together and season with salt and freshly ground black pepper. Melt the remaining butter in a pan until it is sizzling, then quickly pour in the beaten eggs, stirring vigorously with a wooden spoon. Do not let the eggs burn.

3 Stir constantly until the eggs begin to thicken. Just before they have finished cooking, stir in the cream.

4 Remove the pan from the heat and stir in the crème fraîche, add more salt and ground black pepper to taste.

5 Spoon the scrambled eggs on to the smoked salmon and bread on each plate. Top each serving with a spoonful of lumpfish roe or the salmon caviar and garnish with fresh sprigs of dill. Serve immediately.

Egg Crostini with Rouille

Crostini are extremely quick to make so are perfect for brunch parties. The spicy rouille gives them a hint of a Mediterranean flavour, providing the perfect complement to lightly fried eggs.

Serves 8

8 slices of ciabatta bread
extra virgin olive oil, for brushing
90ml/6 tbsp home-made mayonnaise
10ml/2 tsp harissa
8 eggs
8 small slices smoked ham
watercress or salad leaves, to serve

COOK'S TIP
Harissa is a fiery North African chilli paste made from dried red chillies, cumin, garlic, coriander, caraway and olive oil.

1 Preheat the oven to 200°C/400°F/ Gas 6. Use a pastry brush to brush each slice of ciabatta bread lightly with a little olive oil. Place the bread on a baking sheet and bake for 10 minutes, or until crisp and turning golden brown.

VARIATION
You can use four small portions of smoked haddock instead of ham and poach them for 5–7 minutes.

2 Meanwhile, make the rouille. Put the mayonnaise and harissa in a small bowl and mix well together.

3 Fry the eggs lightly in a little oil in a large non-stick frying pan.

4 Top the baked bread with the ham, eggs and a small spoonful of rouille. Serve immediately with watercress or salad leaves.

Eggs Benedict

There is still debate over who created this recipe but the most likely story credits a Mr and Mrs LeGrand Benedict, regulars at New York's Delmonico's restaurant, who complained there was nothing new on the lunch menu. This dish was created as a result.

Serves 4

5ml/1 tsp vinegar
4 eggs
2 English muffins or
    4 rounds of bread
butter, for spreading
4 thick slices cooked ham, trimmed to
    fit the muffins
fresh chives, to garnish

For the sauce
3 egg yolks
30ml/2 tbsp fresh lemon juice
1.5ml/¼ tsp salt
115g/4oz/½ cup butter
30ml/2 tbsp single (light) cream
ground black pepper

1 To make the sauce, place the egg yolks, lemon juice, and salt in a food processor or blender and process for 15 seconds.

2 Melt the butter in a small pan until it bubbles, but do not let it brown. With the motor running, pour the hot butter into the food processor through the feeder tube in a slow, steady stream. Turn off the machine as soon as all the butter has been added.

3 Scrape the sauce into the top of a double boiler or into a heatproof bowl set over barely simmering water. Stir for 2–3 minutes, until thickened. If it curdles, whisk in 15ml/1 tbsp boiling water. Stir in the cream and season to taste with pepper. Keep the sauce warm over the hot water.

4 Bring a shallow pan of water to the boil. Stir in the vinegar. Break each egg in turn, into a cup or jug (pitcher), then slide it carefully into the water. Carefully and gently turn the white around the yolk with a slotted spoon.

5 Cook for about 3–4 minutes, until the egg is set to your taste. Remove from the pan and place on kitchen paper to drain. Very gently cut any ragged edges off the eggs with a small knife or scissors.

6 While the eggs are poaching, split and toast the muffins or bread slices. Spread them with butter while they are still warm.

7 Place a piece of ham, which you may brown in butter if you like, on each muffin half or slice of toast. Place an egg on each ham-topped muffin. Spoon the warm sauce over the eggs, garnish with chives and serve.

COOK'S TIPS

• Use the freshest possible eggs for poaching, or the whites will coagulate immediately and the eggs will not spread out in the water.

• Cook each egg separately, so that they do not merge with each other.

VARIATION

For a special treat grate a little white or black truffle on top before serving.

Chive Scrambled Eggs in **Brioches**

This is an indulgent, truly delicious
dish to serve for brunch.

Serves 4

*115g/4oz/¹/₂ cup unsalted
(sweet) butter
75g/3oz/generous 1 cup brown cap
(cremini) mushrooms, thinly sliced
4 individual brioches
8 eggs
15ml/1 tbsp chopped fresh chives, plus
extra to garnish
salt and ground black pepper*

1 Preheat the oven to 180°C/350°F/
Gas 4. Place a quarter of the butter in
a frying pan and heat until melted.
Add the mushrooms and cook over a
low heat, stirring occasionally, for
about 3 minutes, or until soft, then set
aside and keep warm.

2 Slice the tops off the brioches, then
scoop out the centres and discard.
(Make them into breadcrumbs and
store in the refrigerator for another
recipe.) Put the brioches and lids on a
baking sheet and bake for 5 minutes,
until they are hot and slightly crisp.

3 Meanwhile, beat the eggs lightly
and season to taste with salt and
pepper. Heat the remaining butter in
a heavy pan over a low heat. When
the butter has melted and is foaming
slightly, add the eggs. Using a wooden
spoon, stir constantly to make sure
that the eggs do not stick.

4 Continue to stir fairly gently for
about 2–3 minutes, until about three-
quarters of the egg is semi-solid and
creamy. Remove the pan from the heat
or turn off the heat – the eggs will
continue to cook in the residual heat
from the pan. Stir in the chopped
fresh chives.

5 To serve, spoon a little of the
mushrooms into the base of each
brioche and top with the scrambled
eggs. Sprinkle with extra chopped
chives, balance the brioche lids on top
and serve immediately.

COOK'S TIP
Timing and temperature are crucial for
perfect scrambled eggs. When cooked for
too long over too high a heat, eggs
become dry and crumbly; if they are
undercooked, they will not set and be
sloppy and unappealing.

VARIATION
If fresh chervil is available, use it instead
of the chives.

Poached Eggs Florentine

The term "à la Florentine" means "in the style of Florence", referring to dishes cooked with spinach and topped with mornay sauce.

Serves 4

675g/1½lb spinach
25g/1oz/2 tbsp butter
60ml/4 tbsp double (heavy) cream
pinch of freshly grated nutmeg
salt and ground black pepper

For the topping
25g/1oz/2 tbsp butter
25g/1oz/¼ cup plain
 (all-purpose) flour
300ml/½ pint/1¼ cups hot milk
pinch of ground mace
115g/4oz/1 cup grated Gruyère cheese
4 eggs
15ml/1 tbsp grated Parmesan cheese,
 plus shavings to serve

1 Cut off any tough stalks, then wash the spinach in cold water and drain well. Place it in a large pan with very little water. Cook over a medium heat for 3–4 minutes, or until tender and wilted, then drain thoroughly and chop finely. Return the spinach to the pan, add the butter, cream and grated nutmeg and season to taste with salt and pepper, then heat through gently, stirring occasionally. Spoon the spinach mixture into the base of one large or four small gratin dishes.

2 To make the topping, heat the butter in a small pan, add the flour and cook, stirring constantly, for 1 minute to make a paste. Gradually blend in the hot milk, beating well as it thickens to break up any lumps.

3 Cook for 1–2 minutes, stirring constantly. Remove the pan from the heat and stir in the mace and three-quarters of the Gruyère.

4 Preheat the oven to 200°C/400°F/ Gas 6. Poach the eggs, one at a time, in lightly salted water for 3–4 minutes. Make hollows in the spinach with the back of a spoon, and place a poached egg in each one. Cover with the cheese sauce and sprinkle with the remaining Gruyère and the grated Parmesan. Bake for 10 minutes, or until golden. Serve immediately with Parmesan shavings.

Egg and **Salmon Puff Parcels**

These crisp elegant parcels hide a mouthwatering collection of flavours and textures, and make a delicious lunch dish.

Serves 6

75g/3oz/scant $^1/_2$ cup long grain rice
300ml/$^1/_2$ pint/1$^1/_4$ cups fish stock
350g/12oz piece salmon tail
juice of $^1/_2$ lemon
15ml/1 tbsp chopped fresh dill
15ml/1 tbsp chopped fresh parsley
10ml/2 tsp mild curry powder
6 small eggs, soft-boiled and cooled
425g/15oz flaky pastry, thawed
    if frozen
1 small (US medium) egg, beaten
salt and ground black pepper

1 Cook the rice in the fish stock according to the packet instructions, then drain and set aside to cool. Preheat the oven to 220°C/425°F/Gas 7.

2 Poach the salmon in a large pan with just enough water to cover, then remove and discard the bones and skin. Flake the fish into the rice. Add the lemon juice, dill, parsley and curry powder, then season to taste with salt and pepper and mix well. Shell the soft-boiled eggs.

COOK'S TIP
You can also add a spoonful of cooked spinach to each parcel.

3 Roll out the pastry on a floured surface and cut into six 14–15cm/ 5$^1/_2$–6in squares. Brush the edges with the beaten egg. Place a spoonful of the rice mixture in the middle of each square, push an egg into the middle and top with a little more rice.

4 Pull over the pastry corners to the middle to form a square parcel, squeezing the joins together well to seal. Brush with more beaten egg to glaze, place on a baking sheet and bake the puffs for 20 minutes.

5 Reduce the oven temperature to 190°C/375°F/Gas 5 and cook the puffs for a further 10 minutes, or until golden and crisp underneath.

6 Cool slightly before transferring the puffs to serving plates and serving, with a curry flavoured mayonnaise or hollandaise sauce, if you like. Alternatively, serve them on their own.

Courgette Fritters with Chilli Jam

Chilli jam is hot, sweet and sticky – rather like a thick chutney. It adds a delicious piquancy to these light courgette fritters which are always a popular dish.

Makes 12 fritters

450g/1lb/3½ cups coarsely grated
    courgettes (zucchini)
50g/2oz/⅔ cup freshly grated
    Parmesan cheese
2 eggs, beaten
60ml/4 tbsp plain (all-purpose) flour
vegetable oil, for frying
salt and ground black pepper

For the chilli jam
75ml/5 tbsp olive oil
4 large onions, diced
4 garlic cloves, chopped
1–2 green chillies, seeded and sliced
30ml/2 tbsp dark brown soft sugar

1 First make the chilli jam. Heat the oil in a large, heavy frying pan, then add the onions and the garlic. Reduce the heat to low, then cook for 20 minutes, stirring frequently, until the onions are very soft.

VARIATION

If you don't like chillies or you are short of time, serve the fritters with an easy-to make dip. Chop a bunch of spring onions (scallions) and stir them into a 150ml/ 5fl oz/⅔ cup sour cream or simply mix finely chopped fresh herbs into a bowl of good-quality mayonnaise.

2 Remove the pan from the heat and leave the onion mixture to cool, then transfer to a food processor or blender. Add the chillies and sugar and process until smooth, then return the mixture to the pan. Cook over a low heat for a further 10 minutes, stirring frequently, until the liquid evaporates and the mixture has the consistency of jam. Cool slightly.

3 To make the fritters, squeeze the courgettes in a dishtowel to remove any excess liquid, then combine with the grated Parmesan, eggs and flour and season with salt and pepper.

COOK'S TIP

Stored in an airtight jar in the refrigerator, the chilli jam will keep for up to 1 week.

4 Pour in enough oil to cover the base of a large frying pan and heat. Add 30ml/2 tbsp of the courgette mixture for each fritter and cook three fritters at a time. Cook for 2–3 minutes on each side until golden, then keep warm while you cook the rest of the fritters. Drain well on kitchen paper and serve warm with a spoonful of the chilli jam.

Kansas City Fritters

These tasty fritters are always popular at brunch parties.

Makes 8

210g/7½oz/1¼ cups canned corn
2 eggs, separated
40g/1½oz/⅓ cup plain
   (all-purpose) flour
90ml/6 tbsp milk
1 small courgette (zucchini), grated
2 bacon rashers (strips), diced
2 spring onions (scallions), chopped
good pinch of cayenne pepper
45ml/3 tbsp sunflower oil
salt and ground black pepper
fresh coriander (cilantro) sprigs,
   to garnish

For the salsa
3 tomatoes, peeled, seeded and diced
½ red (bell) pepper, seeded and diced
½ small onion, diced
15ml/1 tbsp lemon juice
15ml/1 tbsp chopped fresh
   coriander (cilantro)
dash of Tabasco sauce

1 To make the salsa, place all the ingredients in a bowl, mix well and season to taste with salt and pepper. Cover with clear film (plastic wrap) and chill until required.

2 To make the fritters, drain the corn, place in a bowl and mix in the egg yolks. Add the flour and blend in with a wooden spoon. When the mixture begins to thicken, gradually blend in the milk.

3 Stir in the grated courgette, bacon, spring onions and cayenne pepper and season with salt and pepper, then set aside until required.

4 Place the egg whites in a clean, grease-free bowl and whisk until stiff. Gently fold the whites into the corn batter mixture with a metal spoon.

5 Heat 30ml/2 tbsp of the oil in a large, heavy frying pan and place four large spoonfuls of the mixture into the oil. Cook over a medium heat for 2–3 minutes on each side until golden, then drain on kitchen paper. Keep warm while you are cooking the remaining four fritters, adding the rest of the oil if necessary.

6 Serve two fritters each, garnished with coriander sprigs and a spoonful of the chilled tomato salsa.

COOK'S TIP
These fritters would also be delicious served with avocado salsa, guacamole or any strongly flavoured salsa spiced with fresh chillies.

Potato and Red Pepper Frittata

For a light and easy-to-make lunch or a quick informal supper with plenty of flavour and colour this frittata will certainly fit the bill. Serve it with a mixed salad to complement the crisp flavours of the fresh mint sprigs and red peppers. You can also make this a day in advance to take to a picnic or serve at a barbecue.

Serves 6–8

900g/2lb small new or salad potatoes
12 eggs
60ml/4 tbsp chopped fresh mint
60ml/4 tbsp olive oil
2 onions, chopped
4 garlic cloves, crushed
4 red (bell) peppers, seeded and
   coarsely chopped
salt and ground black pepper
mint sprigs and crisp bacon, to garnish

1 Cook the potatoes in their skins in a large pan of lightly salted boiling water until they are just tender. Drain and leave to cool slightly, then cut the potatoes into thick slices.

2 Whisk together half the eggs, mint and seasoning in a large bowl, then set aside. Heat 30ml/2 tbsp oil in a large frying pan that can be safely used under the grill (broiler).

3 Add half the onion, garlic, peppers and potatoes to the pan and cook, stirring occasionally, for 5 minutes.

4 Pour the beaten egg mixture into the frying pan and stir gently. Gently push the mixture towards the centre of the pan as it cooks to allow the uncooked liquid egg to run on to the base and cook completely. Continue to cook over a medium heat. Meanwhile, preheat the grill.

5 When the frittata is lightly set, place the pan under the hot grill for 2–3 minutes, or until the top is a light golden brown colour.

6 Make another frittata with the other half of the ingredients.

7 Serve hot or cold, cut into wedges piled high on a serving dish and garnished with mint and crisp bacon.

VARIATIONS

Lightly cooked broccoli florets, cut quite small, are delicious with or instead of peppers in this frittata. Coarsely chopped black olives also go well with both peppers and broccoli.

Risotto Frittata

Half omelette, half risotto, this makes a delightful and satisfying lunch. If possible, cook each frittata separately and preferably in a small, cast-iron pan, so that the eggs cook quickly underneath but stay moist on top. Or cook in one large pan and serve in wedges.

Serves 4

30–45ml/2–3 tbsp olive oil
1 small onion, finely chopped
1 garlic clove, crushed
1 large red (bell) pepper, seeded and
   cut into thin strips
150g/5oz/³/4 cup risotto rice
400–475ml/14–16fl oz/1²/3–2 cups
   simmering vegetable stock
25–40g/1–1¹/2oz/2–3 tbsp butter
175g/6oz/2¹/2 cups button (white)
   mushrooms, thinly sliced
60ml/4 tbsp freshly grated
   Parmesan cheese
6–8 eggs
salt and ground black pepper

1 Heat 15ml/1 tbsp oil in a large frying pan. Add the onion and garlic and cook over a gentle heat, stirring occasionally, for 2–3 minutes, until the onion begins to soften but does not brown. Add the pepper and cook, stirring frequently, for 4–5 minutes, until softened.

2 Stir in the rice and cook gently for 2–3 minutes, stirring constantly, until the grains are evenly coated with oil.

3 Add a quarter of the vegetable stock and season with a little salt and pepper. Stir over a low heat until the stock has been completely absorbed. Continue to add more stock, a little at a time, allowing the rice to absorb the liquid completely before adding more. Continue cooking and adding the stock in this way, stirring constantly, until the rice is *al dente*. This will take about 20 minutes.

4 In a separate small pan, heat a little of the remaining oil and some of the butter. Add the mushrooms and cook quickly over a medium heat until golden. Transfer to a plate.

5 When the rice is tender, remove from the heat and stir in the cooked mushrooms and the Parmesan cheese.

6 Beat the eggs together with 40ml/8 tsp cold water and season well with salt and pepper. Heat the remaining oil and butter in an omelette pan and add the risotto mixture. Spread the mixture out in the pan, then immediately add the beaten eggs, tilting the pan so that the omelette cooks evenly. Cook over a moderately high heat for 1–2 minutes, then transfer to a warmed plate and serve in wedges.

COOK'S TIP
Don't be impatient while cooking the rice. Adding the stock gradually ensures that the rice has a wonderfully creamy consistency. It is important to stir the rice so that it absorbs the stock fully. By the time you have added three-quarters of the stock, you can stop stirring constantly, but must still do so frequently.

Chilli Cheese Tortilla with Tomato Salsa

Good warm or cold, this is like a
quiche without the pastry base.

Serves 8

45ml/3 tbsp sunflower or olive oil
1 small onion, thinly sliced
2–3 green jalapeño chillies, sliced
200g/7oz cold cooked potato, sliced
120g/4¼oz/generous 1 cup grated
   Manchego, Mexican queso blanco
   or Monterey Jack cheese
6 eggs, beaten
salt and ground black pepper
fresh herbs, to garnish

For the salsa
500g/1¼ lb tomatoes, peeled, seeded
   and finely chopped
1 green chilli, seeded and
   finely chopped
2 garlic cloves, crushed
45ml/3 tbsp chopped fresh
   coriander (cilantro)
juice of 1 lime
2.5ml/½ tsp salt

1 Begin by making the salsa. Put the
tomatoes in a bowl and add the chilli,
garlic, coriander, lime juice and salt.
Mix well, cover with clear film (plastic
wrap) and set aside in a cool place.

2 To make the tortilla, heat half the
oil in a large omelette pan. Add the
onion and jalapeños and cook over
a low heat, stirring occasionally, for
5 minutes, until softened. Add the
sliced potato and cook for a further
5 minutes until lightly browned, taking
care to keep the slices whole.

3 Transfer the vegetables to a warm
plate. Wipe the pan with kitchen
paper, then pour in the remaining oil.
Heat well and return the vegetable
mixture to the pan. Sprinkle the grated
cheese evenly over the top.

4 Pour in the beaten eggs, making
sure that they seep underneath the
vegetables. Cook the tortilla over a low
heat until set. Serve in wedges,
garnished with fresh herbs, with the
salsa on the side.

COOK'S TIP
If you cannot find the cheeses listed, use a
medium Cheddar instead.

Quesadillas

These cheese-filled tortillas are the Mexican equivalent of toasted sandwiches. Serve them hot or they will become chewy. If you are making them for a crowd, fill and fold the tortillas ahead of time, but only cook them to order.

Serves 8

400g/14oz mozzarella, Monterey Jack or mild Cheddar cheese
2 fresh fresno chillies (optional)
16 wheat flour tortillas, about 15cm/6in across
onion relish or tomato salsa, to serve

1 If using mozzarella cheese, it must be drained thoroughly and then patted dry and sliced into thin strips. Monterey Jack and Cheddar cheese should both be coarsely grated, as finely grated cheese will melt and ooze away when cooking. Set the cheese aside in a bowl.

2 If using the chillies, spear them on a long-handled metal skewer and roast them over the flame of a gas burner until the skin blisters and darkens. Do not let the flesh burn. Place the roasted chillies in a strong plastic bag and tie the top to keep the steam in. Set aside for 20 minutes for the skin to loosen.

VARIATIONS
Try spreading a thin layer of your favourite salsa on the tortillas before adding the cheese, or add some cooked chicken or prawns (shrimp) before folding the tortillas.

3 Remove the roasted chillies from the bag and carefully peel off the skin. Cut off the stalk, then slit the chillies and scrape out all the seeds. Cut the flesh into 16 even-sized thin strips.

4 Warm a large frying pan or griddle. Place one tortilla on the pan or griddle at a time, sprinkle about one sixteenth of the cheese on to one half and add a strip of chilli, if using. Fold the tortilla over the cheese and press the edges together gently to seal. Cook the filled tortilla for 1 minute, then turn over and cook the other side for 1 minute.

5 Remove the filled tortilla from the frying pan or griddle, cut it into three triangles or four strips and serve immediately while it is still hot, with the onion relish or tomato salsa.

Chicken Fajitas with Grilled Onions

Classic fajitas are fun to eat with friends and make a good choice for an informal supper.

Serves 6

*finely grated rind of 1 lime and the
   juice of 2 limes*
120ml/4fl oz/¹/₂ cup olive oil
1 garlic clove, finely chopped
2.5ml/¹/₂ tsp dried oregano
good pinch of dried red chilli flakes
5ml/1 tsp coriander seeds, crushed
6 chicken breast fillets
3 Spanish onions, thickly sliced
*2 large red, yellow or orange (bell)
   peppers, seeded and cut into strips*
*30ml/2 tbsp chopped fresh
   coriander (cilantro)*
salt and ground black pepper

For the tomato salsa
*450g/1lb tomatoes, peeled, seeded
   and chopped*
2 garlic cloves, finely chopped
1 small red onion, finely chopped
1–2 green chillies, seeded and chopped
finely grated rind of ¹/₂ lime
*30ml/2 tbsp chopped fresh
   coriander (cilantro)*
pinch of caster (superfine) sugar
*2.5–5ml/¹/₂–1 tsp ground roasted
   cumin seeds*

To serve
12–18 soft flour tortillas
guacamole
120ml/4fl oz/¹/₂ cup sour cream
crisp lettuce leaves
*coriander (cilantro) sprigs and
   lime wedges*

1 Mix the lime rind and juice, 75ml/ 5 tbsp of the oil, the garlic, oregano, chilli flakes and coriander seeds in an ovenproof dish and season. Slash the chicken skin several times and turn in the mixture, then cover and set aside to marinate for several hours.

2 To make the salsa, combine the tomatoes, garlic, onion, chillies, lime rind and chopped coriander. Season to taste with salt, pepper, caster sugar and cumin seeds. Set aside for about 30 minutes, then taste and adjust the seasoning, adding more cumin and sugar, if necessary.

3 Preheat the grill (broiler). Thread the onion slices on to a skewer or place them on a grill rack. Brush with 15ml/ 1 tbsp of the remaining oil and season. Grill (broil) until softened and slightly charred in places. Preheat the oven to 200°C/400°F/Gas 6.

4 Cover the dish containing the chicken and marinade and cook in the oven for 20 minutes. Remove from the oven, then grill (broil) for about 8–10 minutes, or until browned and cooked right through.

5 Meanwhile, heat the remaining oil in a large frying pan and cook the peppers for about 10 minutes, or until softened and browned in places. Add the grilled onions and cook for 2–3 minutes.

6 Add the chicken cooking juices and cook over a high heat, stirring frequently, until the liquid evaporates. Stir in the chopped coriander.

7 Heat the tortillas following the instructions on the packet. Using a sharp knife, cut the grilled chicken into strips and transfer to a serving dish. Place the onion and pepper mixture and the salsa in separate dishes.

8 Serve the dishes of chicken, onions and peppers and salsa with the tortillas, guacamole, sour cream, lettuce and coriander for people to help themselves. Serve with lime wedges.

Tortilla Cones with Smoked Salmon and Soft Cheese

These simple yet sophisticated wraps are a must for serving with drinks or as part of a buffet.

Makes 8

115g/4oz/1/2 cup soft white
(farmer's) cheese
30ml/2 tbsp coarsely chopped fresh dill
juice of 1 lemon
1 small red onion
15ml/1 tbsp drained bottled capers
30ml/2 tbsp extra virgin olive oil
30ml/2 tbsp coarsely chopped fresh flat
leaf parsley
115g/4oz sliced smoked salmon
8 small wheat flour tortillas
salt and ground black pepper
lemon wedges, for squeezing

3 Cut the smoked salmon into short, thin strips and add to the red onion mixture. Toss to mix. Season to taste with plenty of pepper.

COOK'S TIP
You can use salted capers in this dish instead of the unsalted variety, but rinse them thoroughly before using.

4 Spread a little of the soft cheese mixture on each tortilla and top with the smoked salmon mixture.

5 Roll up the tortillas into cones and secure with wooden cocktail sticks (toothpicks). Arrange on a serving plate and add some lemon wedges, for squeezing. Serve immediately.

1 Place the soft cheese in a bowl and mix in half the chopped dill. Add a little salt and pepper and a dash of the lemon juice to taste. Reserve the remaining lemon juice in a separate mixing bowl.

2 Finely chop the red onion. Add the onion, capers and olive oil to the lemon juice in the mixing bowl. Add the chopped flat leaf parsley and the remaining dill and gently stir.

VARIATION
Tortilla cones can be filled with a variety of ingredients. Try soft cheese with red pesto and chopped sun-dried tomatoes, or mackerel pâté with slices of cucumber.

Seafood Pancakes

The combination of unsmoked and smoked haddock fillets imparts a wonderful flavour to the filling.

Serves 6

For the pancakes
*115g/4oz/1 cup plain
   (all-purpose) flour
pinch of salt
1 egg plus 1 egg yolk
300ml/¹/₂ pint/1¹/₄ cups milk
15ml/1 tbsp melted butter, plus extra
   for cooking
50–75g/2–3oz Gruyère cheese, grated
frisée lettuce, to serve*

For the filling
*225g/8oz smoked haddock fillet
225g/8oz fresh haddock fillet
300ml/¹/₂ pint/1¹/₄ cups milk
150ml/¹/₄ pint/²/₃ cup single
   (light) cream
40g/1¹/₂ oz/3 tbsp butter
40g/1¹/₂ oz/¹/₄ cup plain
   (all-purpose) flour
freshly grated nutmeg
2 hard-boiled eggs, chopped
salt and ground black pepper*

1 To make the pancakes, sift the flour and salt into a bowl. Make a well in the centre and add the egg and yolk.

2 Whisk the egg, incorporating some of the flour. Gradually whisk in the milk, until the batter is smooth and has the consistency of thin cream. Stir in the measured melted butter.

3 Heat a small crêpe pan or omelette pan until hot, then rub around the inside of the pan with a pad of kitchen paper dipped in melted butter. Pour about 30ml/2 tbsp of the batter into the pan, then immediately tip the pan to coat the base evenly. Cook the pancake over a low to medium heat for about 30 seconds until the top is beginning to set and the underside is golden brown.

4 Flip the pancake over with a spatula and cook on the other side until it is lightly browned. Repeat with the remaining batter to make 12 pancakes, rubbing the pan with melted butter between each pancake. Stack the pancakes as you make them between sheets of baking parchment. Keep the pancakes warm on a plate set over a pan of simmering water.

5 To make the filling, put the haddock fillets in a pan. Add the milk and poach for 6–8 minutes, until tender. Lift out the fish and, when cool enough to handle, remove the skin and any bones. Reserve the milk.

6 Pour the single cream into a measuring jug (cup) then strain enough of the reserved milk into the jug to make the quantity up to 450ml/³/₄ pint/scant 2 cups in total.

7 Melt the butter in a pan, stir in the flour and cook gently, stirring constantly, for 1 minute. Gradually mix in the milk and cream mixture, stirring constantly to make a smooth sauce. Cook for 2–3 minutes, until thickened. Season with salt, black pepper and nutmeg. Coarsely flake the haddock and fold into the sauce with the eggs. Leave to cool.

8 Preheat the oven to 180°C/350°F/ Gas 4. Divide the filling among the pancakes. Fold the sides of each pancake into the centre, then roll them up to enclose the filling completely.

9 Butter six individual ovenproof dishes and then arrange two filled pancakes in each, or butter one large dish for all the pancakes. Brush the tops with melted butter and cook for 15 minutes. Sprinkle over the Gruyère and cook for a further 5 minutes, until warmed through. Serve hot with frisée lettuce leaves.

VARIATION
For a different, but no less delicious flavour, omit the smoked haddock and stir 225g/8oz cooked, peeled prawns (shrimp) or smoked oysters into the sauce with the fresh haddock in step 7.

Leek, Saffron and Mussel Tartlets

Serve these vividly coloured little tarts with cherry tomatoes and a few salad leaves, such as watercress, rocket and frisée.

Makes 12

4 large yellow (bell) peppers, halved
   and seeded
2kg/4½lb mussels
large pinch of saffron threads
   (about 30)
30ml/2 tbsp hot water
4 large leeks, sliced
60ml/4 tbsp olive oil
4 large (US extra large) eggs
600ml/1 pint/2½ cups single
   (light) cream
60ml/4 tbsp finely chopped
   fresh parsley
salt and ground black pepper
salad leaves, to serve

For the pastry
450g/1lb/4 cups plain (all-
   purpose) flour
5ml/1 tsp salt
250g/8oz/1 cup butter, diced
30–45ml/2–3 tbsp water

1 To make the pastry, mix together the flour, salt and butter. Using your fingertips, rub the butter into the flour until the mixture resembles fine breadcrumbs. Mix in the water and knead lightly to form a firm dough. Wrap the dough in clear film (plastic wrap) and chill for 30 minutes.

2 Grill (broil) the pepper halves, skin sides uppermost, until they are black. Place the peppers in a bowl, cover and leave for 10 minutes. When they are cool enough to handle, peel and cut the flesh into thin strips.

3 Scrub the mussel shells with a brush, rinse in cold running water and pull off the beards.

4 Preheat the oven to 190°C/375°F/ Gas 5. Roll out the pastry and use it to line 12 × 10cm/4in tartlet tins (muffin pans), 2.5cm/1in deep. Prick the bases all over with a fork and then line the sides with strips of foil.

5 Bake the pastry cases (pie shells) for 10 minutes. Remove the foil and bake for another 5–8 minutes, or until they are lightly coloured. Remove them from the oven. Reduce the temperature to 180°C/350°F/Gas 4.

6 Soak the saffron in the hot water for 10 minutes. Cook the leeks in the oil over a medium heat for 6–8 minutes until beginning to brown. Add the peppers and cook for 2 minutes.

7 Bring 2.5cm/1in depth of water to a rolling boil in a large pan and add 10ml/2 tsp salt. Discard any open mussels that do not shut when tapped sharply, then throw the rest into the pan. Cover and cook over a high heat, shaking the pan occasionally, for 3–4 minutes, or until the mussels open. Discard any mussels that do not open. Shell the remainder.

8 Beat the eggs, cream and saffron liquid together. Season and whisk in the parsley. Arrange the leeks, peppers and mussels in the cases, add the egg mixture and bake for 20–25 minutes, until just firm. Serve with salad leaves.

Quiche Lorraine

A classic quiche from eastern France that is perfect to serve at a relaxed lunch party. This recipe retains the traditional characteristics that are often forgotten in modern versions, namely very thin pastry, a really creamy and light, egg-rich filling and smoked bacon.

Serves 6–8

*175g/6oz/1½ cups plain
(all-purpose) flour, sifted
pinch of salt
115g/4oz/½ cup unsalted (sweet)
butter, at room temperature, diced
3 eggs, plus 3 yolks
6 smoked streaky (fatty) bacon rashers
(strips), rinds removed
300ml/½ pint/1¼ cups double
(heavy) cream
25g/1oz/2 tbsp unsalted (sweet) butter
salt and ground black pepper*

1 Place the flour, salt, butter and 1 egg yolk in a food processor and process until blended. Tip out on to a floured surface and bring the mixture together into a ball. Leave to rest for 20 minutes.

2 Lightly flour a deep 20cm/8in quiche tin (pan), and place it on a baking tray. Roll out the pastry and use to line the tin, trimming off any overhanging pieces. Press the pastry into the edges of the tin. If the pastry breaks up, just gently push it into shape. Chill for 20 minutes. Preheat the oven to 200°C/400°F/Gas 6.

3 Meanwhile, cut the bacon into thin strips and grill (broil) until the fat runs. Arrange the bacon in the pastry case. Beat together the cream, the remaining eggs and yolks and seasoning, and pour into the pastry case (pie shell).

4 Bake for 15 minutes, then reduce the heat to 180°C/350°F/Gas 4 and bake for a further 15–20 minutes. When the filling is puffed up and golden and the pastry is crisp, remove from the oven and top with knobs (pats) of butter. Stand for 5 minutes before serving.

Wild Mushroom and Fontina Tarts

Italian fontina cheese gives these tarts a creamy, nutty flavour.

Serves 4

25g/1oz/¹/₂ cup dried wild mushrooms
1 red onion, chopped
30ml/2 tbsp olive oil
2 garlic cloves, chopped
30ml/2 tbsp medium-dry sherry
1 egg
120ml/4fl oz/¹/₂ cup single (light) cream
25g/1oz fontina cheese, thinly sliced
salt and ground black pepper
rocket (arugula) leaves, to serve

For the pastry
115g/4oz/1 cup wholemeal
   (whole-wheat) flour
50g/2oz/4 tbsp unsalted (sweet) butter
25g/1oz/¹/₄ cup walnuts, roasted
   and ground
1 egg, lightly beaten

1 To make the pastry, sift the flour into a bowl and rub in butter with your fingertips until the mixture resembles fine breadcrumbs. Add the nuts then the egg and mix to a soft dough. Gather into a ball, wrap, then chill for 30 minutes.

2 Meanwhile, place the dried wild mushrooms in a bowl and add 300ml/ ¹/₂ pint/1¹/₄ cups boiling water. Soak for 30 minutes. Drain well and reserve the liquid. Cook the onion in the oil for 5 minutes, then add the garlic and cook for about 2 minutes, stirring.

3 Add the soaked mushrooms and cook for 7 minutes over a high heat until the edges become crisp. Add the sherry and the reserved mushroom soaking liquid. Cook over a high heat for about 10 minutes, until the liquid has evaporated. Season to taste with salt and pepper and set aside to cool.

COOK'S TIPS
• You can prepare the pastry cases in advance, bake them blind for 10 minutes, then store in an airtight container for up to 2 days.
• Baking beans are small metal weights that help to prevent the pastry case (pie shell) from shrinking and blistering during the initial baking. You can, of course, use real dried beans that are kept especially for the purpose.

4 Preheat the oven to 200°C/400°F/ Gas 6. Lightly grease four 10cm/4in tartlet tins (muffin pans). Roll out the pastry on a lightly floured work surface and use to line the tart tins.

5 Prick the pastry bases all over with a fork, line with baking parchment and baking beans and bake blind for about 10 minutes. Remove the paper and the beans.

6 Whisk the egg and cream to mix, add to the mushroom mixture, then season to taste with salt and pepper. Spoon the filling into the pastry cases (pie shells), top with cheese slices and bake for 15–20 minutes, until the filling is set. Leave to cool slightly, then serve warm with rocket.

Leek and Onion Tartlets

Baking in individual tins makes for easier serving and they look attractive too.

Serves 6

25g/1oz/2 tbsp butter
1 onion, thinly sliced
2.5ml/¹/₂ tsp dried thyme
450g/1lb leeks, thinly sliced
50g/2oz/¹/₂ cup grated Gruyère or
    Emmenthal cheese
3 eggs
300ml/¹/₂ pint/1¹/₄ cups single
    (light) cream
pinch of freshly grated nutmeg
salt and ground black pepper
mixed salad leaves, to serve

For the pastry
175g/6oz/1¹/₃ cup plain
    (all-purpose) flour
75g/3oz/6 tbsp cold butter
1 egg yolk
30–45ml/2–3 tbsp cold water
2.5ml/¹/₂ tsp salt

1 To make the pastry, sift the flour into a bowl and add the butter. Using your fingertips, rub the butter into the flour until it resembles fine breadcrumbs. Make a well in the centre.

2 Beat together the egg yolk, water and salt, pour the mixture into the well and combine the flour and liquid until it begins to stick together. Form into a ball. Wrap in clear film, (plastic wrap) and chill for 30 minutes.

3 Butter six 10cm/4in tartlet tins (muffin pans). On a lightly floured surface, roll out the dough to about 3mm/¹/₈in thick, then using a 12.5cm/5in cutter, cut as many rounds as possible. Gently ease the rounds into the tins, pressing the pastry firmly into the base and sides. Gather up the trimmings, re-roll them and line the remaining tins. Prick the bases all over with a fork and chill in the refrigerator for 30 minutes.

4 Preheat the oven to 190°C/375°F/Gas 5. Line the pastry cases (pie shells) with foil and fill with baking beans. Place them on a baking sheet and bake for 6–8 minutes, until golden brown at the edges. Remove the foil and baking beans and bake for a further 2 minutes, until the bases appear dry. Transfer to a wire rack to cool. Reduce the oven temperature to 180°C/350°F/Gas 4.

5 Melt the butter in a large, heavy frying pan over a medium heat, then add the onion and thyme and cook, stirring occasionally, for 3–5 minutes until the onion is just softened.

6 Add the leeks and cook, stirring occasionally, for 10–12 minutes, until they are soft and tender. Divide the leek and onion mixture among the pastry cases and sprinkle each with cheese, dividing it evenly.

7 Beat the eggs with the cream and nutmeg in a medium bowl and season to taste with salt and pepper. Place the pastry cases on a baking sheet and pour in the egg mixture. Bake for 15–20 minutes, until set and golden.

8 Transfer the tartlets to a wire rack to cool slightly, then remove them from the tins and serve warm or at room temperature with salad leaves.

Vegetable Tarte Tatin

This upside-down tart combines Mediterranean vegetables with rice, garlic, onions and olives.

Serves 4

30ml/2 tbsp sunflower oil
25ml/1½ tbsp olive oil
1 aubergine (eggplant),
   sliced lengthways
1 large red (bell) pepper, seeded and
   cut into long strips
5 tomatoes
2 red shallots, finely chopped
1–2 garlic cloves, crushed
150ml/¼ pint/⅔ cup white wine
10ml/2 tsp chopped fresh basil
225g/8oz/2 cups cooked rice
40g/1½oz/⅔ cup pitted black
   olives, chopped
350g/12oz puff pastry, thawed if frozen
ground black pepper
salad leaves, to serve

1 Preheat the oven to 190°C/375°F/ Gas 5. Heat the sunflower oil with 15ml/1 tbsp of the olive oil. Add the aubergine slices and cook over a medium heat for 4–5 minutes on each side. Drain on kitchen paper.

COOK'S TIP
Modern varieties of aubergine no longer contain bitter juices that must be removed before cooking by salting. However, if you have time, it is still worth doing this because it helps to prevent them from soaking up large amounts of oil during cooking.

2 Add the pepper strips to the oil remaining in the pan, turning them to coat. Cover the pan with a lid or a sheet of foil and sweat the peppers over a moderately high heat for 5–6 minutes, stirring occasionally, until the pepper strips are soft and flecked with brown.

3 Slice two of the tomatoes and set them aside. Place the remaining tomatoes in a bowl, cover with boiling water and leave for 30 seconds, then drain and peel them. Cut them into quarters and remove the cores and seeds. Chop the tomato flesh coarsely.

4 Heat the remaining oil in the frying pan. Add the shallots and garlic and cook over a low heat, stirring occasionally, for 3–4 minutes, until softened but not browned. Then add the chopped tomatoes and cook, for a few minutes, until just softened. Stir in the white wine and basil and season with black pepper to taste. Bring to the boil, then remove the pan from the heat and stir in the cooked rice and black olives.

5 Arrange the tomato slices, the aubergine slices and the peppers in a single layer on the base of a heavy, 30cm/12in, shallow ovenproof dish. Spread the rice and tomato mixture evenly on top.

6 Roll out the pastry to a round slightly larger than the diameter of the dish and place on top of the rice, gently tucking the overlap down inside the dish.

7 Bake for 25–30 minutes, until the pastry is golden and risen. Leave to cool slightly, then invert the tart on to a large, warmed serving plate. Serve in slices, with some salad leaves.

VARIATION
Courgettes (zucchini) and mushrooms could be used as well as, or instead of, the aubergines and pepper. Alternatively, you could use strips of lightly browned chicken.

Dolmades

Stuffed vine leaves are a popular choice for a Greek mezze and will prove a great favourite at parties.

Makes 20–24

*24–28 fresh young vine (grape)
   leaves, soaked*
30ml/2 tbsp olive oil
1 large onion, finely chopped
1 garlic clove, crushed
*225g/8oz/2 cups cooked long grain
   rice, or mixed white and wild rice*
45ml/3 tbsp pine nuts
15ml/1 tbsp flaked (sliced) almonds
*40g/1¹/₂oz/¹/₄ cup sultanas
   (golden raisins)*
15ml/1 tbsp chopped fresh chives
15ml/1 tbsp finely chopped fresh mint
juice of ¹/₂ lemon
150ml/¹/₄ pint/²/₃ cup white wine
*150ml/¹/₄ pint/²/₃ cup hot
   vegetable stock*
salt and ground black pepper
fresh mint sprig, to garnish
garlic yogurt and pitta bread, to serve

1 Bring a large pan of water to the boil and cook the vine leaves for about 2–3 minutes. They will darken and go limp after about 1 minute and then simmering for a further minute or so will make sure that they are pliable. If you are using packet or canned leaves, place them in a bowl, cover with boiling water and leave for about 20 minutes, until the leaves can be separated easily. Rinse and dry well on kitchen paper.

2 Heat the oil in a small frying pan. Add the onion and garlic and cook over a low heat, stirring occasionally, for 3–4 minutes, until soft. Spoon the mixture into a large bowl and add the cooked rice. Stir to combine.

3 Stir in 30ml/2 tbsp of the pine nuts, the almonds, sultanas, chives and mint. Squeeze in the lemon juice. Season with salt and pepper to taste and mix well.

4 Set aside four large vine leaves. Lay a vine leaf on a clean work surface, veined side uppermost. Place a spoonful of filling near the stem, fold the lower part of the vine leaf over it and roll up, folding in the sides as you go. Stuff the rest of the vine leaves in the same way.

5 Line the base of a deep frying pan with the reserved vine leaves. Place the dolmades close together in the pan, seam side down, in a single layer. Pour over the wine and enough stock just to cover. Anchor the dolmades by placing a plate on top of them, then cover the pan and simmer gently for 30 minutes.

6 Transfer the dolmades to a plate. Leave to cool, then chill in the refrigerator. When ready to serve, garnish with the remaining pine nuts and the mint. Serve with a little garlic yogurt and some pitta bread.

COOK'S TIP

Dolmades are delicious served hot but be sure to sprinkle them with fresh lemon juice.

Quail's Eggs in Aspic with Prosciutto

These impressive-looking eggs in jelly are so easy to make, and are great for summer eating. Serve them with salad leaves and some home-made mayonnaise on the side.

Makes 12

20g/³/₄oz aspic powder
45ml/3 tbsp dry sherry
12 quail's eggs
6 slices prosciutto
12 fresh coriander (cilantro) or flat leaf
  parsley leaves
salad leaves, to serve

1 Make up the aspic in a jug (pitcher) following the packet instructions but replace 45ml/3 tbsp water with the dry sherry, to give a greater depth of flavour. Leave the aspic in the refrigerator until it begins to thicken, but not set.

2 Put the quail's eggs in a pan of cold water and bring to the boil over a medium heat. Boil for 1½ minutes only, then pour off the hot water and leave in cold water until cold. This way, the yolks will be a little soft but the whites will be firm enough for you to shell the eggs easily when they are really cold.

3 Rinse 12 dariole moulds in cold water so that they are damp and place them on a tray. Cut the prosciutto into 12 pieces, then roll or fold so they will fit into the moulds.

4 Place a coriander or parsley leaf in the base of each mould, then put a shelled egg on top. As the jelly begins to thicken, pour in enough to nearly cover each egg, holding it steady. Then put the slice of prosciutto on the egg and pour in the rest of the jelly to fill each mould, so that when you turn them out the eggs will be sitting on the prosciutto.

5 Transfer the tray of moulds to a cold place and then leave for 3–4 hours, until completely set and cold. When ready to serve, run a knife blade around the top rim of the jelly to loosen. Dip the base of the moulds into warm, not hot, water and shake or tap gently until they appear loose. Invert on to small plates and serve with salad leaves.

Cheese and Leek Sausages with Chilli and Tomato Sauce

These popular vegetarian sausages served with a spicy sauce flavoured with chilli and balsamic vinegar are bound to be a hit for an informal lunch or supper.

Makes 12

25g/1oz/2 tbsp butter
175g/6oz leeks, finely chopped
90ml/6 tbsp cold mashed potato
115g/4oz/2 cups fresh
    white breadcrumbs
150g/5oz/1¼ cups grated Caerphilly,
    Cheddar or Cantal cheese
30ml/2 tbsp chopped fresh parsley
5ml/1 tsp chopped fresh sage
    or marjoram
2 large (US extra large) eggs, beaten
good pinch of cayenne pepper
65g/2½oz/1 cup dry
    white breadcrumbs
vegetable oil, for shallow frying
salt and ground black pepper

For the sauce
30ml/2 tbsp olive oil
2 garlic cloves, thinly sliced
1 fresh red chilli, seeded and finely
    chopped, or a good pinch of dried
    red chilli flakes
1 small onion, finely chopped
500g/1¼lb tomatoes, peeled,
    seeded and chopped
a few fresh thyme sprigs
10ml/2 tsp balsamic vinegar or red
    wine vinegar
pinch of light muscovado
    (brown) sugar
15–30ml/1–2 tbsp chopped fresh
    marjoram or oregano

COOK'S TIP
These sausages are also delicious when they are served with a fruity chilli salsa and a watercress salad.

1 Melt the butter in a frying pan and cook the leeks for 4–5 minutes, or until softened but not browned. Mix with the mashed potato, fresh breadcrumbs, grated cheese, chopped parsley and sage or marjoram.

2 Add sufficient beaten egg (about two-thirds of the quantity) to bind the mixture together. Season well and add cayenne pepper to taste.

3 Pat or roll the mixture between dampened hands to form 12 sausage shapes. Dip in the remaining egg, then coat in the dry breadcrumbs. Chill the coated sausages.

4 Make the sauce. Heat the oil in a pan and cook the garlic, chilli and onion over a low heat for 3–4 minutes. Add the tomatoes, thyme and vinegar. Season with salt, pepper and sugar.

5 Cook the sauce for 40–50 minutes, or until considerably reduced. Remove the thyme and purée the sauce in a food processor or blender. Reheat with the marjoram or oregano and then adjust the seasoning.

6 Cook the sausages in shallow oil until golden brown on all sides. Drain on kitchen paper and serve with the sauce.

Polpettes

Little fried mouthfuls of potato and tangy-sharp Greek feta cheese, flavoured with dill and lemon juice are ideal to serve for lunch or supper.

Makes 12

500g/1¼lb floury (mealy) potatoes
115g/4oz/1 cup feta cheese
4 spring onions (scallions), chopped
45ml/3 tbsp chopped fresh dill
1 egg, beaten
15ml/1 tbsp lemon juice
plain (all-purpose) flour, for dredging
45ml/3 tbsp olive oil
salt and ground black pepper
fresh dill sprigs and shredded spring
  onions (scallions), to garnish
lemon wedges, to serve

1 Cook the potatoes in their skins in lightly salted, boiling water until soft. Drain and cool slightly, then chop them in half and peel while still warm.

COOK'S TIP

To save time, cook the polpettes in advance, cool and chill until required. Reheat in the oven before serving.

2 Place the potatoes in a bowl and mash until smooth. Crumble the feta cheese into the potatoes and add the spring onions, dill, egg and lemon juice and season with salt and pepper. (The cheese is salty, so taste before you add salt.) Stir well, until combined.

3 Cover and chill until firm. Divide the mixture into walnut-size balls, then flatten them slightly. Dredge with flour, shaking off the excess.

4 Heat the oil in a large frying pan and cook the polpettes, in batches, until golden brown on both sides. Drain on kitchen paper and serve hot, garnished with spring onions and sprigs of dill, and serve with lemon wedges.

Crab Cakes with Tartare Sauce

Sweet crab meat is offset by a piquant tartare sauce.

Serves 4

675g/1¹/₂lb fresh crab meat
1 egg, beaten
30ml/2 tbsp mayonnaise
15ml/1 tbsp Worcestershire sauce
15ml/1 tbsp sherry
30ml/2 tbsp chopped fresh parsley
15ml/1 tbsp chopped fresh chives
salt and ground black pepper
45ml/3 tbsp olive oil
salad leaves, chives and lemon, to garnish

For the sauce

1 egg yolk
15ml/1 tbsp white wine vinegar
30ml/2 tbsp Dijon mustard
250ml/8fl oz/1 cup vegetable oil
30ml/2 tbsp lemon juice
60ml/4 tbsp chopped spring
   onions (scallions)
30ml/2 tbsp chopped drained capers
60ml/4 tbsp chopped sour dill pickles
60ml/4 tbsp chopped fresh parsley

1 Carefully pick over the crab meat, removing any stray pieces of shell or cartilage. Keep the pieces of crab as large as possible.

2 In a mixing bowl, combine the beaten egg with the mayonnaise, Worcestershire sauce, sherry, parsley and chives. Season with a little salt and lots of black pepper. Gently fold in the crab meat.

3 Divide the mixture into eight equal portions and gently form each one into an oval patty. Place them on a baking sheet between layers of baking parchment and chill in the refrigerator for at least 1 hour.

4 Meanwhile, make the sauce. In a medium-size bowl, beat the egg yolk with a wire whisk until smooth. Add the vinegar and mustard, season with salt and pepper to taste and whisk for about 10 seconds to blend. Gradually whisk in the oil.

5 Add the lemon juice, spring onions, capers, pickles and parsley and mix well. Check the seasoning. Cover with clear film (plastic wrap) and chill.

6 Preheat the grill (broiler). Brush the crab cakes with the olive oil. Place on an oiled baking sheet, in one layer.

7 Grill (broil) 15cm/6in from the heat until golden brown, about 5 minutes on each side. Serve the crab cakes with the tartare sauce, garnished with salad leaves, chives and lemon.

COOK'S TIPS

• For easier handling and to make the crab meat go further, add 50g/2oz/1 cup fresh breadcrumbs and 1 more egg to the crab mixture. Divide the mixture into 12 patties to serve six people.
• Fresh crab meat is widely available from supermarkets and fish stores. You can also buy freshly cooked whole crab and remove the meat from the shell yourself. If buying a whole crab, choose one that feels heavy for its size. Shake it before purchase to check whether it contains any water. If it does, reject it. Most of the white meat is found in the claws.

Turkey Croquettes

Smoked turkey gives these crisp croquettes a distinctive flavour. Served with the tangy tomato sauce, crispy bread and salad they make a tasty fork supper.

Makes 8

450g/1lb potatoes, diced
3 eggs
30ml/2 tbsp milk
175g/6oz smoked turkey rashers
 (strips), finely chopped
2 spring onions (scallions), thinly sliced
115g/4oz/2 cups fresh
 white breadcrumbs
vegetable oil, for deep-frying
salt and ground black pepper

For the sauce
15ml/1 tbsp olive oil
1 onion, finely chopped
400g/14oz can tomatoes, drained
30ml/2 tbsp tomato purée (paste)
15ml/1 tbsp chopped fresh parsley

1 Boil the potatoes until tender. Drain and return the pan to a low heat to make sure all the excess water evaporates.

2 Mash the potatoes with two eggs and the milk. Season well with salt and pepper. Stir in the turkey rashers and spring onions. Chill for 1 hour.

3 To make the sauce heat the oil in a frying pan and cook the onion until softened. Add the tomatoes and tomato purée, stir and simmer for 10 minutes. Stir in the parsley and season. Keep the sauce warm.

4 Remove the potato mixture from the refrigerator and divide into eight pieces. Shape each piece into a sausage and dip in the remaining beaten egg and then the breadcrumbs.

5 Heat the vegetable oil in a pan or deep-fryer to 190°C/375°F or until a cube of day-old bread dropped into the hot oil browns in 45 seconds. Deep-fry the croquettes for 5 minutes, or until they are golden and crisp. Drain on kitchen paper. Reheat the sauce gently, if necessary, and serve with the freshly cooked croquettes.

Smoked Salmon and Rice Salad Parcels

Feta, cucumber and tomatoes give a Greek flavour to the salad in these parcels, a combination which goes well with the rice, especially if a little wild rice is added.

Serves 4

175g/6oz/scant 1 cup mixed wild rice and basmati rice
8 slices smoked salmon, total weight about 350g/12oz
10cm/4in piece of cucumber, finely diced
225g/8oz feta cheese, cubed
8 cherry tomatoes, quartered
30ml/2 tbsp mayonnaise
10ml/2 tsp fresh lime juice
15ml/1 tbsp chopped fresh chervil
salt and ground black pepper
lime slices and fresh chervil, to garnish

1 Cook the rice according to the instructions on the packet. Drain, tip into a bowl and leave to cool completely.

2 Line four ramekins with clear film (plastic wrap), then line each ramekin with two slices of smoked salmon, allowing the ends to overlap the edges of the dishes.

VARIATION
You can use other smoked fish in place of the salmon. Smoked trout is an obvious alternative, but you could also try trout, monkfish, freshwater eel or halibut, if you are able to find it.

3 Add the cucumber, cubes of feta and tomato quarters to the rice and stir in the mayonnaise, lime juice and chopped chervil. Mix together well. Season with salt and ground black pepper to taste.

4 Spoon the rice salad mixture into the salmon-lined ramekins. (Any leftover mixture can be used to make a separate rice salad.) Then carefully fold over the overlapping ends of the salmon so that the rice mixture is completely encased.

5 Chill the parcels in the refrigerator for 30–60 minutes, then invert each parcel on to a plate, using the clear film to ease them out of the ramekins. Carefully peel off the clear film, then garnish each parcel with slices of lime and a sprig of fresh chervil and serve.

COOK'S TIP
Wild rice is actually an aquatic grass and is quite expensive, as it is so difficult to harvest. However, a little goes a long way. You can buy packs of mixed wild and long grain rice in most supermarkets.

Salmon Rillettes

This is an economical, but
delightful way of serving salmon.

Serves 6

350g/12oz salmon fillets
175g/6oz/³/₄ cup butter, softened
1 celery stick, finely chopped
1 leek, white part only, finely chopped
1 bay leaf
150ml/¹/₄ pint/²/₃ cup dry white wine
115g/4oz smoked salmon trimmings
generous pinch of ground mace
60ml/4 tbsp fromage frais
   (farmer's cheese)
salt and ground black pepper
salad leaves, to serve
brown bread or oatcakes, to serve

1 Lightly season the salmon fillets.
Melt 25g/1oz/2 tbsp of the butter in a
medium frying pan. Add the celery and
leek and cook over a low heat, stirring
occasionally, for about 5 minutes. Add
the salmon fillets and bay leaf and
pour the wine over. Cover and cook
for 15 minutes, until the fish is tender.

2 Strain the cooking liquid into a pan
and boil until reduced to 30ml/2 tbsp.
Cool. Meanwhile, melt 50g/2oz/4 tbsp
of the remaining butter and gently
cook the smoked salmon until it turns
pale pink. Leave to cool.

3 Remove the skin and any bones
from the salmon fillets. Flake the flesh
into a bowl and add the reduced,
cooled cooking liquid.

4 Beat in the remaining butter, with
the ground mace and the fromage
frais. Break up the cooked smoked
salmon trimmings and fold into the
salmon mixture with all the juices
from the pan. Taste and adjust the
seasoning if you need to.

5 Spoon the salmon mixture into a
dish or terrine and smooth the top
level. Cover with clear film (plastic
wrap) and chill.

COOK'S TIP

If you are preparing the rillettes ahead,
you can store the salmon mixture in the
refrigerator for up to 2 days.

6 To serve the salmon rillettes, shape
the mixture into oval quenelles using
two dessertspoons and arrange them
on individual plates with the salad
leaves. Serve the rillettes accompanied
by slices of brown bread or oatcakes,
if you like.

Pork and **Bacon Rillettes** with **Onion Salad**

These traditional potted meat
rillettes make a great light meal.

Serves 8

1.8kg/4lb belly (side) of pork,
  boned and cut into cubes (reserve
  the bones)
450g/1lb rindless streaky (fatty) bacon,
  finely chopped
5ml/1 tsp salt
1.5ml/¼ tsp freshly ground
  black pepper
4 garlic cloves, finely chopped
2 fresh parsley sprigs
1 bay leaf
2 fresh thyme sprigs
1 fresh sage sprig
300ml/½ pint/1¼ cups water
crusty French bread, to serve

For the onion salad
1 small red onion, halved and
  thinly sliced
2 spring onions (scallions), cut into
  fine strips
2 celery sticks, cut into
  fine strips
15ml/1 tbsp freshly squeezed
  lemon juice
15ml/1 tbsp light olive oil
ground black pepper

1 Mix together the pork, bacon and
salt in a bowl. Cover and leave for 30
minutes. Preheat the oven to 150°C/
300°F/Gas 2. Stir the pepper and garlic
into the meat. Tie the herbs together
and add to the meat.

2 Spread the meat mixture in a roasting
pan and pour in the water. Place the
bones from the pork on top and cover
tightly with foil. Cook for 3½ hours.

3 Discard the bones and herbs, and
ladle the meat mixture into a metal
sieve set over a large bowl. Leave the
liquid to drain through into the bowl,
then turn the meat into a shallow dish.
Repeat until all the meat is drained.
Reserve the liquid. Use two forks to
pull the meat apart into fine shreds.

4 Line a 1.5 litre/2½ pint/6¼ cup terrine
or deep, straight-sided dish with clear
film (plastic wrap) and spoon in the
shredded meat. Strain the reserved
liquid and pour it over the meat.
Leave to cool. Cover and chill in the
refrigerator for at least 24 hours,
or until set.

5 To make the onion salad, place the
sliced onion, spring onions and celery
in a bowl. Add the freshly squeezed
lemon juice and light olive oil and toss
gently. Season with a little freshly
ground black pepper, but do not add
any salt as the rillettes is well salted.

6 Serve the rillettes, cut into thick
slices, on individual plates with a little
onion salad and thick slices of crusty
French bread.

Smoked Salmon Pâté

Making this pâté in individual ramekins wrapped in extra smoked salmon gives a really special presentation. Taste the mousse as you are making it as some people prefer more lemon juice.

Serves 4

350g/12oz thinly sliced
smoked salmon
150ml/¼ pint/⅔ cup double
(heavy) cream
finely grated rind and juice of 1 lemon
salt and ground black pepper
Melba toast, to serve

1 Line four small ramekins with clear film (plastic wrap). Then line the dishes with 115g/4oz of the smoked salmon cut into strips long enough to flop over the edges.

2 In a food processor fitted with a metal blade, process the rest of the salmon with the cream, lemon rind and juice, salt and plenty of pepper.

COOK'S TIP

The quality of smoked salmon is variable. Atlantic salmon is vastly superior to Pacific. Traditional cold smoking over wood still produces the best results.

3 Pack the lined ramekins with the smoked salmon pâté and wrap over the loose strips of salmon. Cover with clear film and chill in the refrigerator for 30 minutes. Invert on to plates and serve with Melba toast.

Smoked Haddock Pâté

The delicate flavour of this pâté makes it the perfect choice for easy entertaining at a light, *al fresco* lunch on a summer's day.

Serves 6

*3 large Arbroath smokies, about
    225g/8oz each
275g/10oz/1¼ cups medium-fat soft
    white (farmer's) cheese
3 eggs, beaten
30–45ml/2–3 tbsp lemon juice
ground black pepper
chervil sprigs, to garnish
lemon wedges and lettuce leaves,
    to serve*

1 Preheat the oven to 160°C/325°F/ Gas 3. Butter six ramekins.

2 Lay the smokies in an ovenproof dish and heat through in the oven for 10 minutes. Carefully remove the skin and bones from the smokies, then flake the flesh into a bowl.

3 Mash the fish with a fork and work in the cheese, then the eggs. Add lemon juice and pepper to taste.

COOK'S TIP

Arbroath smokies, also known as Aberdeen smokies, are small haddock that have been gutted and had their heads removed before being hot smoked over peat. They are a Scottish speciality, but if they are not available, substitute with traditionally smoked haddock.

4 Divide the fish mixture among the ramekins and place in a large-sized roasting pan. Pour hot water into the roasting pan to come halfway up the side of the ramekins. Bake for 30 minutes, until just set.

5 Leave to cool for 2–3 minutes, then run the point of a knife around the edge of each dish and invert on to a warmed plate. Garnish with chervil sprigs and serve with the lemon wedges and lettuce.

Potted Salmon with Lemon and Dill

This sophisticated dish would be ideal for a brunch party. It can be prepared a couple of days in advance and stored in the refrigerator, allowing you to concentrate on cooking any dishes that you plan to serve hot.

Serves 6

350g/12oz cooked salmon
150g/5oz/²/₃ cup butter, softened
rind and juice of 1 large lemon
10ml/2 tsp chopped fresh dill
salt and ground white pepper
75g/3oz/³/₄ cup flaked (sliced)
*   almonds, coarsely chopped*

1 Skin the salmon and remove and discard any bones. Flake the flesh into a bowl and then place in a food processor together with two-thirds of the butter, the lemon rind and juice and half the dill. Season to taste with plenty of salt and pepper. Process until the mixture is quite smooth and thoroughly combined.

2 Mix in the flaked almonds. Check the seasoning and pack the mixture into small ramekins.

3 Sprinkle the remaining dill over the top of each ramekin. Clarify the remaining butter and pour over each ramekin to make a seal. Chill. Serve with crudités or buttered brown bread.

Potted Prawns

The tiny brown shrimp that were
traditionally used for potting are
very awkward to peel. It is easier to
use peeled cooked prawns instead.

Serves 4

*225g/8oz/2 cups cooked peeled
    prawns (shrimp)*
225g/8oz/1 cup butter
pinch of ground mace
salt, to taste
cayenne pepper
fresh dill sprigs, to garnish
*lemon wedges and thin slices of
    brown bread and butter, to serve*

1 Chop a quarter of the prawns. Melt
115g/4oz/½ cup of the butter over a
low heat, carefully skimming off any
foam that rises to the surface with a
metal spoon.

2 Gently stir all the prawns, the
ground mace, salt and cayenne into
the butter and heat gently without
boiling. Pour the prawns and butter
mixture into four individual pots and
leave to cool.

3 Heat the remaining butter in a clean,
small pan, skimming off any foam with
a metal spoon, then carefully spoon
the clear butter over the prawns,
leaving the sediment behind.

4 Leave until the butter is almost set,
then place a dill sprig in the centre of
each pot. Leave to set completely, then
cover and chill.

5 Remove the prawns from the
refrigerator about 30 minutes before
serving to bring them to room
temperature. Serve with lemon
wedges for squeezing over and thin
slices of brown bread and butter.

COOK'S TIP
Use fresh prawns (shrimp), if possible, as
frozen prawns have a fairly unpleasant,
soggy texture. If you have to use frozen,
drain them well and pat dry.

VARIATION
If you prefer, add a pinch of freshly grated
nutmeg in place of the ground mace. The
flavour is similar but it will not colour
the dish. Alternatively, use a blade of
mace and remove it from the mixture
before potting the prawns (shrimp).

Grilled Vegetable Terrine

A colourful, layered terrine, this dish uses all the vegetables that are associated with the Mediterranean.

Serves 6

2 large red (bell) peppers, quartered
*   and seeded*
2 large yellow (bell) peppers, quartered
*   and seeded*
1 large aubergine (eggplant),
*   sliced lengthways*
2 large courgettes (zucchini),
*   sliced lengthways*
90ml/6 tbsp olive oil
1 large red onion, thinly sliced
75g/3oz/¹/₂ cup raisins
15ml/1 tbsp tomato purée (paste)
15ml/1 tbsp red wine vinegar
400ml/14fl oz/1²/₃ cups tomato juice
30ml/2 tbsp powdered gelatine
fresh basil leaves, to garnish

For the dressing
90ml/6 tbsp extra virgin olive oil
30ml/2 tbsp red wine vinegar
salt and ground black pepper

1 Place the peppers skin side up under a hot grill (broiler) and cook until the skins are blackened. Transfer to a bowl and cover with a plate. Leave to cool.

2 Arrange the slices of aubergine and courgette on separate baking sheets. Brush them with a little olive oil and cook under the grill, turning them occasionally, until they are tender and golden brown.

3 Heat the remaining olive oil in a frying pan and add the sliced onion, raisins, tomato purée and red wine vinegar. Cook over a low heat, stirring occasionally, until the mixture is soft and syrupy. Set aside and leave to cool in the frying pan.

4 Line a 1.75 litre/3 pint/7½ cup terrine with clear film (plastic wrap). It helps if you lightly oil the terrine first. Leave a little clear film overhanging the sides of the container.

5 Pour half the tomato juice into a pan and sprinkle with the gelatine. Leave for 5 minutes to soften, then dissolve gently over a low heat, stirring to prevent any lumps from forming.

6 Place a layer of the grilled (broiled) red peppers in the base of the terrine and pour in enough of the tomato juice with gelatine to cover it.

COOK'S TIP
If you don't own a terrine, you can use a loaf tin (pan) instead. It will still need to be lined with clear film (plastic wrap).

7 Continue layering the vegetables, pouring tomato juice over each layer, finishing with a layer of red peppers. Add the remaining tomato juice to the pan and pour into the terrine. Give it a sharp tap, to disperse the juice. Cover and chill until set.

8 To make the dressing, whisk together the oil and vinegar, then season to taste. Turn out the terrine and remove the clear film. Serve in thick slices, drizzled with dressing and garnished with basil leaves.

VARIATION
Use orange and green peppers along with or in place of the red and yellow ones. Green beans, simply boiled first, would make a tasty addition, as would a colourful layer of peas or corn.

Roast Pepper Terrine

This terrine is perfect for all kinds of entertaining because it tastes better if made ahead. Prepare the salsa on the day of serving. Serve with Italian bread.

Serves 8

8 (bell) peppers (red, yellow
    and orange)
675g/1½lb/3 cups mascarpone cheese
3 eggs, separated
30ml/2 tbsp each coarsely chopped
    flat leaf parsley and shredded basil
2 large garlic cloves, coarsely chopped
2 red, yellow or orange (bell) peppers,
    seeded and coarsely chopped
30ml/2 tbsp extra virgin olive oil
10ml/2 tsp balsamic vinegar
a few fresh basil sprigs
salt and ground black pepper

1 Place the whole peppers under a hot grill (broiler) for 8–10 minutes, turning them frequently, until blackened and charred. Then put into a plastic bag, tie the top and leave until cold before peeling and seeding them. Slice seven of the peppers lengthways into thin strips and reserve the eighth.

2 Put the mascarpone cheese in a bowl with the egg yolks, parsley, basil and half the garlic. Season with salt and pepper to taste. Beat well. In a separate, grease-free bowl, whisk the egg whites to a soft peak, then fold into the cheese mixture until they are evenly incorporated.

3 Preheat the oven to 180°C/350°F/ Gas 4. Line the base of a lightly oiled 900g/2lb loaf tin (pan). Put one-third of the cheese mixture in the tin and spread evenly, levelling the surface. Arrange half the pepper strips on top in an even layer. Repeat until all the cheese and pepper strips have been used, ending with a layer of the mascarpone cheese mixture.

4 Cover the tin with foil and place in a roasting pan. Pour in boiling water to come halfway up the sides of the loaf tin. Bake for 1 hour. Remove from the oven and leave the terrine to cool in the water bath, then lift out and chill overnight in the refrigerator.

5 A few hours before serving, make the salsa. Place the remaining peeled pepper and fresh peppers in a food processor. Add the remaining garlic, oil and vinegar. Set aside a few basil leaves for garnishing and add the rest to the processor. Process until finely chopped. Tip the mixture into a bowl, season with salt and pepper to taste and mix well. Cover with clear film (plastic wrap) and chill in the refrigerator until ready to serve.

6 Turn out the terrine on to a chopping board, peel off the lining paper and slice thickly. Garnish with the reserved basil leaves and serve cold, with the sweet pepper salsa.

Asparagus and Egg Terrine

For a special occasion, this terrine is a delicious choice yet it is very light. Make the hollandaise sauce well in advance and warm through gently when required.

Serves 8

150ml/¼ pint/⅔ cup milk
150ml/¼ pint/⅔ cup double
   (heavy) cream
40g/1½oz/3 tbsp butter
40g/1½oz/3 tbsp plain
   (all-purpose) flour
75g/3oz herbed or garlic cream cheese
675g/1½ lb asparagus spears, cooked
vegetable oil, for brushing
2 eggs, separated
15ml/1 tbsp chopped fresh chives
30ml/2 tbsp chopped fresh dill
salt and ground black pepper
fresh dill sprigs, to garnish

For the orange hollandaise sauce
15ml/1 tbsp white wine vinegar
15ml/1 tbsp fresh orange juice
4 black peppercorns
1 bay leaf
2 egg yolks
115g/4oz/½ cup butter, melted and
   cooled slightly

1 Put the milk and cream into a small pan and heat to just below boiling point. Melt the butter in a medium pan, stir in the flour and cook over a low heat, stirring constantly, to a thick paste. Gradually stir in the milk, whisking as it thickens. Stir in the cream cheese, season to taste with salt and ground black pepper and leave to cool slightly.

2 Trim the asparagus to fit the width of a 1.2 litre/2 pint/5 cup loaf tin (pan) or terrine. Lightly oil the tin and then base line with baking parchment. Preheat the oven to 180°C/350°F/Gas 4.

3 Beat the egg yolks into the sauce mixture. Whisk the whites until stiff and fold in with the chives, dill and seasoning. Layer the asparagus and egg mixture in the tin, starting and finishing with asparagus. Cover the top with foil.

4 Place the terrine in a roasting pan and half fill with hot water. Cook for 45–55 minutes, until firm.

5 When the terrine is just firm to the touch, remove from the oven and leave to cool, then chill.

6 To make the sauce, put the vinegar, orange juice, peppercorns and bay leaf in a small pan and heat gently until reduced by half.

7 Cool the sauce slightly, then whisk in the egg yolks, then the butter, with a balloon whisk over a very gentle heat. Season to taste with salt and pepper and continue whisking until thick. Keep the sauce warm over a pan of hot water.

8 Invert the terrine on to a serving dish, remove the paper and garnish with the dill. Cut into slices and pour over the warmed sauce.

Haddock and Smoked Salmon Terrine

This is a fairly substantial terrine, so serve modest slices, perhaps accompanied by fresh dill mayonnaise or a fresh mango salsa. It would be perfect for a summer lunch party.

Serves 10–12

15ml/1 tbsp sunflower oil, for greasing
350g/12oz thinly sliced oak-
*   smoked salmon*
900g/2lb haddock fillets
2 eggs, lightly beaten
105ml/7 tbsp crème fraîche
30ml/2 tbsp drained capers
30ml/2 tbsp drained soft green or
*   pink peppercorns*
salt and ground white pepper
crème fraîche, peppercorns and fresh
*   dill and rocket (arugula), to garnish*

1 Preheat the oven to 200°C/400°F/ Gas 6. Grease a 1 litre/1¾ pint/4 cup loaf tin (pan) or terrine with the sunflower oil. Use some of the smoked salmon slices to line the loaf tin or terrine, allowing the ends to overhang the rim of the mould slightly. Set aside the remaining smoked salmon until it is needed.

2 Skin the haddock fillets. Using a sharp knife, cut two long slices of haddock the same length as the loaf tin or terrine and set aside. Cut the remaining haddock fillets into small pieces. Season all of the haddock with salt and ground white pepper.

3 Combine the eggs, crème fraîche, capers and green or pink peppercorns in a bowl. Add salt and pepper and stir in the haddock pieces. Spoon the mixture into the mould until it is about one-third full. Smooth the surface with a spatula.

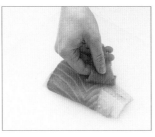

4 Wrap the long haddock slices in the reserved smoked salmon. Lay them on top of the layer of the fish mixture in the tin or terrine.

5 Cover with the rest of the fish mixture, smooth the surface and fold the overhanging pieces of smoked salmon over the top. Cover tightly with a double thickness of foil. Tap the terrine to settle the contents.

6 Stand the loaf tin or terrine in a roasting pan and pour in boiling water to come halfway up the sides of the tin or terrine. Place in the oven and cook for 45 minutes–1 hour, until the filling is just set.

7 Take the terrine out of the water bath, but do not remove the foil cover. Place two or three large heavy cans on the foil to weigh it and leave until cold. Chill in the refrigerator for 24 hours.

8 About an hour before serving, remove the terrine from the refrigerator, lift off the weights and remove the foil. Carefully invert on to a serving plate and garnish with crème fraîche, peppercorns and sprigs of dill and rocket leaves.

COOK'S TIP
If you are going to slice a side of salmon yourself, you will need a very sharp knife with a thin 25cm/10in blade.

VARIATION
Use any thick white fish fillets for this terrine. Try cod, whiting, hake, or hoki.

Striped Fish Terrine

Serve this terrine cold or just warm, with a hollandaise sauce if you like.

Serves 8

15ml/1 tbsp sunflower oil
450g/1lb salmon fillet
450g/1lb sole fillets
3 egg whites
105ml/7 tbsp double (heavy) cream
15ml/1 tbsp finely chopped
    fresh chives
2.5ml/¹⁄₂ tsp grated nutmeg
juice of 1 lemon
115g/4oz/1 cup peas, cooked
5ml/1 tsp chopped fresh mint
salt and ground white pepper
thinly sliced cucumber, salad cress and
    whole fresh chives, to garnish

1 Grease a 1 litre/1¾ pint/4 cup loaf tin (pan) or terrine with the oil. Skin the salmon and sole fillets. Using a sharp knife, slice the salmon thinly; then cut it and the sole into long strips, 2.5cm/1in wide. Preheat the oven to 200°C/400°F/Gas 6.

2 Line the terrine neatly with alternate strips of salmon and sole, leaving the ends overhanging the edge. You should be left with about a third of the salmon and half the sole. Set aside until required.

COOK'S TIP
You can use fresh or frozen peas, but both must be cooked first.

3 In a clean grease-free bowl, whisk the egg whites with a pinch of salt until they form soft peaks. Place the reserved sole strips in a food processor and process until smooth. Spoon into a bowl, season with salt and ground white pepper, then fold in two-thirds of the egg whites, followed by two-thirds of the cream. Put half the mixture into a second bowl; stir in the chives. Add nutmeg to the first bowl.

4 Place the reserved salmon strips in the food processor and process until smooth. Scrape the purée into a bowl and add the lemon juice and seasoning. Fold in the remaining whisked egg whites, then the remaining cream.

5 Place the cooked peas and the mint in the food processor and process until smooth. Season the mixture to taste with salt and pepper and spread it over the base of the loaf tin or terrine, smoothing the surface with a spatula. Spoon over the sole with chives mixture and spread that layer evenly with a spatula.

6 Add the salmon mixture, then finish with the sole and nutmeg mixture, spreading them both evenly. Cover with the overhanging fish fillets and make a lid of oiled foil. Stand the loaf tin or terrine in a roasting pan and pour in enough boiling water to come halfway up the sides of the terrine.

7 Bake for 15–20 minutes, until the top fillets are just cooked and the mousse feels springy. Remove the foil, lay a wire rack over the top of the loaf tin or terrine and invert both rack and terrine on to a lipped baking sheet to catch the cooking juices that drain out. Keep these to make fish stock or soup.

8 Leaving the container in place, let the terrine stand for about 15 minutes, then turn it over again, invert it on to a serving dish and lift off the tin or terrine carefully. Serve warm, or chill in the refrigerator first and serve cold. Garnish with thinly sliced cucumber, salad cress and chives before serving.

VARIATION
While Dover sole has an incomparable flavour, you could also use the slightly less expensive lemon sole or, even more economically, substitute brill. Also known in some places as Torbay sole, this much underrated fish has an exquisite flavour.

Chicken and Pork Terrine

This elegant terrine is flecked with parsley and green peppercorns, which give it a lovely subtle flavour.

Serves 6–8

225g/8oz rindless, streaky
  (fatty) bacon
375g/13oz skinless, boneless chicken
  breast portions
15ml/1 tbsp lemon juice
225g/8oz lean minced (ground) pork
1/2 small onion, finely chopped
2 eggs, beaten
30ml/2 tbsp chopped fresh parsley
5ml/1 tsp salt
5ml/1 tsp green peppercorns, crushed
vegetable oil, for greasing
salad leaves, radishes and lemon
  wedges, to serve

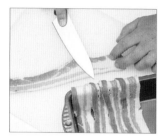

1 Preheat the oven to 160°C/325°F/ Gas 3. Put the bacon on a board and stretch it using the back of a knife before arranging it in overlapping slices over the base and sides of a 900g/2lb loaf tin (pan).

2 Cut 115g/4oz of the chicken into strips about 10cm/4in long. Sprinkle with lemon juice and set aside. Put the rest of the chicken in a food processor or blender with the minced pork and the onion. Process until fairly smooth.

3 Add the eggs, parsley, salt and peppercorns to the meat mixture and process again briefly. Spoon half the mixture into the loaf tin and then level the surface.

4 Arrange the reserved chicken strips on top, then spoon in the remaining meat mixture and smooth the top. Give the tin a couple of sharp taps on the work surface to knock out any pockets of air.

5 Cover the loaf tin with a piece of oiled foil and put it in a roasting pan. Pour in enough hot water to come halfway up the sides of the loaf tin. Bake for about 45–50 minutes, until the terrine is firm.

6 Leave the terrine to cool in the tin before turning out on to a plate and chilling in the refrigerator.

7 Serve the terrine in slices, with salad leaves, radishes and wedges of lemon for squeezing.

COOK'S TIP

For a slightly sharper flavour, substitute chopped fresh coriander (cilantro) for the parsley. It goes particularly well with the flavour of lemon.

Turkey, Juniper and Peppercorn Terrine

This can be made several days in advance. If you prefer, arrange some of the pancetta and pistachio nuts as a layer in the middle of the terrine.

Serves 10–12

225g/8oz chicken livers, trimmed
450g/1lb minced (ground) turkey
450g/1lb minced (ground) pork
225g/8oz pancetta, cubed
50g/2oz/$^{1}/_{2}$ cup shelled pistachio nuts,
   coarsely chopped
5ml/1 tsp salt
2.5ml/$^{1}/_{2}$ tsp ground mace
2 garlic cloves, crushed
5ml/1 tsp drained green peppercorns
   in brine
5ml/1 tsp juniper berries
120ml/4fl oz/$^{1}/_{2}$ cup dry white wine
30ml/2 tbsp gin
finely grated rind of 1 orange
8 large vine (grape) leaves in brine
vegetable oil, for greasing
pickle or chutney, to serve

1 Chop the chicken livers finely. Put them in a bowl and add the turkey, pork, pancetta, pistachio nuts, salt, mace and garlic. Mix well.

2 Lightly crush the peppercorns and juniper berries in a mortar with a pestle or with the end of a rolling pin and add them to the mixture. Stir in the wine, gin and orange rind. Cover with clear film (plastic wrap) and chill overnight to allow the flavours to mingle.

3 Preheat the oven to 160°C/325°F/ Gas 3. Rinse the vine leaves under cold running water. Drain them thoroughly and pat dry. Lightly oil a 1.2 litre/ 2 pint/5 cup pâté terrine or loaf tin (pan). Line the terrine or tin with the vine leaves, letting the ends overhang the sides. Pack the meat mixture into the terrine or tin and fold the overhanging leaves over to enclose the filling completely. Brush the top lightly with a little oil.

4 Cover the terrine with its lid or the loaf tin with foil. Place it in a roasting pan and pour in boiling water to come halfway up the sides of the terrine. Bake for 1¾ hours, checking the level of the water occasionally, so that the roasting pan does not dry out.

5 Leave the terrine to cool, then pour off the surface juices. Cover with clear film (plastic wrap), then foil and place weights on top. Chill in the refrigerator overnight. Serve at room temperature with a pickle or chutney, such as spiced kumquats or red bell pepper and chilli jelly.

COOK'S TIP

A pâté terrine is usually made of cast iron, which is ideal for even cooking. Its traditional long shape makes it easier to cut the terrine into neat slices.

Hot Crab Soufflés

These delicious little soufflés must be served as soon as they are ready, so seat your guests at the table before taking the soufflés out of the oven.

Serves 6

50g/2oz/¼ cup butter
45ml/3 tbsp fine wholemeal
    (whole-wheat) breadcrumbs
4 spring onions (scallions),
    finely chopped
15ml/1 tbsp Malayan or mild Madras
    curry powder
25g/1oz/2 tbsp plain
    (all-purpose) flour
105ml/7 tbsp coconut milk or milk
150ml/¼ pint/⅔ cup whipping cream
4 egg yolks
225g/8oz white crab meat
mild green Tabasco sauce
6 egg whites
salt and ground black pepper

1 Use some of the butter to grease six ramekins or a 1.75 litre/3 pint/7½ cup soufflé dish. Sprinkle the breadcrumbs in the dishes or dish and roll them around to coat the base and sides completely, then tip out the excess breadcrumbs. Preheat the oven to 200°C/400°F/Gas 6.

2 Melt the remaining butter in a pan, add the spring onions and Malayan or mild Madras curry powder and cook over a low heat, stirring frequently, for about 1 minute, until softened. Stir in the flour and cook, stirring constantly, for 1 minute more.

3 Gradually add the coconut milk or milk and the cream, stirring constantly. Cook over a low heat, still stirring, until smooth and thick. Remove the pan from the heat, stir in the egg yolks, then the crab. Season to taste with salt, black pepper and Tabasco sauce.

4 In a clean grease-free bowl, whisk the egg whites with a pinch of salt until they are stiff. Using a metal spoon, stir one-third of the whites into the crab mixture to slacken, then fold in the remainder. Spoon into the dishes or dish.

5 Bake the soufflés until well risen, golden brown and just firm to the touch. Individual soufflés will take about 8 minutes, while a large, single soufflé will take 15–20 minutes. Serve immediately.

Twice-baked Gruyère and Potato Soufflé

This recipe can be prepared in advance and given its second baking just before you serve it up.

Serves 4

225g/8oz floury (mealy) potatoes
2 eggs, separated
175g/6oz/1¹/₂ cups grated
  Gruyère cheese
50g/2oz/¹/₂ cup self-raising
  (self-rising) flour
50g/2oz spinach leaves
butter, for greasing
salt and ground black pepper

1 Preheat the oven to 200°C/400°F/ Gas 6. Peel the potatoes and cook in lightly salted, boiling water for 20 minutes, until very tender. Drain well and mash with the egg yolks, using a potato masher or a fork.

2 Stir in half of the Gruyère cheese and all of the flour. Season to taste with salt and ground black pepper.

COOK'S TIP
Never attempt to mash potatoes with an electric mixer. It breaks down the starch and turns the potatoes into a sticky mess with the texture of wallpaper paste. Use a potato masher or fork to pound them by hand or a potato ricer which will produce an even, lump-free, fine mash.

3 Finely chop the spinach and fold into the potato mixture.

VARIATION
Try replacing the Gruyère with a crumbled blue cheese, such as Stilton or Shropshire Blue, which have a stronger flavour.

4 Whisk the egg whites in a clean, grease-free bowl until they form soft peaks. Fold a little of the egg white into the mixture to slacken it slightly, then, using a large spoon, fold the remaining egg white into the mixture.

5 Grease four large ramekins. Pour the mixture into the dishes and place on a baking sheet. Bake for 20 minutes. Remove the dishes from the oven and leave to cool.

6 Turn the soufflés out on to a baking sheet and sprinkle with the remaining cheese. Bake again for 5 minutes and serve immediately.

Leek Roulade with Cheese, Walnut and Sweet Pepper Filling

This roulade is easy to prepare and is ideal for brunch or a vegetarian main course, served with home-made tomato sauce.

Serves 6

butter or oil, for greasing
30ml/2 tbsp dry white breadcrumbs
75g/3oz/1 cup grated Parmesan cheese
50g/2oz/¼ cup butter
2 leeks, thinly sliced
40g/1½oz/⅓ cup plain
  (all-purpose) flour
250ml/8fl oz/1 cup milk
5ml/1 tsp Dijon mustard
1.5ml/¼ tsp freshly grated nutmeg
2 large (US extra large) eggs,
  separated, plus 1 egg white
2.5ml/½ tsp cream of tartar
salt and ground black pepper
rocket (arugula) and balsamic dressing,
  to serve

For the filling
2 large red (bell) peppers
350g/12oz/1½ cups ricotta cheese or
  soft goat's cheese
90g/3½oz/scant 1 cup chopped walnuts
4 spring onions (scallions), chopped
15g/½oz/½ cup fresh basil leaves

1 Grease and line a 30 × 23cm/ 12 × 9in Swiss roll tin (jelly roll pan) with baking parchment, then sprinkle with the breadcrumbs and 30ml/2 tbsp of the grated Parmesan. Preheat the oven to 190°C/375°F/Gas 5.

2 Melt the butter in a pan and cook the leeks for 5 minutes, until softened.

3 Stir in the flour and cook over a low heat, stirring constantly, for 2 minutes, then gradually stir in the milk. Cook for 3–4 minutes, stirring constantly to make a thick sauce.

4 Stir in the mustard and nutmeg and season with salt and plenty of pepper. Reserve 30–45ml/2–3 tbsp of the remaining Parmesan, then stir the rest into the sauce. Cool slightly.

5 Beat the egg yolks into the sauce. In a clean, grease-free bowl, whisk the egg whites and cream of tartar until stiff. Stir 2–3 spoonfuls of the whites into the leek mixture, then carefully fold in the remaining egg whites.

6 Pour the mixture into the tin and gently level it out using a spatula. Bake for 15–18 minutes, until risen and just firm to a light touch in the centre. If the roulade is to be served hot, increase the oven temperature to 200°C/400°F/ Gas 6 after removing the roulade.

7 Preheat the grill (broiler). Halve and seed the peppers, grill (broil) them, skin sides up, until black. Place in a bowl, cover and leave for 10 minutes. Peel and cut the flesh into strips. Mix the cheese, nuts and spring onions. Chop half the basil and stir into the mixture.

8 Sprinkle the remaining Parmesan on to a large sheet of baking parchment. Turn out the roulade on to it. Strip off the lining paper and allow the roulade to cool. Spread the cheese mixture over it and top with the red pepper strips. Sprinkle the remaining basil leaves over the top. Roll up the roulade and place on a platter. If serving hot, roll it on to a baking sheet, cover with a tent of foil and bake for 15–20 minutes. Serve with rocket and drizzle with dressing.

Smoked Fish and **Asparagus Mousse**

This elegant mousse looks good with its studding of asparagus and smoked salmon. Serve a mustard and dill dressing separately if you like.

Serves 8

15ml/1 tbsp powdered gelatine
juice of 1 lemon
105ml/7 tbsp fish stock
50g/2oz/¼ cup butter, plus extra
   for greasing
2 shallots, finely chopped
225g/8oz smoked trout fillets
105ml/7 tbsp sour cream
225g/8oz/1 cup soft white
   (farmer's) cheese
1 egg white
12 spinach leaves, blanched
12 fresh asparagus spears,
   lightly cooked
115g/4oz smoked salmon, cut in strips
salt
shredded beetroot (beet) and beetroot
   leaves, to garnish

1 Sprinkle the gelatine over the lemon juice and leave until spongy. In a small pan, heat the fish stock, then add the soaked gelatine and stir to dissolve completely. Set aside. Melt the butter in a pan, add the shallots and cook gently until softened but not coloured.

2 Break up the smoked trout fillets and put them in a food processor with the shallots, sour cream, stock mixture and cheese. Process until smooth, then spoon into a bowl.

3 In a clean bowl, beat the egg white with a pinch of salt to soft peaks. Fold into the fish. Cover the bowl; chill for 30 minutes, or until starting to set.

4 Grease a 1 litre/1¾ pint/4 cup loaf tin (pan) or terrine with butter, then line it with the spinach leaves. Carefully spread half the trout mousse over the spinach-covered base, arrange the asparagus spears on top, then cover with the remaining trout mousse.

5 Arrange the smoked salmon strips lengthways on the mousse and fold over the overhanging spinach leaves. Cover with clear film (plastic wrap) and chill for 4 hours, until set. To serve, remove the clear film, turn out on to a serving dish and garnish with the shredded beetroot and leaves.

COOK'S TIP
Use a serrated knife with a fine-toothed blade to cut the mousse into neat slices.

Risotto alla Milanese

This classic risotto is often served
with the hearty veal stew, osso
bucco, but it also makes a delicious
light meal in its own right.

Serves 5–6

*about 1.2 litres/2 pints/5 cups beef or
   chicken stock*
good pinch of saffron threads
75g/3oz/6 tbsp butter
1 onion, finely chopped
275g/10oz/1½ cups risotto rice
*75g/3oz/1 cup freshly grated
   Parmesan cheese*
salt and ground black pepper

1 Bring the stock to the boil in a large
pan, then reduce to a low simmer.
Ladle a little hot stock into a small
bowl. Add the saffron threads and set
aside to infuse (steep).

2 Melt 50g/2oz/4 tbsp of the butter
in a large, heavy pan until foaming.
Add the onion and cook over a low
heat, stirring occasionally, for about
3 minutes, until softened and
translucent but not browned.

3 Add the rice. Stir until the grains are
coated with butter and starting to swell
and burst, then add a few ladlefuls of
the hot stock, with the saffron liquid and
salt and pepper to taste. Stir constantly
over a low heat until all the stock has
been absorbed. Add the remaining
stock, a few ladlefuls at a time, allowing
the rice to absorb all the liquid before
adding more, and stirring constantly.
After about 20–25 minutes, the rice
should be just tender and the risotto
golden yellow, moist and creamy.

4 Gently stir in about two-thirds of the
grated Parmesan and the remaining
butter. Heat through gently until the
butter has melted, then taste and
adjust the seasoning, if necessary.
Transfer the risotto to a warmed
serving bowl or platter and serve hot,
with the remaining grated Parmesan
served separately.

COOK'S TIP
Italians always cook with unsalted
(sweet) butter.

Risotto with **Four Cheeses**

This is a very rich dish. Serve it with a light, dry sparkling white wine.

Serves 4–6

40g/1^1/$_2$oz/3 tbsp butter
1 small onion, finely chopped
1.2 litres/2 pints/5 cups chicken stock
350g/12oz/1^3/$_4$ cups risotto rice
200ml/7fl oz/scant 1 cup dry
     white wine
50g/2oz/^{1}/$_2$ cup grated Gruyère cheese
50g/2oz/^{1}/$_2$ cup diced taleggio cheese
50g/2oz/^{1}/$_2$ cup diced
     Gorgonzola cheese
50g/2oz/^{2}/$_3$ cup freshly grated
     Parmesan cheese
salt and ground black pepper
chopped fresh flat leaf parsley,
     to garnish

1 Melt the butter in a large, heavy pan or deep frying pan. Add the onion and cook over a low heat, stirring occasionally, for about 4–5 minutes, until softened and lightly browned. Meanwhile, pour the stock into a separate pan, bring to the boil, then lower the heat to a simmer.

2 Add the rice to the pan with the onion, stir until the grains are coated with butter and starting to swell and burst, then add the wine. Stir until it stops sizzling and most of it has been absorbed by the rice.

3 Pour in a little of the hot stock. Season with salt and ground black pepper to taste. Stir the rice over a low heat until all the stock has been absorbed.

4 Gradually add the remaining stock, a little at a time, allowing the rice to absorb the liquid before adding more, and stirring constantly. After about 20–25 minutes, the rice will be tender and the risotto will be creamy.

5 Turn off the heat under the pan, then add the Gruyère, taleggio, Gorgonzola and 30ml/2 tbsp of the Parmesan. Stir gently until the cheeses have melted, then taste and adjust the seasoning, if necessary. Spoon the risotto into a warm serving bowl and garnish with parsley. Serve the remaining Parmesan separately.

Pancakes with Leek, Chicory and Squash Stuffing

Serve a chunky tomato sauce with these melt-in-the-mouth pancakes.

Serves 8

225g/8oz/2 cups plain
   (all-purpose) flour
115g/4oz/1 cup yellow corn meal
5ml/1 tsp salt
5ml/1 tsp chilli powder
4 large (US extra large) eggs
900ml/1½ pint/3¾ cups milk
50g/2oz/4 tbsp butter, melted
vegetable oil, for greasing

For the filling
60ml/4 tbsp olive oil
900g/2lb butternut squash (peeled
   weight), seeded and diced
large pinch of dried red chilli flakes
4 large leeks, thickly sliced
5ml/1 tsp chopped fresh thyme
6 chicory (Belgian endive) heads, sliced
225g/8oz goat's cheese, cut into cubes
200g/7oz/1¾ cups walnuts, chopped
60ml/4 tbsp chopped fresh
   flat leaf parsley
50g/2oz/⅔ cup grated Parmesan cheese
90ml/6 tbsp melted butter or olive oil
salt and ground black pepper

1 Sift the flour, corn meal, salt and chilli powder into a bowl and make a well in the centre. Add the eggs and a little milk. Whisk together, gradually adding the remaining milk.

2 When ready to cook the pancakes, whisk the melted butter into the batter. Heat a lightly greased or oiled 18cm/7in heavy frying pan or crêpe pan. Pour about 60ml/4 tbsp batter into the pan and cook over a medium heat for 2–3 minutes, until set and lightly browned underneath. Turn and cook the pancake on the second side for 2–3 minutes. Lightly grease the pan after every second pancake.

3 To make the filling, heat the oil in a large frying pan. Add the squash and cook, stirring frequently, for about 10 minutes, until almost tender. Add the chilli flakes and cook, stirring, for 1–2 minutes. Stir in the leeks and thyme and cook for 4–5 minutes.

4 Add the chicory and cook, stirring frequently, for 4–5 minutes, until the leeks are cooked and the chicory is hot, but still has some bite. Cool slightly, then stir in the cheese, walnuts and parsley. Season to taste.

5 Preheat the oven to 200°C/400°F/Gas 6. Lightly grease an ovenproof dish. Spoon 30–45ml/2–3 tbsp filling on to each pancake. Roll or fold each pancake to enclose the filling, then place in the prepared dish.

6 Sprinkle the Parmesan over the pancakes and drizzle the melted butter or olive oil over. Bake for 10–15 minutes, until the cheese is bubbling. Serve hot.

Indian Mee Goreng

This colourful noodle dish is truly international, combining Indian, Chinese and Western ingredients. In Singapore and Malaysia, it can be bought from many street stalls.

Serves 6

450g/1lb fresh yellow egg noodles
115g/4oz fried or plain tofu
60–90ml/4–6 tbsp vegetable oil
2 eggs
30ml/2tbsp water
1 onion sliced
1 garlic clove, crushed
15ml/1 tbsp light soy sauce
30–45ml/2–3 tbsp tomato ketchup
15ml/1 tbsp chilli sauce (or to taste)
1 large cooked potato, diced
4 spring onions (scallions), shredded
1–2 fresh green chillies, seeded and
    thinly sliced (optional)

1 Bring a large pan of water to the boil, add the fresh egg noodles and cook for just 2 minutes. Drain the noodles and immediately rinse them under cold water to stop any further cooking. Drain again and set aside.

COOK'S TIP

Nowadays, many supermarkets provide a guide to the heat of the chillies on sale. This is helpful, but not always completely reliable, as even different pods from the same plant may vary. As a general rule, dark green chillies tend to be hotter than pale green ones and pointed, thin chillies hotter than larger, blunt ones.

2 If using fried tofu, cut each cube in half, refresh it in a pan of boiling water, then drain well Heat 30ml/2 tbsp of the oil in a large frying pan. If using using plain tofu, cut into cubes, add to the pan and cook until brown, then lift it out with a slotted spoon and set aside.

3 Beat the eggs with the water. Add to the the frying pan and cook without stirring until just set. Flip over, cook the other side briefly, then slide it out of the pan, roll up and slice thinly into narrow strips.

4 Heat the remaining oil in a wok. Add the onion and garlic and stir-fry for 2–3 minutes. Ad the drained noodles, soy sauce, tomato ketchup and chilli sauce. Toss well over medium heat for 2 minutes, then add the diced potato. Reserve half the spring onions for the garnish and stir the remainder into the noodles with the chilli, if using, and the tofu.

5 When hot, stir in the omelette strips. Transfer to a hot platter and serve immediately, garnished with the remaining spring onions.

Black Pasta with Ricotta

This is designer pasta – which is coloured with squid or cuttlefish ink – at its most dramatic, the kind of dish you are most likely to see at a fashionable Italian restaurant. Serve it for a smart party supper – it will create a great talking point.

Serves 4

300g/11oz dried black pasta
60ml/4 tbsp ricotta cheese
60ml/4 tbsp extra virgin
* olive oil*
1 small fresh red chilli, seeded and
* finely chopped*
small handful of fresh basil leaves
salt and ground black pepper

1 Cook the pasta in a large pan of lightly salted, boiling water for about 8–10 minutes, until tender but still firm to the bite.

2 Meanwhile, put the ricotta in a bowl, season with salt and pepper to taste and use a little of the hot water from the pasta pan to mix it to a smooth, creamy consistency.

3 Drain the pasta. Heat the olive oil gently in a clean pan and add the pasta with the chilli and salt and pepper to taste. Toss quickly over a high heat to combine.

4 Divide the pasta equally among four warmed bowls, then top with the ricotta cheese. Sprinkle with the basil leaves and serve immediately. Each diner tosses their own portion of pasta and cheese.

VARIATION
If you prefer, use green spinach-flavoured pasta or red tomato-flavoured pasta in place of the black pasta. Alternatively, for an equally dramatic contrast, try magenta pasta, flavoured with beetroot (beet) or golden brown wild-mushroom pasta.

Paglia e Fieno with Walnuts and Gorgonzola

Cheese and nuts are popular ingredients for pasta sauces. The combination is very rich. The contrasting colours make this dish look particularly attractive. It needs no accompaniment other than wine – a dry white would be good.

Serves 4

25g/1oz/2 tbsp butter
5ml/1 tsp finely chopped fresh sage, or
* 2.5ml/1/2 tsp dried, plus fresh sage*
* leaves, to garnish (optional)*
115g/4oz/1 cup diced
* Gorgonzola cheese*
45ml/3 tbsp mascarpone cheese
75ml/5 tbsp milk
275g/10oz dried paglia e fieno
50g/2oz/1/2 cup walnut halves, ground
30ml/2 tbsp freshly grated
* Parmesan cheese*
ground black pepper

1 Melt the butter in a large, heavy pan over a low heat, add the sage and stir it around. Sprinkle in the diced Gorgonzola and then add the mascarpone. Stir the ingredients with a wooden spoon until the cheeses are starting to melt. Pour in the milk and keep stirring.

2 Meanwhile, cook the pasta in a large pan of lightly salted, boiling water for about 8–10 minutes, until tender but still firm to the bite.

3 Sprinkle the walnuts and grated Parmesan into the cheese mixture and add plenty of black pepper. Continue to stir over a low heat until the mixture forms a creamy sauce. Do not let it boil or the nuts will taste bitter, and do not cook the sauce for longer than a few minutes or the nuts will begin to discolour it.

4 Drain the pasta, tip it into a warmed bowl, then add the sauce and toss well. Serve immediately, with more black pepper ground on top. Garnish with sage leaves, if using.

COOK'S TIP
To cook pasta to perfection, bring the pan of water back to the boil after adding it and time the cooking from that moment. Pasta needs to boil, not simmer, so do not turn the heat right down. Test the pasta for readiness by biting a small piece.

sensational soups

Sharing a large dish with a few
accompaniments or dipping into a classic
one-pot meal is a sure way of having a
memorable no-fuss meal with friends.

Vichyssoise with **Watercress Cream**

Classic soups, such as this cold French version of leek and potato soup, will always remain firm favourites for dinner parties.

Serves 6

50g/2oz/¼ cup butter
1 onion, sliced
450g/1lb leeks, sliced
225g/8oz potatoes, sliced
750ml/1¼ pints/3 cups chicken stock
300ml/½ pint/1¼ cups milk
45ml/3 tbsp single (light) cream
salt and ground black pepper
fresh chervil, to garnish

For the watercress cream
1 bunch watercress, about 75g/3oz,
    stalks removed
small bunch of fresh chervil,
    finely chopped
150ml/¼ pint/⅔ cup double
    (heavy) cream
pinch of freshly grated nutmeg

1 Melt the butter in a pan. Add the onion and leeks, cover and cook gently for 10 minutes, stirring occasionally, until softened. Stir in the potatoes and stock, and bring to the boil. Reduce the heat and simmer for 20 minutes, or until the potatoes are tender. Cool slightly.

2 Process the soup in a food processor or blender until smooth, then press through a sieve into a clean pan.

3 Stir in the milk and single cream. Season the soup well and chill for at least 2 hours.

4 To make the watercress cream, process the watercress in a food processor or blender until finely chopped, then stir in the chervil and cream. Pour into a bowl and stir in the nutmeg with seasoning to taste.

5 Ladle the vichyssoise into bowls and spoon the watercress cream on top. Garnish with chervil and serve.

COOK'S TIP
The soup is also delicious served hot in winter, especially sprinkled with a little grated nutmeg.

Iced Melon Soup with Melon and Mint Sorbet

You can use different melons for the cool soup and ice sorbet to create a subtle contrast in flavour and colour. Try a combination of Charentais and Ogen or cantaloupe and piel de sapo. This soup is refreshing and ideal for formal and informal summer dinner parties, and *al fresco* dining.

Serves 6–8

2.25kg/5lb very ripe melon
45ml/3 tbsp orange juice
30ml/2 tbsp lemon juice
fresh mint leaves, to garnish

For the melon and mint sorbet (sherbet)
25g/1oz/2 tbsp sugar
120ml/4fl oz/½ cup water
2.25kg/5lb very ripe melon
juice of 2 limes
30ml/2 tbsp chopped fresh mint

1 To make the melon and mint sorbet, put the sugar and water into a pan and heat gently until the sugar dissolves. Bring to the boil and simmer for 4–5 minutes, then leave to cool.

2 Halve the melon. Scrape out the seeds, then cut it into large wedges and cut the flesh out of the skin. It should weigh about 1.6kg/3½lb.

3 Process the melon flesh in a food processor or blender with the cooled syrup and lime juice.

4 If you are using an ice cream maker: stir in the mint and pour in the melon mixture. Churn, following the maker's instructions, or until the sorbet is smooth and firm. By hand: stir in the mint and pour the mixture into a freezerproof container. Freeze until icy at the edges. Transfer to a food processor and process until smooth. Repeat this process until the mixture is smooth and holding its shape, then freeze until firm.

5 To make the chilled melon soup, prepare the melon as in step 2 and process until smooth in a food processor or blender. Pour the purée into a bowl and stir in the orange and lemon juice. Place the soup in the refrigerator for 30–40 minutes, but do not chill it for too long as this will dull its flavour.

6 Ladle the soup into bowls and add a large scoop of the melon and mint sorbet to each. Garnish with mint leaves and serve immediately.

COOK'S TIP
The soup also looks impressive served in large wine glasses, with small balls of sorbet (sherbet) instead of large scoops. Keep the glasses cool by standing them in bowls filled with ice cubes.

Chilled Asparagus Soup

This soup provides a delightful way to enjoy a favourite seasonal vegetable. Choose bright, crisp-looking asparagus with firm stalks.

Serves 6

900g/2lb fresh asparagus
60ml/4 tbsp butter or olive oil
175g/6oz/1 1/2 cups sliced leeks or
*   spring onions (scallions)*
45ml/3 tbsp plain (all-purpose) flour
1.5 litres/2 1/2 pints/6 1/4 cups chicken
*   stock or water*
120ml/4fl oz/1/2 cup single (light)
*   cream or plain (natural) yogurt*
salt and ground black pepper
15ml/1 tbsp minced (ground) fresh
*   tarragon or chervil*

3 Heat the butter or olive oil in a heavy pan. Add the leeks or spring onions and cook over a low heat, stirring occasionally, for 5–8 minutes, until softened and translucent.

4 Stir in the chopped asparagus stalks, cover and cook gently for a further 6–8 minutes.

5 Add the flour and stir well to blend. Cook for 3–4 minutes, uncovered, stirring constantly.

6 Gradually stir in the chicken stock or water and bring to the boil, stirring frequently, then reduce the heat and simmer for 30 minutes. Season to taste with salt and pepper.

7 Process the soup in a food processor or blender. If necessary, strain it through a fine sieve to remove any coarse fibres. Stir in the asparagus tips, most of the cream or yogurt, and the herbs. Cool, then chill well. Stir thoroughly before serving and check the seasoning. Garnish with the remaining cream or yogurt.

1 Cut the top 6cm/2 1/2in off the asparagus spears. Blanch these tips in a small pan of boiling water for about 5–6 minutes, until they are just tender. Drain well. Cut each tip into two or three pieces, and set aside.

2 Trim the ends of the stalks, removing any brown or woody parts. Chop the asparagus stalks into 1cm/1/2in pieces.

COOK'S TIP
Chilled soups can require extra seasoning, so remember to check the taste just before you serve.

Chilled Tomato and Sweet Pepper Soup

This recipe was inspired by the Spanish gazpacho, the difference being that this soup is cooked first, and then chilled.

Serves 4

2 red (bell) peppers, halved and seeded
45ml/3 tbsp olive oil
1 onion, finely chopped
2 garlic cloves, crushed
675g/1 1/2 lb ripe well-flavoured tomatoes
150ml/1/4 pint/2/3 cup red wine
600ml/1 pint/2 1/2 cups chicken stock
salt and ground black pepper
chopped fresh chives, to garnish

For the croûtons
2 slices white bread, crusts removed
60ml/4 tbsp olive oil

1 Cut each red pepper half into quarters. Place skin side up on a grill (broiler) rack and cook until the skins are charred. Transfer to a bowl and cover with a plate or put into a plastic bag and seal.

2 Heat the oil in a large pan. Add the onion and garlic and cook over a low heat, stirring occasionally, for about 5 minutes, until soft. Meanwhile, remove the skin from the peppers and coarsely chop the flesh. Cut the tomatoes into chunks.

3 Add the peppers and tomatoes to the pan, then cover and cook gently for 10 minutes. Add the wine and cook for a further 5 minutes, then add the stock and season with salt and pepper to taste and continue to simmer for 20 minutes.

4 To make the croûtons, cut the bread into cubes. Heat the oil in a small frying pan, add the bread and cook, stirring and tossing frequently, until golden brown all over. Drain well on kitchen paper, leave to cool and then store in an airtight box until you are ready to serve.

5 Process the soup in a blender or food processor until smooth. Pour it into a clean glass or ceramic bowl, cover with clear film (plastic wrap) and leave to cool thoroughly before chilling in the refrigerator for at least 3 hours. When the soup is cold, taste and adjust the seasoning, if necessary.

6 Serve the soup in bowls, topped with the croûtons and garnished with chopped chives.

Gazpacho with **Avocado Salsa**

Tomatoes, cucumber and peppers form the basis of this classic, chilled soup. Add a spoonful of chunky, fresh avocado salsa and a sprinkling of croûtons for a delicious summer appetizer. This is quite a substantial soup, so follow with a light main course, such as grilled fish or chicken.

Serves 4–6

2 slices day-old bread
600ml/1 pint/2½ cups chilled water
1kg/2¼ lb tomatoes
1 cucumber
1 red (bell) pepper, seeded
* and chopped*
1 fresh green chilli, seeded
* and chopped*
2 garlic cloves, chopped
30ml/2 tbsp extra virgin olive oil
juice of 1 lime and 1 lemon
few drops Tabasco sauce
salt and ground black pepper
handful of fresh basil, to garnish
8–12 ice cubes, to serve

For the croûtons
2–3 slices day-old bread,
* crusts removed*
1 garlic clove, halved
15–30ml/1–2 tbsp olive oil

For the avocado salsa
1 ripe avocado
5ml/1 tsp lemon juice
2.5cm/1in piece cucumber, diced
½ fresh red chilli, finely chopped

1 Make the soup first. Place the bread in a shallow bowl, add 150ml/¼ pint/ ⅔ cup of the chilled water and leave to soak for 5 minutes.

COOK'S TIP
For a superior flavour, choose Haas avocados with the rough-textured, almost black skins.

2 Meanwhile, place the tomatoes in a heatproof bowl; cover with boiling water. Leave for 30 seconds, then peel, seed and chop the flesh.

3 Thinly peel the cucumber, cut in half lengthways and scoop out the seeds with a teaspoon. Discard the seeds and chop the flesh.

4 Place the soaked bread, tomatoes, cucumber, red pepper, chilli, garlic, oil, citrus juices, Tabasco and 450ml/ ¾ pint/scant 2 cups chilled water in a food processor or blender. Blend until mixed but still chunky. Season with salt and pepper and chill well.

5 To make the croûtons, rub the slices of bread with the cut surface of the garlic clove. Cut the bread into cubes and place in a plastic bag with the olive oil. Seal the bag and shake until the bread cubes are coated with the oil. Heat a large non-stick frying pan and cook the croûtons over a medium heat until crisp and golden. Remove from the pan and drain thoroughly on kitchen paper. Store in an airtight box until ready to serve.

6 Just before serving make the avocado salsa. Halve the avocado and twist it apart, remove the stone (pit) with the point of the knife, then peel and dice the flesh. Toss the avocado in the lemon juice to prevent it from turning brown, then mix with the cucumber and chilli.

7 Ladle the soup into individual bowls, add the ice cubes, and top each bowl with a spoonful of avocado salsa. Garnish with the basil and hand around the croûtons separately.

Cold Cucumber and Yogurt Soup

This refreshing cold soup uses the classic combination of cucumber and yogurt, with the added flavours of garlic and crunchy walnuts.

Serves 5–6

1 cucumber
4 garlic cloves
2.5ml/¹/₂ tsp salt
75g/3oz/³/₄ cup walnut pieces
40g/1¹/₂ oz day-old bread, torn into pieces
30ml/2 tbsp walnut or sunflower oil
400ml/14fl oz/1²/₃ cups sheep's or cow's yogurt
120ml/4fl oz/¹/₂ cup cold water or chilled still mineral water
5–10ml/1–2 tsp lemon juice
40g/1¹/₂oz/scant ¹/₂ cup walnuts, chopped, to garnish
olive oil, for drizzling
fresh dill sprigs, to garnish

1 Cut the cucumber into two and peel one half of it. Dice the cucumber flesh and set aside.

2 Using a large pestle and mortar, crush the garlic and salt together well, then add the walnuts and bread.

3 When the mixture is smooth, add the walnut or sunflower oil slowly and combine well.

4 Transfer the walnut and bread mixture to a large bowl, then beat in the cow's or sheep's yogurt and the diced cucumber.

5 Add the cold water or mineral water and lemon juice to taste. Chill until ready to serve.

6 Ladle the soup into chilled soup bowls to serve. Garnish with the chopped walnuts, drizzling a little olive oil over them, and with sprigs of dill.

COOK'S TIP
If you prefer your soup smooth, purée it in a food processor or blender before serving.

Chilled Prawn and Cucumber Soup

If you've never served a chilled soup before, this is the one to try first. Delicious and light, it's the perfect way to celebrate summer.

Serves 4

25g/1oz/2 tbsp butter
2 shallots, finely chopped
2 garlic cloves, crushed
1 cucumber, peeled, seeded and diced
300ml/½ pint/1¼ cups milk
225g/8oz cooked peeled prawns
    (shrimp)
15ml/1 tbsp each finely chopped fresh
    mint, dill, chives and chervil
300ml/½ pint/1¼ cups whipping cream
salt and ground white pepper

For the garnish
30ml/2 tbsp crème fraîche (optional)
4 large, cooked prawns (shrimp),
    peeled with tails intact
chopped fresh chives and dill

1 Melt the butter in a pan. Add the shallots and garlic and cook over a low heat, stirring occasionally, for about 4 minutes, until soft but not coloured. Add the cucumber and cook the vegetables gently, stirring frequently, until tender.

2 Stir in the milk, bring almost to the boil, then lower the heat and simmer for 5 minutes. Tip the soup into a blender or food processor and process until very smooth. Season to taste with salt and ground white pepper.

3 Pour the soup into a bowl and set aside to cool. When cool, stir in the prawns, chopped herbs and the whipping cream. Cover the bowl with clear film (plastic wrap) and chill in the refrigerator for at least 2 hours.

4 To serve, ladle the soup into four individual bowls and top each portion with a spoonful of crème fraîche, if using. Place a prawn over the edge of each bowl. Garnish the soup with the chives and dill.

VARIATIONS
• For a change try fresh or canned crab meat or cooked, flaked salmon fillet instead of the prawns.
• If crème fraîche is not available, use sour cream.
• Garnish the soup with a sprinkling of salmon or sea trout roe or, for a truly special occasion, a little caviar.

Hot-and-sour Soup

This light and invigorating soup is traditionally served at the start of a formal Thai meal.

Serves 4

2 carrots
900ml/1 1/2 pints/3 3/4 cups
 vegetable stock
2 Thai chillies, seeded and thinly sliced
2 lemon grass stalks, each cut into
 3 pieces
4 kaffir lime leaves
2 garlic cloves, finely chopped
4 spring onions (scallions), thinly sliced
5ml/1 tsp sugar
juice of 1 lime
45ml/3 tbsp chopped fresh
 coriander (cilantro)
salt
130g/4 1/2 oz/1 cup Japanese tofu,
 sliced

1 To make carrot flowers, cut each carrot in half crossways, then, using a sharp knife, cut four V-shaped channels lengthways. Slice the carrots into thin rounds and set aside.

COOK'S TIPS

• Kaffir lime leaves have a distinctive citrus flavour. The fresh leaves can be bought from Asian stores, and some supermarkets now sell them dried.
• Before using lemon grass stalks, remove and discard the tough outer layers.
• Thai chillies are notorious for their intense heat, so if you prefer a milder flavour, use only one.

2 Pour the vegetable stock into a large pan. Reserve 2.5ml/1/2 tsp of the chillies and add the rest to the pan with the lemon grass, lime leaves, garlic and half the spring onions. Bring to the boil, then reduce the heat and simmer for 20 minutes. Strain the stock and discard the flavourings.

3 Return the stock to the pan, add the reserved chillies and spring onions, the sugar, lime juice and coriander and season with salt to taste.

4 Simmer for 5 minutes, then add the carrot flowers and tofu slices, and cook the soup for a further 2 minutes, until the carrot is just tender. Ladle into warm bowls and serve hot.

Pear and Watercress Soup

The pears in the soup are complemented beautifully by Stilton croûtons.

Serves 6

1 bunch watercress
4 pears, sliced
900ml/1½ pints/3¾ cups
   chicken stock
120ml/4fl oz/½ cup double
   (heavy) cream
juice of 1 lime
salt and ground black pepper

For the croûtons
25g/1oz/2 tbsp butter
15ml/1 tbsp olive oil
200g/7oz/3 cups cubed stale bread
150g/5oz/1 cup chopped Stilton

1 Reserve about one-third of the watercress leaves. Place the rest of the leaves and stalks in a pan with the pear slices, stock and a little salt and pepper. Simmer gently for about 15–20 minutes. Set aside some of the reserved watercress leaves for garnishing, then add the rest of the leaves to the soup. Process in a blender or food processor until smooth.

2 Put the mixture into a bowl and stir in the cream and the lime juice to mix the flavours thoroughly. Season again to taste. Pour all the soup back into a pan and reheat, stirring gently until warmed through.

3 To make the croûtons, melt the butter and oil in a frying pan. Add the bread cubes and cook, stirring and tossing them frequently, until golden brown. Drain well on kitchen paper.

4 Spread them out on a baking sheet, sprinkle the cheese over them and heat under a hot grill (broiler) until bubbling. Reheat the soup and pour into bowls. Divide the croûtons and the reserved watercress leaves among them and serve immediately.

Baby Carrot and Fennel Soup

Sweet tender carrots find their moment of glory in this delicately spiced soup. Fennel provides a very subtle aniseed flavour.

Serves 4

50g/2oz/4 tbsp butter
1 small bunch spring onions
(scallions), chopped
150g/5oz fennel bulb, chopped
1 celery stick, chopped
450g/1lb new carrots, grated
2.5ml/½ tsp ground cumin
150g/5oz new potatoes, diced
1.2 litres/2 pints/5 cups chicken or
vegetable stock
60ml/4 tbsp double (heavy) cream
salt and ground black pepper
60ml/4 tbsp chopped fresh parsley,
to garnish

1 Melt the butter in a large pan and add the spring onions, fennel, celery, carrots and cumin. Cover and cook over a low heat for about 5 minutes, or until soft.

COOK'S TIP
For convenience, you can prepare the soup in advance and freeze, in portions if you like, before adding the cream, seasoning and parsley.

2 Add the diced potatoes and chicken or vegetable stock and increase the heat to medium. Bring to the boil, then lower the heat, re-cover the pan and simmer the mixture gently for a further 10 minutes.

3 Purée the soup in the pan with a hand-held blender. Stir in the cream and season to taste with salt and pepper. Ladle into individual soup bowls and garnish with chopped parsley. Serve immediately.

Broccoli Soup with **Garlic Toast**

This is an Italian recipe, originating from Rome. For the best flavour and brightest colour, use the freshest broccoli you can find.

Serves 6

675g/1½ lb broccoli spears
1.75 litres/3 pints/7½ cups chicken or
    vegetable stock
30ml/2 tbsp fresh lemon juice
salt and ground black pepper
freshly grated Parmesan cheese
    (optional), to serve

For the garlic toast
6 slices white bread
1 large garlic clove, halved

1 Using a small sharp knife, peel the broccoli stems, starting from the base of the stalks and pulling gently up towards the florets. (The peel comes off very easily.) Chop the broccoli into small chunks.

2 Bring the stock to the boil in a large pan over a medium heat. Add the chopped broccoli, lower the heat and simmer for 30 minutes, or until soft.

COOK'S TIP
As this is an Italian recipe, choose a really good-quality Parmesan cheese, if you are using it. The very best is Italy's own Parmigiano-Reggiano. Alternatively, as it is Roman, substitute Pecorino Romano, which is made from sheep's milk. Both should be freshly grated.

3 Remove the pan from the heat and leave the soup to cool slightly, then transfer about half of it to a blender or food processor. Process to a smooth purée. Return the puréed soup to the pan and mix it into the rest of the soup. Stir in lemon juice and season to taste with salt and pepper.

4 Just before serving, gently reheat the soup to just below boiling point. Toast the bread, rub with the cut surfaces of the garlic and cut into quarters. Place three or four pieces of toast in the base of each soup plate. Ladle on the soup. Serve immediately, with grated Parmesan cheese if you like.

Split Pea Soup

This tasty winter soup is a perfect for informal entertaining.

Serves 4–6

25g/1oz/2 tbsp butter
1 large onion, chopped
1 large celery stalk with leaves, chopped
2 carrots, chopped
1 smoked gammon (cured ham)
  knuckle, 450g/1lb
2 litres/3¹/₂ pints/8¹/₂ cups water
350g/12oz/1¹/₂ cups split peas
30ml/2 tbsp chopped fresh parsley,
  plus extra to garnish
2.5ml/¹/₂ tsp dried thyme
1 bay leaf
about 30ml/2 tbsp lemon juice
salt and ground black pepper

3 After 2 hours, once the split peas are very tender, remove the gammon knuckle from the soup. Leave it to cool slightly, then, with a sharp knife, remove the skin and cut the meat from the bones. Discard the skin and bones, then cut the meat into chunks as evenly sized as possible.

4 Return the chunks of gammon to the soup. Remove and discard the bay leaf. Taste and adjust the seasoning with more lemon juice, salt and pepper, if necessary.

5 Ladle the soup into warm bowls and serve, sprinkled with fresh parsley.

1 Melt the butter in a large, heavy pan. Add the onion, celery and carrots and cook over a medium heat, stirring occasionally, until softened.

2 Add all the rest of the ingredients to the pan. Bring to the boil, cover the pan, then lower the heat and simmer gently for 2 hours.

Corn Soup

This is a simple to make, yet very flavoursome soup. It is sometimes made with sour cream and cream cheese. Poblano chillies may be added, but these are rather difficult to locate outside Mexico. However, you may be able to find them in cans.

Serves 4

30ml/2 tbsp corn oil
1 onion, finely chopped
*1 red (bell) pepper, seeded
   and chopped*
*450g/1lb corn kernels, thawed
   if frozen*
750ml/1¼ pints/3 cups chicken stock
250ml/8fl oz/1 cup single (light) cream
salt and ground black pepper
*½ red (bell) pepper, seeded and finely
   diced, to garnish*

1 Heat the oil in a frying pan. Add the onion and red pepper and cook over a low heat, stirring occasionally, for about 5 minutes, until softened but not browned. Add the corn and cook for 2 minutes.

2 Carefully tip the contents of the pan into a food processor or blender. Process until the mixture is smooth, scraping down the sides and adding a little of the stock, if necessary.

3 Transfer the mixture to a clean pan and stir in the stock. Season to taste with salt and pepper, bring to a simmer and cook for 5 minutes.

4 Gently stir in the cream. Serve the soup hot or chilled, with the diced red pepper sprinkled over. If serving hot, reheat gently after adding the cream, but do not allow the soup to boil.

Courgette Soup

This soup is so simple – in terms of ingredients and preparation. It would provide an elegant start to a dinner party.

Serves 4

30ml/2 tbsp butter
1 onion, finely chopped
*450g/1lb young courgettes (zucchini),
   trimmed and chopped*
750ml/1¼ pints/3 cups chicken stock
*120ml/4fl oz/½ cup single (light)
   cream, plus extra to serve*
salt and ground black pepper

1 Melt the butter in a large, heavy pan. Add the onion and cook over a low heat, stirring occasionally, for about 5 minutes, until it is softened but not browned. Add the courgettes and cook, stirring occasionally, for about 1–2 minutes.

2 Add the chicken stock. Bring to the boil over a medium heat and then simmer for about 5 minutes, or until the courgettes are just tender.

COOK'S TIPS
• Always use the smallest courgettes (zucchini) available, as these have the best flavour.
• Be careful to prevent the soup from boiling once you have added the cream. Single (light) cream has a tendency to curdle if it is overheated.

3 Strain the stock into a clean pan, saving the vegetable solids in the sieve. Place the solids in a food processor and process until smooth, then add them to the pan. Season to taste with salt and pepper.

4 Stir the cream into the soup and heat through very gently without allowing it to come to the boil. Ladle into warm bowls and serve the soup immediately with a little extra cream swirled in to garnish.

Curried Parsnip Soup

The spices impart a delicious, mild curry flavour which carries an exotic hint of India.

Serves 4

30ml/2 tbsp butter
1 garlic clove, crushed
1 onion, chopped
5ml/1 tsp ground cumin
5ml/1 tsp ground coriander
4 parsnips, peeled and sliced
10ml/2 tsp medium curry paste
450ml/³/4 pint/scant 2 cups chicken stock
450ml/³/4 pint/scant 2 cups milk
60ml/4 tbsp sour cream
squeeze of lemon juice
salt and ground black pepper
fresh chives, to garnish
ready-made garlic and coriander naan
  bread, to serve

1 Melt the butter in a large, heavy pan until foaming. Add the garlic and onion and cook over a medium heat, stirring occasionally, for 4–5 minutes, until softened and lightly golden. Stir in the ground cumin and coriander and cook, stirring frequently, for a further 1–2 minutes.

2 Add the parsnip slices and stir until thoroughly coated with the butter, then stir in the curry paste, followed by the stock. Cover the pan, lower the heat and simmer for 15 minutes, until the parsnips are tender.

3 Remove the pan from the heat and leave the soup to cool slightly. Ladle the soup into a food processor or blender and then process until smooth, scraping down the sides if necessary.

4 Return the soup to the pan and stir in the milk. Heat very gently for about 2–3 minutes, then add half the sour cream and a generous squeeze of fresh lemon juice. Season to taste with salt and pepper.

5 Serve in warm bowls topped with swirls of the remaining sour cream and garnished the chopped fresh chives, accompanied by the naan bread.

Avocado Soup

To add a subtle garlic flavour, rub the cut side of a garlic clove around the soup bowls before adding the soup.

Serves 4

2 large ripe avocados
1 litre/1¾ pints/4 cups chicken stock
250ml/8fl oz/1 cup single (light) cream
salt and ground white pepper
15ml/1 tbsp finely chopped coriander
  (cilantro), to garnish (optional)

2 Heat the chicken stock with the cream in a pan. When the mixture is hot, but not boiling, whisk it into the puréed avocado.

3 Season to taste with salt and pepper. Serve immediately, sprinkled with the coriander, if using. Alternatively, leave the soup to cool, then cover and chill in the refrigerator before serving.

1 Cut the avocados in half, twist to separate, then remove the stones (pits) with the point of the knife. Mash the flesh (see Cook's Tips). Put the flesh into a sieve and press it through with the back of a wooden spoon into a warmed bowl.

COOK'S TIPS
• The easiest way to mash the avocados is to hold each seeded half in turn in the palm of one hand and mash the flesh in the shell with a fork, before scooping it into the bowl. This prevents the avocado flesh from slithering about when it is being mashed.
• Avocados are harvested when the fruit is mature but before it is ripe. You cannot tell if an avocado has ripened by looking at it because of the variation in colour, although black spots on the skin are some indication. Cradle the fruit gently in your hand. If it yields to gentle pressure, then it is fully ripened. However, do not squeeze it, as this will bruise the delicate flesh.

Tomato and **Blue Cheese Soup** with **Bacon**

As blue cheese is rather salty, it is important to use unsalted stock for this flavoursome soup.

Serves 4

1.3kg/3lb ripe tomatoes, peeled,
    quartered and seeded
2 garlic cloves, crushed
30ml/2 tbsp vegetable oil or butter
1 leek, chopped
1 carrot, chopped
1 litre/1¾ pints/4 cups unsalted
    chicken stock
115g/4oz Danish blue cheese, crumbled
45ml/3 tbsp whipping cream
several large fresh basil leaves, or
    1–2 fresh parsley sprigs
salt and ground black pepper
175g/6oz bacon, cooked and
    crumbled, to garnish

1 Preheat the oven to 200°C/400°F/ Gas 6. Spread out the tomato quarters in an ovenproof dish. Sprinkle with the garlic and some salt and ground black pepper. Place in the oven and bake for 35 minutes.

2 Heat the oil or butter in a large pan. Add the leek and carrot and season lightly with salt and pepper. Cook over a low heat, stirring frequently, for about 10 minutes, or until softened.

COOK'S TIP

Don't be tempted to use unripe tomatoes for this soup, as their lack of sweetness and flavour will spoil it.

3 Stir in the chicken stock and baked tomatoes. Bring to the boil, lower the heat, cover and simmer for 20 minutes.

VARIATION

Danish blue cheese, also known as Danablu, has a very sharp, almost metallic taste, which some people dislike intensely, while others love it. If you prefer, you could use a milder blue cheese, such as Dolcelatte or Bleu de Causses.

4 Add the blue cheese, cream and basil or parsley. Remove from the heat and leave to cool slightly, then transfer the soup to a food processor or blender and process until smooth, working in batches if necessary. Taste and adjust the seasoning, if you like.

5 If necessary, reheat the soup, but do not let it boil. Ladle into warmed bowls and sprinkle the crumbled bacon over.

Fresh Tomato Soup

Intensely flavoured sun-ripened tomatoes need little embellishment in this fresh-tasting soup. If you buy from the supermarket, choose the juiciest looking ones and add the amount of sugar and vinegar necessary, depending on their natural sweetness.

Serves 6

1.3–1.6kg/3–3¹/₂ lb ripe tomatoes
400ml/14fl oz/1²/₃ cups chicken or
   vegetable stock
45ml/3 tbsp sun-dried tomato paste
30–45ml/2–3 tbsp balsamic vinegar
10–15ml/2–3 tsp caster
   (superfine) sugar
small handful of basil leaves
salt and ground black pepper
basil leaves, to garnish
toasted cheese croûtes and crème
   fraîche, to serve

1 Plunge the tomatoes into boiling water for 30 seconds, then refresh in cold water. Peel off the skins and quarter the tomatoes. Put them in a large, heavy pan and pour over the chicken or vegetable stock. Bring just to the boil, reduce the heat, cover and simmer the mixture gently for about 10 minutes, until the tomatoes are thickened and pulpy.

COOK'S TIP

This Italian soup may be left to cool and then chilled in the refrigerator before serving in a hot day.

2 Stir in the tomato paste, vinegar, sugar and basil. Season with salt and pepper, then cook gently, stirring, for 2 minutes. Process the soup in a blender or food processor, then return to the pan and reheat gently.

3 Serve in bowls topped with one or two toasted cheese croûtes and a spoonful of crème fraîche, garnished with basil leaves.

French Onion and Morel Soup

French onion soup is appreciated for its light beefy taste. There are few improvements to be made to this classic soup, but a few richly scented morel mushrooms will impart a worthwhile flavour.

Serves 4

50g/2oz/4 tbsp unsalted (sweet)
*   butter, plus extra for spreading*
15ml/1 tbsp vegetable oil
3 onions, sliced
900ml/1¹⁄₂ pints/3³⁄₄ cups beef stock
75ml/5 tbsp Madeira or sherry
8 dried morel mushrooms
4 slices French bread
75g/3oz Gruyère, Beaufort or Fontina
*   cheese, grated*
30ml/2 tbsp chopped fresh parsley

1 Melt the butter with the oil in a large frying pan, then add the sliced onions and cook over a low heat for 10–15 minutes, until the onions are a rich mahogany brown colour.

2 Transfer the browned onions to a large pan, pour in the beef stock, add the Madeira or sherry and the dried morels, then simmer for 20 minutes.

3 Preheat the grill (broiler) to medium and toast the French bread on both sides. Spread one side with butter and heap with the grated cheese.

4 Ladle the soup into four flameproof bowls, float the cheese-topped toasts on top and grill (broil) until they are crisp and brown and the cheese is bubbling. Alternatively, grill the cheese-topped toast, then place one slice in each warmed soup bowl before ladling the hot soup over it. The toast will float to the surface. Sprinkle over the chopped fresh parsley and serve.

COOK'S TIP
The flavour and richness of this soup will improve with keeping. Store in the refrigerator for up to 5 days.

Spanish Garlic Soup

This is a simple and satisfying soup, made with one of the most popular ingredients in the Mediterranean region – garlic.

Serves 4

30ml/2 tbsp olive oil
4 large garlic cloves, peeled
4 slices French bread, 5mm/¹⁄₄ in thick
15ml/1 tbsp paprika
1 litre/1³⁄₄ pints/4 cups beef stock
1.5ml/¹⁄₄ tsp ground cumin
pinch of saffron threads
4 eggs
salt and ground black pepper
chopped fresh parsley, to garnish

1 Preheat the oven to 230°C/450°F/ Gas 8. Heat the oil in a large pan. Add the whole garlic cloves and cook over a low heat until golden. Remove with a slotted spoon and set aside.

2 Add the bread to the pan and cook on both sides until golden. Remove from the pan and set aside.

COOK'S TIP
Use home-made beef stock for the best flavour or buy prepared stock from your supermarket – you'll find it in the chilled counter. Never use stock (bouillon) cubes as most of them contain too much salt.

3 Add the paprika to the pan and cook for a few seconds, stirring constantly. Stir in the beef stock, cumin and saffron, then add the reserved fried garlic, crushing the cloves with the back of a wooden spoon. Season with salt and ground black pepper to taste then cook over a low heat for about 5 minutes.

4 Ladle the soup into four individual ovenproof bowls and gently break an egg into each one. Place the slices of fried French bread on top of the eggs and place the bowls in the oven for about 3–4 minutes, or until the eggs are just set. Sprinkle with chopped fresh parsley to garnish and serve the soup immediately.

Tortellini Chanterelle Broth

The savoury-sweet quality of chanterelle mushrooms combines well in a simple broth with spinach-and-ricotta-filled tortellini. The addition of a little sherry creates a lovely warming effect.

Serves 4

1.2 litres/2 pints/5 cups chicken stock
75ml/5 tbsp dry sherry
175g/6oz fresh chanterelle
  mushrooms, trimmed and sliced, or
  15g/¹/₂ oz/¹/₂ cup dried chanterelles
350g/12oz fresh spinach and ricotta
  tortellini, or 175g/6oz dried
chopped fresh parsley, to garnish

1 Bring the chicken stock to the boil, add the dry sherry and fresh or dried mushrooms and simmer over a low heat for 10 minutes.

2 Cook the tortellini according to the packet instructions.

3 Drain the tortellini, add to the stock and mushroom mixture, then ladle the broth into four warmed soup bowls, making sure each contains the about same proportions of tortellini and mushrooms. Garnish with the chopped parsley and serve immediately.

Cream of **Mushroom Soup** with **Goat's Cheese Crostini**

Classic cream of mushroom soup is still a firm favourite, especially with the addition of crisp and garlicky croûtes with tangy goat's cheese.

Serves 6

25g/1oz/2 tbsp butter
1 onion, chopped
1 garlic clove, chopped
450g/1lb/6 cups chestnut or brown cap (cremini) mushrooms, some whole, some coarsely chopped
15ml/1 tbsp plain (all-purpose) flour
45ml/3 tbsp dry sherry
900ml/1½ pints/3¾ cups vegetable stock
150ml/¼ pint/⅔ cup double (heavy) cream
salt and ground black pepper
fresh chervil sprigs, to garnish

For the crostini
15ml/1 tbsp olive oil, plus extra for brushing
1 shallot, chopped
115g/4oz/2 cups button (white) mushrooms, finely chopped
15ml/1 tbsp chopped fresh parsley
6 brown cap (cremini) mushrooms
6 slices baguette
1 small garlic clove
115g/4oz/1 cup soft goat's cheese

1 Melt the butter. Cook the onion and garlic for 5 minutes. Add the mushrooms, cover, cook for 10 minutes.

2 Add the flour and cook, stirring, for 1 minute. Stir in the dry sherry and stock and bring to the boil, then simmer for 15 minutes. Cool slightly, then process the mixture in a food processor or blender until smooth.

3 Meanwhile, prepare the crostini. Heat the oil in a small pan. Add the shallot and button mushrooms, and cook for 8–10 minutes, until softened. Drain well and transfer to a food processor or blender. Add the fresh parsley and process the mushroom mixture until finely chopped.

4 Preheat the grill (broiler). Brush the brown cap mushrooms with oil and grill (broil) for 5–6 minutes.

5 Toast the slices of baguette, rub with the garlic and put a spoonful of cheese on each. Top the grilled mushrooms with the mushroom mixture and place on the crostini.

6 Return the soup to the pan and stir in the cream. Season, then reheat gently. Ladle the soup into six bowls. Float a crostini in the centre of each and garnish with chervil.

Spinach and Rice Soup

Use very fresh, young spinach leaves in the preparation of this light and fresh-tasting soup.

Serves 4

675g/1¹/₂ lb fresh spinach, washed
45ml/3 tbsp extra virgin olive oil
1 small onion, finely chopped
2 garlic cloves, finely chopped
1 small fresh red chilli, seeded and
*   finely chopped*
115g/4oz/generous 1 cup risotto rice
1.2 litres/2 pints/5 cups
*   vegetable stock*
salt and ground black pepper
60ml/4 tbsp grated Pecorino cheese

1 Place the spinach in a large pan with just the water that clings to its leaves after washing. Add a large pinch of salt. Heat gently until the spinach has wilted, then remove from the heat and drain, reserving any liquid.

2 Either chop the spinach finely using a large knife or place it in a food processor and process briefly to a fairly coarse purée.

COOK'S TIP

Pecorino, made from sheep's milk, has a slightly sharper taste than its cow's-milk counterpart, Parmesan. However, if you cannot find it, use Parmesan instead.

VARIATION

Substitute young Swiss chard leaves or sorrel for the spinach if you like.

3 Heat the oil in a large pan. Add the onion, garlic and chilli and cook over a low heat, stirring occasionally, for 4–5 minutes, until softened. Stir in the rice until well coated, then pour in the stock and reserved spinach liquid. Bring to the boil, lower the heat and simmer for 10 minutes. Add the spinach, with salt and ground black pepper to taste. Cook for a further 5–7 minutes, until the rice is tender. Check the seasoning and adjust if necessary. Serve immediately with the Pecorino cheese.

Vermicelli Soup

The inclusion of fresh coriander adds a piquancy to this soup and complements the tomato flavour.

Serves 4

30ml/2 tbsp olive or corn oil
50g/2oz vermicelli
1 onion, coarsely chopped
1 garlic clove, chopped
450g/1lb tomatoes, peeled, seeded
  and coarsely chopped
1 litre/1³/4 pints/4 cups chicken stock
1.5ml/¹/4 tsp sugar
15ml/1 tbsp finely chopped fresh
  coriander (cilantro), plus extra
  to garnish
salt and ground black pepper
25g/1oz/¹/4 cup freshly grated
  Parmesan cheese, to serve

1 Heat the oil in a large, heavy frying pan. Add the vermicelli and cook over a medium heat until golden brown. Take care not to let the strands burn. Remove the vermicelli with a slotted spoon or tongs and drain well on kitchen paper.

2 Place the onion, garlic and tomatoes in a food processor or blender and process until smooth. Return the frying pan to the heat. When the oil is hot again, add the vegetable purée to the pan. Cook, stirring constantly to prevent sticking, for about 5 minutes, or until thick.

3 Transfer the purée to a pan. Add the vermicelli and pour in the stock. Stir in the sugar and season to taste with salt and pepper. Stir in the coriander, bring to the boil, then lower the heat, cover the pan and simmer the soup gently, until the vermicelli is tender.

4 Ladle the soup into warmed bowls, sprinkle with chopped fresh coriander and serve immediately. Offer the grated Parmesan cheese separately.

COOK'S TIP
Vermicelli will burn very easily, so move it about constantly in the frying pan with a wooden spoon and remove it from the heat the moment it has turned a golden brown colour.

Spinach and Tofu Soup

This soup is really delicious. If fresh spinach is not in season, watercress or lettuce can be used instead.

Serves 4

1 cake tofu, 7.5cm/3in sq. and
  2.5cm/1in thick
115g/4oz spinach leaves
750ml/1¼ pints/3 cups
  vegetable stock
15ml/1 tbsp light soy sauce
salt and ground black pepper

1 Rinse the tofu then cut into 12 small pieces, each about 5mm/¼in thick. Wash the spinach leaves and cut them into small pieces.

2 Pour the vegetable stock into a wok or large, heavy pan and bring to a rolling boil over a medium heat. Add the pieces of tofu and the soy sauce, stir carefully without breaking up the tofu, bring back to the boil, then lower the heat and simmer gently for about 2 minutes.

3 Add the pieces of spinach, and simmer for a further 1–2 minutes. Skim the surface of the soup to remove any foam and to make it clear, then season with salt and ground black pepper to taste. Ladle the soup into warm bowls or a tureen and serve immediately.

Fish Soup with Rouille

Making this soup is simplicity itself, yet the flavour suggests it is the product of painstaking preparation and complicated cooking. Rouille, a spicy Provençal paste, makes a colourful addition.

Serves 6

1kg/2¼lb mixed fish, skinned
30ml/2 tbsp olive oil
1 onion, chopped
1 carrot, chopped
1 leek, chopped
2 large ripe tomatoes, chopped
1 red (bell) pepper, seeded
 and chopped
2 garlic cloves, peeled
150g/5oz/²/₃ cup tomato purée (paste)
1 large fresh bouquet garni,
 containing 3 parsley sprigs, 3 small
 celery sticks and 3 bay leaves
300ml/½ pint/1¼ cups dry white wine
salt and ground black pepper

For the rouille

2 garlic cloves, coarsely chopped
5ml/1 tsp coarse salt
1 thick slice of white bread, crust
 removed, soaked in water and then
 squeezed dry
1 fresh red chilli, seeded and
 coarsely chopped
45ml/3 tbsp olive oil
salt
pinch of cayenne pepper (optional)

For the garnish

12 slices of baguette, toasted in
 the oven
50g/2oz/½ cup finely grated
 Gruyère cheese

COOK'S TIP

Any firm fish, such as monkfish, sea bass or snapper, can be used for this recipe, but avoid oily types. If you use whole fish, include the heads, which enhance the flavour of the soup.

1 Cut the fish into 7.5cm/3in chunks, removing any obvious bones. Heat the olive oil in a large, heavy pan, then add the chunks of fish, onion, carrot, leek, tomatoes, red pepper and garlic. Stir gently over a medium heat until the vegetables begin to colour.

2 Add the tomato purée, bouquet garni and white wine, then pour in just enough cold water to cover the mixture. Season well with salt and pepper and bring to just below boiling point, then lower the heat so that the soup is barely simmering, cover and cook for 1 hour.

3 Meanwhile, make the rouille. Put the garlic and coarse salt in a mortar and crush to a paste with a pestle. Add the soaked bread and chilli and pound until smooth, or process in a food processor to a purée.

4 Whisk in the olive oil, a drop at a time to begin with, to make a smooth, shiny sauce that resembles mayonnaise in consistency. Season to taste with salt and add a pinch of cayenne if you like. Set aside.

5 Lift out and discard the bouquet garni. Process the soup, in batches, in a food processor, then strain through a fine sieve into a clean pan, pushing the solids through with a ladle.

6 Reheat the soup but do not allow it to boil. Taste and adjust the seasoning, if necessary, and ladle into individual bowls. Top each with two slices of toasted baguette, a spoonful of rouille and some grated Gruyère.

Salmon Chowder

This salmon version of a traditional fish chowder is quite exquisite.

Serves 4–6

20g/³⁄₄oz/1¹⁄₂ tbsp butter or margarine
1 onion, minced (ground)
1 leek, minced (ground)
50g/2oz/¹⁄₂ cup minced (ground)
   bulb fennel
60ml/4 tbsp plain (all-purpose) flour
1.5 litres/2¹⁄₂ pints 6¹⁄₄ cups fish stock
225g/8oz potatoes, cut into 1cm/¹⁄₂in
   cubes (about 2 medium-size potatoes)
salt and ground black pepper
450g/1lb boneless, skinless salmon,
   cut into 2cm/³⁄₄in cubes
175ml/6fl oz/³⁄₄ cup milk
120ml/4fl oz/¹⁄₂ cup whipping cream
30ml/2 tbsp chopped fresh dill

1 Melt the butter or margarine in a large, heavy pan. Add the onion, leek and fennel and cook over a medium heat, stirring occasionally, for about 5–8 minutes, until all the vegetables are softened.

2 Stir in the flour. Reduce the heat to low and cook, stirring constantly to prevent any lumps forming, for 3 minutes.

3 Gradually stir in the stock and add potatoes. Season to taste with salt and ground black pepper. Bring to the boil, then reduce the heat, cover and simmer for about 20 minutes, until the potatoes are tender.

4 Add the cubed salmon and then simmer for about 3–5 minutes, until just cooked through and tender. The salmon cubes should remain intact, not fall apart.

5 Stir in the milk, cream and dill. Cook until just warmed through, but do not allow the soup to boil. Taste and adjust the seasoning, if necessary, then ladle into warm bowls and serve.

Cappuccino of **Puy Lentils, Lobster** and **Tarragon**

Here is a really impressive soup to start a dinner party with. Adding ice-cold butter a little at a time is the secret of whipping up the good froth that gives the soup its clever cappuccino effect.

Serves 6

450–675g/1–1½lb live lobster
150g/5oz/⅔ cup Puy lentils
1 carrot, halved
1 celery stick, halved
1 small onion, halved
1 garlic clove
1 bay leaf
large bunch of tarragon, tied firmly
1 litre/1¾ pints/4 cups fish stock
120ml/4fl oz/½ cup double
  (heavy) cream
25g/1oz/2 tbsp butter, finely diced and
  chilled until ice cold
salt and ground black pepper
fresh tarragon sprigs,
  to garnish

1 Bring a large stockpot of water to the boil. Lower the live lobster into the water and cover the pan. Cook for 15–20 minutes, then drain the lobster and leave to cool.

2 Put the Puy lentils in a large pan and pour in enough cold water to cover. Add the carrot, celery, onion, garlic and herbs. Bring the water to the boil and simmer for 20 minutes.

3 Drain the lentils and discard the herbs and vegetables. Process the lentils in a food processor until smooth. Set aside.

4 Break the claws off the lobster, crack them open and remove all the meat from inside. Break off the tail, split it open and remove the meat. Cut all the meat into bitesize pieces.

5 Pour the fish stock into a large clean pan and bring to the boil. Lightly stir in the lentil purée and cream, but do not mix too much at this point otherwise you will not be able to create the frothy effect. The mixture should still be quite watery in places. Season well.

6 Using either a hand-held blender or electric beater, whisk the soup mixture, adding the butter, one piece at a time, until it is very frothy.

7 Divide the lobster meat among the bowls and carefully pour in the soup. Garnish with sprigs of tarragon and serve immediately.

COOK'S TIP

Instead of adding the live lobster to the pan, kill it first by freezing it overnight. Cook from frozen, allowing 30 minutes in the boiling water. The other way of killing lobster is by stabbing it in the back of the head, where the tail shell meets the head.

dinner party appetizers

These tempting first courses are all visually appealing and perfect for setting the right tone at the beginning of a special meal.

Pears and Stilton

This is a traditional English dish and a marriage made in heaven. The flavours and textures of pears and cheese are simply superb together.

Serves 4

4 ripe pears, lightly chilled
75g/3oz blue Stilton
50g/2oz curd (farmer's) cheese
ground black pepper
watercress sprigs, to garnish

For the dressing
45ml/3 tbsp light olive oil
15ml/1 tbsp lemon juice
10ml/2 tsp toasted poppy seeds
salt and ground black pepper

2 Cut the pears in half lengthways, then scoop out the cores and cut away the calyx from the rounded end.

3 Place the Stilton and curd cheese in a bowl and beat together, then season with a little pepper and beat lightly again. Divide this mixture among the cavities in the pears.

4 Shake the dressing to mix it again, then spoon it over the pears. Serve garnished with some watercress sprigs.

VARIATION

Stilton is the classic British blue cheese, but you could use Blue Cheshire or even a non-British cheese, such as Gorgonzola or Roquefort, if you like.

1 First make the dressing, place the olive oil and lemon juice, poppy seeds and seasoning to taste in a screw-top jar and then shake together vigorously until emulsified.

COOK'S TIPS

• Comice pears are a good choice for this dish, being very juicy and aromatic. For a dramatic colour contrast, select the excellent sweet and juicy Red Williams or Red Bartletts.

• You can mix the cheese filling in advance and store, covered with clear film (plastic wrap) in the refrigerator. Similarly, mix the dressing ahead of time, but bring it to room temperature to serve. However, don't halve the pears until just before serving or the flesh will discolour, becoming an unappetizing brown.

Asparagus with **Raspberry Dressing**

Asparagus and raspberries complement each other. The sauce gives this appetizer a real zing.

Serves 4

675g/1¹/₂lb thin asparagus spears
30ml/2 tbsp raspberry vinegar
2.5ml/¹/₂ tsp salt
5ml/1 tsp Dijon mustard
25ml/1¹/₂ tbsp sunflower oil
30ml/2 tbsp sour cream or
    natural (plain) yogurt
ground white pepper
175g/6oz/1 cup fresh raspberries

1 Fill a large wide frying pan or wok with water 10cm/4in deep and bring to the boil.

4 Using a fish slice or metal spatula, carefully remove the asparagus bundles from the frying pan or wok and immerse them in cold water to stop any further cooking. Drain, then untie the bundles. Pat the spears dry with kitchen paper. Chill the asparagus in the refrigerator for at least 1 hour.

5 Put the vinegar and salt into a bowl and stir with a fork until the salt has dissolved. Stir in the Dijon mustard. Gradually stir in the oil until it is blended. Add the sour cream or yogurt and season with pepper to taste.

6 To serve, arrange the asparagus on individual plates, dividing the spears equally, and drizzle the dressing across the middle of them. Garnish with the fresh raspberries.

COOK'S TIP
Adding Dijon or other mustard to salad dressings not only provides flavour, but also helps the oil and vinegar mixture to combine and emulsify.

2 Trim off the tough ends of the asparagus spears. If you like, remove the "scales" on the stems, using a vegetable peeler.

3 Tie the asparagus spears into two bundles. Lower the bundles into the boiling water and cook for about 2 minutes, until just tender.

Tomato and Courgette Timbales

Timbales are baked savoury custards typical of the south of France, and mainly made with light vegetables. This combination is delicious as an appetizer. It can be served warm or cool.

Serves 4

butter, for greasing
2 courgettes (zucchini), about
  175g/6oz
2 firm, ripe vine tomatoes, sliced
2 eggs plus 2 egg yolks
45ml/3 tbsp double (heavy) cream
15ml/1 tbsp fresh tomato sauce or
  passata (bottled strained tomatoes)
10ml/2 tsp chopped fresh basil or
  oregano or 5ml/1 tsp dried oregano
salt and ground black pepper
salad leaves, to serve

1 Preheat the oven to 180°C/350°F/ Gas 4. Lightly butter four large ramekins. Trim the courgettes, then cut them into thin slices. Put them into a steamer and steam over boiling water for 4–5 minutes.

2 Drain the courgette slices well in a colander, then layer them in the prepared ramekins alternating with the sliced tomatoes.

3 Whisk together the eggs, cream, tomato sauce or passata and basil or oregano in a bowl. Season to taste with salt and pepper.

4 Pour the egg mixture into the ramekins. Place them in a roasting pan and half fill the pan with hot water. Bake the ramekins for 20–30 minutes, until the custard is just firm.

5 Cool slightly, then run a knife blade around the rims of the ramekins and carefully turn out on to small plates. Serve with salad leaves.

COOK'S TIP
Don't overcook the timbales or the texture of the savoury custard will become rubbery.

Lemon, Thyme and Bean Stuffed Mushrooms

Portabello mushrooms have a rich flavour and a meaty texture that go well with this fragrant herb-and-lemon stuffing. The garlicky pine nut accompaniment is a traditional Middle Eastern dish with a smooth, creamy consistency similar to that of hummus.

Serves 4–6

200g/7oz/1 cup dried or 400g/14oz/
   2 cups drained, canned aduki beans
45ml/3 tbsp olive oil, plus extra
   for brushing
1 onion, finely chopped
2 garlic cloves, crushed
30ml/2 tbsp fresh chopped thyme or
   5ml/1 tsp dried
8 large field mushrooms, such as
   portabello mushrooms, stalks
   finely chopped
50g/2oz/1 cup fresh wholemeal
   (whole-wheat) breadcrumbs
juice of 1 lemon
185g/6^{1}/2 oz/^{3}/4 cup crumbled
   goat's cheese
salt and ground black pepper

For the pine nut sauce
50g/2oz/^{1}/2 cup pine nuts, toasted
50g/2oz/1 cup cubed white bread
2 garlic cloves, chopped
200ml/7fl oz/scant 1 cup milk
45ml/3 tbsp olive oil
15ml/1 tbsp chopped fresh parsley, to
   garnish (optional)

1 If using dried beans, place them in a bowl, add cold water to cover and leave to soak overnight, then drain and rinse well. Place the beans in a pan, add enough water to cover and bring to the boil. Boil vigorously for 10 minutes, then reduce the heat, cook for about 30 minutes, until tender, then drain. If using canned beans, rinse under cold running water, drain well, then set aside.

2 Preheat the oven to 200°C/400°F/ Gas 6. Heat the oil in a large, heavy frying pan. Add the onion and garlic and cook, stirring occasionally, for about 5 minutes, until softened. Add the thyme and the mushroom stalks and cook for a further 3 minutes, stirring occasionally, until tender.

3 Stir in the beans, breadcrumbs and lemon juice, season well with salt and pepper, then cook for 2 minutes, until heated through. Mash two-thirds of the beans with a fork or potato masher, leaving the remaining beans whole.

4 Brush an ovenproof dish and the base and sides of the mushrooms with olive oil, then top each one with a spoonful of the bean mixture. Place the mushrooms in the dish, cover with foil and bake for 20 minutes.

5 Remove the foil. Top each mushroom with some of the goat's cheese and bake for a further 15 minutes, or until the goat's cheese is melted and bubbly and the mushrooms are tender.

6 To make the pine nut sauce, place all the ingredients in a food processor or blender and process or blend until smooth and creamy. Add more milk if the mixture appears too thick. Sprinkle with parsley, if using, and serve with the stuffed mushrooms.

Hard-boiled Eggs with Tuna Sauce

The combination of eggs and tasty tuna mayonnaise makes a nourishing first course that is quick and easy to prepare.

Serves 6

6 large (US extra large) eggs
200g/7oz can tuna in olive oil
3 anchovy fillets
15ml/1 tbsp capers, drained
lemon juice
30ml/2 tbsp olive oil
salt and ground black pepper
drained capers and anchovy fillets, to
garnish (optional)

For the mayonnaise

1 egg yolk, at room temperature
5ml/1 tsp Dijon mustard
5ml/1 tsp white wine vinegar or
lemon juice
150ml/¼ pint/⅔ cup olive oil

1 Cook the eggs in a pan of boiling water for 12–14 minutes. Drain and rinse under cold water. Shell carefully and set aside.

2 Make the mayonnaise by whisking the egg yolk, Dijon mustard and white wine vinegar or lemon juice together in a small bowl. Whisk in the olive oil, a few drops at a time to begin with, until 45–60ml/3–4 tbsp of the oil have been incorporated. Pour in the remaining oil in a slow, steady stream, whisking constantly until thickened and fully incorporated.

3 Place the tuna with its oil, the anchovies, capers, lemon juice and olive oil in a blender or a food processor. Process until smooth.

4 Fold the tuna and anchovy mixture into the mayonnaise. Season with black pepper, and extra salt if necessary. Chill for at least 1 hour.

5 To serve, cut the eggs in half lengthways. Arrange them on a serving platter. Spoon over the sauce, and garnish with capers and anchovy fillets, if using. Serve the eggs chilled.

COOK'S TIP
If hard-boiled eggs are left to cool in their shells, the yolks will discolour.

Salmon Cakes with Butter Sauce

Salmon fish cakes make a real treat for the start of a dinner party. They are also economical as you could use any small tail pieces which are on special offer from your local fish store or supermarket.

Makes 6

225g/8oz salmon tail piece, cooked
30ml/2 tbsp chopped fresh parsley
2 spring onions (scallions), chopped
grated rind and juice of 1/2 lemon
225g/8oz mashed potato (not too soft)
1 egg
50g/2oz/1 cup fresh white breadcrumbs
75g/3oz/6 tbsp butter, plus extra for
*   frying (optional)*
oil, for frying (optional)
salt and ground black pepper
courgette (zucchini) and carrot slices
*   and coriander (cilantro), to garnish*

1 Remove and discard all the skin and bones from the fish and mash or flake the flesh well.

2 Place the fish in a bowl and add the fresh parsley, onions and 5ml/1 tsp of the lemon rind, then season with salt and plenty of black pepper.

3 Gently work in the mashed potato and then, with lightly dampened hands, shape the mixture into six rounds, triangles or croquettes. Place the salmon cakes on a platter and chill them in the refrigerator for 20 minutes to firm up.

4 Preheat the grill (broiler). Beat the egg in a shallow dish and spread out the breadcrumbs. When chilled, coat the salmon cakes well in egg and then in the breadcrumbs. Grill (broil) gently for 5 minutes on each side, or until golden, or fry in butter and oil.

5 To make the butter sauce, melt the butter, whisk in the remaining lemon rind, the lemon juice, 15–30ml/ 1–2 tbsp water and season to taste with salt and pepper. Simmer for a few minutes, whisking, and serve with the hot fish cakes, garnished with slices of courgette and carrot and a sprig of fresh coriander.

Prawn, Egg and Avocado Mousses

A light and creamy mousse with lots of chunky texture and a great mix of flavours.

Serves 6

a little olive oil
juice and rind of 1 lemon
1 sachet gelatine
60ml/4 tbsp good-quality mayonnaise
60ml/4 tbsp chopped fresh dill
5ml/1 tsp anchovy essence (extract)
5ml/1 tsp Worcestershire sauce
1 large avocado, ripe but just firm
4 hard-boiled eggs, shelled
   and chopped
175g/6oz/1 cup cooked peeled prawns
   (shrimp), coarsely chopped if large
250ml/8fl oz/1 cup double (heavy) or
   whipping cream, lightly whipped
2 egg whites, whisked
salt and ground black pepper
fresh dill or parsley sprigs, to garnish
warm bread or toast, to serve

1 Prepare six small ramekins. Lightly grease the dishes with olive oil, then wrap a greaseproof (wax) paper collar around the top of each and secure with tape. This makes sure that you can fill the dishes as high as you like, and the extra mixture will be supported while it is setting. The mousses will look really dramatic when you remove the paper. Alternatively, prepare just one medium soufflé dish.

2 Put the lemon juice into a small, heatproof bowl, stir in 15ml/1 tbsp hot water and sprinkle over the gelatine. Leave for 5 minutes, until spongy, then set the bowl over hot water, until clear, stirring occasionally. Leave to cool slightly, then blend in the lemon rind, mayonnaise, dill, anchovy essence and Worcestershire sauce.

3 Cut the avocado in half, twist to separate and remove the stone (pit) with the point of the knife. In a medium bowl mash the avocado flesh, then mix in the eggs and prawns. Stir in the gelatine mixture and then fold in the cream and egg whites. Season to taste with salt and pepper. When evenly blended, spoon into the ramekins or soufflé dish and chill for 3–4 hours.

4 Garnish with the dill or parsley and serve the mousse with bread or toast.

COOK'S TIP
Other fish can make a good alternative to prawns (shrimp). Try substituting the same quantity of smoked trout or salmon, or cooked crab meat.

Sea Trout Mousse

This deliciously creamy mousse makes a little sea trout go a long way. It is equally good made with salmon if sea trout is unavailable. Serve with crisp Melba toast or triangles of lightly toasted pitta bread.

Serves 6

250g/9oz sea trout fillet
120ml/4fl oz/¹/₂ cup fish stock
2 gelatine leaves, or 15ml/1 tbsp
   powdered gelatine
juice of ¹/₂ lemon
30ml/2 tbsp dry sherry or dry vermouth
30ml/2 tbsp freshly grated Parmesan
300ml/¹/₂ pint/1 ¹/₄ cups whipping cream
2 egg whites
15ml/1 tbsp sunflower oil, for greasing
salt and ground white pepper

For the garnish
5cm/2in piece cucumber, with peel,
   thinly sliced and halved
fresh dill or chervil

1 Put the sea trout in a large, shallow pan. Pour in the fish stock and heat gently to simmering point. Poach the fish for about 3–4 minutes, until it is lightly cooked. Carefully strain the stock into a jug (pitcher) and leave the sea trout to cool slightly.

2 Add the gelatine to the reserved hot stock and stir well until it has dissolved completely. Cover and set aside until required.

3 When the sea trout is cool enough to handle, remove and discard the skin and any stray bones, then flake the flesh. Pour the stock into a food processor or blender. Process briefly, then gradually add the flaked sea trout, lemon juice, sherry or vermouth and Parmesan through the feeder tube, continuing to process the mixture until it is smooth. Scrape into a large bowl and leave to cool completely.

4 Lightly whip the cream in a bowl, then fold it into the cold trout mixture. Season to taste with salt and pepper, then cover with clear film (plastic wrap) and chill until the mousse is just starting to set. It should have the consistency of mayonnaise.

5 In a clean, grease-free bowl, beat the egg whites with a pinch of salt until they form soft peaks. Then using a large metal spoon or rubber spatula, stir about one-third of the egg whites into the sea trout mixture to slacken it slightly, then carefully fold in the remainder.

6 Lightly grease six ramekins or similar individual serving dishes. Divide the mousse equally among the prepared dishes and level the surface. Place in the refrigerator for 2–3 hours, until set. Just before serving, arrange a few slices of cucumber and a small herb sprig on top of each mousse and, finally, sprinkle over a little chopped dill or chervil.

Monkfish Packages

Notoriously ugly, the monkfish makes delicious eating with its faintly shellfish-like flavour. You could use a cheaper fish, but you'll lose that special taste.

Serves 4

175g/6oz/1½ cups strong white
*   bread flour*
2 eggs
115g/4oz skinless monkfish fillet, diced
grated rind of 1 lemon
1 garlic clove, chopped
1 fresh red chilli, seeded and sliced
45ml/3 tbsp chopped fresh parsley
30ml/2 tbsp single (light) cream
salt and ground black pepper

For the tomato oil

2 tomatoes, peeled, seeded and
*   finely diced*
45ml/3 tbsp extra virgin olive oil
15ml/1 tbsp lemon juice

1 Pulse the flour, eggs and 2.5ml/ ½ tsp salt in a blender or food processor to form a soft dough. Knead for 2–3 minutes. Wrap in clear film (plastic wrap) and chill for 20 minutes.

2 Place the diced monkfish, lemon rind, garlic, chilli and parsley in the clean food processor and process until very finely chopped. Add the cream and season with plenty of salt and ground black pepper, then process again until a very thick paste is formed. Scrape into a bowl.

3 Make the tomato oil by stirring the diced tomatoes with the olive oil and lemon juice in a bowl. Season with salt to taste. Cover with clear film and chill in the refrigerator until ready to serve.

COOK'S TIPS

• If the dough is sticky, sprinkle a little flour into the bowl of the food processor.
• Make sure that you remove the grey membrane that surrounds the monkfish fillet before dicing.

4 Roll out the dough thinly on a lightly floured surface and cut out 32 rounds, using a 4cm/1½in plain cutter. Divide the monkfish filling equally among half the rounds, then cover them with the remaining rounds. Pinch the edges tightly to seal, trying to exclude as much air as possible.

5 Bring a large pan of water to the boil, then lower the heat to a simmer. Add the fish packages, in batches, and poach for 2–3 minutes, or until they rise to the surface. Remove with a slotted spoon, drain well and keep hot while you cook the remaining packages. Serve hot, drizzled with the tomato oil.

Scallop and Mussel Kebabs

These delightfully crispy seafood skewers are served with hot toast spread with a lovely fresh herb butter.

Serves 4

65g/2¹/₂oz/5 tbsp butter, at
   room temperature
30ml/2 tbsp minced (ground) fresh
   fennel or parsley
15ml/1 tbsp lemon juice
32 small scallops
24 large mussels, in the shell
8 bacon rashers (strips)
50g/2oz/1 cup fresh breadcrumbs
50ml/2fl oz/¹/₄ cup olive oil
salt and ground black pepper
hot toast, to serve

1 Make the flavoured butter by combining the butter with the minced herbs and lemon juice in a bowl. Season with salt and pepper to taste. Mix well and set aside.

2 Cook the scallops in their own liquor in a small pan until they begin to shrink. If there is no scallop liquor – retained from the shells after shucking – use a little fish stock or white wine. Drain the scallops well and then pat dry with kitchen paper.

COOK'S TIP
When shucking scallops, wrap the hand that is holding the shell in a dishtowel to protect it, as the sharp knife required for the process can easily slip.

3 Scrub the mussels and remove their beards, then rinse under cold running water. Discard any that do not shut when sharply tapped. Place in a large pan with about 2.5cm/1in of water in the base. Cover tightly and steam over a medium heat, shaking the pan occasionally, for about 5 minutes, until they open. When cool enough to handle, remove them from their shells, and pat dry using kitchen paper. Discard any mussels that have not opened during cooking.

4 Take eight 15cm/6in wooden or metal skewers. Thread on each one, alternately, four scallops and three mussels. As you are doing this, weave a rasher of bacon between the scallops and mussels.

5 Preheat the grill (broiler). Spread the breadcrumbs on a plate. Brush the seafood with olive oil and roll in the crumbs to coat all over.

6 Place the skewers on the grill rack. Grill (broil) for 4–5 minutes on each side, until crisp and lightly browned. Serve immediately with hot toast and the flavoured butter.

Salmon and Scallop Brochettes

With their delicate colours and really superb flavour, these skewers make the perfect first course.

Serves 4

8 lemon grass stalks
225g/8oz salmon fillet, skinned
8 shucked queen scallops, with their
*   corals if possible*
8 baby (pearl) onions, blanched
1/2 yellow (bell) pepper, seeded and cut
*   into 8 squares*
25g/1oz/2 tbsp butter
juice of 1/2 lemon
salt, ground white pepper and paprika

For the sauce

30ml/2 tbsp dry vermouth
50g/2oz/1/4 cup butter
5ml/1 tsp chopped fresh tarragon

1 Preheat the grill (broiler) to medium-high. Cut off the top 7.5–10cm/3–4in of each lemon grass stalk to make "skewers" for the brochettes. Reserve the bulb ends for another dish. Cut the salmon fillet into twelve 2cm/3/4in cubes. Thread the salmon cubes, scallops, corals if available, onions and pepper squares on to the lemon grass stalks and arrange the brochettes in a grill pan.

2 Melt the butter in a small pan, add the lemon juice and a pinch of paprika and then brush all over the brochettes. Grill (broil) the skewers for about 2–3 minutes on each side, turning and basting the brochettes every minute, until the fish and scallops are just cooked, but are still very juicy. Transfer to a platter and keep hot while you make the tarragon butter sauce.

3 To make the sauce, pour the dry vermouth and the leftover cooking juices from the brochettes into a pan, bring to the boil and boil fiercely to reduce by half. Lower the heat, add the butter and melt, then stir in the chopped fresh tarragon and season with salt and ground white pepper. Pour the tarragon butter sauce over the brochettes and serve.

Coquilles St Jacques

A classic French first course that calls for the best quality scallops possible to produce a truly wonderful result. Select firm, white shellfish and check that they have not previously been frozen before buying them to avoid their being watery and flabby. You will need eight scallop shells to serve this dish.

Serves 8

900g/2lb potatoes, chopped
115g/4oz/½ cup butter
8 large or 16 small scallops
250ml/8fl oz/1 cup fish stock
fresh dill sprigs, to garnish
grilled (broiled) lemon wedges, to serve

For the sauce
50g/2oz/4 tbsp butter
50g/2oz/½ cup plain (all-purpose) flour
600ml/1 pint/2½ cups milk
60ml/4 tbsp single (light) cream
250g/8oz/2 cups grated mature (sharp)
   Cheddar cheese
salt and ground black pepper

1 Preheat oven to 200°C/400°F/Gas 6. Place the chopped potatoes in a large pan, cover with lightly salted water and boil for 15 minutes, or until tender. Drain and mash with the butter.

2 Spoon the mixture into a piping (pastry) bag fitted with a star nozzle. Pipe the potatoes around the outside of a cleaned scallop shell. Repeat the process, making eight in total.

3 Simmer the scallops in the fish stock for about 3 minutes, or until just firm. Do not allow the stock to boil but poach the scallops gently, otherwise they will become tough and rubbery. Drain and slice the scallops thinly. Set them aside.

4 To make the sauce, melt the butter in a small pan, add the flour and cook over a low heat, stirring constantly, for a couple of minutes, gradually add the milk and cream, stirring constantly, and cook until thickened.

5 Stir in the cheese and cook until melted. Season to taste with salt and pepper. Spoon a little sauce in the base of each shell. Divide the scallops between the shells and then pour the remaining sauce over the scallops.

6 Bake the scallops for 10 minutes, or until golden. Garnish with dill and serve with grilled lemon wedges.

Grilled Scallops with Brown Butter

This is a very striking dish as the scallops are served on the half shell, still sizzling from the grill. Reserve it for a special occasion – and special guests.

Serves 4

50g/2oz/¼ cup unsalted (sweet)
 butter, diced
8 scallops, prepared on the half shell
15ml/1 tbsp chopped fresh parsley
salt and ground black pepper
lemon wedges, to serve

COOK'S TIP

If you can't get hold of scallops in their shells, you can use shelled, fresh scallops if you cook them on the day of purchase. Avoid frozen scallops, as they have a flabby texture.

1 Preheat the grill (broiler) to high. Melt the butter in a small pan over a medium heat. Continue to heat it gently until it is pale golden brown. Remove the pan from the heat immediately – the butter must not be allowed to burn. Arrange the scallops in their half shells in a single layer in a large casserole or a shallow roasting pan. Brush a little of the brown butter over them.

2 Grill (broil) the scallops for 4 minutes – it will not be necessary to turn them. Pour over the remaining brown butter, then season with a little salt and pepper and sprinkle the parsley over them. Serve immediately, with lemon wedges for squeezing over.

Fried Squid

The squid is simply dusted in flour and dipped in egg before being fried, so the coating is light and does not mask the flavour.

Serves 2

115g/4oz prepared squid, cut
 into rings
30ml/2 tbsp seasoned plain
 (all-purpose) flour
1 egg
30ml/2 tbsp milk
olive oil, for frying
sea salt, to taste
lemon wedges, to serve

VARIATION

For a crisper coating, dust the rings in flour, then dip them in batter instead of this simple egg and flour coating.

1 Toss the squid rings in the seasoned flour in a bowl or strong plastic bag. Beat the egg and milk together in a shallow bowl. Heat the oil in a large, heavy frying pan.

COOK'S TIP

Keep the squid warm in the oven while you cook the rest.

2 Dip the floured squid rings, one at a time, into the egg mixture, shaking off any excess liquid. Add to the hot oil, in batches if necessary, and cook for 2–3 minutes on each side, until evenly golden all over.

3 Drain the fried squid on kitchen paper, then sprinkle with salt. Transfer to a small warm plate and serve with the lemon wedges.

Scallop-stuffed Roast Peppers with Pesto

Serve these scallop-and-pesto-filled sweet red peppers with Italian bread, such as ciabatta or focaccia, to mop up the garlicky juices.

Serves 4

4 squat red (bell) peppers
2 large garlic cloves, cut into
thin slivers
60ml/4 tbsp olive oil
4 shelled scallops
45ml/3 tbsp pesto sauce
salt and ground black pepper
freshly grated Parmesan cheese, to serve
salad leaves and basil sprigs, to garnish

1 Preheat the oven to 180°C/350°F/ Gas 4. Cut the peppers in half lengthways, through their stalks. Scrape out and discard the cores and seeds. Wash the pepper shells and pat dry with kitchen paper.

2 Put the peppers, cut side up, in an oiled roasting pan. Divide the slivers of garlic equally among them and sprinkle with salt and ground black pepper to taste. Then spoon the olive oil into the peppers and roast for 40 minutes.

VARIATION
You could also prepare this dish using red pesto sauce, which is made with sun-dried tomatoes.

3 Using a sharp knife, carefully cut each of the shelled scallops in half horizontally to make two flat discs, each with a piece of coral. When cooked, remove the peppers from the oven and place a scallop half in each pepper half. Then top the scallops with the pesto sauce.

4 Return the roasting pan to the oven and roast for 10 minutes more. Transfer the peppers to individual serving plates, sprinkle with grated Parmesan and garnish each plate with a few salad leaves and basil sprigs. Serve warm.

COOK'S TIP
Scallops are available from most fishmongers and supermarkets with fresh fish counters. Never cook scallops for longer than the time stated in the recipe or they will be tough and rubbery. The orange-coloured corals – scallop roe – are regarded by many as a delicacy, although in the United States and some other countries they are usually discarded.

Marinated Asparagus and Langoustines

For an even more extravagant treat, you could make this attractive salad with medallions of fresh lobster. For a slightly more economical version, use large prawns, allowing six per serving.

Serves 4

16 langoustines
16 fresh asparagus spears, trimmed
2 carrots
30ml/2 tbsp olive oil
1 garlic clove, peeled
salt and ground black pepper
4 fresh tarragon sprigs and some
*   chopped fresh tarragon, to garnish*

For the dressing
30ml/2 tbsp tarragon vinegar
120ml/4fl oz/¹/₂ cup olive oil

1 Peel the langoustines and keep the discarded parts for making shellfish stock. Set the tail meat aside.

2 Steam the asparagus over a pan of boiling salted water until just tender, but still a little crisp. Refresh under cold water, drain well and place in a shallow dish.

3 Peel the carrots and cut into fine julienne shreds. Cook in a pan of lightly salted, boiling water for about 3 minutes, until tender but still retaining some crunch. Drain, refresh under cold water and drain again. Add to the asparagus.

4 Make the dressing. Whisk the tarragon vinegar with the olive oil in a jug (pitcher). Season to taste with salt and pepper. Pour the dressing over the asparagus and carrots, cover and set aside to marinate.

5 Heat the oil with the garlic in a frying pan until very hot. Add the langoustines and sauté quickly until just heated through. Discard the garlic.

6 Arrange four asparagus spears and a quarter of the carrots on each of four individual plates. Drizzle over the dressing remaining in the dish and top each portion with four langoustine tails. Top with the tarragon sprigs and sprinkle the chopped tarragon on top. Serve immediately.

COOK'S TIP

Langoustines are also known as Dublin Bay prawns, Norway lobster and, when sold already peeled, scampi. Most of the langoustines we buy have been cooked at sea, a necessary act because the flesh deteriorates rapidly after death. Bear this in mind when you cook the shellfish. Because it has already been cooked, it will need to be only lightly sautéed until heated through. If you are lucky enough to buy live langoustines, kill them quickly by immersing them in boiling water, then sauté until cooked through.

Tiger Prawns with **Mint, Dill** and **Lime**

A wonderful combination – mint, dill and lime blend together to make a magical concoction to flavour succulent tiger prawns that will delight everyone who tries it.

Serves 4

4 large sheets filo pastry
75g/3oz/¹/₃ cup butter
16 large tiger prawns (jumbo shrimp),
   cooked and peeled
15ml/1 tbsp chopped fresh mint, plus
   extra to garnish
15ml/1 tbsp chopped fresh dill
juice of 1 lime
8 cooked unpeeled tiger prawns
   (jumbo shrimp) and lime wedges,
   to serve

1 Keep the sheets of filo pastry covered with a dry, clean dishtowel to keep them moist. Melt the butter in a small pan over a low heat, then remove the pan from the heat. Cut one sheet of filo pastry in half widthways and brush with some of the melted butter. Place one half on top of the other.

2 Preheat the oven to 230°C/450°F/ Gas 8. Cut the tiger prawns in half down the back of the prawn and remove the dark vein.

3 Place four prawns in the centre of the double layer of filo pastry and sprinkle a quarter of the mint, dill and lime juice over the top. Fold over the sides, brush with butter and roll up to make a parcel.

4 Make three more parcels in the same way. Place all the parcels, join side down, on a lightly greased baking sheet. Bake for 10 minutes, or until golden. Serve immediately, garnished with whole tiger prawns, lime wedges and extra chopped mint.

Prawn Cocktail

There is no nicer appetizer than a good, fresh prawn cocktail – and nothing nastier than one in which soggy prawns swim in a thin, vinegary sauce embedded in limp lettuce. This recipe shows just how good a prawn cocktail can be.

Serves 6

60ml/4 tbsp double (heavy) cream, lightly whipped
60ml/4 tbsp mayonnaise, preferably home-made
60ml/4 tbsp tomato ketchup
5–10ml/1–2 tsp Worcestershire sauce
juice of 1 lemon
¹/₂ cos or romaine lettuce
450g/1lb/4 cups cooked peeled prawns (shrimp)
salt, ground black pepper and paprika
6 large whole cooked unpeeled prawns (shrimp), to garnish (optional)
thinly sliced brown bread and lemon wedges, to serve

1 Mix together the whipped cream, mayonnaise and ketchup in a bowl. Add Worcestershire sauce to taste. Stir in enough lemon juice to make a really tangy cocktail sauce.

VARIATION

You can also use this mixture for filling vol-au-vents, cold puff pastry cases, to serve as appetizers, canapés or party snacks. The prawns (shrimp) should be chopped before they are mixed with the sauce. Fill the cases just before serving, otherwise they will become soggy and liable to collapse.

2 Finely shred the lettuce and fill six individual glasses one-third full. Gently stir the prawns into the sauce, then taste and adjust the seasoning, if necessary. Spoon the prawn mixture generously over the lettuce.

3 If you like, drape a whole cooked prawn over the edge of each glass (see Cook's Tip). Sprinkle each of the cocktails with ground black pepper and some paprika. Serve the cocktails immediately, with thinly sliced brown bread and butter and lemon wedges for squeezing over.

COOK'S TIP

To prepare the garnish, remove the heads and peel the body shells from the prawns, including the legs, and leave the tail "fan" for decoration.

Garlic Prawns in Filo Tartlets

Tartlets made with crisp layers of filo pastry and filled with garlic prawns make a tempting appetizer.

Serves 4

50g/2oz/4 tbsp butter, melted
2–3 large sheets filo pastry

For the filling
115g/4oz/¹/₂ cup butter
2–3 garlic cloves, crushed
1 fresh red chilli, seeded
  and chopped
350g/12oz/3 cups cooked peeled
  prawns (shrimp)
30ml/2 tbsp chopped fresh parsley or
  fresh chives
salt and ground black pepper

1 Preheat the oven to 200°C/400°F/ Gas 6. Brush four 7.5cm/3in flan tins (quiche pans) with melted butter.

2 Cut the filo pastry into twelve 10cm/ 4in squares and brush them with the melted butter.

3 Place three squares inside each tin, overlapping them at slight angles and frilling the edges and points while forming a good hollow in each centre.

4 Bake for 10–15 minutes, until crisp and golden. Leave to cool slightly, then remove the pastry cases (pie shells) from the tins.

5 Meanwhile, make the filling. Melt the butter in a large frying pan, then add the garlic, chilli and prawns and cook quickly for 1–2 minutes to warm through. Stir in the fresh parsley or chives and season with salt and plenty of black pepper.

6 Spoon the prawn filling into the tartlets and serve immediately, perhaps with some sour cream.

Sautéed Mussels with Garlic and Herbs

These mussels are served without their shells, in a delicious paprika-flavoured sauce. Eat them with cocktail sticks or toothpicks.

Serves 4

900g/2lb fresh mussels
1 lemon slice
90ml/6 tbsp olive oil
2 shallots, finely chopped
1 garlic clove, finely chopped
15ml/1 tbsp chopped fresh parsley
2.5ml/1/2 tsp sweet paprika
1.5ml/1/4 tsp dried chilli flakes

COOK'S TIP

The reason for discarding mussels that do not shut when they are being scrubbed and debearded is because they will certainly be dead and probably toxic.

1 Scrub the mussels and pull off their beards, discarding any damaged ones or ones that do not close when sharply tapped with a knife. Put the mussels in a large pan, with 250ml/8fl oz/1 cup water and the slice of lemon. Bring to the boil and cook for 3–4 minutes, removing the mussels as they open. Discard any that remain closed. Take the mussels out of the shells and drain on kitchen paper.

2 Heat the oil in a sauté pan, add the mussels and cook, stirring constantly, for 1 minute. Remove from the pan. Add the shallots and garlic and cook, covered, over a low heat for about 5 minutes, or until softened. Remove from the heat and stir in the parsley, paprika and chilli.

3 Return to the heat and stir in the mussels. Cook briefly to heat through. Remove from the heat and cover for 1–2 minutes to let the flavours mingle, before serving.

VARIATION

This recipe also works well with clams, especially the flavoursome, rough-shelled varieties. You may need to cook them slightly longer in step 2 to make sure that they are completely tender.

Mussels and Clams with Lemon Grass

Lemon grass has an incomparable flavour and is excellent used with a medley of seafood.

Serves 6

1.8–2kg/4–4¹/₂ lb fresh mussels
450g/1lb baby clams, washed
120ml/4fl oz/¹/₂ cup dry white wine
1 bunch spring onions
 (scallions), chopped
2 lemon grass stalks, chopped
6 kaffir lime leaves, chopped
10ml/2 tsp Thai green curry paste
200ml/7fl oz/scant 1 cup coconut cream
30ml/2 tbsp chopped fresh
 coriander (cilantro)
salt and ground black pepper
whole garlic chives, to garnish

1 Scrub the mussels and pull off the beards. Discard any that are broken or stay open when tapped.

2 Put the wine, spring onions, lemon grass, lime leaves and curry paste in a pan. Simmer over a low heat until the wine has almost evaporated.

COOK'S TIPS

• Buy a few extra mussels just in case there are any which have to be discarded.
• Small, smooth-shelled clams just need rinsing in cold water, but the larger, rough-shelled varieties should be well scrubbed. Like mussels, discard any with broken shells or that are open and do not shut immediately when sharply tapped with a knife.

3 Add the mussels and clams to the pan, cover with a tight-fitting lid and steam the shellfish over a high heat, shaking the pan occasionally, for about 5–6 minutes, until all the shells have opened.

4 Using a slotted spoon, transfer the mussels and clams to a warmed serving bowl and keep hot. Discard any shellfish that remain closed. Strain the cooking liquid through a sieve lined with muslin (cheesecloth) into a clean pan. Set over a low heat and simmer to reduce the quantity to about 250ml/8fl oz/1 cup.

5 Stir in the coconut cream and coriander and season with salt and pepper to taste. Heat through. Pour the sauce over the seafood and serve immediately, garnished with whole garlic chives.

Prosciutto with **Potato Rémoulade**

Lime juice brings a contemporary twist to this cream-enriched version of the classic piquant rémoulade dressing. It is best made when the new season's asparagus is available.

Serves 8

*4 potatoes, each weighing about
    350g/12oz, quartered lengthways
300ml/½ pint/1¼ cup mayonnaise
300ml/½ pint/1¼ cup double
    (heavy) cream
10–15ml/2–3 tsp Dijon mustard
juice of 1 lime
60ml/4 tbsp olive oil
24 prosciutto slices
900g/2lb asparagus spears, halved
salt and ground black pepper
50g/2oz wild rocket (arugula),
    to garnish
extra virgin olive oil, to serve*

1 Put the potatoes in a pan. Add water to cover and bring to the boil. Add salt, then simmer for about 15 minutes, or until the potatoes are tender, but do not let them get too soft. Drain thoroughly and leave to cool, then cut into long, thin strips.

2 Beat together the mayonnaise, cream, mustard, lime juice and seasoning in a large bowl. Add the potatoes and stir carefully to coat them with the dressing.

3 Heat the oil in a griddle or frying pan and cook the prosciutto, in batches, until crisp and golden. Remove with a slotted spoon, draining each piece well.

4 Cook the asparagus in the olive oil remaining in the pan for 3 minutes, or until tender and golden.

5 Put a generous spoonful of potato rémoulade on each plate and top with several slices of prosciutto. Add the asparagus and garnish with rocket. Serve immediately, offering olive oil to drizzle over.

VARIATION
Use a mixture of potatoes and celeriac instead of all potatoes. For an inexpensive salad, use mixed root vegetables and omit the asparagus, adding fresh or roasted cherry tomatoes instead.

Stuffed Garlic Mushrooms with Prosciutto

Field mushrooms can vary greatly in size. Try to find similar-sized specimens with undamaged edges.

Serves 4

8 field (portabello) mushrooms
15g/¹/₂oz/¹/₄ cup dried ceps, bay
   boletus or saffron milk-caps, soaked
   in warm water for 20 minutes
75g/3oz/6 tbsp unsalted (sweet) butter
1 onion, chopped
1 garlic clove, crushed
75g/3oz/³/₄ cup fresh breadcrumbs
1 egg
75ml/5 tbsp chopped fresh parsley
15ml/1 tbsp chopped fresh thyme
salt and ground black pepper
115g/4oz prosciutto di Parma or San
   Daniele, thinly sliced
fresh parsley, to garnish

1 Preheat the oven to 190°C/375°F/ Gas 5. Carefully break off the stems of the field mushrooms, without damaging the caps. Set the caps aside. Finely chop the stems. Drain the dried mushrooms and chop finely.

2 Melt half the butter in a large, heavy frying pan until foaming. Add the onion and cook over a low heat, stirring occasionally, for 6–8 minutes, until softened but not coloured.

3 Add the garlic, dried mushroom and chopped mushroom stems to the pan and cook, stirring occasionally, for about 2–3 minutes.

4 Transfer the mixture to a bowl, add the breadcrumbs, egg, parsley and thyme and season to taste with salt and pepper. Melt the remaining butter in a small pan and generously brush over the reserved mushroom caps. Arrange the mushroom caps on a baking sheet and spoon in the filling. Bake for 20–25 minutes, until they are well browned and tender.

5 Top each mushroom with a slice of prosciutto, garnish with parsley and serve immediately.

COOK'S TIPS
• Garlic mushrooms can be easily prepared in advance ready to go into the oven when your guests arrive.
• Fresh breadcrumbs can be made and then frozen. They can be taken from the freezer as they are required and do not need to be thawed first.
• Prosciutto is a dry-cured ham and opinions on whether Parma or San Daniele ham is superior differ. You could also use Jambon de Bayonne, Lomo Ahumado or Smithfield ham.

Grilled Asparagus with Salt-cured Ham

Serve this classic Spanish tapas when asparagus is plentiful and not too expensive.

Serves 4

6 slices of Serrano ham
12 asparagus spears
15ml/1 tbsp olive oil
sea salt and coarsely ground
black pepper

COOK'S TIP

If you can't find Serrano ham, the best variety of which is called Jamón de Jabugo, you can use Italian prosciutto or Portuguese presunto instead.

1 Preheat the grill (broiler) to high. Cut each slice of ham lengthways in half and wrap one half around each of the asparagus spears.

2 Brush the ham and asparagus lightly with oil and season to taste with salt and pepper. Place on the grill rack. Grill (broil), turning frequently but carefully with tongs, for 5–6 minutes, until the asparagus is tender but still firm. Serve immediately.

dinner party and festive main courses

Classic dishes are sure winners for dinner parties
and celebrations, especially with a clever twist
of seasoning or a contemporary garnish.

Tempura

This flavourful Japanese dish of crunchy battered vegetables and crispy squid rings is served with a piquant dipping sauce. Tempura can be cooked at the table over a special spill-proof spirit burner making it ideal for a party.

Serves 4

2 medium aubergines (eggplant)
4 red (bell) peppers, seeded
500g/1¼ lb/5 cups plain (all-purpose) flour, plus extra for dusting
8 baby squid, cut into rings
400g/14oz green beans, trimmed
24 mint sprigs
oil, for deep-frying
4 egg yolks
1 litre/1¾ pints/4 cups iced water
10ml/2 tsp salt
gari (Japanese pickled ginger) or grated fresh root ginger, and grated mooli (daikon) or pink radishes, to serve

For the dipping sauce
400ml/14fl oz/1⅔ cups water
90ml/6 tbsp mirin or sweet sherry
20g/½oz bonito flakes (see Cook's Tip)
90ml/6 tbsp soy sauce

1 To make the dipping sauce, mix the sauce ingredients together in a pan, bring to the boil and then strain into serving saucers and leave to cool.

COOK'S TIP
If you cannot get hold of bonito flakes, an acceptable substitute would be to use 200ml/7fl oz/scant 1 cup fish stock instead of the water to make the dipping sauce.

VARIATIONS
• Any seafood is suitable for cooking in a tempura batter. Try mussels, clams, prawns (shrimp) or scallops, or slices of salmon, cod, tuna or haddock.
• Cauliflower, broccoli, and mangetouts (snow peas) work well, too.

2 Cut the aubergine and peppers into fine julienne strips using a sharp knife or a mandolin. Put the flour for dusting into a plastic bag and add the squid. Shake the bag to coat the squid with a little flour, then place on a serving dish. Repeat with the vegetables and mint.

3 When you are ready to serve, heat the oil for deep-frying in a wok or deep pan to 190°C/375°F or until a cube of day-old bread dropped into the hot oil browns in 45 seconds. Transfer the wok or pan to a burner at the table. Never leave it unattended.

4 When ready to eat, beat the egg yolks and the iced water together. Tip in the flour and salt, and stir briefly. It is important that the tempura is lumpy and not mixed to a smooth batter.

5 Each diner dips the food into the batter and then immediately into the hot oil, using chopsticks, long fondue forks or wire baskets. Deep-fry for about 2 minutes, or until crisp.

6 Serve the tempura dipped in the sauce and accompanied by gari or ginger and mooli or radishes.

Swiss Cheese Fondue with **Vegetables**

This classic, richly flavoured fondue is traditionally served with cubes of bread, but here it is updated with herbed vegetable dippers and toasted garlic croûtes.

Serves 4–6

2 French batons or 1 baguette
1–2 garlic cloves, halved
1 small head broccoli, divided
    into florets
1 small head cauliflower, divided
    into florets
200g/7oz mangetouts (snow peas)
    or green beans, trimmed
115g/4oz baby carrots, trimmed,
    or 2 medium carrots, cut into wedges
250ml/8fl oz/1 cup dry white wine
115g/4oz/1 cup grated Gruyère cheese
250g/9oz/2¼ cups grated
    Emmenthal cheese
15ml/1tbsp cornflour (cornstarch)
30ml/2tbsp Kirsch
freshly grated nutmeg
salt and ground black pepper

For the dressing
30ml/2 tbsp extra virgin olive oil
rind and juice of 2 lemons
25g/1oz/1 cup chopped fresh parsley
25g/1oz/1 cup chopped fresh mint
1 red chilli, seeded and finely chopped

1 Cut the batons or baguette on the diagonal into 1cm/½in slices, then toast on both sides. Rub one side of each slice with the cut side of a garlic clove, if you like, and transfer to a platter.

2 Blanch the vegetables for 2 minutes in a large pan of lightly salted, boiling water, then place them in a large bowl. While they are hot, add all the dressing ingredients, season and toss together.

3 Rub the inside of the fondue pot with the cut side of a garlic clove. Pour in the white wine and heat gently on the stove. Gradually add the grated cheeses to the pot, stirring constantly until melted. Mix the cornflour with the Kirsch and add to the pot, then stir until thickened.

4 Season with salt, ground black pepper and grated nutmeg to taste. When the fondue is hot and smooth, but not boiling, transfer to a burner at the table. Do not leave unattended.

5 Each diner dips the vegetables and toasted bread into the fondue.

VARIATIONS
• Use fresh chopped basil instead of mint.
• Use crunchy, fresh vegetables such as pink radishes, mushrooms, baby corn and red or yellow (bell) peppers.

Mongolian Firepot

Cooking at the table in a firepot is a fun and sociable way to enjoy a meal with family or friends. It calls for plenty of participation by guests, who cook the assembled ingredients, dipping the meats in a variety of different sauces.

Serves 6–8

900g/2lb boned leg of lamb, preferably
    bought thinly sliced
225g/8oz lamb's liver and/or kidneys
900ml/1½ pints/3¾ cups lamb stock
    (see Cook's Tip)
900ml/1½ pints/3¾ cups chicken stock
1cm/½in piece fresh root ginger,
    peeled and thinly sliced
45ml/3 tbsp rice wine or
    medium-dry sherry
½ head Chinese leaves (Chinese
    cabbage), rinsed and shredded
few young spinach leaves
250g/9oz fresh firm tofu,
    diced (optional)
115g/4oz cellophane noodles
salt and ground black pepper

For the dipping sauce
50ml/2fl oz/¼ cup red wine vinegar
7.5ml/1½ tsp dark soy sauce
1cm/½in piece fresh root ginger,
    peeled and finely shredded
1 spring onion (scallion), shredded

To serve
bowls of tomato sauce, sweet chilli
    sauce, mustard oil and sesame oil
dry-fried coriander seeds, crushed

COOK'S TIP
To make lamb stock, place the leg bones in a large pan with water to cover. Bring to the boil and skim the surface. Add 1 peeled onion, 2 carrots, 1cm/½in piece of peeled and bruised ginger, 5ml/1 tsp salt and ground black pepper. Bring back to the boil, then simmer for about 1 hour. Strain, cool, then skim and use.

1 When buying the lamb, ask your butcher to slice it thinly on a slicing machine, if possible. If you have had to buy the lamb in one piece, however, put it in the freezer for about an hour, so that it is easier to slice thinly.

2 Trim the liver and remove the skin and core from the kidneys, if using. Place them in the freezer, too. If you managed to buy sliced lamb, keep it in the refrigerator until needed.

3 Mix both types of stock in a large pan. Add the sliced ginger and rice wine or sherry, with salt and pepper to taste. Heat to simmering point and simmer for 15 minutes.

4 Slice all the meats thinly and arrange them attractively on a large platter.

5 Place the shredded Chinese leaves, spinach leaves and the diced tofu on a separate platter.

6 Soak the noodles in warm or hot water, following the instructions given on the packet.

7 Make the dipping sauce by mixing all the ingredients in a small bowl. The other sauces and the crushed coriander seeds should be spooned into separate small dishes and placed on a serving tray or on the table.

8 When you are ready to eat, set the firepot on the dining table and light the burner. Fill the moat of the hotpot with the simmering stock. Alternatively, fill a fondue pot and place it over a burner. Remember never to leave the lighted burner unattended. Each guest selects a portion of meat from the platter and cooks it in the hot stock, using chopsticks, a little wire basket (usually sold alongside firepots) or a fondue fork. The meat is then dipped in one of the sauces and coated with the coriander seeds (if you like).

9 When most of the meat has been eaten, top up the stock if necessary, then add the vegetables, tofu and drained noodles. Cook until the noodles are tender and the vegetables retain a little crispness. Serve the soup in warmed bowls.

Peppers filled with **Spiced Vegetables**

Indian spices season the potato and aubergine stuffing in these colourful baked peppers. They are good with plain rice and a lentil dhal, or a salad, Indian breads and a cucumber or mint and yogurt raita.

Serves 6

*6 large evenly shaped red or yellow
(bell) peppers
500g/1¼lb waxy potatoes
1 small onion, chopped
4–5 garlic cloves, chopped
5cm/2in piece fresh root
ginger, chopped
1–2 fresh green chillies, seeded
and chopped
105ml/7 tbsp water
90–105ml/6–7 tbsp groundnut
(peanut) oil
1 aubergine (eggplant), cut into
1cm/½in dice
10ml/2 tsp cumin seeds
5ml/1 tsp kalonji (nigella) seeds
2.5ml/½ tsp ground turmeric
5ml/1 tsp ground coriander
5ml/1 tsp ground toasted cumin seeds
pinch of cayenne pepper
about 30ml/2 tbsp lemon juice
salt and ground black pepper
30ml/2 tbsp chopped fresh coriander
(cilantro), to garnish*

2 Bring a large pan of lightly salted water to the boil. Add the peppers and cook for 5–6 minutes. Drain and leave upside down in a colander.

3 Cook the potatoes in lightly salted, boiling water for 10–12 minutes, until just tender. Drain, cool and peel, then cut into 1cm/½in dice.

4 Put the onion, garlic, ginger and green chillies in a food processor or blender with 60ml/4 tbsp of the water and process to a purée.

5 Heat 45ml/3 tbsp of the oil in a large, deep frying pan and cook the aubergine over a medium heat, stirring occasionally, until browned on all sides. Remove from the pan and set aside. Add another 30ml/2 tbsp of the oil to the pan and cook the diced potatoes until lightly browned. Remove from the pan and set aside.

6 If necessary, add another 15ml/1 tbsp oil to the pan, then add the cumin and kalonji seeds. Cook briefly until the seeds darken, then add the turmeric, coriander and ground cumin. Cook for 15 seconds. Stir in the onion and garlic purée and cook, scraping the pan with a spatula, until it begins to brown.

7 Return the potatoes and aubergines to the pan, season with salt, pepper and 1–2 pinches of cayenne. Add the remaining water and 15ml/1 tbsp lemon juice and then cook, stirring, until the liquid evaporates. Preheat the oven to 190°C/375°F/Gas 5.

8 Fill the peppers with the potato mix and place on a lightly greased baking tray. Brush the peppers with a little oil and bake for 30–35 minutes, until the peppers are cooked. Leave to cool, then sprinkle with a little more lemon juice, garnish with the coriander and serve.

1 Cut the tops off the red or yellow peppers then remove and discard the seeds. Cut a thin slice off the base of the peppers, if necessary, to make them stand upright.

Goat's Cheese Soufflé

The mellow flavour of roasted garlic pervades this simple, but elegant soufflé. Balance this rich dish with a crisp green salad, including peppery leaves.

Serves 6–8

4 large heads of garlic
6 fresh thyme sprigs
30ml/2 tbsp olive oil
475ml/16fl oz/2 cups milk
2 fresh bay leaves
4 × 1cm/½in thick onion slices
4 cloves
115g/4oz/½ cup butter
75g/3oz/⅔ cup plain (all-purpose)
*   flour, sifted*
cayenne pepper
6 eggs, separated, plus 1 egg white
300g/11oz goat's cheese, crumbled
115g/4oz/1⅓ cups freshly grated
*   Parmesan cheese*
5–10ml/1–2 tsp chopped fresh thyme
5ml/1 tsp cream of tartar
salt and ground black pepper

1 Preheat the oven to 180°C/350°F/ Gas 4. Place the garlic and thyme sprigs on a piece of foil. Sprinkle with the oil and close the foil around the garlic, then bake for about 1 hour, until the garlic is soft. Leave to cool.

2 Squeeze the garlic out of its skin. Discard the thyme and garlic skins, then purée the garlic flesh with the oil.

3 Meanwhile, place the milk, bay leaves, onion slices and cloves in a medium pan. Bring to the boil, then remove from the heat. Cover and leave to stand for 30 minutes.

4 Melt 75g/3oz/6 tbsp of the butter in another pan. Stir in the flour and cook gently for 2 minutes, stirring. Reheat and strain the milk, then gradually stir it into the flour and butter.

5 Cook the sauce very gently for 10 minutes, stirring frequently. Season with salt, pepper and a pinch of cayenne. Cool slightly. Preheat the oven to 200°C/400°F/Gas 6.

6 Beat the egg yolks into the sauce, one at a time. Then beat in the goat's cheese, all but 30ml/2 tbsp of the Parmesan and the chopped thyme. Use the remaining butter to grease a large soufflé dish (1 litre/1¾ pints/ 4 cups) or eight ramekins (about 125ml/4fl oz/½ cup).

7 Whisk the egg whites and cream of tartar in a clean, grease-free bowl until firm, but not dry. Stir 90ml/6 tbsp of the egg whites into the sauce, then gently, but thoroughly, fold in the remainder using a rubber spatula.

8 Pour the mixture into the prepared dish or dishes. Run a knife around the edge of each dish, pushing the mixture away from the rim. Sprinkle with the reserved Parmesan.

9 Place the dish or dishes on a baking sheet and cook for 25–30 minutes for a large soufflé or 20 minutes for small soufflés. The mixture should be risen and firm to a light touch in the centre; it should not wobble excessively when given a light push. Serve immediately.

COOK'S TIP

Whisked egg whites give a soufflé its characteristic airy texture. But the lightness can be destroyed if they are folded in too roughly. Fold whites in using a rubber spatula and a cutting and scooping action. Turn the bowl a little after each stroke.

Roasted Garlic and Aubergine Custards with Red Pepper Dressing

These make a splendid main course for a special vegetarian dinner. Serve fresh, warm bread and steamed broccoli as accompaniments.

Serves 6

2 large heads of garlic
6–7 fresh thyme sprigs
60ml/4 tbsp extra virgin olive oil, plus
    extra for greasing
350g/12oz aubergines (eggplant),
    cut into 1cm/½in dice
2 large red (bell) peppers, halved
    and seeded
pinch of saffron threads
300ml/½ pint/1¼ cups whipping cream
2 large (US extra large) eggs
pinch of caster (superfine) sugar
30ml/2 tbsp shredded fresh basil leaves
salt and ground black pepper

For the dressing
90ml/6 tbsp extra virgin oil
15–25ml/1–1½ tbsp balsamic vinegar
pinch of caster (superfine) sugar
115g/4oz tomatoes, peeled, seeded
    and finely diced
½ small red onion, finely chopped
generous pinch of ground toasted
    cumin seeds
handful of fresh basil leaves

1 Preheat the oven to 190°C/375°F/ Gas 5. Place the garlic on a piece of foil with the thyme and sprinkle with 15ml/ 1 tbsp of the oil. Wrap the foil around the garlic and cook for 35–45 minutes, or until the garlic is soft. Cool slightly. Reduce the oven temperature to 180°C/350°F/Gas 4.

2 Meanwhile, heat the remaining olive oil in a heavy pan. Add the diced aubergines and cook over a medium heat, stirring frequently, for 5–8 minutes, or until they are browned and cooked.

3 Grill (broil) the peppers, skin sides uppermost, until they are black. Place the peppers in a bowl, cover and leave for 10 minutes.

4 When the peppers are cool enough to handle, peel and dice them. Soak the saffron in 15ml/1 tbsp hot water for 10 minutes.

5 Unwrap the roasted garlic and separate the cloves, then squeeze the flesh out of its skin into a blender or food processor. Discard the thyme sprigs. Add the oil from cooking the garlic, the cream and eggs to the garlic. Process until smooth. Add the soaked saffron with its liquid, and season well with salt, pepper and a pinch of sugar. Stir in half the diced red pepper and the shredded basil leaves.

6 Lightly grease six large ovenproof ramekins (about 200–250ml/7–8fl oz/ 1 cup capacity) and line the base of each with a disc of baking parchment. Grease the baking parchment.

7 Divide the aubergines among the dishes. Pour the egg mixture into the ramekins, then place them in a roasting pan. Cover each dish with foil and make a little hole in the centre of the foil to allow steam to escape. Pour hot water into the tin to come halfway up the outsides of the ramekins. Bake for 25–30 minutes, or until the custards are just set in the centre.

8 Make the dressing while the custards are cooking. Whisk the oil and vinegar with salt, pepper and a pinch of sugar. Stir in the tomatoes, red onion, the remaining red pepper and the cumin. Set aside some of the basil leaves for garnishing, then chop the rest and add to the dressing.

9 Leave the custards to cool for about 5 minutes. Slide a knife around the insides of the ramekins and invert the custards on to warmed serving plates. Spoon the dressing around the custards and garnish each with the reserved fresh basil leaves.

Potato and Leek Filo Pie

This filo pastry pie, filled with a wonderful mixture of potatoes, leeks, cheese, cream and herbs, makes an attractive and unusual centrepiece for a vegetarian buffet. Serve it cold, together with a choice of different salads.

Serves 8

800g/1¾lb new potatoes, sliced
400g/14oz leeks (trimmed weight)
75g/3oz/6 tbsp butter
15g/½ oz/¼ cup finely chopped
    fresh parsley
60ml/4 tbsp chopped mixed fresh
    herbs, such as chervil, chives,
    a little tarragon and basil
12 sheets filo pastry, thawed if frozen
150g/5oz white Cheshire, Lancashire
    or Sonoma Jack cheese, sliced
2 garlic cloves, finely chopped
250ml/8fl oz/1 cup double
    (heavy) cream
2 large (US extra large) egg yolks
salt and ground black pepper

1 Preheat the oven to 190°C/375°F/ Gas 5. Cook the potatoes in lightly salted, boiling water for 3–4 minutes, then drain and set aside.

2 Thinly slice the leeks. Melt 25g/1oz/ 2 tbsp of the butter in a frying pan and cook the leeks gently over a low heat, stirring occasionally, until softened. Remove from the heat and season with pepper and stir in half the parsley and half the mixed herbs.

3 Melt the remaining butter. Line a 23cm/9in loose-based metal cake tin (pan) with six sheets of filo pastry, brushing each layer with melted butter. Allow the edges of the filo pastry to overhang the tin.

4 Layer the potatoes, leeks and cheese in the tin, sprinkling a few herbs and the garlic between the layers. Season.

5 Flip the overhanging pastry over the filling and cover with another two sheets of filo pastry, tucking in the sides to fit, and brush with melted butter as before. Cover the pie loosely with foil and bake for 35 minutes. (Keep the remaining pastry covered with a plastic bag and a damp cloth.)

6 Meanwhile beat the cream, egg yolks and remaining herbs together. Make a hole in the centre of the pie and gradually pour in the eggs and cream.

7 Arrange the remaining pastry on top, teasing it into swirls and folds, then brush with melted butter.

8 Reduce the oven temperature to 180°C/350°F/Gas 4 and bake the pie for another 25–30 minutes, or until the top is golden and crisp. Leave to cool before serving.

COOK'S TIP

To make a spicy tomato sauce to serve with the pie, cook 1 chopped onion in 15ml/ 1 tbsp olive oil for 3 minutes, add 1 chopped garlic clove and cook for 2 minutes. Stir in 400g/14oz can chopped tomatoes and 5ml/1 tsp hot chilli powder. Simmer for 15–20 minutes, or until thickened.

VARIATIONS

• Reduce the quantity of leeks to 225g/ 8oz. Cook 1kg/2¼lb washed spinach leaves in a covered pan over a high heat for 3–4 minutes, gently shaking the pan frequently. Drain, chop and mix with the cooked leeks.

• Reduce the quantity of leeks to 225g/ 8oz. Blanch 450g/1lb small broccoli florets in boiling water for 1 minute. Drain and add to the leeks.

• For a punchy flavour, use Stilton or Danish blue cheese instead of white cheese. Crumble the cheese rather than slicing it.

Tofu and Vegetable Thai Curry

Traditional Thai ingredients – chillies, galangal, lemon grass and kaffir lime leaves – give this vegetarian curry a wonderfully fragrant aroma. It makes an excellent main course when served with boiled jasmine rice or noodles.

Serves 8

350g/12oz tofu, drained
90ml/6 tbsp dark soy sauce
30ml/2 tbsp sesame oil
10ml/2 tsp chilli sauce
5cm/2in piece fresh root ginger,
    finely grated
450g/1lb cauliflower
450g/1lb broccoli
60ml/4 tbsp vegetable oil
2 onions, peeled and sliced
750ml/1¼ pints/3 cups coconut milk
300ml/½ pint/1¼ cups water
2 red (bell) peppers, seeded
    and chopped
350g/12oz green beans, halved
225g/8oz/3 cups shiitake or button
    (white) mushrooms, halved
shredded spring onions (scallions),
    to garnish
boiled jasmine rice or noodles,
    to serve

For the curry paste
4 chillies, seeded and chopped
2 lemon grass stalks, chopped
5cm/2in piece fresh galangal, chopped
4 kaffir lime leaves
20ml/4 tsp ground coriander
a few fresh coriander (cilantro) sprigs,
    including the stalks

1 Cut the drained tofu into 2.5cm/1in cubes and place in an ovenproof dish. Mix together the soy sauce, sesame oil, chilli sauce and ginger and pour over the tofu. Toss gently, then marinate for at least 2 hours or overnight, turning and basting the tofu occasionally.

2 To make the curry paste, blend the chopped chillies, lemon grass, galangal, kaffir lime leaves, ground and fresh coriander in a food processor for a few seconds. Add 90ml/6 tbsp water and process to a thick paste.

3 Preheat the oven to 190°C/375°F/ Gas 5. Using a sharp knife cut the cauliflower and broccoli into florets and cut any stalks into thin slices.

4 Heat the vegetable oil in a frying pan, add the sliced onions and cook gently for about 8 minutes, or until soft and lightly browned. Stir in the curry paste and the coconut milk. Add the water and bring to the boil.

5 Stir in the red peppers, green beans, cauliflower and broccoli. Transfer to a casserole. Cover and place in the oven.

6 Stir the tofu and marinade, then place the dish in the top of the oven and cook for 30 minutes. Add the marinade mixture and mushrooms to the curry. Reduce the oven temperature to 180°C/ 350°F/Gas 4 and cook for 15 minutes, or until the vegetables are tender. Garnish the curry with shredded spring onions. Serve immediately with boiled jasmine rice or noodles.

Malaysian Seafood Stew

This Malaysian stew of fish, seafood and vegetables with noodles is wonderfully tasty. If you prefer a hot and spicy version, add a little chilli powder instead of some of the paprika.

Serves 8–10

4 medium-hot fresh red
    chillies, seeded
6–8 garlic cloves
10ml/2 tsp mild paprika
20ml/4 tsp fermented shrimp paste
45ml/3 tbsp chopped fresh root
    ginger or galangal
500g/1¼ lb small red shallots
50g/2oz fresh coriander (cilantro),
    preferably with roots
90ml/6 tbsp groundnut (peanut) oil
10ml/2 tsp fennel seeds, crushed
4 fennel bulbs, cut into
    thin wedges
1.2 litres/2 pints/5 cups fish stock
600g/1 lb 6oz thin vermicelli
    rice noodles
900ml/1½ pints/3¾ cups coconut milk
juice of 2–4 limes
60–90ml/4–6 tbsp Thai fish sauce
900g/2lb firm white fish fillet, such as
    monkfish, halibut or snapper
900g/2lb large raw prawns (shrimp)
    (about 40), shelled and deveined
bunch of fresh basil
4 spring onions (scallions),
    thinly sliced

1 Process the chillies, garlic, paprika, shrimp paste, ginger or galangal and four shallots to a paste in a food processor, blender or spice grinder. Remove the roots and stems from the coriander and add them to the paste; chop and reserve the coriander leaves. Add 30ml/2 tbsp of the groundnut oil to the paste and process again until fairly smooth.

2 Heat the remaining oil in a large pan or stockpot. Add the remaining shallots, the fennel seeds and fennel wedges. Cook until lightly browned, then add 90ml/6 tbsp of the paste and stir-fry for about 2 minutes. Pour in the fish stock and bring to the boil. Reduce the heat and simmer for 8–10 minutes.

3 Meanwhile, cook the vermicelli rice noodles according to the instructions on the packet. Drain and set aside.

4 Pour the coconut milk into the pan of shallots, stirring constantly to prevent them from sticking, then add the juice of two limes, with 60ml/4 tbsp of the fish sauce. Stir well to combine. Bring to a simmer and taste, adding more of the curry paste, lime juice or fish sauce as necessary.

5 Cut the fish into chunks and add to the pan. Cook for 3–4 minutes, then add the prawns and cook until they turn pink. Chop most of the basil and add to the pan with the reserved chopped coriander leaves.

6 Divide the noodles equally among 8–10 bowls, then ladle in the stew. Sprinkle with spring onions and the remaining basil leaves and serve.

Fillets of Sea Bream in Filo Pastry

Any firm fish fillets can be used for this dish. Each little parcel is a meal in itself and can be prepared several hours in advance, which makes them ideal for entertaining.

Serves 8

16 small waxy salad potatoes
400g/14oz sorrel, stalks removed
60ml/4 tbsp olive oil
32 sheets of filo pastry, thawed
  if frozen
8 sea bream fillets, about 175g/6oz
  each, scaled but not skinned
115g/4oz/½ cup butter, melted
250ml/8fl oz/1 cup fish stock
475ml/16fl oz/2 cups double
  (heavy) cream
salt and ground black pepper
finely diced red (bell) pepper, to garnish

1 Preheat the oven to 200°C/400°F/ Gas 6. Cook the salad potatoes in lightly salted, boiling water for about 15–20 minutes, or until just tender. Drain and set aside to cool.

2 Shred half the sorrel leaves by piling up six or eight at a time, rolling them up like a fat cigar and cutting them with a sharp knife, into very fine slices: shake these out.

3 Thinly slice the potatoes lengthways. Brush a baking tray with a little oil. Lay a sheet of filo pastry on the tray, brush it with oil then lay a second sheet crossways over the first. Repeat with two more sheets. Arrange one-eighth of the sliced potatoes in the centre of the pastry, season well and add one-eighth of the shredded sorrel. Lay a bream fillet on top, skin side up. Season to taste again.

4 Loosely fold the filo pastry up and over to make a neat parcel. Make seven more parcels in the same way. Place on the baking tray and brush them with half the butter. Bake for 20 minutes, or until the filo has fully puffed up and is golden brown.

5 Meanwhile, make the sorrel sauce. Heat the remaining butter in a small pan, add the reserved sorrel and cook until it wilts. Stir in the fish stock and cream. Heat almost to boiling point, stirring constantly. Season and keep hot. Serve the fish parcels garnished with red pepper and offer the sauce separately in its own bowl.

Malaysian Prawn Laksa

This spicy prawn and noodle stew tastes just as good when made with fresh crab meat or any flaked cooked fish.

Serves 3–4

115g/4oz rice vermicelli or stir-fry rice noodles
15ml/1 tbsp vegetable or groundnut (peanut) oil
600ml/1 pint/2¹/₂ cups fish stock
400ml/14fl oz/1²/₃ cups thin coconut milk
30ml/2 tbsp Thai fish sauce
¹/₂ lime
16–24 cooked peeled prawns (shrimp)
salt and cayenne pepper
60ml/4 tbsp chopped fresh coriander (cilantro), to garnish

For the spicy paste
2 lemon grass stalks, finely chopped
2 fresh red chillies, seeded and chopped
2.5cm/1in piece fresh root ginger, peeled and sliced
2.5ml/¹/₂ tsp dried shrimp paste
2 garlic cloves, chopped
2.5ml/¹/₂ tsp ground turmeric
30ml/2 tbsp tamarind paste

1 Cook the rice vermicelli or noodles in a large pan of lightly salted, boiling water according to the instructions on the packet. Tip into a large sieve or colander, then rinse under cold water to stop any further cooking and drain. Set aside and keep warm.

2 To make the spicy paste, place the lemon grass, chillies, ginger, shrimp paste, garlic, turmeric and tamarind paste in a mortar and pound with a pestle until smooth. Alternatively, if you prefer, put all the ingredients in a food processor or blender and then process until a smooth paste is formed.

3 Heat the oil in a large pan, add the spicy paste and cook over a low heat, stirring constantly, for a few moments to release all the flavours, but be careful not to let it burn.

4 Add the fish stock and coconut milk and bring to the boil. Stir in the Thai fish sauce, then simmer for 5 minutes. Season with salt and cayenne to taste, adding a squeeze of lime juice. Add the prawns and heat through gently for a few seconds.

5 Divide the noodles among three or four soup plates. Pour the soup over, making sure that each portion includes an equal number of prawns. Garnish with the chopped coriander and serve piping hot.

Red Chicken Curry with Bamboo Shoots

Bamboo shoots have a lovely crunchy texture and make a delightful, contrasting texture to the chicken in this Thai curry. It is perfect served with jasmine rice.

Serves 6

1 litre/1¾ pints/4 cups coconut milk
30ml/2 tbsp red curry paste
450g/1lb skinless chicken breast fillets,
* cut into bitesize pieces*
30ml/2 tbsp Thai fish sauce
15ml/1 tbsp sugar
225g/8oz canned whole bamboo
* shoots, rinsed, drained and sliced*
5 kaffir lime leaves, torn
salt and ground black pepper
chopped fresh red chillies and kaffir
* lime leaves, to garnish*

For the red curry paste
5ml/1 tsp roasted coriander seeds
2.5ml/½ tsp roasted cumin seeds
6–8 fresh red chillies, seeded
* and chopped*
4 shallots, thinly sliced
2 garlic cloves, chopped
15ml/1 tbsp fresh galangal, peeled
* and chopped*
2 lemon grass stalks, chopped
4 fresh coriander (cilantro) roots
10 black peppercorns
pinch of ground cinnamon
5ml/1 tsp ground turmeric
2.5ml/½ tsp shrimp paste
5ml/1 tsp salt
30 ml/2 tbsp vegetable oil

1 To make the red curry paste, put all the ingredients except the oil into a mortar or food processor and pound or process to a paste. Add the oil, a little at a time, mixing or processing well after each addition. If you are not using the paste immediately, transfer it to a jar and keep in the refrigerator until you are ready to use it. For a hotter paste, add a few chilli seeds.

2 Pour half of the coconut milk into a wok or large pan over a medium heat. Bring to the boil, stirring constantly, with large cooking chopsticks or a spoon until it has separated.

3 Add the red curry paste and cook the mixture for 2–3 minutes. Stir the paste constantly to prevent it from sticking to the base of the pan.

4 Add the chicken pieces, fish sauce and sugar to the pan. Stir well, then cook for 5–6 minutes, or until the chicken changes colour and is cooked through. Continue to stir during cooking to prevent the mixture from sticking to the base of the pan and to cook the chicken evenly.

5 Pour the remaining coconut milk into the pan, then add the sliced bamboo shoots and torn kaffir lime leaves. Bring back to the boil over a medium heat, stirring constantly to prevent the mixture from sticking, then taste and add salt and pepper if necessary.

6 To serve, spoon the curry into a warmed serving dish and garnish with chopped chillies and kaffir lime leaves.

COOK'S TIP
Preparing a double or larger quantity of paste in a food processor or blender makes the blending of the ingredients easier and the paste will be smoother. Store surplus curry paste in the freezer.

VARIATIONS
• For green curry paste, process 12–15 green chillies, 2 chopped lemon grass stalks, 3 sliced shallots, 2 garlic cloves, 15ml/1 tbsp chopped galangal, 4 chopped kaffir lime leaves, 2.5ml/½ tsp grated kaffir rind, 5ml/1 tsp each of chopped coriander (cilantro) root, salt, roasted coriander seeds, roasted cumin seeds and shrimp paste, 15ml/1 tbsp sugar, 6 black peppercorns and 15ml/1 tbsp vegetable oil until a paste forms.
• For yellow curry paste, process 6–8 yellow chillies, 1 chopped lemon grass stalk, 2 sliced shallots, 4 garlic cloves, 15ml/1 tbsp chopped fresh root ginger, 5ml/1 tsp ground cinnamon, 15ml/1 tbsp light brown sugar and 30ml/2 tbsp vegetable oil until a paste forms.
• Use turkey or pork instead of chicken.

Herb-crusted Rack of Lamb with Puy Lentils

This roast is easy to prepare, yet impressive when served – the perfect choice when entertaining.

Serves 8

4 × 6-bone racks of lamb, chined
115g/4oz/2 cups fresh
* white breadcrumbs*
4 large garlic cloves, crushed
40g/1½ oz chopped mixed fresh herbs,
* such as rosemary, thyme, flat leaf*
* parsley and marjoram, plus extra*
* sprigs to garnish*
115g/4oz/½ cup butter, melted
salt and ground black pepper

For the Puy lentils
2 red onions, chopped
60ml/4 tbsp olive oil
2 × 400g/14oz cans Puy or green
* lentils, rinsed and drained*
2 × 400g/14oz cans
* chopped tomatoes*
60ml/4 tbsp chopped fresh parsley

1 Preheat the oven to 220°C/425°F/Gas 7. Trim off any excess fat from the racks of lamb, and season well with salt and ground black pepper.

2 Mix together the breadcrumbs, garlic, herbs and butter and press on to the fat-sides of the lamb. Place in a roasting pan and roast for 25 minutes. Cover with foil and leave to stand for 5 minutes before carving.

COOK'S TIP
Boiled or steamed new potatoes and broccoli are good accompaniments.

3 To make the Puy lentils, cook the onion in the olive oil until softened. Add the lentils and tomatoes and cook gently for 5 minutes, or until the lentils are piping hot. Stir in the parsley and season to taste.

4 Cut each rack of lamb in half and serve with the lentils. Garnish with the extra herb sprigs.

VARIATION
Add the grated rind of 1 lemon and 30ml/2 tbsp finely chopped walnuts to the crumb mixture.

Moussaka

Layers of minced lamb, aubergines, tomatoes and onions are topped with a creamy yogurt and cheese sauce in this delicious, authentic eastern Mediterranean recipe. Serve with a simple, mixed leaf, green salad.

Serves 8

900g/2lb aubergines (eggplant)
300ml/½ pint/1¼ cups olive oil
2 large onions, chopped
4–6 garlic cloves, finely chopped
1.3kg/3lb lean minced (ground) lamb
30ml/2 tbsp plain (all-purpose) flour
2 × 400g/14oz cans
   chopped tomatoes
60ml/4 tbsp chopped mixed fresh
   herbs, such as parsley, marjoram
   and oregano
salt and ground black pepper

For the topping
600ml/1 pint/2½ cups natural
   (plain) yogurt
4 eggs
50g/2oz feta cheese, crumbled
50g/2oz/⅔ cup grated Parmesan cheese

1 Cut the aubergines into thin slices and layer them in a colander, sprinkling each layer with salt. Cover them with a plate and a weight, then leave to drain for about 30 minutes. Drain and rinse well to remove all traces of salt, then pat dry with kitchen paper.

2 Heat 90ml/6 tbsp of the olive oil in a large, heavy pan. Cook the chopped onion and garlic until softened, but not coloured. Add the lamb and cook over a high heat, stirring frequently, until lightly browned.

3 Stir in the flour until mixed, then stir in the tomatoes, herbs and seasoning. Bring to the boil, reduce the heat and simmer gently for 20 minutes.

4 Meanwhile, heat a little of the remaining oil in a large frying pan. Add as many aubergine slices as can be laid in the pan, then cook until golden on both sides. Set the cooked aubergines aside. Heat more oil and continue cooking the aubergines, in batches, adding oil as necessary.

5 Preheat the oven to 180°C/350°F/ Gas 4. Arrange half the aubergine slices in a large, shallow ovenproof dish or divide among two smaller dishes.

6 Top the aubergine slices with about half of the meat and tomato mixture, then add the remaining aubergine slices. Spread the remaining meat mixture over the aubergines.

7 Beat together the yogurt and eggs, mix in the feta and Parmesan cheeses, and spread the mixture over the meat.

8 Transfer the moussaka to the oven and bake for 35–40 minutes, or until golden and bubbling.

Tagine of **Lamb** with **Couscous**

A tagine is a classic Moroccan stew which is traditionally served with couscous. Its warm and fruity flavourings create a rich and sumptuous sauce that is perfect for serving at winter evening dinner parties.

Serves 6

1kg/2¼lb lean boneless lamb,
    such as shoulder or neck fillet
25g/1oz/2 tbsp butter
15ml/1 tbsp sunflower oil
1 large onion, chopped
2 garlic cloves, chopped
2.5cm/1in piece fresh root ginger,
    peeled and finely chopped
1 red (bell) pepper, seeded
    and chopped
900ml/1½ pints/3¾ cups lamb stock
    or water
250g/9oz/generous 1 cup
    ready-to-eat prunes
juice of 1 lemon
15ml/1 tbsp clear honey
1.5ml/¼ tsp saffron threads
1 cinnamon stick, broken in half
50g/2oz/½ cup flaked (sliced)
    almonds, toasted
salt and ground black pepper

To serve
450g/1lb/2⅔ cups couscous
25g/1oz/2 tbsp butter
30ml/2 tbsp chopped fresh
    coriander (cilantro)

1 Trim the lamb and cut it into 2.5cm/1in cubes. Heat the butter and oil in a large flameproof casserole until foaming. Add the onion, garlic and ginger and cook, stirring occasionally, until softened but not coloured.

2 Add the lamb and red pepper and mix well. (The meat is not sealed in batches over high heat for an authentic tagine.) Pour in the stock or water.

3 Add the prunes, lemon juice, honey, saffron threads and cinnamon. Season to taste with salt and pepper and stir well. Bring to the boil, then reduce the heat and cover the casserole. Simmer for 1½–2 hours, stirring occasionally, or until the meat is melt-in-the-mouth tender.

4 Meanwhile, cook the couscous according to packet instructions, usually by placing in a large bowl and pouring in boiling water to cover the "grains" by 2.5cm/1in. Stir well, then cover and leave to stand for 5–10 minutes. The couscous absorbs the water and swells to become tender and fluffy. Stir in the butter, chopped fresh coriander and seasoning to taste.

5 Taste the stew for seasoning and add more salt and pepper if necessary. Pile the couscous into a large, warmed serving dish or on to individual warmed bowls or plates. Ladle the stew on to the couscous and sprinkle the toasted flaked almonds over the top.

Beef Carbonade

This rich, dark stew of beef, cooked slowly with lots of onions, garlic and beer, is a classic one-pot casserole from the north of France and Belgium. Serve with roasted potatoes, if you like.

Serves 6

45ml/3 tbsp vegetable oil
3 onions, sliced
45ml/3 tbsp plain (all-purpose) flour
2.5ml/½ tsp mustard powder
*1kg/2¼lb stewing beef, such as shin
  (shank) or chuck, cut into large cubes*
2–3 garlic cloves, finely chopped
*300ml/½ pint/1¼ cups dark beer
  or ale*
150ml/¼ pint/⅔ cup water
5ml/1 tsp dark brown sugar
1 fresh thyme sprig
1 fresh bay leaf
1 piece celery stick
salt and ground black pepper

For the topping
50g/2oz/½ cup butter
1 garlic clove, crushed
15ml/1 tbsp Dijon mustard
45ml/3 tbsp chopped fresh parsley
6–12 slices baguette or ficelle loaf

1 Preheat the oven to 160°C/325°F/ Gas 3. Heat 30ml/2 tbsp of the oil in a frying pan and cook the onions over a low heat until softened. Remove from the pan and set aside.

2 Meanwhile, mix together the flour and mustard and season. Toss the beef in the flour. Add the remaining oil to the pan and heat over a high heat. Brown the beef all over, then transfer it to a casserole.

COOK'S TIP
When making more than double the quantity, limit the garlic cloves to 8 in total, otherwise the flavour is too strong.

3 Reduce the heat and return the onions to the pan. Add the garlic, cook, then add the beer or ale, water and sugar. Tie the thyme and bay leaf together and add to the pan with the celery. Bring to the boil, stirring, then season.

4 Pour the sauce over the beef and mix. Cover, then place in the oven for 2½ hours. Check the beef to make sure that it is not too dry, adding water, if necessary. Test for tenderness, allowing an extra 30–40 minutes cooking time.

5 To make the topping, cream the butter together with the garlic, mustard and 30ml/2 tbsp of the parsley. Spread the butter thickly over the bread.

6 Increase the oven temperature to 190°C/375°F/Gas 5. Taste and season the casserole, then arrange the bread slices, buttered side uppermost, on top. Bake for 20–25 minutes, until the bread is browned. Sprinkle the remaining parsley over the top and serve.

Lasagne with Three Cheeses

Mozzarella, ricotta and Parmesan cheeses make this lasagne rich and filling. Pasta meals such as these are always popular with adults and children alike so they make good fare for gatherings of family and friends.

Serves 6–8

25g/1oz/2 tbsp butter
15ml/1 tbsp olive oil
225–250g/8–9oz/2–2¼ cups button
  (white) mushrooms, quartered
30ml/2 tbsp chopped fresh flat
  leaf parsley
250–350ml/8–12fl oz/1–1½ cups hot
  beef stock
9–12 fresh or no pre-cook dried
  lasagne sheets
450g/1lb/2 cups ricotta cheese
1 large (US extra large) egg
3 × 130g/4½oz packets mozzarella
  cheese, drained and thinly sliced
115g/4oz/1⅓ cups freshly grated
  Parmesan cheese
salt and ground black pepper

For the bolognese sauce
45ml/3 tbsp olive oil
1 onion, finely chopped
1 small carrot, finely chopped
1 celery stick, finely chopped
2 garlic cloves, finely chopped
400g/14oz minced (ground) beef
120ml/4fl oz/½ cup red wine
200ml/7fl oz/scant 1 cup passata
  (bottled, strained tomatoes)
15ml/1 tbsp tomato purée (paste)
5ml/1 tsp dried oregano
15ml/1 tbsp chopped fresh flat
  leaf parsley
350ml/12fl oz/1½ cups beef stock
8 baby Italian tomatoes (optional)
salt and ground black pepper

VARIATION
Grated mature (sharp) Cheddar cheese can be used instead of the grated Parmesan.

1 Preheat the oven to 190°C/375°F/Gas 5. Melt the butter in the oil in a frying pan. Add the mushrooms, with salt and pepper to taste, and toss over a medium to high heat for 5–8 minutes, until the mushrooms are tender and quite dry. Remove the pan from the heat and stir in the parsley.

2 To make the bolognese sauce, heat the oil in a large pan, add the chopped vegetables and cook over a low heat, stirring frequently, for 5–7 minutes.

3 Add the minced beef and cook for 5 minutes, stirring frequently. Stir in the wine and mix well.

4 Cook for 1–2 minutes, then add the passata, tomato purée, herbs and 60ml/4 tbsp of the stock. Season with salt and pepper to taste. Stir well and bring to the boil.

5 Cover the pan, and cook over a low heat for 30 minutes, adding more stock as necessary and stirring occasionally. Add the fresh tomatoes, if using, and simmer for 5–10 minutes more.

6 Stir in enough hot beef stock to make the sauce quite runny. (This is particularly important if using the no pre-cook sheets of dried lasagne).

7 Stir in the mushroom and parsley mixture, then spread about a quarter of this sauce over the base of an ovenproof dish. Cover with three or four sheets of lasagne.

8 Beat together the ricotta and egg in a bowl, with salt and pepper to taste, then spread about a third of the mixture over the lasagne sheets. Cover with a third of the mozzarella slices, then sprinkle with about a quarter of the grated Parmesan.

9 Repeat these layers twice, using half the remaining bolognese sauce each time, and finishing with the remaining Parmesan cheese.

10 Bake for 30–40 minutes, or until the cheese topping is golden brown and bubbling. Leave the lasagne to stand for about 10 minutes before serving straight from the dish.

Beef Wellington

Tender fillet of beef baked in puff pastry makes a sophisticated main course for a formal dinner. Start preparing the dish well in advance to allow time for the meat to cool before it is wrapped in the pastry.

Serves 6

1.5kg/3¼lb fillet (tenderloin) of beef
45ml/3 tbsp sunflower oil
115g/4oz/1½ cups mushrooms,
  chopped
2 garlic cloves, crushed
175g/6oz smooth liver pâté
30ml/2 tbsp chopped fresh parsley
400g/14oz puff pastry
beaten egg, to glaze
salt and ground black pepper
fresh flat leaf parsley, to garnish

1 Tie the fillet of beef at regular intervals with string so that it stays in a neat shape during cooking.

2 Heat 30ml/2 tbsp of the sunflower oil in a large frying pan, and cook the beef over a high heat for about 10 minutes, until brown on all sides. Transfer to a roasting pan, bake for 20 minutes. Leave to cool.

3 Heat the remaining oil in a frying pan and cook the mushrooms and garlic for about 5 minutes. Beat the mushroom mixture into the pâté with the parsley, season well. Set aside to cool.

4 Roll out the pastry into a sheet large enough to enclose the beef, plus a strip to spare. Trim off the spare pastry, trim the other edges to neaten. Spread the pâté mix down the middle of the pastry. Untie the beef and lay it on the pâté.

5 Preheat the oven to 220°C/425°F/ Gas 7. Brush the edges of the pastry with beaten egg and fold it over the meat to enclose it in a neat parcel. Place the parcel on a baking sheet with the join in the pastry underneath. Cut leaf shapes from the reserved pastry. Brush the parcel with egg, garnish with pastry leaves. Chill for 10 minutes.

6 Bake the Beef Wellington for 50–60 minutes, covering it loosely with foil after about 30 minutes to prevent the pastry from burning. Serve cut into thick slices garnished with parsley.

Boeuf Bourguignonne

This classic French dish of beef cooked in Burgundy style with red wine, small pieces of bacon, baby onions and mushrooms, is a favourite choice for a dinner party.

Serves 6

175g/6oz rindless streaky (fatty) bacon
    rashers (strips), chopped
900g/2lb lean braising steak
30ml/2 tbsp plain (all-purpose) flour
45ml/3 tbsp sunflower oil
25g/1oz/2 tbsp butter
12 baby (pearl) onions
2 garlic cloves, crushed
175g/6oz/2⅓ cups mushrooms, sliced
450ml/¾ pint/scant 2 cups red wine
150ml/¼ pint/⅔ cup beef stock
    or consommé
1 bay leaf
2 sprigs each of fresh thyme, parsley
    and marjoram
salt and ground black pepper
creamed potatoes and celeriac,
    to serve

1 Preheat the oven to 160°C/325°F/ Gas 3. Heat a large flameproof casserole, then add the bacon and cook, stirring occasionally, until the fat runs and the cooked pieces are crisp and golden brown.

2 Meanwhile, cut the meat into 2.5cm/ 1in cubes. Season the flour and use to coat the meat. Use a slotted spoon to remove the bacon from the casserole and set aside. Add the oil and heat, then brown the beef, in batches, and set aside with the bacon (cooking too much at once reduces the temperature of the oil drastically).

3 Add the butter to the fat remaining in the casserole. Cook the onions and garlic until just starting to colour, then add the mushrooms and cook for a further 5 minutes. Replace the bacon and meat, and stir in the wine and stock or consommé. Tie the bay leaf, thyme, parsley and marjoram together into a bouquet garni and add to the casserole.

4 Cover and cook in the oven for 1½ hours, or until the meat is tender, stirring once or twice. Season to taste and serve the casserole with creamy mashed root vegetables, such as celeriac and potatoes.

Seared Tuna Steaks with Red Onion Salsa

Red onions are ideal for this salsa, not only for their mild and sweet flavour, but also because they look so appetizing. Salad, rice or bread and a bowl of thick yogurt flavoured with chopped fresh herbs are good accompaniments.

Serves 8

8 tuna steaks, about 175–200g/
   6–7oz each
10ml/2 tsp cumin seeds, toasted
   and crushed
pinch of dried red chilli flakes
grated rind and juice of 2 limes
60–75ml/4–5 tbsp extra virgin
   olive oil
salt and ground black pepper
lime wedges and fresh coriander
   (cilantro) sprigs, to garnish

For the salsa

2 small red onions, finely chopped
400g/14oz red or yellow cherry
   tomatoes, coarsely chopped
2 avocados, peeled, stoned, (pitted)
   and chopped
4 kiwi fruit, peeled and chopped
2 fresh red chillies, seeded and
   finely chopped
25g/1oz/½ cup chopped fresh
   coriander (cilantro)
12 fresh mint sprigs, leaves
   only, chopped
10–15ml/2–3 tsp Thai fish sauce
about 10ml/2 tsp muscovado
   (molasses) sugar

1 Wash the tuna steaks and pat dry with kitchen paper. Sprinkle with half the cumin, the dried chilli flakes, salt, pepper and half the lime rind. Rub in 60ml/4 tbsp of the oil and set aside in a dish for about 30 minutes.

COOK'S TIP
The spicy fruity salsa also goes well with salmon steaks cooked on the barbecue.

2 Meanwhile, make the salsa. Mix the onions, tomatoes, avocados, kiwi fruit, fresh chilli, chopped coriander and mint. Add the remaining cumin, the rest of the lime rind and half the lime juice. Add the Thai fish sauce and sugar to taste. Set aside for 15–20 minutes, then add more Thai fish sauce, lime juice and olive oil if required.

3 Heat a griddle. Cook the tuna, allowing about 2 minutes on each side for rare tuna or a little longer for a medium result.

4 Serve the tuna steaks garnished with lime wedges and coriander sprigs. Serve the salsa separately or spoon it next to the tuna.

Lobster Thermidor

One of the classic French dishes, lobster thermidor makes a little lobster go a long way. It is best to use large lobsters rather than small ones, as they will contain a higher proportion of flesh and the meat will be sweeter.

Serves 6

3 large lobsters, about 800g–1kg/
  1¾–2¼lb, boiled
120ml/4fl oz/½ cup brandy
75g/3oz/6 tbsp butter
6 shallots, finely chopped
350g/12oz/4½ cups button (white)
  mushrooms, thinly sliced
50ml/3 tbsp plain (all-purpose) flour
350ml/12fl oz/1½ cups fish stock
350ml/12fl oz/1½ cups double
  (heavy) cream
15ml/1 tbsp Dijon mustard
6 egg yolks, beaten
120ml/9 tbsp dry white wine
115g/4oz/1⅓ cups freshly grated
  Parmesan cheese
salt, ground black pepper and
  cayenne pepper
steamed rice and salad leaves, to serve

1 Split each lobster in half lengthways; crack the claws. Discard the stomach sac, and keep the coral for another dish. Keeping each half-shell intact, extract the meat from the tail and claws, then cut into large dice. Place in a shallow dish and sprinkle over the brandy. Cover and set aside. Wipe and dry the half-shells and set them aside.

2 Melt the butter in a pan and cook the shallots over a low heat until soft. Add the mushrooms and cook until just tender, stirring constantly. Stir in the flour and a pinch of cayenne pepper; cook, stirring, for 2–3 minutes. Gradually add the stock, stirring until the sauce boils and thickens.

3 Stir in the cream and mustard and continue to cook until the sauce is smooth and thick. Season to taste with salt, black pepper and cayenne. Pour half the sauce on to the egg yolks, stir well and return the mixture to the pan. Stir in the wine. Taste and adjust the seasoning, being generous with the cayenne pepper.

4 Preheat the grill (broiler) to medium-high. Stir the diced lobster and the brandy into the sauce. Arrange the lobster half-shells in a grill pan and divide the mixture among them. Sprinkle with Parmesan and place under the grill until browned. Serve with the rice and salad leaves.

Baked Salmon with Watercress Sauce

A whole baked salmon makes a
stunning centrepiece for a buffet.
Baking it in foil is easier than
poaching and yet the flesh has
a similar melting quality. If you
decorate the fish with thin slices
of cucumber it will add a delicate
touch to its appearance.

Serves 6–8

2–3kg/4½–6½lb salmon, cleaned
    with head and tail left on
3–5 spring onions (scallions),
    thinly sliced
1 lemon, thinly sliced
1 cucumber, thinly sliced
fresh dill sprigs, to garnish
lemon wedges, to serve
salt and ground black pepper

For the sauce
3 garlic cloves, chopped
200g/7oz watercress leaves,
    finely chopped
40g/1½oz/¾ cup finely chopped
    fresh tarragon
300g/11oz mayonnaise
15–30ml/1–2 tbsp freshly squeezed
    lemon juice
200g/7oz/scant 1 cup unsalted
    (sweet) butter

1 Preheat the oven to 180°C/350°F/
Gas 4. Rinse the salmon and lay it on a
large piece of foil. Stuff the fish with
the sliced spring onions and layer the
lemon slices inside and around the fish,
then sprinkle with salt and pepper.

2 Loosely fold the foil around the fish
and fold the edges over to seal. Bake
for about 1 hour.

3 Remove the fish from the oven and
leave it to stand, still wrapped in the
foil, for about 15 minutes. Then
unwrap the foil parcel and leave
the salmon to cool.

4 When the fish is cool, carefully lift it
on to a large plate, still covered with
lemon slices. Cover the fish tightly with
clear film (plastic wrap) and chill for
several hours in the refrigerator.

5 Use a blunt knife to lift up the edge
of the skin and carefully peel the skin
away from the flesh, avoiding tearing
the flesh. Pull out any fins at the same
time. Carefully turn over the salmon
and repeat on the other side. Leave
the head on for serving, if you wish.
Discard the skin.

6 Arrange the cucumber slices in
overlapping rows along the length of
the fish, so that they look like large
fish scales.

7 To make the sauce, put the garlic,
watercress, tarragon, mayonnaise and
lemon juice in a food processor or
blender or a bowl, and process or mix
well to combine.

8 Melt the butter, then add to the
watercress mixture, a little at a time,
processing or stirring, until the butter
has been incorporated and the sauce is
thick and smooth. Cover and chill
before serving.

9 Serve the fish, garnished with dill
and lemon wedges, and the watercress
sauce alongside.

COOK'S TIP
Do not prepare the sauce more than a
few hours ahead of serving as the
watercress will discolour it.

VARIATION
If you prefer to poach the fish rather than
baking it, you will need to use a fish
kettle. Place the salmon on the rack, in the
kettle. Cover with cold water and bring
to a simmer, cook for 5–10 minutes per
450g/1lb until tender.

Celebration Paella

This paella is a marvellous mixture of some of the finest Spanish ingredients and makes a colourful one-pot party dish.

Serves 6–8

6–8 large raw prawns (shrimp), peeled,
    or 12–16 smaller raw prawns
450g/1lb fresh mussels
90ml/6 tbsp white wine
150g/5oz green beans, cut into
    2.5cm/1in lengths
115g/4oz/1 cup frozen broad
    (fava) beans
6 small skinless chicken breast fillets,
    cut into large pieces
30ml/2 tbsp plain (all-purpose) flour,
    seasoned with salt and pepper
about 90ml/6 tbsp olive oil
150g/5oz pork fillet (tenderloin), cut
    into bitesize pieces
2 onions, chopped
2–3 garlic cloves, crushed
1 red (bell) pepper, seeded and sliced
2 ripe tomatoes, peeled, seeded
    and chopped
900ml/1½ pints/3¾ cups well-
    flavoured chicken stock
good pinch of saffron threads,
    dissolved in 30ml/2 tbsp hot water
350g/12oz/1¾ cups Spanish rice or
    risotto rice
225g/8oz chorizo, sliced
115g/4oz/1 cup frozen peas
6–8 stuffed green olives,
    thickly sliced
salt and ground black pepper

COOK'S TIP

Ideally, you should use a paella pan for this recipe and the paella should not be stirred during cooking. However, you may find that the rice cooks in the centre but not around the outside. To make sure it cooks evenly stir occasionally, or cook the paella on the bottom of a preheated 190°C/375°F/Gas 5 oven for about 15–18 minutes.

1 Make a shallow cut down the centre of the curved back of each of the large prawns. Pull out the black veins with a cocktail stick (toothpick) or your fingers, then rinse the prawns thoroughly and set them aside.

2 Scrub the mussel shells with a stiff brush and rinse thoroughly under cold running water. Scrape off any barnacles and remove the "beards" with a small knife. Rinse well. Discard any mussels that are open and do not close when sharply tapped.

3 Place the mussels in a large pan with the wine, bring to the boil, then cover the pan tightly and cook, shaking the pan occasionally, for 3–4 minutes, or until the mussels have opened. Drain, reserving the liquid and discarding any mussels that remain closed.

4 Briefly cook the green beans and broad beans in separate pans of boiling water for 2–3 minutes. Drain. As soon as the broad beans are cool enough to handle, pop the bright green inner beans out of their skins.

5 Dust the chicken with the seasoned flour. Heat half the oil in a paella pan or frying pan and cook the chicken until browned all over. Transfer to a plate. Cook the prawns briefly, adding more oil if needed, use a slotted spoon to transfer them to a plate. Heat a further 30ml/2 tbsp of the oil in the pan and brown the pork. Transfer to a plate.

6 Heat the remaining oil and cook the onions and garlic for 3–4 minutes, or until golden brown. Add the red pepper, cook for 2–3 minutes, then add the chopped tomatoes and cook until the mixture is fairly thick.

7 Stir in the chicken stock, the reserved mussel liquid and the saffron liquid. Season well with salt and pepper and bring to the boil. When the liquid is bubbling, add the rice. Stir once, then add the chicken pieces, pork, prawns, beans, chorizo and peas. Cook over a moderately high heat for 12 minutes, then lower the heat and cook for 8–10 minutes more, until all the liquid has been absorbed.

8 Add the mussels and olives and cook for a further 3–4 minutes to heat through. Remove the pan from the heat, cover with a clean, damp dishtowel and leave the paella to stand for 10 minutes before serving straight from the pan.

Roasted Stuffed Turkey

Serve this classic roast with stuffing balls, bacon rolls, roast potatoes, vegetables and gravy.

Serves 8

4.5kg/10lb oven-ready turkey, with
    giblets, thawed, if frozen
1 large onion, peeled and studded
    with 6 whole cloves
50g/2oz/¼ cup butter, softened
10 chipolata sausages
salt and ground black pepper

For the stuffing

225g/8oz rindless streaky (fatty)
    bacon, chopped
1 large onion, finely chopped
450g/1lb pork sausage meat
    (bulk sausage)
25g/1oz/⅓ cup rolled oats
30ml/2 tbsp chopped fresh parsley
10ml/2 tsp dried mixed herbs
1 large (US extra large) egg, beaten
115g/4oz/1 cup ready-to-eat dried
    apricots, finely chopped

For the gravy

25g/1oz/¼ cup plain (all-purpose) flour
450ml/¾ pint/scant 2 cups giblet stock

1 Preheat the oven to 200°C/400°F/Gas 6. To make the stuffing, cook the bacon and onion over a gentle heat in a frying pan until the bacon is crisp and the onion is tender but not browned. Transfer to a large bowl and add the remaining stuffing ingredients. Season well and mix to combine.

2 Stuff the neck end of the turkey only, tucking the flap of skin under and securing it with a small skewer or stitching it in place with a thread. Do not overstuff the turkey or the skin will burst during cooking. Reserve any remaining stuffing and set aside.

3 Put the onion studded with cloves in the body cavity of the turkey and tie the legs together with string to hold them in place. Weigh the stuffed bird and calculate the cooking time: allow 15 minutes per 450g/1lb plus an extra 15 minutes. Place the turkey in a large roasting pan.

4 Brush the turkey with the butter and season well with salt and pepper. Cover it loosely with foil and cook it for 30 minutes. Baste the turkey with the pan juices. Then lower the oven temperature to 180°C/350°F/Gas 4 and cook for the remainder of the calculated cooking time. Baste the turkey every 30 minutes or so and check for any small bubbles of fat, pricking them with a fork to release the fat from the skin.

5 Remove the foil from the turkey for the last hour of cooking and baste. With wet hands, shape the remaining stuffing into small balls or pack it into a greased ovenproof dish. Cook in the oven for 20 minutes, or until golden brown and crisp. About 20 minutes before the end of cooking, put the chipolata sausages into an ovenproof dish and put them in the oven. The turkey is cooked if the juices run clear when the thickest part of the thigh is pierced with a skewer.

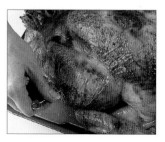

6 Transfer the turkey to a serving plate, cover it with foil and let it stand for 15 minutes before carving. To make the gravy, spoon off the fat from the roasting pan, leaving the meat juices. Blend in the flour and cook on the stove for 2 minutes. Gradually stir in the stock and bring to the boil. Check the seasoning. Pour into a sauce boat.

7 To serve the turkey, remove the skewer and pour any juices into the gravy. Surround the turkey with chipolata sausages and stuffing and carve it at the table.

Turkey and Cranberry Pie

This is ideal for using up leftovers and the cranberries add a tart layer to this attractive pie. It needs to be made the day before, and it can even be frozen in advance.

Serves 8

450g/1lb pork sausage meat
   (bulk sausage)
450g/1lb/2 cups minced (ground) pork
15ml/1 tbsp ground coriander
15ml/1 tbsp mixed dried herbs
finely grated rind of 2 large oranges
10ml/2 tsp grated fresh root ginger or
   2.5ml/½ tsp ground ginger
450g/1lb turkey breast fillets, skinned
115g/4oz/1 cup fresh cranberries
salt and ground black pepper

For the pastry

450g/1lb/4 cups plain (all-purpose) flour
5ml/1 tsp salt
150g/5oz/10 tbsp white cooking fat
150ml/¼ pint/⅔ cup mixed milk
   and water

To finish

1 egg, beaten
300ml/½ pint/1¼ cups aspic jelly, made
   up as packet instructions

1 Preheat the oven to 180°C/350°F/Gas 4. Place a large baking tray in the oven to preheat. In a large bowl, mix together the sausage meat, minced pork, coriander, mixed dried herbs, orange rind and ginger with plenty of salt and ground black pepper.

2 To make the pastry, put the flour into a large bowl with the salt. Heat the fat in a small pan with the milk and water until just beginning to boil. Set aside and leave to cool slightly.

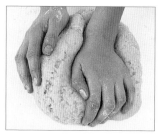

3 Using a spoon, stir the liquid into the flour until a stiff dough forms. Turn on to a work surface and knead until smooth. Cut one-third off the dough for the lid, wrap it in clear film (plastic wrap), and keep it in a warm place.

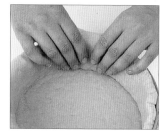

4 Roll out the large piece of dough on a floured surface and line the base and sides of a well-greased 20cm/8in loose-based, springform cake tin (pan). Work the dough while it is warm, as it will crack and break if it is left to get cold.

5 Thinly slice the turkey fillets and put between two pieces of clear film and flatten with a rolling pin to a 3mm/⅛in thickness. Spoon half the pork mixture into the base of the tin, pressing it into the edges. Cover with half of the turkey slices and then the cranberries, followed by the remaining turkey and finally the rest of the pork mixture.

6 Roll out the rest of the dough and cover the filling, trimming any excess and sealing the edges with beaten egg. Make a steam hole in the lid and decorate with pastry trimmings. Brush with beaten egg. Bake for 2 hours. Cover the pie with foil if it gets too brown. Place the pie on a wire rack to cool. When cold, use a funnel to fill the pie with aspic jelly. Leave to set for a few hours before unmoulding the pie.

COOK'S TIPS

• Stand the springform pan on a baking tray with a shallow rim to catch any juices that may seep from the pie during baking.
• Leave the pie to cool in the pan until the pastry has firmed up slightly before transferring it to a wire rack.

Duck with Plum Sauce

This is an updated version of an old English dish, which is quite quick to prepare and cook, and ideal formal dinner party fare. Make it when plums are in season, when they will be ripe and juicy.

Serves 8

8 duck quarters
2 large red onions, finely chopped
1kg/2¼lb ripe plums, stoned (pitted) and quartered
60ml/4 tbsp redcurrant jelly
salt and ground black pepper

COOK'S TIP

It is important that the plums used in this dish are very ripe, otherwise the mixture will be too dry and the sauce will be extremely tart.

1 Prick the duck skin all over with a fork to release the fat during cooking and help give a crisp result, then place the portions in a heavy frying pan, skin sides down.

2 Cook the duck pieces for 10 minutes on each side, or until golden brown and cooked right through. Remove the duck from the frying pan using a slotted spoon, and keep warm.

3 Pour away all but 30ml/2 tbsp of the duck fat, then stir-fry the onion for 5 minutes, or until golden. Add the plums and cook, stirring frequently, for a further 5 minutes. Add the redcurrant jelly and mix well.

4 Replace the duck portions and cook for a further 5 minutes, or until thoroughly reheated. Season with salt and pepper to taste before serving.

Wild Duck with **Olives**

Compared to farmed duck, wild duck, which has a brilliant flavour, is worth the extra expense for a special occasion meal. They are often quite small birds, so allow two pieces per portion. Mashed parsnips and green vegetables are good accompaniments.

Serves 4

2 wild ducks, weighing about 1.5kg/
    3¼lb, each cut into 4 portions
2 onions, chopped
2 carrots, chopped
4 celery sticks, chopped
6 garlic cloves, sliced
2 bottles red wine
600ml/1 pint/2½ cups well-flavoured
    game stock
handful of fresh thyme leaves
5ml/1 tsp arrowroot
450g/1lb/4 cups pitted green olives
225g/8oz passata (bottled
    strained tomatoes)
salt and ground black pepper

1 Preheat the oven to 220°C/425°F/ Gas 7. Season the duck portions generously with salt and ground black pepper and place them in a large flameproof casserole.

2 Roast the duck portions for 25–30 minutes, then remove the casserole from the oven. Use a slotted spoon to remove the duck from the casserole, reserving the cooking fat, and set aside. Reduce the oven temperature to 160°C/325°F/Gas 3.

3 Carefully transfer the casserole to the stove and heat the duck fat until it is sizzling. Add the chopped onions, carrots, celery sticks and garlic cloves, and cook for 10 minutes, or until the vegetables have softened. Pour in the red wine and boil until it has reduced by about half.

4 Add the stock and thyme leaves, then replace the duck portions in the casserole. Bring to the boil, skim the surface, then cover the casserole and place in the oven for about 1 hour, or until the duck is tender. Remove the duck portions and keep warm.

5 Skim the excess fat from the cooking liquid, strain it and return it to the casserole, then bring it to the boil. Skim the liquid again, if necessary.

VARIATION
Process 225g/8oz canned tomatoes in a blender and use instead of the passata.

6 Mix the arrowroot to a thin paste with a little cold water and whisk it into the simmering sauce. Add the olives and passata and replace the duck, then cook, uncovered, for 15 minutes. Check the seasoning and serve.

Roast Goose with Caramelized Apples

Tender goose served with sweet apples makes this a perfect celebration main course.

Serves 8

4.5–5.5kg/10–12lb goose, with giblets, thawed, if frozen
salt and ground black pepper

For the apple and nut stuffing
225g/8oz/1 cup prunes
150ml/¼ pint/⅔ cup port or red wine
675g/1½ lb cooking apples, peeled, cored and cubed
1 large onion, chopped
4 celery sticks, sliced
15ml/1 tbsp mixed dried herbs
finely grated rind of 1 orange
goose liver, chopped
450g/1lb pork sausage meat (bulk sausage)
115g/4oz/1 cup chopped pecan nuts
2 eggs

For the caramelized apples
50g/2oz/¼ cup butter
60ml/4 tbsp redcurrant jelly
30ml/2 tbsp red wine vinegar
9 small eating apples, peeled and cored

For the gravy
30ml/2 tbsp plain (all-purpose) flour
600ml/1 pint/2½ cups giblet stock
juice of 1 orange

1 Soak the prunes in the port or red wine for 24 hours. Stone (pit) and cut each prune into four. Reserve the liquid.

2 The next day, mix the prunes with all the remaining stuffing ingredients and season well. Moisten with half the reserved port or red wine.

3 Preheat the oven to 200°C/400°F/Gas 6. Stuff the neck-end of the goose, tucking the flap of skin under and securing it with a small skewer. Remove the excess fat from the cavity and pack it with the stuffing. Tie the legs together to hold them in place.

4 Weigh the stuffed goose to calculate the cooking time: allow 15 minutes for each 450g/1lb plus an extra15 minutes. Put the bird on a rack in a roasting pan and rub the skin with salt. Prick the skin all over to help the fat run out. Roast for 30 minutes, then reduce the heat to 180°C/350°F/Gas 4 and roast for the remaining cooking time. Occasionally check and pour off any fat produced during cooking into a bowl. The goose is cooked when the juices run clear when the thickest part of the thigh is pierced with a skewer. Pour a little cold water over the breast halfway through the cooking time to crisp up the skin.

5 Meanwhile, prepare the apples. Melt the butter, redcurrant jelly and vinegar in a small roasting pan or a shallow ovenproof dish. Put in the apples, baste them well and cook in the oven for 15–20 minutes. Baste the apples halfway through the cooking time. Do not cover them or they will collapse.

6 Lift the goose on to a serving dish and let it stand for 15 minutes before carving. Pour off the excess fat from the roasting pan, leaving any sediment in the base. Stir in the flour, cook gently until brown, and then blend in the stock. Bring to the boil, add the remaining reserved port, orange juice and seasoning. Simmer gently for 2–3 minutes. Strain into a gravy boat.

7 Surround the goose with the caramelized apples and spoon over the redcurrant glaze. Serve with the gravy.

COOK'S TIP
Do not overestimate the yield from a goose – the bird often looks big but there is a lot of fat and not too much meat on it for its size.

Glazed Poussins

Golden poussins make an impressive main course. Serve them with traditional roast accompaniments or a refreshing side salad.

Serves 6

75g/3oz/6 tbsp butter
15ml/1 tbsp mixed (pumpkin pie) spice
45ml/3 tbsp clear honey
grated rind and juice of 3 clementines
6 poussins, each weighing
* about 450g/1lb*
1 large onion, finely chopped
2 garlic cloves, chopped
25ml/1½ tbsp plain (all-purpose) flour
75ml/2½ fl oz/⅓ cup Marsala
450ml/¾ pint/scant 2 cups
* chicken stock*
bunch of fresh coriander (cilantro),
* to garnish*

VARIATION
You can stuff each poussin, before roasting, with a quartered clementine.

1 Preheat the oven to 220°C/425°F/ Gas 7. To make the glaze, heat the butter, mixed spice, honey and clementine rind and juice until the butter has melted, stirring to mix well. Remove from the heat.

2 Place the poussins in a large roasting pan, brush them with the glaze, then roast for 40 minutes. Brush with any remaining glaze and baste occasionally with the pan juices during cooking. Transfer the poussins to a serving platter, cover with foil and leave to stand for 10 minutes.

3 Skim off all but 15ml/1 tbsp of the fat from the roasting pan. Add the onion and garlic to the juices in the pan and cook on the stove, stirring occasionally, until beginning to brown. Stir in the flour, then gradually pour in the Marsala, followed by the stock, whisking constantly. Bring to the boil and simmer for 3 minutes to make a smooth, rich gravy.

4 Transfer the poussins to warm plates or leave on the serving platter and garnish with coriander. Serve at once, offering the gravy separately.

Medallions of Venison with Herbed Horseradish Dumplings

Venison is lean and full-flavoured, and tastes simply wonderful with these piquant dumplings.

Serves 8

1.2 litres/2 pints/5 cups venison stock
250ml/8fl oz/1 cup port
30ml/2 tbsp sunflower oil
8 medallions of venison, about
*   175g/6oz each*
chopped fresh parsley, to garnish
steamed baby vegetables, to serve

For the dumplings
150g/5oz/1¼ cup self-raising
*   (self-rising) flour*
75g/3oz beef suet (US chilled
*   grated shortening)*
30ml/2 tbsp chopped mixed herbs
10ml/2 tsp creamed horseradish
90–120ml/6–8 tbsp water

1 First make the dumplings: mix the flour, suet and herbs and make a well in the centre. Add the horseradish and water, then mix to make a soft but not sticky dough. Shape the dough into walnut-size balls and chill in the refrigerator for up to 1 hour.

2 Boil the venison stock in a pan until reduced by half. Add the port and continue boiling until reduced again by half, then pour the reduced stock into a frying pan. Heat the stock until it is simmering and add the dumplings. Poach them for 5–10 minutes, or until risen and cooked through. Use a slotted spoon to remove the dumplings.

COOK'S TIP
Serve a variety of steamed vegetables with the venison such as carrots, courgettes (zucchini) and turnips.

3 Smear the sunflower oil over a non-stick griddle, heat until very hot. Add the venison, cook for 2–3 minutes on each side. Place the venison medallions on warmed serving plates and pour the sauce over. Serve with the dumplings and vegetables, garnished with parsley.

VARIATION
Beef fillet (tenderloin) medallions can be used instead of the venison. Replace the venison stock with beef stock.

Rich Game Pie

Smart enough for a formal wedding buffet but also terrific for a stylish picnic, this rich game pie looks spectacular when baked in a fluted raised pie mould. Some specialist kitchen stores hire the moulds so you can avoid the expense of purchasing one; alternatively a 20cm/8in round deep, loose-based tin can be used. Serve the pie garnished with salad leaves.

Serves 10

25g/1oz/2 tbsp butter
1 onion, finely chopped
2 garlic cloves, finely chopped
900g/2lb mixed boneless game meat,
*   such as skinless pheasant and/or*
*   pigeon (US squab) breast, venison*
*   and rabbit, diced*
30ml/2 tbsp chopped mixed fresh
*   herbs, such as parsley, thyme*
*   and marjoram*
salt and ground black pepper

For the pâté
50g/2oz/¼ cup butter
2 garlic cloves, finely chopped
450g/1lb chicken livers, rinsed,
*   trimmed and chopped*
60ml/4 tbsp brandy
5ml/1 tsp ground mace

For the pastry
675g/1½lb/6 cups strong white
*   bread flour*
5ml/1 tsp salt
115ml/3½fl oz/scant ½ cup milk
115ml/3½fl oz/scant ½ cup water
115g/4oz/½ cup white cooking
*   fat, diced*
115g/4oz/½ cup butter, diced
beaten egg, to glaze

For the jelly
300ml/½ pint/1¼ cups game or
*   beef consommé*
2.5ml/½ tsp powdered gelatine

1 Melt the butter in a small pan until foaming, then add the onion and garlic, and cook until softened but not coloured. Remove from the heat and mix with the diced game meat and the chopped mixed herbs. Season well, cover and chill.

2 To make the pâté, melt the butter in a pan until foaming. Add the garlic and chicken livers and cook until the livers are just browned. Remove the pan from the heat and stir in the brandy and mace. Process the mixture in a blender or food processor until smooth, then set aside and leave to cool completely.

3 To make the pastry, sift the flour and salt into a bowl and make a well in the centre. Place the milk and water in a pan. Add the white cooking fat and butter and heat gently until melted, then bring to the boil and remove from the heat as soon as the mixture begins to bubble. Pour the hot liquid into the well in the flour and beat until smooth. Cover and leave until the dough is cool enough to handle.

4 Preheat the oven to 200°C/400°F/ Gas 6. Roll out two-thirds of the pastry and use to line a 23cm/9in raised pie mould. Press the pastry into the flutes and around the edge. Patch any thin areas with offcuts (scraps) from the top edge. Spoon in half the mixture and press it down evenly. Add the pâté and then top with the remaining game.

5 Roll out the remaining pastry to form a lid. Brush the edge of the pastry lining the tin with a little water and cover the pie with the pastry lid. Trim off excess pastry from around the edge. Pinch the edges together to seal in the filling. Make two holes in the centre of the lid and glaze with egg. Use pastry trimmings to roll out leaves to garnish the pie. Brush with egg.

6 Bake the pie for 20 minutes, then cover it with foil and cook for a further 10 minutes. Reduce the oven temperature to 150°C/300°F/Gas 2. Glaze the pie again with beaten egg and cook for a further 1½ hours, with the top covered loosely with foil.

7 Remove the pie from the oven and leave it to stand for 15 minutes. Increase the oven temperature to 200°C/400°F/Gas 6. Stand the tin on a baking sheet and remove the sides. Quickly glaze the sides of the pie with beaten egg and cover the top with foil, then cook for a final 15 minutes to brown the sides. Leave to cool completely, then chill the pie overnight.

8 To make the jelly, heat the game or beef consommé in a small pan until just beginning to bubble, whisk in the gelatine until dissolved and leave to cool until just setting. Using a small funnel, carefully pour the jellied consommé into the holes in the pie. Chill until set. This pie will keep in the refrigerator for up to 3 days.

Fillet of Beef with Ratatouille

This succulent beef is served cold
with a colourful garlicky ratatouille.

Serves 8

675–900g/1½–2lb fillet (tenderloin)
  of beef
45ml/3 tbsp olive oil
300ml/½ pint/1¼ cups aspic jelly, made
  up as packet instructions

For the marinade

30ml/2 tbsp sherry
30ml/2 tbsp olive oil
30ml/2 tbsp soy sauce
10ml/2 tsp grated fresh root ginger
2 garlic cloves, crushed

For the ratatouille

60ml/4 tbsp olive oil
1 onion, sliced
2–3 garlic cloves, crushed
1 large aubergine (eggplant), cubed
1 small red (bell) pepper, seeded
  and sliced
1 small green (bell) pepper, seeded
  and sliced
1 small yellow (bell) pepper, seeded
  and sliced
225g/8oz courgettes (zucchini), sliced
450g/1lb tomatoes, peeled
15ml/1 tbsp chopped fresh mixed herbs
30ml/2 tbsp French dressing
salt and ground black pepper

1 Mix all the marinade ingredients
together and pour over the beef. Cover
the dish with clear film (plastic wrap)
and leave for 30 minutes.

2 Preheat the oven to 220°C/425°F/
Gas 7. Using a large slotted spoon, lift
the beef out of the marinade and pat it
dry with kitchen paper. Heat the oil in a
frying pan until smoking hot and then
brown the beef all over to seal it.

3 Transfer the beef to a roasting pan
and roast for 10–15 minutes, basting it
occasionally with the marinade. Lift
the beef out on to a large plate and
leave it to cool.

4 Meanwhile, for the ratatouille, heat
the oil in a large casserole and cook the
onion and garlic over a low heat, until
tender, without letting the onions
become brown. Add the aubergine
cubes to the casserole and cook for a
further 5 minutes, until soft.

5 Add the sliced peppers and the
courgettes and cook for 2 minutes
more. Then add the tomatoes and
chopped herbs, and season well with
salt and pepper. Cook for a few
minutes longer. Turn the ratatouille into
a dish and set aside to cool. Drizzle
with a little French dressing.

6 Slice the beef fillet and arrange
overlapping slices on a large serving
platter. Brush the slices of beef with a
little cold aspic jelly that is just on the
point of setting.

7 Leave the beef until the aspic jelly has
set completely, then brush the slices
with a second coat. Spoon the cooled
ratatouille around the beef slices on
the platter and serve immediately.

COOK'S TIP
Ratatouille is a traditional French recipe
that is at its best when made with the
choicest fresh ingredients. It makes a
wonderful side dish for a buffet or can be
eaten as a snack or as a vegetarian filling
for jacket potatoes.

VARIATIONS
• Instead of marinating the beef in
soy sauce and ginger, add 15ml/1 tbsp
chopped fresh marjoram to the mixture,
increase the quantity of sherry to 60ml/
4 tbsp and add 15ml/1 tbsp crushed
juniper berries.
• Use pork instead of beef and increase
the roasting time to 20–30 minutes.

Cider-glazed Ham

A succulent gammon joint with a sweet cider glaze that looks impressive and tastes wonderful. Served with a zesty cranberry sauce, it would be ideal for a Christmas or Thanksgiving buffet.

Serves 8–10

2kg/4½lb middle gammon (smoked or
    cured ham) joint
1 large or 2 small onions
about 30 whole cloves
3 bay leaves
10 black peppercorns
1.3 litres/2¼ pints/5⅔ cups
    medium-dry (hard) cider
45ml/3 tbsp soft light brown sugar
bunch of flat leaf parsley, to garnish

For the sauce

350g/12oz/3 cups cranberries
175g/6oz/¾ cup soft light brown sugar
grated rind and juice of 2 clementines
30ml/2 tbsp port

1 Weigh the gammon joint and calculate the cooking time: allow 20 minutes per 450g/1lb, then place it in a large casserole or pan. Stud the onion or onions with 5–10 of the cloves and add to the casserole or pan with the bay leaves and peppercorns.

VARIATION

Use clear honey in place of the soft brown sugar for the glaze and serve the gammon with redcurrant sauce or jelly instead of the cranberry sauce.

2 Add 1.2 litres/2 pints/5 cups of the cider and enough water to just cover the gammon. Heat until simmering and then carefully skim off the scum that rises to the surface using a large spoon. Start timing the cooking from the moment the stock begins to simmer.

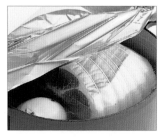

3 Cover with a lid or foil and simmer gently for the calculated time. Towards the end of the cooking time, preheat the oven to 220°C/425°F/Gas 7.

4 Heat the sugar and remaining cider in a pan; stir until the sugar has dissolved. Simmer for 5 minutes to make a dark, sticky glaze. Remove the pan from the heat and leave to cool for 5 minutes.

COOK'S TIPS

• A large stock pot or preserving pan can be used for cooking the gammon.
• Leave the gammon until it is just cool enough to handle before removing the rind. Snip off the string, then carefully slice off the rind, leaving a thin, even layer of fat. Use a narrow-bladed, sharp knife for the best results.

5 Lift the gammon out of the casserole or pan with a slotted spoon and a large fork. Carefully and evenly, cut off the rind, then score the fat into a neat diamond pattern. Place the gammon in a roasting pan or ovenproof dish.

6 Press a clove into the centre of each diamond, then carefully spoon over the glaze. Bake for 20–25 minutes, or until the fat is brown, glistening and crisp.

7 Simmer all the sauce ingredients in a heavy pan for 15–20 minutes, stirring frequently. Pour into a jug (pitcher).

8 Serve the ham hot or cold, garnished with parsley and with the cranberry sauce accompaniment.

stylish salads

A repertoire of exciting salads is every cook's

standby for colourful first courses,

refreshing side dishes or buffet pizzazz.

Pear and Parmesan Salad

This is great when pears are at their seasonal best. Try Packhams or Comice when plentiful, drizzled with a poppy-seed dressing and topped with shavings of Parmesan.

Serves 4

4 just-ripe dessert pears
50g/2oz piece Parmesan cheese
watercress, to garnish
water biscuits (crackers) or rye bread,
    to serve (optional)

For the dressing

30ml/2 tbsp extra virgin olive oil
15ml/1 tbsp sunflower oil
30ml/2 tbsp cider vinegar or white
    wine vinegar
2.5ml/½ tsp soft light brown sugar
good pinch of dried thyme
15ml/1 tbsp poppy seeds
salt and ground black pepper

1 Cut the pears in quarters and remove the cores. Cut each pear quarter in half lengthways and arrange them on four small serving plates. Peel the pears if you wish, though they look more attractive unpeeled.

COOK'S TIP

Always buy Parmesan cheese in a piece. It will keep for months in the refrigerator. If you have bought a large piece, freeze half of it. You can, in fact, make Parmesan shavings and grate it from frozen.

2 Make the dressing. Mix the olive oil, sunflower oil, vinegar, sugar, thyme and seasoning in a jug (pitcher). Whisk well, then tip in the poppy seeds. Trickle the dressing over the pears. Garnish with watercress and shave Parmesan over the top. Serve with water biscuits or thinly sliced rye bread, if you like.

VARIATION

Blue cheeses and pears also have a natural affinity. Stilton, Dolcelatte, Gorgonzola or Danish blue are all good substitutes. Allow about 200g/7oz and cut into wedges or cubes.

Pear and Roquefort Salad

Choose ripe, firm Comice or Williams pears for this salad.

Serves 4

3 ripe pears
lemon juice, for tossing
about 175g/6oz mixed salad leaves
175g/6oz Roquefort cheese
50g/2oz/¹/₂ cup hazelnuts, toasted
  and chopped

For the dressing
30ml/2 tbsp hazelnut oil
45ml/3 tbsp olive oil
15ml/1 tbsp cider vinegar
5ml/1 tsp Dijon mustard
salt and ground black pepper

1 To make the dressing, mix together the hazelnut oil, olive oil, vinegar and mustard in a bowl or screw-top jar. Season with salt and black pepper to taste. Stir or shake well.

2 Peel, core and slice the pears and toss them in lemon juice.

3 Arrange the salad leaves on serving plates, then place the pears on top. Crumble the cheese and sprinkle it over the salad with the hazelnuts. Stir or shake the dressing again, pour it over the salad and serve immediately.

Asparagus and **Orange Salad**

A simple dressing of olive oil and
sherry vinegar mingles with the
orange and tomato flavours with
great results.

Serves 4

225g/8oz asparagus, trimmed and cut
*   into 5cm/2in pieces*
2 large oranges
2 well-flavoured ripe tomatoes, cut
*   into eighths*
50g/2oz romaine lettuce leaves, shredded
30ml/2 tbsp extra virgin olive oil
2.5ml/¹/₂ tsp sherry vinegar
salt and ground black pepper

1 Cook the asparagus in lightly salted,
boiling water for 3–4 minutes, until
just tender. Drain and refresh under
cold water. Set aside.

2 Grate the rind from half an orange
and reserve. Peel both oranges and cut
into segments, leaving the membrane
behind. Squeeze out the juice from
the membrane and reserve the juice.

COOK'S TIP
Sherry vinegar is golden brown with a
rounded and full flavour. It is matured in
wooden barrels in much the same way as
sherry itself.

3 Put the asparagus pieces, segments
of orange, tomatoes and lettuce into
a salad bowl. Mix together the olive
oil and sherry vinegar and add
15ml/1 tbsp of the reserved orange
juice and 5ml/1 tsp of the grated
orange rind, whisking well to combine.
Season with a little salt and plenty of
ground black pepper. Just before
serving, pour the dressing over the
salad and mix gently to coat.

Melon and **Prosciutto Salad**

Sections of cool fragrant melon wrapped with slices of air-dried ham make a delicious salad appetizer. If strawberries are in season, serve with a savoury-sweet strawberry salsa and watch it disappear.

Serves 4

1 large cantaloupe, Charentais or
*   Galia melon*
175g/6oz prosciutto or Serrano ham,
*   thinly sliced*

For the salsa
225g/8oz/2 cups strawberries
5ml/1 tsp caster (superfine) sugar
30ml/2 tbsp sunflower oil
15ml/1 tbsp orange juice
2.5ml/¹/₂ tsp finely grated orange rind
2.5ml/¹/₂ tsp finely grated fresh
*   root ginger*
salt and ground black pepper

1 Halve the melon, scoop out the seeds with a spoon and discard. Cut the rind away with a paring knife, then slice the melon thickly. Chill in the refrigerator until ready to serve.

2 For the salsa, hull the strawberries and cut them into large dice. Place in a small mixing bowl with the sugar and crush very lightly to release the juices. Add the sunflower oil, orange juice, orange rind and grated ginger. Season with a little salt and plenty of ground black pepper.

3 Arrange the melon slices on a serving plate, lay the prosciutto or Serrano ham over the top and then serve with a bowl of salsa, handed around separately.

Moroccan Orange, Onion and Olive Salad

This is a refreshing salad to add to a selection of buffet dishes.

Serves 6

5 large oranges
90g/3½oz/scant 1 cup black olives
1 red onion, thinly sliced
1 large fennel bulb, thinly sliced,
*   feathery tops reserved*
15ml/1 tbsp chopped fresh mint, plus
*   a few extra sprigs to garnish*
15ml/1 tbsp chopped fresh coriander
*   (cilantro), plus extra to garnish*
60ml/4 tbsp olive oil
10ml/2 tsp lemon juice
2.5ml/½ tsp ground toasted
*   coriander seeds*
2.5ml/½ tsp orange flower water
salt and ground black pepper

1 Peel the oranges with a sharp knife, making sure that you remove all the white pith, and cut them into 5mm/¼in slices. Remove any pips (seeds) and work over a bowl to catch all the orange juice. Set the juice aside for adding to the salad dressing.

2 Pit the olives, if you like. In a bowl, toss the orange slices, onion and fennel together with the olives, chopped fresh mint and coriander.

3 Make the dressing: in a bowl or jug (pitcher), whisk together the olive oil, 15ml/1 tbsp of the reserved fresh orange juice and the lemon juice. Add the ground toasted coriander seeds and season to taste with a little salt and pepper. Whisk thoroughly to mix.

4 Toss the dressing into the salad, cover and leave to stand in a cool place for 30–60 minutes.

5 To serve, drain off any excess dressing and place the salad in a serving dish or bowl. Sprinkle with the chopped herbs and reserved fennel tops, and sprinkle with the orange flower water.

Tomato, Mozzarella and Red Onion Salad with Basil and Caper Dressing

Sweet tomatoes and the heady scent of basil capture the essence of summer in this simple salad.

Serves 8

10 large ripe tomatoes
4 small packets mozzarella di bufala
*   cheese, drained and sliced*
2 small red onions, chopped
fresh basil and parsley sprigs, to garnish

For the dressing
1 small garlic clove, peeled
25g/1oz/1 cup fresh basil
60ml/4 tbsp chopped fresh flat
*   leaf parsley*
45ml/3 tbsp salted capers, rinsed
5ml/1 tsp mustard
150ml/¼ pint/⅔ cup extra virgin
*   olive oil*
15ml/1tbsp balsamic vinegar
salt and ground black pepper

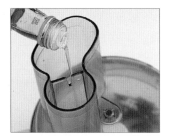

1 First make the dressing. Put the garlic, basil, parsley, half the capers and the mustard in a food processor or blender and process briefly to chop. Then, with the motor running, gradually pour in the olive oil through the feeder tube to make a smooth purée with a dressing consistency. Add the balsamic vinegar to taste and season with ground black pepper. Alternatively, the dressing can be made by pounding the ingredients in a mortar and adding the oil by hand.

2 Slice the tomatoes thinly. Arrange the tomato and mozzarella slices overlapping alternately on a large plate. Sprinkle the onion over the top and season with a little pepper.

3 Drizzle the dressing over the salad, then sprinkle a few basil leaves, parsley sprigs and the remaining capers on top.

4 Leave the salad to marinate for 10–15 minutes for the flavours to develop before serving.

Tricolour Salad

A popular salad, this dish depends for its success on the quality of its ingredients. Mozzarella di bufala is the best cheese to serve uncooked. Whole ripe plum tomatoes give up their juice to blend with extra virgin olive oil for a natural dressing.

Serves 4

300g/11oz mozzarella di bufala
cheese, thinly sliced
8 large plum tomatoes, sliced
1 large avocado
about 15 basil leaves or a small
handful of flat leaf parsley leaves
90–120ml/6–8 tbsp extra virgin olive oil
ground black pepper
ciabatta and sea salt flakes, to serve

1 Arrange the mozzarella cheese slices and tomato slices randomly on four salad plates. Crush over a few good pinches of sea salt flakes. This will help to draw out some of the juices from the plum tomatoes. Cover with clear film (plastic wrap), set aside in a cool place and leave to marinate for about 30 minutes.

2 Just before serving, cut the avocado in half lengthways, using a large, sharp knife and twist the halves to separate them. Lift out the stone (pit) with the point of the knife and remove the peel.

3 Carefully slice the avocado flesh crossways into half moons, or cut it into large chunks if that is easier.

4 Place the avocado slices on the salad, then sprinkle with the basil or parsley. Drizzle over the olive oil, add a little more salt if you like and season well with black pepper. Serve the salad at room temperature, with chunks of crusty Italian ciabatta or other country bread for mopping up the dressing.

Green Bean and Sweet Red Pepper Salad

Serrano chillies are very fiery so be cautious about their use.

Serves 4

350g/12oz cooked green beans
2 red (bell) peppers, seeded
2 spring onions (scallions), chopped
1 or more drained pickled serrano
  chillies, rinsed, seeded and chopped
1 iceberg lettuce, coarsely shredded
olives, to garnish

For the dressing
45ml/3 tbsp red wine vinegar
135ml/9 tbsp olive oil
salt and ground black pepper

1 Cut the cooked green beans into quarters and chop the peppers. Combine the beans, peppers, spring onions and chillies in a bowl.

2 Make the salad dressing. Pour the red wine vinegar into a bowl or jug (pitcher). Add salt and ground black pepper to taste, then gradually whisk in the olive oil until well combined. Alternatively, combine the vinegar and oil in a screw-top jar, add salt and pepper to taste, close the lid and shake vigorously to mix.

COOK'S TIPS
Although jars of pickled chillies may be labelled "mild" or "hot", as opposed to "very hot", do not assume that you have the same tolerance to their heat as the people in the country that pickled them.

3 Pour the salad dressing over the prepared vegetables and toss lightly together to mix and coat thoroughly. Set aside at room temperature until you are ready to serve.

4 Line a large serving platter with the shredded iceberg lettuce leaves and arrange the salad vegetables attractively on top. Garnish with the olives and serve immediately.

Roasted Tomato and Mozzarella Salad

Roasting the tomatoes brings out their sweetness and adds a new dimension to this salad. Make the basil oil just before serving to retain its fresh flavour and lovely vivid colour.

Serves 4

olive oil, for brushing
6 large plum tomatoes
2 fresh mozzarella cheese balls, cut into 8–12 slices
salt and ground black pepper
fresh basil leaves, to garnish

For the basil oil
25 fresh basil leaves
60ml/4 tbsp extra virgin olive oil
1 garlic clove, crushed

1 Preheat the oven to 200°C/400°F/ Gas 6 and brush a baking sheet with olive oil. Cut the tomatoes in half lengthways and remove and discard the seeds. Place the tomato halves, skin side down, on the baking sheet, brush with a little oil and roast for about 20 minutes, or until the tomatoes are very tender but still retain their shape.

2 Meanwhile, make the basil oil. Place the basil leaves, olive oil and garlic in a food processor or blender and process until smooth. You will need to scrape down the sides once or twice to make sure that the mixture is processed properly. Transfer to a bowl, cover with clear film (plastic wrap) and chill until required.

3 For each serving, place the tomato halves on top of two or three slices of mozzarella and drizzle over the basil oil. Season to taste with salt and pepper. Garnish with fresh basil leaves and serve immediately.

Mixed Herb Salad with Toasted Mixed Seeds

This simple salad is the perfect antidote to a rich, heavy meal, as it contains fresh herbs that can ease the digestion. Balsamic vinegar adds a rich, sweet taste to the dressing, but red or white wine vinegar could be used instead.

Serves 4

90g/3¹/₂oz/4 cups mixed salad leaves
50g/2oz/2 cups mixed salad herbs, such as coriander (cilantro), parsley, basil, chervil and rocket (arugula)
45ml/3 tbsp pumpkin seeds
45ml/3 tbsp sunflower seeds

For the dressing
60ml/4 tbsp extra virgin olive oil
15ml/1 tbsp balsamic vinegar
2.5ml/¹/₂ tsp Dijon mustard
salt and ground black pepper

1 To make the dressing, combine the ingredients in a bowl or screw-top jar. Mix with a small whisk or fork, or shake well, until completely combined.

2 Put the salad leaves and herb leaves in a large bowl. Toss with your fingers to mix together.

3 Toast the pumpkin and sunflower seeds in a dry frying pan over a medium heat for about 2 minutes, until golden, tossing frequently to prevent them from burning. Leave the seeds to cool slightly before sprinkling them over the salad.

4 Pour the dressing over the salad and toss with your hands until the leaves are well coated, then serve.

Orange and **Red Onion Salad** with **Cumin**

Cumin and mint give this refreshing salad a typically Middle Eastern flavour. Choose small seedless oranges.

Serves 6

6 oranges
2 red onions
15ml/1 tbsp cumin seeds
5ml/1 tsp coarsely ground
  black pepper
15ml/1 tbsp chopped fresh mint
90ml/6 tbsp olive oil
salt

To serve
fresh mint sprigs
black olives

1 Slice the oranges thinly, working over a bowl to catch any juice. Then, holding each orange slice in turn over the bowl, cut round with scissors to remove the peel and pith. Slice the onions thinly and separate the rings.

2 Arrange the orange and onion slices in layers in a shallow dish, sprinkling each layer with cumin seeds, black pepper, chopped mint, olive oil and salt to taste. Pour over any orange juice collected when slicing the oranges.

3 Cover the salad with clear film (plastic wrap) and set aside to marinate in a cool place for about 2 hours. Just before serving, sprinkle the salad with the mint sprigs and black olives.

Spanish Salad with **Olives** and **Capers**

Make this refreshing salad in the summer when tomatoes are sweet and full of flavour. The dressing gives it a lovely tang.

Serves 4

4 tomatoes
1/2 cucumber
1 bunch spring onions
1 bunch purslane or watercress, washed
8 pimiento-stuffed olives
30ml/2 tbsp drained capers

For the dressing
30ml/2 tbsp red wine vinegar
5ml/1 tsp paprika
2.5ml/1/2 tsp ground cumin
1 garlic clove, crushed
75ml/5 tbsp olive oil
salt and ground black pepper

1 To peel the tomatoes, place them in a heatproof bowl, add boiling water to cover and leave for 1 minute. Lift the tomatoes out with a slotted spoon and plunge into a bowl of cold water. Leave for 1 minute, then drain. Slip the skins off the tomatoes and dice the flesh finely. Put in a salad bowl.

2 Peel the cucumber, dice it finely and add it to the tomatoes. Trim and chop half the spring onions, add them to the salad bowl and mix lightly.

3 Break the purslane or watercress into small sprigs. Add to the tomato mixture, with the olives and capers.

4 To make the dressing, mix the wine vinegar, paprika, cumin and garlic in a bowl. Whisk in the oil and season with salt and pepper to taste. Pour the dressing over the salad and toss lightly to coat. Serve with the remaining spring onions on the side.

Warm Broad Bean and Feta Salad

This recipe is loosely based on a typical medley of fresh-tasting Greek salad ingredients – broad beans, tomatoes and feta cheese. It's delicious, served warm or cold.

Serves 4–6

900g/2lb broad (fava) beans, shelled, or 350g/12oz shelled frozen broad (fava) beans
60ml/4 tbsp olive oil
75g/3oz plum tomatoes, halved, or quartered if large
4 garlic cloves, crushed
115g/4oz firm feta cheese, cut into large, even-size chunks
45ml/3 tbsp chopped fresh dill, plus extra to garnish
12 black olives
salt and ground black pepper

1 Cook the fresh or frozen broad beans in lightly salted, boiling water until just tender. Drain and refresh under cold water, then set aside.

2 Meanwhile, heat the olive oil in a large, heavy frying pan and add the tomatoes and garlic. Cook over a medium heat, turning occasionally, until the tomatoes are beginning to colour, but not collapse.

3 Add the feta cheese to the pan and toss the ingredients together for 1 minute. Mix with the drained beans, dill, olives and salt and pepper. Serve garnished with chopped dill.

COOK'S TIP
Much of the feta cheese commonly available is made from cow's, rather than the traditional sheep's milk. Try to find the authentic cheese for this recipe.

Halloumi and Grape Salad

In Eastern Europe, firm salty halloumi cheese is often served fried for breakfast or supper. In this recipe for an unusual salad, it's tossed with sweet, juicy grapes which really complement its distinctive sweet and salty flavour.

Serves 4

150g/5oz mixed green salad leaves
75g/3oz seedless green grapes
75g/3oz seedless black grapes
250g/9oz halloumi cheese
45ml/3 tbsp olive oil
fresh young thyme leaves or dill, to garnish

For the dressing
60ml/4 tbsp olive oil
15ml/1 tbsp lemon juice
2.5ml/1/2 tsp caster (superfine) sugar
salt and ground black pepper
5ml/1 tsp chopped fresh thyme or dill

1 To make the dressing, mix together the olive oil, lemon juice and sugar in a bowl. Season to taste with salt and ground black pepper. Stir in the thyme or dill and set aside.

2 Toss together the salad leaves and the green and black grapes, then transfer to a large serving plate.

COOK'S TIP
If the cheese goes cold before it is served, it will become rubbery.

3 Thinly slice the halloumi cheese. Heat the oil in a large frying pan. Add the cheese and cook briefly until it turns golden on the underside. Turn the cheese with a fish slice or metal spatula and cook the other side.

4 Arrange the cheese over the salad. Pour over the dressing and garnish with thyme or dill. Serve immediately.

Potato Salad with Curry Plant Mayonnaise

Potato salad can be made well in advance and is therefore a useful dish for serving as an unusual appetizer or accompaniment at a party. Its popularity means that there are very rarely any leftovers to be cleared away at the end of the day.

Serves 6

1kg/2¼lb new potatoes
300ml/½ pint/1¼ cups mayonnaise
6 curry plant leaves, coarsely chopped
salt and ground black pepper
mixed lettuce leaves or other salad
*   leaves, to serve*

1 Wash, but do not peel the potatoes. Place them in a pan of lightly salted water, cover and bring to the boil, then lower the heat and simmer gently for about 15 minutes, or until tender. Drain well, place in a large bowl and leave to cool slightly.

2 Mix the mayonnaise with the curry plant leaves and season with black pepper to taste. Stir the dressing into the potatoes while they are still warm. Leave to cool completely, then serve on a bed of mixed lettuce leaves or other assorted salad leaves.

Panzanella Salad

If sliced, juicy tomatoes layered with day-old bread sounds strange for a salad, don't be deceived – it's quite delicious. A popular Italian salad, this dish is ideal for entertaining.

Serves 4–6

4 thick slices day-old bread, either
white, brown or rye
1 small red onion
450g/1lb ripe tomatoes, thinly sliced
115g/4oz mozzarella cheese,
thinly sliced
5ml/1 tbsp fresh basil, shredded, or
fresh marjoram
120ml/4fl oz/¹/₂ cup extra virgin
olive oil
45ml/3 tbsp balsamic vinegar
juice or 1 small lemon
salt and ground black pepper
pitted and sliced black olives or salted
capers, to garnish

1 Dip the bread briefly in a shallow dish of cold water, then carefully squeeze out the excess water. Arrange the bread in the base of a shallow salad bowl.

2 Thinly slice the onion, then soak the slices in a separate bowl of cold water for about 10 minutes while you prepare the other ingredients. This helps to reduce the astringency of the onion, so that it does not overpower the other flavours. Drain and reserve.

3 Layer the tomatoes, cheese, onion, basil or marjoram in the salad bowl, seasoning well with salt and pepper in between each layer. Sprinkle the salad with the olive oil, balsamic vinegar and lemon juice.

4 Top with the olives or capers. Cover with clear film (plastic wrap) and chill the salad in the refrigerator for at least 2 hours, or overnight, if possible.

New York Deli Coleslaw

The key to a good coleslaw is a zesty dressing and an interesting selection of vegetables. Serve at barbecues, picnics or buffets.

Serves 6–8

1 large white or green cabbage, very
   thinly sliced
3–4 carrots, coarsely grated
½ red (bell) pepper, chopped
½ green (bell) pepper, chopped
1–2 celery sticks, finely chopped or
   5–10ml/1–2 tsp celery seeds
1 onion, chopped
2–3 handfuls of raisins or sultanas
   (golden raisins)
45ml/3 tbsp white wine vinegar or
   cider vinegar
60–90ml/4–6 tbsp sugar
175–250ml/6–8fl oz/
   ¾–1 cup mayonnaise
salt and ground black pepper

1 Put the cabbage, carrots, peppers, celery or celery seeds, onion, and raisins or sultanas in a salad bowl and mix to combine well. Add the vinegar and sugar to taste. Season with salt and pepper and toss together. Leave to stand for about 1 hour.

COOK'S TIP
The salad can be prepared beforehand to the end of step 1 and chilled overnight. Next day, it can be dressed with the mayonnaise before serving.

2 Stir enough mayonnaise into the salad to bind the ingredients lightly together. Taste the salad for seasoning and sweet-and-sour flavour, adding more sugar, salt and pepper if necessary. Chill for about 1 hour.

3 Drain off any excess liquid that has formed before serving.

VARIATION
Use low-fat crème fraîche for a lighter dressing.

Potato Salad with Egg, Mayonnaise and Olives

This version of potato salad includes a mustard mayonnaise, chopped eggs and green olives.

Serves 6–8

1kg/2¼lb waxy salad potatoes, cleaned
1 red, brown or white onion,
   finely chopped
2–3 celery sticks, finely chopped
60–90ml/4–6 tbsp chopped parsley
15–20 pimiento-stuffed olives, halved
3 hard-boiled eggs, chopped
60ml/4 tbsp extra virgin olive oil
60ml/4 tbsp white wine vinegar
15–30ml/1–2 tbsp mild or
   wholegrain mustard
celery seeds, to taste (optional)
175–250ml/6–8fl oz/
   ¾–1 cup mayonnaise
salt and ground black pepper
paprika, to garnish

1 Cook the potatoes in a pan of lightly salted boiling water until tender. Drain, return to the pan and leave for 2–3 minutes to cool and dry a little.

2 When the potatoes are cool enough to handle but still warm, cut them into chunks and place in a salad bowl.

VARIATION
Instead of potatoes, use 400g/14oz cooked macaroni.

3 Sprinkle the potatoes with salt and pepper, then add the onion, celery, parsley, olives and the chopped eggs to the salad bowl.

4 In a jug (pitcher), combine the olive oil, vinegar, mustard and celery seeds, if using. Pour over the salad and toss to combine thoroughly. Add enough mayonnaise to bind the salad together. Chill for about 1 hour before serving, sprinkled with a little paprika.

Goat's Cheese Salad

Goat's cheese has a strong, tangy flavour, so choose robust salad leaves to accompany it.

Serves 4

30ml/2 tbsp olive oil
4 slices of French bread,
    1cm/½ in thick
8 cups mixed salad leaves, such as
    frisée lettuce, radicchio and red oak
    leaf, torn in small pieces
4 firm goat's cheese rounds, about
    50g/2oz each, rind removed
1 yellow or red (bell) pepper, seeded
    and finely diced
1 small red onion, thinly sliced
45ml/3 tbsp chopped fresh parsley
30ml/2 tbsp chopped fresh chives

For the dressing
30ml/2 tbsp white wine vinegar
1.5ml/¼ tsp salt
5ml/1 tsp wholegrain mustard
75ml/5 tbsp olive oil
ground black pepper

1 To make the dressing, mix the vinegar and salt in a bowl or jug (pitcher), stirring with a fork until the salt has dissolved. Stir in the mustard. Gradually whisk in the olive oil until blended. Season to taste with pepper and set aside until needed.

2 Preheat the grill (broiler). Heat the oil in a frying pan. Add the bread slices and cook for about 1 minute, until the undersides are golden. Turn and cook on the other side for about 30 seconds more. Drain well on kitchen paper and set aside.

3 Place the salad leaves in a bowl. Add 45ml/3 tbsp of the dressing and toss to coat well. Divide the dressed leaves among four salad plates.

4 Place the goat's cheeses, cut sides up, on a baking sheet and grill (broil) for about 1–2 minutes, until bubbling and golden.

COOK'S TIP
Cheese made entirely from goat's milk is usually labelled "pure" or, if French, "chèvre". Milder cheeses are made with a mixture of cow's and goat's milk.

5 Set a goat's cheese on each slice of bread and place in the centre of each plate. Sprinkle the diced pepper, red onion, parsley and chives over the salad. Drizzle with the remaining dressing and serve.

Caesar Salad

This is a well-known and much
enjoyed salad invented by a chef
called Caesar Cardini. Be sure to
use crisp lettuce and add the very
soft eggs at the last minute.

Serves 6

175ml/6fl oz/³⁄₄ cup salad oil,
preferably olive oil
115g/4oz French or Italian bread, cut
in 2.5cm/1in cubes
1 large garlic clove, crushed with the
flat side of a knife
1 cos or romaine lettuce
2 eggs, boiled for 1 minute
120ml/4fl oz/¹⁄₂ cup lemon juice
50g/2oz/²⁄₃ cup freshly grated
Parmesan cheese
6 canned anchovy fillets, drained and
finely chopped (optional)
salt and ground black pepper

1 Heat 50ml/2fl oz/¹⁄₄ cup of the oil in
a large frying pan. Add the bread
cubes and garlic. Cook over a medium
heat, stirring and turning constantly,
until the bread cubes are golden
brown all over. Drain well on kitchen
paper. Discard the garlic.

2 Tear large lettuce leaves into smaller
pieces. Put all the lettuce in a bowl.

COOK'S TIP
Do not boil the eggs for longer than
1 minute. The whites should be milky,
while the yolks remain raw.

3 Add the remaining oil to the lettuce
and season with salt and plenty of
ground black pepper. Toss well to coat
the leaves.

4 Break the eggs on top. Sprinkle
with the lemon juice. Toss thoroughly
again to combine.

5 Add the Parmesan cheese and
anchovies, if using. Toss gently to mix.

6 Sprinkle the fried bread cubes on
top and serve immediately.

VARIATIONS
• To make a tangier dressing mix 30ml/
2 tbsp white wine vinegar, 15ml/1 tbsp
Worcestershire sauce, 2.5ml/¹⁄₂ tsp
mustard powder, 5ml/1 tsp sugar, salt and
pepper in a screw-top jar, then add the oil
and shake well.
• If you are worried about the safety of
eating very lightly cooked eggs, you can
substitute quartered hard-boiled eggs.
However, the dressing will not be as
creamy without the runny egg yolk.

Avocado and Smoked Fish Salad

Avocado and smoked fish make a good combination, and flavoured with herbs and spices, create a delectable and elegant salad.

Serves 4

15g/¹/₂oz/1 tbsp butter
   or margarine
¹/₂ onion, thinly sliced
5ml/1 tsp mustard seeds
225g/8oz smoked mackerel, flaked
30ml/2 tbsp chopped fresh
   coriander (cilantro)
2 firm tomatoes, peeled
   and chopped
15ml/1 tbsp lemon juice

For the salad
2 avocados, halved, stoned (pitted)
   and peeled
¹/₂ cucumber
15ml/1 tbsp lemon juice
2 firm tomatoes
1 green chilli
salt and ground black pepper

1 Melt the butter or margarine in a heavy frying pan, add the onion and mustard seeds and cook over a low heat, stirring occasionally, for about 5 minutes, until the onion is soft but not browned.

2 Add the flaked mackerel, chopped coriander, tomatoes and lemon juice and cook over a low heat for about 2–3 minutes. Remove the pan from the heat and leave to cool.

COOK'S TIP
Although smoked mackerel has a very distinctive flavour, smoked haddock or cod can also be used in this salad, or a mixture of mackerel and haddock. For a speedy salad when time is short, canned tuna makes an easy and convenient substitute.

3 To make the salad, thinly slice the avocados and cucumber. Place them together in a bowl and sprinkle with the lemon juice to prevent the avocado flesh from discolouring.

4 Slice the tomatoes and seed and finely chop the chilli.

5 Place the fish mixture in the centre of a serving plate.

6 Arrange the avocado slices, cucumber and tomatoes decoratively around the outside of the fish mixture. Alternatively, spoon a quarter of the fish mixture on to each of four individual serving plates and divide the avocados, cucumber and tomatoes equally among them. Then sprinkle with the chopped chilli, season with a little salt and ground black pepper and serve immediately.

Salade Niçoise

Made with the freshest ingredients, this classic Provençal salad makes a simple yet unbeatable summer dish. Serve with country-style bread and chilled white wine for a Mediterannean treat.

Serves 4–6

115g/4oz green beans
1 tuna steak, about 175g/6oz
olive oil, for brushing
115g/4oz mixed salad leaves
1/2 small cucumber, thinly sliced
4 ripe tomatoes, quartered
50g/2oz can anchovies, drained and
    halved lengthways
4 hard-boiled eggs, quartered
1/2 bunch radishes, trimmed
50g/2oz/1/2 cup small black olives
salt and ground black pepper
flat leaf parsley, to garnish

For the dressing
90ml/6 tbsp virgin olive oil
2 garlic cloves, crushed
15ml/1 tbsp white wine vinegar
salt and ground black pepper

1 To make the dressing, whisk together the oil, garlic and vinegar in a bowl, then season to taste with salt and pepper.

2 Preheat the grill (broiler). Brush the tuna steak with olive oil and season with salt and black pepper. Grill (broil) for 3–4 minutes on each side, until cooked through. Set aside to cool.

3 Trim and halve the green beans. Cook them in a pan of boiling water for 2 minutes, until only just tender, then drain, refresh under cold water and leave to cool.

4 Mix together the salad leaves, sliced cucumber, tomatoes and green beans in a large, shallow bowl. Flake the cooled tuna steak with your fingers or two forks.

5 Sprinkle the tuna, anchovies, eggs, radishes and olives over the salad. Pour over the dressing and toss together lightly. Serve garnished with parsley.

COOK'S TIP

For an authentic touch, use black Nice olives and Nice mesclun – a mixture of frisée lettuce, lamb's lettuce, dandelion, rocket (arugula), chervil, purslane, young spinach leaves and oak leaf lettuce.

Smoked Trout Pasta Salad

The little pasta shells catch the
trout, creating tasty mouthfuls.

Serves 8

15g/¹/₂oz/1 tbsp butter
175g/6oz/1 cup minced (ground)
    bulb fennel
6 spring onions (scallions), 2 minced
    (ground) and the rest thinly sliced
225g/8oz skinless smoked trout
    fillets, flaked
45ml/3 tbsp chopped fresh dill
120ml/4fl oz/¹/₂ cup mayonnaise
10ml/2 tsp fresh lemon juice
30ml/2 tbsp whipping cream
450g/1lb/4 cups small pasta shells
salt and ground black pepper
fresh dill sprigs, to garnish

1 Melt the butter in a small pan. Add
the fennel and minced spring onions
and cook for 3–5 minutes. Transfer to
a large bowl and cool slightly.

2 Add the sliced spring onions, trout,
dill, mayonnaise, lemon juice and
cream. Season to taste with salt and
pepper and mix.

3 Bring a large pan of lightly salted
water to the boil. Add the pasta, bring
back to the boil and cook for about
8–10 minutes, until tender but still
firm to the bite. Drain thoroughly and
leave to cool.

4 Add the pasta to the vegetable
and trout mixture and toss to coat
evenly. Taste and adjust the seasoning,
if necessary. Serve the salad lightly
chilled or at room temperature,
garnished with sprigs of dill.

Crab Salad with Rocket

Garnish these salads with strips of lemon rind, if you like.

Serves 8

8 dressed crabs
2 red (bell) peppers, seeded
and chopped
2 small red onions, finely chopped
60ml/4 tbsp fresh coriander (cilantro)
60ml/4 tbsp drained capers
grated rind and juice of 3 lemons
Tabasco sauce, to taste
salt and ground black pepper

For the salad
75g/3oz rocket (arugula) leaves
60ml/4 tbsp sunflower oil
30ml/2 tbsp fresh lime juice

1 Remove all the white and brown meat from the crab. Put it into a large mixing bowl with the chopped peppers, onions and coriander. Add the capers, lemon rind and juice, and toss gently to mix everything thoroughly together. Season with a few drops of Tabasco sauce, according to taste, and a little salt and pepper.

2 To make the salad, wash the rocket leaves and pat them dry on kitchen paper. Divide among eight plates. Mix together the oil and lime juice in a small bowl. Dress the rocket leaves with the oil and lime juice.

3 Pile the crab salad on top and serve garnished with lemon rind strips.

Thai Prawn Salad with Garlic Dressing and Frizzled Shallots

In this intensely flavoured salad, sweet prawns and mango are partnered with a sweet-sour garlic dressing heightened with the hot taste of chilli. The crisp frizzled shallots are a traditional addition to Thai salads.

Serves 4–6

675g/1½lb raw prawns (shrimp),
   shelled and deveined with tails on
finely shredded rind of 1 lime
½ fresh red chilli, seeded and chopped
30ml/2 tbsp olive oil, plus extra
   for brushing
1 ripe but firm mango
2 carrots, cut into long thin shreds
10cm/4in piece cucumber, sliced
1 red onion, halved and thinly sliced
a few fresh coriander (cilantro) sprigs
a few fresh mint sprigs
45ml/3 tbsp roasted peanuts, chopped
4 shallots, sliced and fried until crisp in
   30ml/2 tbsp peanut (groundnut) oil
salt and ground black pepper

For the dressing
1 large garlic clove, chopped
10–15ml/2–3 tsp caster
   (superfine) sugar
juice of 2 limes
15–30ml/1–2 tbsp Thai fish sauce
1 red chilli, seeded
5–10ml/1–2 tsp light rice vinegar

1 Place the prawns in a glass or china dish with the lime rind and chilli. Spoon the oil over them and season. Toss well and leave to marinate for 30 minutes.

2 For the dressing, place the garlic in a mortar with 10ml/2 tsp caster sugar and pound until smooth, then work in the juice of 1½ limes and 15ml/1 tbsp of the Thai fish sauce.

3 Transfer to a jug (pitcher). Finely chop half the chilli and add to the dressing. Taste and add more sugar, juice, fish sauce and the vinegar to taste.

COOK'S TIP
To devein prawns, make a shallow cut down the back of the prawn using a small, sharp knife. Using the tip of the knife, lift out the thin, black vein, then rinse the prawn under cold water.

4 Peel and stone (pit) the mango, then cut it into very fine strips.

5 Toss together the mango, carrots, cucumber and onion, and half the dressing. Arrange on plates or in bowls.

6 Heat a ridged, cast-iron griddle pan or heavy frying pan until very hot. Brush with a little oil, then sear the prawns for 2–3 minutes on each side, until they turn pink and are patched with brown on the outside. Arrange the prawns on the salads.

7 Sprinkle the remaining dressing over the salads and sprinkle the sprigs of coriander and mint over. Finely shred the remaining chilli and sprinkle it over the salads with the peanuts and crisp-fried shallots. Serve immediately.

Mixed Seafood Salad

If you cannot find all the seafood included in this dish in fresh form, then it's all right to use a combination of fresh and frozen, but do use what is in season first.

Serves 6–8

350g/12oz small squid
1 small onion, cut into quarters
1 bay leaf
200g/7oz raw prawns (shrimp)
675g/1½lb fresh mussels, in the shell
450g/1lb small fresh clams
175ml/6fl oz/¾ cup white wine
1 fennel bulb

For the dressing
75ml/5 tbsp extra virgin olive oil
45ml/3 tbsp lemon juice
1 garlic clove, finely chopped
salt and ground black pepper

1 Working near the sink, clean the squid by first peeling off the thin skin from the body section. Rinse well. Pull the head and tentacles away from the sac section. Some of the intestines will come away with the head. Remove and discard the translucent quill and any remaining insides from the sac. Sever the tentacles from the head. Discard the head and intestines. Remove the small hard beak from the base of the tentacles. Rinse the body sac and tentacles of the squid well under cold running water. Drain thoroughly in a colander.

2 Bring a large pan of water to the boil over a medium heat. Add the onion and bay leaf. Drop in the squid and cook for about 10 minutes, or until tender. Remove with a slotted spoon and leave to cool before slicing into rings about 1cm/½in wide. Cut each tentacle section into two pieces. Set aside.

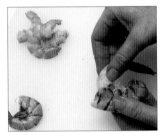

3 Drop the prawns into the same pan of boiling water and cook for about 2 minutes, until they have turned pink. Remove with a slotted spoon. Pull off the heads, peel and devein the prawns. (The cooking liquid may be strained and kept for using to make soup. When it is cool, store it in the freezer if not using immediately.)

4 Pull off the "beards" from the mussels. Scrub and rinse the mussels and clams well in several changes of cold water. Place in a large pan with the wine. Cover and steam over a high heat, shaking the pan occasionally, for 3–5 minutes, until all the shells have opened. Discard any that do not open. Lift the clams and mussels out.

5 Remove all the clams from their shells with a small spoon. Place in a large serving bowl. Remove all but eight of the mussels from their shells, and add them to the clams in the bowl. Leave the remaining mussels in their half shells and set aside.

6 Cut off the green fronds from the fennel, chop finely and set aside. Chop the fennel bulb into bitesize pieces, and add it to the serving bowl with the squid and prawns.

7 Make a dressing by combining the oil, lemon juice, garlic and chopped fennel fronds in a small bowl. Season with salt and pepper to taste. Pour the dressing over the salad and toss well. Decorate with the remaining mussels in the half shell. This salad may be served either at room temperature or lightly chilled.

COOK'S TIP
Fresh squid is available most of the year, but you can use frozen, if necessary. Squid is one of the few kinds of seafood that freezes without much loss of quality.

Mushroom Salad with Prosciutto

Pancake ribbons create a lovely light texture to this salad. Use whatever edible wild mushrooms you can find, or substitute interesting cultivated varieties if you need to.

Serves 4

40g/1¹/₂ oz/3 tbsp unsalted (sweet) butter
450g/1lb assorted wild and cultivated mushrooms such as chanterelles, ceps, bay boletus, oyster, field (portabello) and Paris mushrooms, trimmed and sliced
60ml/4 tbsp Madeira or sherry
juice of ¹/₂ lemon
¹/₂ oak leaf lettuce
¹/₂ frisée lettuce
30ml/2 tbsp walnut oil
salt and ground black pepper

For the pancake and ham ribbons
25g/1oz/3 tbsp plain (all-purpose) flour
75ml/5 tbsp milk
1 egg
60ml/4 tbsp freshly grated Parmesan cheese
60ml/4 tbsp chopped fresh herbs such as parsley, thyme, marjoram or chives
salt and ground black pepper
butter, for frying
175g/6oz prosciutto, thickly sliced

1 To make the pancakes, blend the flour and the milk. Beat in the egg, cheese, herbs and some seasoning. Heat the butter in a frying pan and pour enough of the mixture to coat the base. When the batter has set, turn the pancake over and cook until firm.

2 Turn out and cool. Roll up the pancake and slice to make 1cm/¹/₂in ribbons. Cook the remaining batter the same way and cut the ham into similar sized ribbons. Toss with the pancake ribbons. Set aside.

3 Gently soften the mushrooms in the butter for 6–8 minutes, until the moisture has evaporated. Add the Madeira or sherry and lemon juice and season to taste.

4 Toss the salad leaves in the oil and arrange on four plates. Place the prosciutto and pancake ribbons in the centre, spoon on the mushrooms and serve immediately.

Wilted Spinach and Bacon Salad

The hot dressing in this salad wilts the spinach and provides a taste sensation.

Serves 6

450g/1lb fresh young spinach leaves
25ml/1½ tbsp vegetable oil
225g/8oz bacon rashers (strips)
60ml/4 tbsp red wine vinegar
60ml/4 tbsp water
20ml/4 tsp caster (superfine) sugar
5ml/1 tsp mustard powder
8 spring onions (scallions), thinly sliced
6 radishes, thinly sliced
2 hard-boiled eggs, coarsely grated
salt and ground black pepper

1 Pull any coarse stalks from the spinach leaves and rinse well. Put the leaves in a large salad bowl.

VARIATION
For extra flavour, use hard-boiled duck eggs instead of hen's eggs.

2 Heat the oil in a frying pan and cook the bacon until crisp and brown. Remove with tongs and drain well on kitchen paper. Reserve the cooking fat in the pan. Chop the bacon and set aside until needed.

3 Combine the vinegar, water, sugar, mustard, and salt and ground black pepper in a bowl and stir until smoothly blended. Add to the fat in the frying pan and stir to mix. Bring the dressing to the boil over a medium heat, stirring constantly.

4 Pour the hot dressing evenly over the spinach leaves. Sprinkle the bacon, spring onions, radishes and eggs over, and toss, then serve.

eating outdoors

Discover great dishes for making barbecues

and *al fresco* eating as delicious and easy

as they are fun and informal.

Country Pasta Salad

Colourful, tasty and nutritious, this is the ideal pasta salad for a picnic.

Serves 6

300g/11oz/2¾ cups dried fusilli
150g/5oz green beans, trimmed and
*   cut into 5cm/2in lengths*
1 potato, about 150g/5oz, diced
200g/7oz baby tomatoes, halved
2 spring onions (scallions),
*   finely chopped*
90g/3½oz/scant 1¼ cups diced or
*   coarsely shaved Parmesan cheese*
6–8 pitted black olives, cut into rings
15–30ml/1–2 tbsp capers, to taste

For the dressing
90ml/6 tbsp extra virgin olive oil
15ml/1 tbsp balsamic vinegar
15ml/1 tbsp chopped fresh flat
*   leaf parsley*
salt and ground black pepper

1 Cook the pasta in lightly salted boiling water for 8–10 minutes, until tender. Drain in a colander, rinse under cold running water, then shake the colander to remove as much water as possible. Leave to drain and dry, shaking the colander occasionally so that it does not stick.

2 Cook the beans and diced potato in a pan of lightly salted, boiling water for 5–6 minutes, or until tender. Drain and leave to cool.

3 To make the dressing, put all the ingredients in a large bowl with salt and pepper to taste and whisk well until thoroughly combined.

4 Add the baby tomatoes, spring onions, Parmesan, olive rings and capers to the dressing, then the cold pasta, beans and potato. Toss well to mix all the ingredients. Cover the salad and leave to stand for about 30 minutes. Season to taste with salt and pepper before serving.

Salad with **Watermelon** and **Feta Cheese**

The combination of sweet and juicy watermelon with salty feta cheese was inspired by the Turkish tradition of eating watermelon with salty white cheese in the hot summer months. It is ideal for barbecues and picnics.

Serves 6–8

30–45ml/2–3 tbsp extra virgin olive oil
juice of ½ lemon
5ml/1 tsp vinegar of choice
sprinkling of fresh thyme
pinch of ground cumin
4 large slices of watermelon, chilled
1 frisée lettuce, core removed
130g/4½ oz feta cheese, preferably
  sheep's milk feta, cut into
  bitesize pieces
handful of lightly toasted
  pumpkin seeds
handful of sunflower seeds
10–15 black olives

1 Pour the extra virgin olive oil, lemon juice and vinegar into a bowl or jug (pitcher). Add the fresh thyme and ground cumin, and whisk until well combined. Set the dressing aside until you are ready to serve the salad.

2 Cut the rind off the watermelon and remove as many seeds as possible.

COOK'S TIP
Use plump black Mediterranean olives, such as kalamata, for this recipe or other shiny, dry-cured black olives.

3 Cut the flesh into bitesize triangular-shaped chunks.

4 Put the lettuce leaves in a bowl, pour over the dressing and toss together. Arrange the leaves on a serving dish or individual plates and add the watermelon, feta cheese, pumpkin and sunflower seeds and black olives. Serve the salad immediately.

VARIATION
Use Galia, cantaloupe or Charentais melon instead of the watermelon.

Peruvian Salad

This really is a spectacular-looking salad. If you serve it in a deep, glass salad bowl, the guests can then see the various layers of rice and green salad leaves, topped by the bright colours of the peppers, corn, eggs and olives.

Serves 8

450g/1lb/4 cups cooked long grain
  brown or white rice
30ml/2 tbsp chopped fresh parsley
2 red (bell) peppers
2 onions, sliced
olive oil, for sprinkling
250g/9oz green beans, halved
115g/4oz/²⁄₃ cup baby corn
8 quail's eggs, hard-boiled
75g/3oz Serrano ham, cut into
  thin slices (optional)
2 small avocados
lemon juice, for sprinkling
150g/5oz mixed salad leaves
30ml/2 tbsp capers
about 20 stuffed olives, halved

For the dressing
2 garlic cloves, crushed
120ml/4fl oz/¹⁄₂ cup olive oil
90ml/6 tbsp sunflower oil
60ml/4 tbsp lemon juice
90ml/6 tbsp natural (plain) yogurt
5ml/1 tsp mustard
5ml/1 tsp granulated sugar
salt and ground black pepper

1 Make the dressing by placing all the ingredients in a bowl and whisking with a fork until smooth. Alternatively, shake the ingredients together in a screw-top jar.

COOK'S TIP
To hard-boil quail's eggs, place them in a pan of simmering water, bring the water back to simmering point and cook for 4 minutes. Drain the eggs and rinse in cold water, then shell.

2 Put the cooked rice into a large bowl and spoon in half the dressing. Add the chopped parsley, stir well and set aside.

3 Cut the peppers in half, remove the seeds and pith, then place the halves, cut side down, in a small roasting pan. Add the onion rings. Sprinkle with a little olive oil, place the pan under a hot grill (broiler) and grill (broil) for 5–6 minutes, or until the peppers blacken and blister and the onion turns golden. You may need to stir the onion once or twice so that it cooks evenly.

4 Stir the onion into the rice. Put the peppers in a bowl, cover and leave until cool. Peel the peppers and cut the flesh into thin strips.

5 Cook the green beans in boiling water for 2 minutes, then add the corn and cook for 1–2 minutes more, until tender. Drain both vegetables, refresh them under cold water, then drain again. Place in a large mixing bowl and add the red pepper strips, quail's eggs and ham, if using.

6 Peel each avocado, remove the stone (pit), and cut the flesh into slices or chunks. Sprinkle with the lemon juice. Put the salad leaves in a separate bowl, add the avocado and mix lightly. Arrange the salad on top of the rice.

7 Stir about 45ml/3 tbsp of the remaining dressing into the green bean and pepper mixture. Pile this on top of the salad.

8 Sprinkle the capers and stuffed olives on top and serve the salad with the remaining dressing.

VARIATION
Use couscous instead of rice. Place in a bowl and cover with 2.5cm/1in boiling water. Leave to stand for 10–15 minutes.

Egg and Fennel Tabbouleh with Nuts

Tabbouleh is a Middle Eastern
salad of steamed bulgur wheat,
flavoured with lots of parsley, mint
and garlic. It goes very well with
almost all barbecue dishes,
especially chicken.

Serves 4

250g/9oz/1¼ cups bulgur wheat
4 small (US medium) eggs
1 fennel bulb
1 bunch spring onions
(scallions), chopped
25g/1oz/½ cup sun-dried
tomatoes, sliced
45ml/3 tbsp chopped fresh parsley
30ml/2 tbsp chopped fresh mint
75g/3oz/½ cup black olives
60ml/4 tbsp olive oil, preferably Greek
or Spanish
30ml/2 tbsp garlic oil
30ml/2 tbsp lemon juice
salt and ground black pepper

1 Place the bulgur wheat in a bowl,
cover with boiling water and leave to
soak for 15 minutes. Transfer to a
metal sieve, place over a pan of
boiling water, cover and steam for
10 minutes. Spread out on a metal tray
and leave to cool while you cook the
eggs and fennel.

2 Hard-boil the eggs for 8 minutes.
Cool under running water, shell and
quarter. Alternatively, using an egg
slicer, slice them but not quite all the
way through.

3 Halve and then thinly slice the
fennel. Boil in salted water for
6 minutes, drain and cool under
running water.

4 Combine the egg quarters, fennel,
spring onions, sun-dried tomatoes,
parsley, mint and olives with the
bulgur wheat. If you have sliced the
eggs, arrange them on top of the
salad. Dress the tabbouleh with olive
oil, garlic oil and lemon juice. Season
well with salt and pepper.

COOK'S TIP
Small whole eggs, such as gull, quail,
plover or guinea fowl, would also be
good in this dish.

Tortilla Wrap with Tabbouleh and Avocado

To be successful, tabbouleh needs lemon juice, plenty of fresh herbs and lots of freshly ground black pepper.

Serves 6

175g/6oz/1 cup bulgur wheat
30ml/2 tbsp chopped fresh mint
30ml/2 tbsp chopped fresh flat
*   leaf parsley*
1 bunch spring onions
*   (scallions), sliced*
¹/₂ cucumber, diced
50ml/2fl oz/¹/₄ cup extra virgin olive oil
juice of 1 large lemon
1 ripe avocado, stoned (pitted), peeled
*   and diced*
juice of ¹/₂ lemon
¹/₂ red chilli, seeded and sliced
1 garlic clove, crushed
¹/₂ red (bell) pepper, seeded and
*   finely diced*
salt and ground black pepper
4 wheat tortillas, to serve
flat leaf parsley, to garnish (optional)

1 To make the tabbouleh, place the bulgur wheat in a large heatproof bowl and pour over enough boiling water to cover. Leave for 30 minutes until the grains are tender but still retain a little resistance to the bite. Drain thoroughly in a sieve, then tip back into the bowl.

2 Add the mint, parsley, spring onions and cucumber to the bulgur wheat and mix thoroughly. Blend together the olive oil and lemon juice in a jug (pitcher) and pour over the tabbouleh, season to taste with salt and pepper and toss well to mix. Cover with clear film (plastic wrap) and chill in the refrigerator for 30 minutes to allow the flavours to mingle.

COOK'S TIP
The soaking time for bulgur wheat can vary. For the best results, follow the instructions on the packet and taste the grain every now and again to check whether it is tender enough.

3 To make the avocado mixture, place the avocado in a bowl and add the lemon juice, chilli and garlic. Season to taste with salt and pepper and mash with a fork to form a smooth purée. Stir in the red pepper.

4 Warm the tortillas in a dry frying pan and serve either flat, folded or rolled up with the tabbouleh and avocado mixture. Garnish with parsley, if using.

Summer Vegetables with Yogurt Pesto

Chargrilled summer vegetables make a meal on their own, or are delicious served as a Mediterranean-style accompaniment to grilled meats and fish.

Serves 8

4 small aubergines (eggplant)
4 large courgettes (zucchini)
2 red (bell) peppers
2 yellow (bell) peppers
2 fennel bulbs
2 red onions
300ml/½ pint/1¼ cups Greek
*   (US strained plain) yogurt*
90ml/6 tbsp pesto
olive oil, for brushing
salt and ground black pepper

1 Cut the aubergines into 1cm/½in slices. Sprinkle with salt and leave to drain for about 30 minutes. Rinse well in cold running water and pat dry.

2 Use a sharp kitchen knife to cut the courgettes in half lengthways. Cut the peppers in half, removing the seeds but leaving the stalks in place.

3 Slice the fennel bulbs and the red onions into thick wedges, using a sharp kitchen knife.

4 Prepare the barbecue. Stir the yogurt and pesto lightly together in a bowl, to make a marbled sauce. Spoon the yogurt pesto into a serving bowl, cover and set aside.

5 Arrange the vegetables on the hot barbecue, brush generously with olive oil and sprinkle with plenty of salt and ground black pepper.

6 Cook the vegetables until golden brown and tender, turning occasionally. The aubergines and peppers will take 6–8 minutes to cook, the courgettes, onion and fennel 4–5 minutes. Serve the vegetables as soon as they are cooked, with the yogurt pesto.

COOK'S TIP

Baby vegetables are excellent for cooking whole on the barbecue, so look for baby aubergines (eggplant) and (bell) peppers, in particular. There's no need to salt the aubergines if they are small.

Aubergine and Smoked Mozzarella Rolls

Slices of grilled aubergine are stuffed with smoked mozzarella, tomato and fresh basil to make an attractive hors-d'oeuvre.

Serves 4

1 large aubergine (eggplant)
45ml/3 tbsp olive oil, plus extra for
    drizzling (optional)
165g/5¹/2 oz smoked mozzarella
    cheese, cut into 8 slices
2 plum tomatoes, each cut into
    4 even-size slices
8 large basil leaves
balsamic vinegar, for
    drizzling (optional)
salt and ground black pepper

1 Cut the aubergine lengthways into 10 thin slices and discard the two outermost slices. Sprinkle the slices with salt and set them aside for 20 minutes. Rinse well under cold running water to remove all traces of salt, then drain and pat dry with kitchen paper.

2 Prepare the barbecue or preheat the grill (broiler) and line the rack with foil. Place the aubergine slices on the rack and brush liberally with oil. Cook for 8–10 minutes until tender and golden, turning once.

3 Remove the aubergine slices from the heat, then place a slice of mozzarella, a slice of tomato and a basil leaf in the centre of each aubergine slice, and season to taste. Fold the aubergine over the filling and return to the heat, seam side down, until heated through and the mozzarella begins to melt. Serve drizzled with olive oil and a little balsamic vinegar, if using.

Chicken Liver Pâté with Garlic

This smooth pâté is indulgent and absolutely delicious. Start preparation the day before so that the flavour can develop fully.

Serves 6–8

225g/8oz/1 cup unsalted (sweet) butter
400g/14oz chicken livers, chopped
45–60ml/3–4 tbsp Madeira
3 large shallots, chopped
2 large garlic cloves, finely chopped
5ml/1 tsp finely chopped fresh thyme
pinch of ground allspice
30ml/2 tbsp double (heavy)
    cream (optional)
salt and ground black pepper
small fresh bay leaves or fresh thyme
    sprigs, to garnish
toast and small pickled gherkins,
    to serve

1 Melt 75g/3oz/6 tbsp butter in a small pan over a low heat, then leave it to bubble gently until it is clear. Pour off the clarified butter into a bowl.

2 Melt 40g/1½oz/3 tbsp butter in a frying pan and cook the chicken livers for 4–5 minutes, or until browned. Stir frequently to make sure that the livers cook evenly. Do not overcook them or they will be tough.

3 Add 45ml/3 tbsp Madeira and set it alight, then scrape the contents of the pan into a food processor or blender.

4 Melt 25g/1oz/2 tbsp butter in the pan over a low heat and cook the shallots for 5 minutes, or until soft. Add the garlic, thyme and allspice and cook for another 2–3 minutes. Add this mixture to the livers with the remaining butter and cream, if using, then process until smooth.

5 Add about 7.5ml/1½ tsp each of salt and black pepper and more Madeira to taste. Scrape the pâté into a serving dish and place a few bay leaves or thyme sprigs on top. Melt the clarified butter, if necessary, then pour it over the pâté. Cool and chill the pâté for 4 hours or overnight.

VARIATIONS
• Cognac, Armagnac or port can be used instead of Madeira.
• Use duck livers instead of chicken and add 2.5ml/½ tsp grated orange rind.
• Use chopped fresh tarragon instead of the thyme.

Herbed Liver Pâté Pie

Serve this highly flavoured pâté with a glass of Pilsner beer for a change from wine.

Serves 10

675g/1½ lb minced (ground) pork
350g/12oz pork liver
350g/12oz/2 cups diced cooked ham
1 small onion, finely chopped
30ml/2 tbsp chopped fresh parsley
5ml/1 tsp German mustard
30ml/2 tbsp Kirsch
5ml/1 tsp salt
beaten egg, for sealing and glazing
25g/1oz sachet (envelope) aspic jelly
250ml/8fl oz/1 cup boiling water
ground black pepper
mustard, crusty bread and dill pickles,
    to serve

For the pastry
450g/1lb/4 cups plain
    (all-purpose) flour
pinch of salt
275g/10oz/1¼ cups butter
2 eggs plus 1 egg yolk
30ml/2 tbsp water

1 Preheat the oven to 200°C/400°F/ Gas 6. To make the pastry, sift the flour and salt and rub in the butter. Beat the eggs, egg yolk and water, add to the dry ingredients and mix.

2 Knead the dough briefly until smooth. Roll out two-thirds on a lightly floured surface and use to line a 10 × 25cm/4 × 10in hinged loaf tin (pan). Trim any excess dough.

3 Process half the pork and all of the liver until fairly smooth. Stir in the remaining minced pork, ham, onion, parsley, mustard, Kirsch, salt and black pepper to taste.

4 Spoon the filling into the tin and level the surface.

5 Roll out the remaining pastry on the lightly floured surface and use it to top the pie, brushing the edges with some of the beaten egg to seal. Decorate with the pastry trimmings and brush with the remaining beaten egg to glaze. Using a fork, make three or four holes in the top, for the steam to escape during cooking.

6 Bake for 40 minutes, then reduce the oven temperature to 180°C/350°F/ Gas 4 and cook for a further hour. Cover the pastry with foil if the top begins to brown too much. Leave the pie to cool in the tin.

7 Make up the aspic jelly, using the boiling water or according to the packet instructions. Stir to dissolve, then leave to cool.

8 Make a small hole near the edge of the pie with a skewer, then pour in the aspic through a greaseproof paper funnel. Chill in the refrigerator for at least 2 hours before slicing and serving the pie with mustard, crusty bread and dill pickles.

Summer Herb Ricotta Flan

Infused with aromatic herbs, this flan makes a delightful picnic dish.

Serves 8

olive oil, for greasing and glazing
800g/1³/₄lb/3½ cups ricotta cheese
75g/3oz/1 cup grated Parmesan cheese
3 eggs, separated
60ml/4 tbsp torn fresh basil leaves
60ml/4 tbsp chopped fresh chives
45ml/3 tbsp fresh oregano leaves
2.5ml/½ tsp paprika
salt and ground black pepper
fresh herb leaves, to garnish

For the tapenade

400g/14oz/3½ cups pitted black olives,
*   rinsed and halved, reserving a few*
*   whole to garnish (optional)*
5 garlic cloves, crushed
75ml/5 tbsp olive oil

1 Preheat the oven to 180°C/350°F/ Gas 4 and lightly grease a 23cm/9in springform cake tin (pan) with oil. Mix together the ricotta cheese, Parmesan and egg yolks in a food processor or blender. Add the herbs and seasoning, and blend until smooth and creamy.

2 Whisk the egg whites in a large bowl until they form soft peaks. Gently fold the egg whites into the ricotta cheese mixture using a rubber spatula, taking care not to knock out too much air. Spoon the ricotta mixture into the prepared tin and smooth the top.

3 Bake for 1 hour 20 minutes, or until the flan is risen and the top is golden. Remove from the oven and brush lightly with olive oil, then sprinkle with paprika. Leave the flan to cool before removing it from the pan.

4 Make the tapenade by placing the olives and garlic in a food processor or blender and process until finely chopped. Gradually add the olive oil and blend to a coarse paste, then transfer to a serving bowl. Garnish the flan with fresh herbs leaves and serve with the tapenade.

VARIATION
Sprinkle 25g/1oz chopped, drained sun-dried tomatoes over the flan as a garnish.

Red Onion and Goat's Cheese Pastries

These attractive little pastries are ideal for picnics and buffets and couldn't be easier to make. Serve simply with a mixed green salad dressed with balsamic vinegar and extra virgin olive oil.

Serves 8

30ml/2 tbsp olive oil
900g/2lb red onions, sliced
60ml/4 tbsp fresh thyme or
*   20ml/4 tsp dried*
30ml/2 tbsp balsamic vinegar
850g/1lb 14oz ready-rolled puff pastry
225g/8oz/1 cup goat's cheese, cubed
2 eggs, beaten
salt and ground black pepper
fresh thyme sprigs,
*   to garnish (optional)*
mixed green salad leaves and
*   cherry tomatoes, to serve*

1 Heat the olive oil in a large heavy frying pan, add the sliced red onions and cook over a gentle heat for about 10 minutes, or until softened, stirring occasionally with a wooden spoon to prevent them from browning.

2 Add the thyme, seasoning and balsamic vinegar, and cook the onions for a further 5 minutes. Remove the frying pan from the heat and leave to cool.

3 Preheat the oven to 220°C/425°F/ Gas 7. Unroll the puff pastry and using a 15cm/6in plate as a guide, cut out eight equal rounds. Place the pastry rounds on dampened baking sheets and, using the point of a sharp knife, score a border, 2cm/¾in inside the edge of each round.

4 Divide the onions among the pastry rounds and top with the cubes of goat's cheese. Brush the edge of each round with beaten egg and bake for 25–30 minutes, until golden. Garnish with the fresh thyme, if using. Serve with the salad leaves and tomatoes.

VARIATION
Ring the changes by spreading the pastry base with 45ml/3 tbsp pesto or tapenade (see recipe above) before you add the onion filling.

Herbed Greek Pies

Mixed fresh herbs give these
little pies a delicate flavour.

Makes 8

115g/4oz/1 cup plain (all-purpose) flour
50g/2oz/4 tbsp butter, diced
15–25ml/1–1½ tbsp water

For the filling
45–60ml/3–4 tbsp tapenade or
    sun-dried tomato paste
1 large (US extra large) egg
100g/3¾oz/scant ½ cup thick Greek
    (US strained plain) yogurt
90ml/6 tbsp milk
1 garlic clove, crushed
30ml/2 tbsp chopped mixed herbs,
    such as thyme, basil and parsley
salt and ground black pepper

1 To make the pastry, mix together the
flour, a pinch of salt and the butter.
Using the fingertips or a pastry blender,
rub the butter into the flour until the
mixture resembles fine breadcrumbs.
Mix in the water using a round-bladed
knife and knead lightly to form a
firm dough. Wrap the dough in clear
film (plastic wrap) and chill in the
refrigerator for 30 minutes.

2 Preheat the oven to 190°C/375°F/
Gas 5. Roll out the pastry thinly and cut
out eight rounds using a 7.5cm/3in
cutter. Line deep patty tins (muffin
pans) with the pastry rounds, then
line each one with a piece of baking
parchment. Bake blind for 15 minutes.
Remove the baking parchment and
cook for a further 5 minutes, or until
the cases are crisp.

3 To make the filling, spread a little
tapenade or tomato paste in the base of
each pastry case. Whisk together the egg,
yogurt, milk, garlic, herbs and seasoning.
Spoon into the pastry cases and bake
for 25–30 minutes, or until the filling is
just firm and the pastry golden. Leave
the pies to cool slightly before carefully
removing from the tins and serving.

Tomato and Black Olive Tart

This delicious tart has a fresh, rich
Mediterranean flavour and is ideal
for picnics and buffets. Using a
rectangular tin makes the tart
easier to transport and divide
into portions.

Serves 8

250g/9oz/1 cup plain (all-purpose)
    flour, plus extra for dusting
2.5ml/½ tsp salt
130g/4½oz/1 cup butter, diced
45ml/3 tbsp water

For the filling
3 eggs, beaten
300ml/½ pint/1¼ cups milk
30ml/2 tbsp chopped fresh herbs,
    such as parsley, marjoram or basil
6 firm plum tomatoes
75g/3oz ripe Brie
about 16 black olives, pitted
salt and ground black pepper

1 Preheat the oven to 190°C/375°F/
Gas 5. To make the pastry, mix together
the flour, salt and butter. Using your
fingertips or a pastry blender, rub the
butter into the flour until the mixture
resembles fine breadcrumbs. Mix in
the water and knead lightly to form a
firm dough. Roll out the pastry thinly
on a lightly floured surface. Line a
28 × 18cm/11 × 7in loose-based
rectangular flan tin (quiche pan),
trimming off any overhanging edges.

2 Line the pastry case with baking
parchment and baking beans, and
bake blind for 15 minutes. Remove the
baking parchment and baking beans
and bake for a further 5 minutes, or
until the base is crisp.

VARIATION
This tart is delicious made with other
cheeses. Try slices of Gorgonzola or
Camembert for a slightly stronger flavour.

3 To make the filling, beat the eggs
with the milk, seasoning and herbs.
Slice the tomatoes and olives and cube
the cheese. Add to the prepared flan
case (pie shell). Then pour over the
egg mixture.

4 Transfer the tart carefully to the oven
and bake for about 40 minutes, or until
the filling is just firm and turning
golden. Serve the tart warm or cold,
cut into slices.

Greek Aubergine and Spinach Pie

Aubergines layered with spinach, feta cheese and rice make a flavoursome and dramatic filling for a pie. It can be served warm or cold in elegant slices.

Serves 12

375g/13oz shortcrust pastry, thawed
  if frozen
45–60ml/3–4 tbsp olive oil
1 large aubergine (eggplant), sliced
  into rounds
1 onion, chopped
1 garlic clove, crushed
175g/6oz spinach
4 eggs
75g/3oz/¹/₂ cup crumbled feta cheese
40g/1¹/₂oz/¹/₂ cup freshly grated
  Parmesan cheese
60ml/4 tbsp natural (plain) yogurt
90ml/6 tbsp creamy milk
225g/8oz/2 cups cooked white or
  brown long grain rice
salt and ground black pepper

2 Heat 30–45ml/2–3 tbsp of the oil in a frying pan. Add the aubergine slices and cook over a medium heat for 6–8 minutes on each side, until golden. You may need to add a little more oil at first, but this will be released as the flesh softens. Remove from the pan with a spatula and drain well on kitchen paper.

3 Add the onion and garlic to the oil remaining in the pan then cook over a gentle heat for 4–5 minutes, until soft, adding a little extra oil if necessary.

5 Spread the cooked rice in an even layer over the base of the part-baked pastry case (pie shell). Reserve a few aubergine slices for the top, and arrange the remainder in an even layer over the rice.

6 Spoon the spinach and feta mixture over the aubergines and place the remaining aubergine slices on top. Bake for 30–40 minutes, until lightly browned. Serve the pie while warm, or leave it to cool completely before transferring to a serving plate.

1 Preheat the oven to 180°C/350°F/ Gas 4. Roll out the pastry thinly on a lightly floured surface and use to line a 25cm/10in flan tin (quiche pan). Prick the base all over with a fork and bake for 10–12 minutes, until the pastry is pale golden. (Alternatively, bake blind, having lined the pastry with baking parchment and weighted it with a handful of baking beans.)

4 Rinse the spinach in cold water, drain well and pat dry with kitchen paper. Remove and discard any tough stalks, then chop the spinach leaves finely with a sharp knife or in a food processor. Beat the eggs in a large mixing bowl, then add the spinach, feta, Parmesan, yogurt, milk and the onion mixture. Season to taste with salt and ground black pepper and stir thoroughly to mix.

COOK'S TIP
Courgettes (zucchini) could be used in place of the aubergines (eggplant), if you prefer. Cook the sliced courgettes in a little olive oil over a medium heat for 3–4 minutes, until they are evenly golden. You will need to use three or four standard courgettes. Alternatively, choose baby courgettes instead and slice them horizontally.

Roasted Vegetable and Garlic Sausage Loaf

Stuffed with cured meat and roasted vegetables, this crusty cob loaf makes a colourful centrepiece for a casual summer lunch or picnic. Serve with fresh green salad leaves.

Serves 6

1 large cob loaf
2 red (bell) peppers, quartered
　　and seeded
1 large leek, sliced
90ml/6 tbsp olive oil
175g/6oz green beans, blanched
　　and drained
75g/3oz garlic sausage, sliced
2 eggs, hard-boiled and quartered
115g/4oz/1 cup cashew nuts, toasted
75g/3oz/⅓ cup soft white (farmer's)
　　cheese with garlic and herbs
salt and ground black pepper

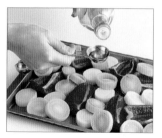

1 Preheat the oven to 220°C/425°F/ Gas 7. Slice the top off the loaf using a large serrated knife and set it aside, then cut out the soft centre, leaving the crust intact. Stand the crusty shell on a baking sheet.

COOK'S TIP
Do not throw away the soft centre of the loaf. It can be made into breadcrumbs and frozen for use in another recipe.

2 Put the red peppers and sliced leek into a roasting pan with the olive oil and cook for 25–30 minutes, turning occasionally, or until the peppers have softened.

3 Spoon half of the pepper and leek mixture into the base of the loaf shell, pressing it down firmly with the back of a spoon. Add the green beans, garlic sausage slices, egg quarters and cashew nuts, packing the layers down well. Season each layer with salt and ground black pepper to taste before adding the next. Dot the soft cheese with garlic and herbs over the filling and top with the remaining pepper and leek mixture.

4 Replace the top of the loaf and bake it for 15–20 minutes, or until the filling is warmed through. Serve, cut into wedges or slices.

VARIATION
You can use a variety of different-shaped loaves, such as a large, uncut white or wholemeal (whole-wheat) sandwich loaf, for this recipe. Hollow out the loaf and fill as above, then cut into slices.

Potato Skewers with Mustard Dip

When potatoes are cooked on the barbecue, they have a great flavour and crisp skin. Try these delicious kebabs served with a thick, garlic-rich dip for an unusual start to a meal.

Serves 6

1kg/2¼ lb small new potatoes
200g/7oz shallots, halved
30ml/2 tbsp olive oil
15ml/1 tbsp sea salt

For the dip
4 garlic cloves, crushed
2 egg yolks
30ml/2 tbsp lemon juice
300ml/½ pint/1¼ cups extra virgin
*   olive oil*
10ml/2 tsp wholegrain mustard
salt and ground black pepper

1 Prepare the barbecue or preheat the grill (broiler). To make the dip place the garlic, egg yolks and lemon juice in a blender or a food processor fitted with a metal blade and process for just a few seconds until the mixture is smooth and combined.

COOK'S TIPS
• Only early or "new" potatoes and salad potatoes have the firmness necessary to stay on the skewer.
• Lightly oil the skewers before threading the potatoes and shallots to make the process easier.

2 Keep the blender or food processor motor running and add the oil very gradually, pouring it in a thin stream, until the mixture forms a thick, glossy cream. Transfer to a bowl, add the mustard and stir to combine, then season to taste with salt and pepper. Cover with clear film (plastic wrap) and chill until ready to use.

3 Par-boil the potatoes in their skins in a pan of boiling water for 5 minutes. Drain well and then thread them on to metal skewers alternating with the shallot halves.

4 Brush the skewers with olive oil and sprinkle with sea salt. Cook on the barbecue or grill (broil) for about 10–12 minutes, turning occasionally. Serve with the mustard dip.

Ceviche

You can use any firm-fleshed fish for this South American dish, provided that is perfectly fresh. The fish is "cooked" by the action of the acidic lime juice.

Serves 6

675g/1½ lb halibut, turbot, sea bass or
    salmon fillets, skinned
juice of 3 limes
1–2 fresh red chillies, seeded and very
    finely chopped
15ml/1 tbsp olive oil
salt

For the garnish
1 ripe avocado
4 large firm tomatoes, peeled, seeded
    and diced
15ml/1 tbsp lemon juice
30ml/2 tbsp olive oil
30ml/2 tbsp fresh coriander
    (cilantro) leaves

1 Cut the fish into strips measuring about 5 × 1cm/2 × ½in. Lay these in a shallow, non-metallic dish and pour over the lime juice, turning the fish strips to coat them all over in the juice. Cover with clear film (plastic wrap) and leave for 1 hour.

2 Meanwhile, prepare the garnish. Cut the avocado in half lengthways and twist to separate the halves. Remove the stone (pit) with the point of the knife, then peel and finely dice the flesh.

3 Place the avocado in a bowl and add the tomatoes, lemon juice and olive oil and mix gently. Cover with clear film and set aside.

4 Season the fish with salt and sprinkle over the chillies. Drizzle with the olive oil. Toss the fish in the mixture, then replace the cover. Leave to marinate in the refrigerator for 15–30 minutes more. To serve, divide the avocado and tomato garnish among six plates. Arrange the ceviche, then sprinkle with coriander.

Three-colour Fish Kebabs

Don't leave the fish to marinate for more than an hour. The lemon juice will start to break down the fibres of the fish after this time.

Serves 4

120ml/4fl oz/¹/₂ cup olive oil
finely grated rind and juice of
*   1 large lemon*
5ml/1 tsp crushed chilli flakes
350g/12oz monkfish fillet, skinned
*   and cubed*
350g/12oz swordfish fillet, skinned
*   and cubed*
350g/12oz thick salmon fillet or
*   steak, skinned and cubed*
2 red, yellow or orange (bell) peppers,
*   seeded and cut into squares*
30ml/2 tbsp finely chopped fresh flat
*   leaf parsley*
salt and ground black pepper

**For the sweet tomato and
chilli salsa**
225g/8oz ripe tomatoes,
*   finely chopped*
1 garlic clove, crushed
1 fresh red chilli, seeded and chopped
45ml/3 tbsp extra virgin olive oil
15ml/1 tbsp lemon juice
15ml/1 tbsp finely chopped fresh flat
*   leaf parsley*
pinch of sugar

1 Put the oil in a large, shallow glass or china dish and add the lemon rind and juice, the chilli flakes and pepper to taste. Whisk well to combine, then add all the fish chunks and turn to coat them evenly.

2 Add the pepper squares, stir, then cover with clear film (plastic wrap) and leave to marinate in a cool place for 1 hour, turning the fish occasionally with a slotted spoon.

3 Prepare the barbecue or preheat the grill (broiler) to medium. Thread the chunks of fish and pepper squares on to eight oiled metal skewers, reserving the marinade.

4 Cook the skewers on the barbecue or under the grill, turning once, for 5–8 minutes, until the fish is tender and light golden brown.

5 Meanwhile, make the salsa by mixing the tomatoes, garlic, chilli, olive oil, lemon juice, parsley and sugar in a bowl. Season to taste.

6 Heat the reserved marinade in a small pan to boiling point, then remove the pan from the heat and stir in the parsley and season with salt and pepper to taste.

7 Transfer the kebabs to warm plates, spoon the marinade over them and serve immediately, accompanied by the salsa.

VARIATION

Use tuna instead of swordfish, if you like. It has a similar meaty texture and will be equally successful.

Moroccan Grilled Fish Brochettes

Serve these delicious skewers with strips of red peppers, potatoes and aubergine slices, which can also be cooked on the barbecue. Accompany them with warm, soft flour tortillas.

Serves 6

5 garlic cloves, chopped
2.5ml/½ tsp paprika
2.5ml/½ tsp ground cumin
2.5–5ml/½–1 tsp salt
2–3 pinches of cayenne pepper
60ml/4 tbsp olive oil
30ml/2 tbsp lemon juice
30ml/2 tbsp chopped fresh coriander
    (cilantro) or parsley
675g/1½ lb firm-fleshed white fish,
    such as haddock, halibut, sea bass or
    snapper, cut into 2.5–5cm/
    1–2in cubes
3–4 green (bell) peppers, cut into
    2.5–5cm/1–2in pieces
2 lemon wedges, to serve

1 Put the garlic, paprika, cumin, salt, cayenne pepper, oil, lemon juice and coriander or parsley in a large bowl and mix together.

2 Add the fish and toss to coat. Leave to marinate for at least 30 minutes, and preferably 2 hours, at room temperature, or chill overnight.

COOK'S TIP
If you are using wooden skewers, soak them in cold water for 30 minutes before using to stop them burning.

3 Thread the fish cubes and pepper pieces alternately on to six wooden or metal skewers.

4 About 40 minutes before you are going to cook the brochettes, prepare and light the barbecue. It will be ready when the flames subside and the coals have turned white and grey.

5 Grill the brochettes on the barbecue for 2–3 minutes on each side, or until the fish is tender and lightly browned. Serve with lemon wedges.

Grilled Squid Stuffed with Feta Cheese

A large, fresh leafy salad or a vegetable dish, such as fresh green beans with tomato sauce could be served with the grilled squid.

Serves 8

8 medium squid, total weight about 900g/2lb
8–12 finger-length slices of feta cheese
175ml/6fl oz/³⁄₄ cup olive oil
4 garlic cloves, crushed
6–8 fresh marjoram sprigs, leaves removed and chopped
salt and ground black pepper
lemon wedges, to serve

1 To prepare the squid, wash it carefully. If there is any ink on the body, rinse it off so that you can see what you are doing. Holding the body firmly, pull away the head and tentacles. If the ink sac is still intact, remove it. Either keep it for cooking or discard it.

2 Pull out all the innards, including the long transparent stick or "quill". Peel off and discard the thin purple skin on the body, but keep the two small fins on the sides, if you like. Slice the head across just under the eyes, severing the tentacles. Discard the rest of the squid's head. Squeeze the tentacles at the head end to push out the round beak in the centre. Throw this away. Rinse the body sac inside and out and the tentacles very thoroughly under cold running water. Drain well and pat dry on kitchen paper.

3 Lay the squid bodies and tentacles in a large shallow dish that will hold them in a single layer. Tuck the pieces of cheese between the squid.

4 To make the marinade, pour the olive oil into a jug (pitcher) or bowl and whisk in the fresh garlic and marjoram sprigs. Season to taste with salt and pepper. Pour the marinade over the squid and the cheese, then cover with foil and leave in a cool place to marinate for 2–3 hours to allow the flavours to develop, turning once.

5 Insert one or two pieces of cheese and a few bits of marjoram from the marinade into each squid and place them in a lightly oiled grill (broiler) pan or tray. Thread the tentacles on to wooden skewers that have been soaked in water for half an hour (this prevents them from burning).

6 Preheat the grill (broiler) to a low setting or prepare a barbecue. Cook the stuffed squid for about 6 minutes, then turn them over. Cook them for 1–2 minutes more, then add the skewered tentacles. Cook them for 2 minutes on each side, until they start to scorch. Serve the stuffed squid with the tentacles and a few lemon wedges.

COOK'S TIP
Tentacles are often left whole for frying, but can be chopped into short lengths.

Scallops Wrapped in Prosciutto

Cook these lovely skewers on the barbecue for *al fresco* summer dining. Serve with lime wedges for a sharper flavour.

Serves 4

24 shucked medium-size scallops,
  corals removed
lemon juice
8–12 prosciutto slices, cut lengthways
  into 2 or 3 strips
olive oil, for brushing
ground black pepper
lemon wedges, to serve

1 Prepare the barbecue in advance or preheat the grill (broiler) when you make the skewers.

2 Sprinkle the scallops with lemon juice. Wrap a strip of prosciutto around each scallop. Thread them on to eight metal or wooden skewers.

3 Brush the wrapped scallops with olive oil. Arrange the skewers on a baking sheet if you are going to grill (broil) them. Cook for 3–5 minutes on each side, or until the scallops have just turned opaque. Be careful not to overcook them or they will become tough and inedible.

4 Set two skewers on each of four warmed serving plates. Sprinkle the scallops with freshly ground black pepper and serve immediately with lemon wedges for squeezing over.

COOK'S TIP
Use a short sturdy knife to prise scallop shells open and to cut the roof muscle and the muscle under the skirt. Discard the membrane, organs and gristle at the side of the white meat. Set the coral aside for another dish, if you like. Rinse the scallops well under cold running water and pat dry with kitchen paper.

Italian Prawn Skewers

Parsley and lemon are all that is required to create a lovely tiger prawn dish. Grill them or cook on the barbecue for an informal *al fresco* summer appetizer.

Serves 4

900g/2lb raw tiger prawns (jumbo
   shrimp), peeled
60ml/4 tbsp olive oil
45ml/3 tbsp vegetable oil
75g/3oz/1¼ cups very fine
   dry breadcrumbs
1 garlic clove, crushed
15ml/1 tbsp chopped fresh parsley
salt and ground black pepper
lemon wedges, to serve

1 Slit the prawns down their backs and remove the dark vein with the point of the knife. Rinse in cold water and pat dry on kitchen paper.

2 Put the olive oil and vegetable oil in a large bowl and add the prawns, mixing them to coat evenly. Add the breadcrumbs, garlic and parsley and season with salt and pepper. Toss the prawns thoroughly, to give them an even coating of breadcrumbs. Cover and leave to marinate for 1 hour.

3 Thread the tiger prawns on to four metal or wooden skewers, curling them up slightly as you work, so that the tails are skewered neatly and securely in the middle.

4 Prepare the barbecue or preheat the grill (broiler). Cook the skewers for about 2 minutes on each side, until the breadcrumbs are golden. Serve with lemon wedges.

King Prawns in Sherry

This dish just couldn't be simpler. The sherry brings out the sweetness of the seafood perfectly.

Serves 4

12 raw king prawns (jumbo shrimp)
30ml/2 tbsp olive oil
30ml/2 tbsp sherry
few drops of Tabasco sauce
salt and ground black pepper

COOK'S TIP
King prawns are known as tiger prawns in Britain, jumbo shrimp in the United States and leader prawns in Australia.

1 Pull off the heads and peel the prawns. Using a very sharp knife, make a shallow cut down the back of each prawn, then pull out and discard the dark intestinal tract with the point of the knife or a cocktail stick (toothpick).

2 Heat the oil in a frying pan and cook the prawns for about 2–3 minutes, until pink. Pour over the sherry and season with Tabasco sauce and salt and pepper. Turn into a dish and serve the prawns immediately.

Sizzling Prawns

This dish works especially well with tiny prawns that can be eaten whole, but any type of unpeeled prawns will be fine. Choose a small casserole or frying pan that can be taken to the table for serving while the garlicky prawns are still sizzling and piping hot.

Serves 4

2 garlic cloves, halved
25g/1oz/2 tbsp butter
1 small fresh red chilli, seeded and
    finely sliced
115g/4oz/1 cup unpeeled cooked
    prawns (shrimp)
sea salt and coarsely ground
    black pepper
lime wedges, to serve

COOK'S TIP
Wear gloves when handling chillies, or wash your hands thoroughly afterwards, as the juices can cause severe irritation to sensitive skin, especially around the eyes, nose and mouth.

1 Rub the cut surfaces of the garlic cloves over the base and sides of a frying pan, then throw the garlic cloves away. Add the butter to the pan and melt over a fairly high heat until it just begins to turn golden brown.

2 Toss in the sliced red chilli and the prawns. Stir-fry for 1–2 minutes, until heated through, then season to taste with sea salt and plenty of black pepper. Serve directly from the pan with lime wedges for squeezing over.

Grilled King Prawns with Romesco Sauce

This sauce, originally from the Catalan region of Spain, is served with seafood. Its main ingredients are sweet pepper, tomatoes, garlic and almonds.

Serves 6–8

24 raw king prawns (jumbo shrimp)
30–45ml/2–3 tbsp olive oil
flat leaf parsley, to garnish
lemon wedges, to serve

For the sauce
2 well-flavoured tomatoes
60ml/4 tbsp olive oil
1 onion, chopped
4 garlic cloves, chopped
1 canned pimiento, chopped
2.5ml/1/2 tsp dried chilli flakes or powder
75ml/5 tbsp fish stock
30ml/2 tbsp white wine
10 blanched almonds
15ml/1 tbsp red wine vinegar
salt

3 Toast the almonds under the grill (broiler) until golden. Transfer to a blender or food processor and grind coarsely. Add the remaining 30ml/ 2 tbsp of the olive oil, the vinegar and the last garlic clove and process until evenly combined. Add the tomato and pimiento sauce and process until smooth. Season with salt to taste.

COOK'S TIP
You can cook the prawns (shrimp) on the barbecue if you thread them on skewers.

4 Remove the heads from the prawns leaving them otherwise unpeeled and, with a sharp knife, slit each one down the back and remove the dark vein with the point of the knife or a cocktail stick (toothpick). Rinse and pat dry on kitchen paper. Preheat the grill. Toss the prawns in olive oil, then spread out in the grill pan. Grill (broil) for about 2–3 minutes on each side, until pink. Arrange on a serving platter with the lemon wedges, and the sauce in a small bowl. Serve immediately, garnished with parsley.

1 To make the sauce, place the tomatoes in a bowl, cover with boiling water and leave for about 30 seconds, then refresh them under cold water. Peel off the skins and coarsely chop the tomato flesh.

2 Heat 30ml/2 tbsp of the oil in a pan, add the onion and three of the garlic cloves and cook until soft. Add the pimiento, tomatoes, chilli, fish stock and wine, then cover and simmer for 30 minutes.

Clams with **Chilli** and **Yellow Bean Sauce**

This delicious Thai-inspired dish is simple to prepare. It can be made in a matter of minutes so will not keep you away from your guests for very long.

Serves 4–6

1kg/2¼ lb fresh clams
30ml/2 tbsp vegetable oil
4 garlic cloves, finely chopped
15ml/1 tbsp grated fresh root ginger
4 shallots, finely chopped
30ml/2 tbsp yellow bean sauce
6 fresh red chillies, seeded
  and chopped
15ml/1 tbsp Thai fish sauce
pinch of granulated sugar
handful of fresh basil leaves, plus extra
  to garnish

1 Wash and scrub the clams. Heat the oil in a wok or large frying pan. Add the garlic and ginger and stir-fry over a medium heat for 30 seconds, then add the shallots and stir-fry for a further minute.

2 Add the clams to the pan. Using a fish slice or spatula, turn them a few times to coat all over with the oil. Stir in the yellow bean sauce and half the chopped red chillies.

3 Continue to cook, stirring frequently, for 5–7 minutes, or until all the clams are open. Discard any that remain shut. You may need to add a splash of water. Adjust the seasoning with the fish sauce and a little sugar.

4 Finally add the basil leaves and stir to mix. Transfer the clams to individual bowls or a serving platter. Garnish with the remaining red chillies and basil leaves. Serve immediately.

Lamb Tikka

Creamy yogurt and ground nuts go wonderfully with the spices in these little Indian meatballs.

Makes about 20

450g/1lb lamb fillet
2 spring onions (scallions), chopped

For the marinade
350ml/12fl oz/1½ cups yogurt
15ml/1 tbsp ground almonds, cashew
*   nuts or peanuts*
15ml/1 tbsp vegetable oil
2–3 garlic cloves, finely chopped
juice of 1 lemon
5ml/1 tsp garam masala or curry powder
2.5ml/½ tsp ground cardamom
1.5ml/¼ tsp cayenne pepper
15–30ml/1–2 tbsp chopped fresh mint

1 To prepare the marinade, put all the ingredients in a bowl and stir well to mix. Reserve about 120ml/4fl oz/½ cup of the mixture in a separate bowl to use as a dipping sauce.

2 With a sharp knife, cut the lamb fillet into small pieces and put in the bowl of a food processor with the spring onions. Process, using the pulse action, until the meat is finely chopped. Add 30–45ml/2–3 tbsp of the marinade and process again.

3 Test to see if the mixture holds together by pinching a little between your fingertips. Add a little more marinade if necessary, but do not make the mixture too wet and soft.

4 With moistened palms, form the meat mixture into slightly oval-shaped balls, measuring about 4cm/1½in long, and arrange them in a shallow dish. Spoon over the remaining marinade, cover with clear film (plastic wrap) and chill the meatballs in the refrigerator for 8–10 hours or overnight.

5 Preheat the grill (broiler) and line a baking sheet with foil. Thread each meatball on to a skewer and arrange on the baking sheet. Grill (broil) for 4–5 minutes, turning the skewers occasionally, until crisp and golden on all sides. Serve with the reserved marinade as a dipping sauce.

Barbecue-glazed Chicken Skewers

Known as yakitori in Japan, these skewers are popular throughout the country and are often served as an appetizer with drinks.

Makes 12 skewers and 8 wing pieces

8 chicken wings
4 chicken thighs, skinned
4 spring onions (scallions), blanched
  and cut into short lengths

For the basting sauce
60ml/4 tbsp sake
75ml/5 tbsp/¹/₃ cup dark soy sauce
30ml/2 tbsp tamari sauce
15ml/1 tbsp mirin, or sweet sherry
15ml/1 tbsp sugar

1 Remove the wing tip of the chicken at the first joint. Chop through the second joint, revealing the two narrow bones. Take hold of the bones with a clean cloth and pull, turning the meat around the bones inside out. Remove the smaller bone and discard. Repeat with the remaining wings and then set them aside.

2 Bone the chicken thighs and cut the meat into large dice. Thread the spring onions and thigh meat on to 12 metal or wooden skewers.

3 Measure the ingredients for the basting sauce into a stainless-steel or enamel pan and simmer gently until reduced by two-thirds. Remove from the heat and leave to cool.

4 Heat the grill (broiler) to moderately high. Grill (broil) the wings and skewers without applying any oil. When juices begin to emerge from the chicken, baste liberally with the sauce. Allow a further 3 minutes for the chicken on skewers and cook about 5 minutes for the chicken wings.

Barbecue Chicken

A fragrant marinade of Thai spices and coconut milk gives this chicken a superb flavour. It makes ideal party food for outdoor eating with a difference.

Serves 6

1 chicken, about 1.5kg/3¼lb, cut into
   8–10 pieces
lime wedges and fresh red chillies,
   to garnish

For the marinade
2 lemon grass stalks, roots removed
2.5cm/1in piece fresh root ginger,
   peeled and thinly sliced
6 garlic cloves, coarsely chopped
4 shallots, coarsely chopped
½ bunch coriander (cilantro)
   roots, chopped
15ml/1 tbsp palm sugar
120ml/4fl oz/½ cup coconut milk
30ml/2 tbsp Thai fish sauce
30ml/2 tbsp light soy sauce

1 To make the marinade, cut off the lower 5cm/2in of the lemon grass stalks and chop them coarsely. Put into a food processor or blender along with all the other marinade ingredients and process until the mixture has reached a smooth consistency.

COOK'S TIP
You can buy coconut milk fresh, in cans or cartons, or use 50g/2oz creamed coconut, available in packets, and dissolve in 120ml/4fl oz/½ cup warm water.

2 Place the chicken pieces in a fairly deep dish, pour the marinade over them and stir to mix well, turning the chicken pieces over to coat thoroughly. Cover the dish with clear film (plastic wrap) and leave in a cool place to marinate for at least 4 hours or in the refrigerator overnight.

3 Prepare the barbecue. Cook the chicken over the barbecue for 20–30 minutes, or until the pieces are cooked and golden brown. Turn the pieces and brush with the marinade once or twice during cooking. Transfer to a serving platter and garnish with lime wedges and red chillies to serve.

Turkey Patties

Minced turkey makes deliciously light patties, which are ideal for summer meals. Serve the patties in split and toasted buns or between thick pieces of crusty bread, with chutney, salad leaves and chunky fries or potato wedges.

Serves 6

675g/1½lb minced (ground) turkey
1 small red onion, finely chopped
grated rind and juice of 1 lime
small handful of fresh thyme leaves
15–30ml/1–2 tbsp olive oil
salt and ground black pepper

1 Mix together the turkey, onion, lime rind and juice, thyme and seasoning. Cover and chill for up to 4 hours to allow the flavours to infuse (steep), then divide the mixture into six equal portions and shape into round patties.

2 Preheat a griddle. Brush the patties with oil, then place them on the griddle and cook for 10–12 minutes. Turn the patties over, brush with more oil and cook for 10–12 minutes on the second side, or until cooked through.

Lamb Burgers with **Red Onion** and **Tomato Relish**

A sharp-sweet red onion relish works well with burgers based on Middle-Eastern style lamb. The burgers can be made a day ahead and chilled. Serve them with pitta bread and tabbouleh or a crisp green salad.

Serves 8

50g/2oz/⅓ cup bulgur wheat
1kg/2¼lb lean minced (ground) lamb
2 small red onions, finely chopped
4 garlic cloves, finely chopped
2 fresh green chillies, seeded and
    finely chopped
10ml/2 tsp ground toasted cumin seeds
5ml/1 tsp ground sumac
25g/1oz/½ cup chopped fresh flat
    leaf parsley
60ml/4 tbsp chopped fresh mint
olive oil, for frying
salt and ground black pepper

For the relish
4 red (bell) peppers, halved
    and seeded
4 red onions, cut into 5mm/¼in
    thick slices
150ml/¼ pint/⅔ cup olive oil
700g/1lb 9oz cherry tomatoes, chopped
1 fresh red or green chilli, seeded and
    finely chopped (optional)
60ml/4 tbsp chopped fresh mint
60ml/4 tbsp chopped fresh parsley
30ml/2 tbsp chopped fresh oregano
    or marjoram
5ml/1 tsp ground toasted cumin seeds
5ml/1 tsp ground sumac
juice of 1 lemon
caster (superfine) sugar, to taste

1 Pour 300ml/½ pint/1¼ cups hot water over the bulgur wheat in a bowl and leave to stand for 15 minutes, then drain in a sieve and squeeze out the excess moisture.

2 Place the bulgur wheat in a bowl and add the minced lamb, onion, garlic, chilli, cumin, sumac, parsley and mint. Mix the ingredients thoroughly together by hand, then season with 10ml/2 tsp salt and plenty of black pepper and mix again. Form the mixture into 16 small burgers and set aside while you make the relish.

3 Grill (broil) the peppers, skin side up, until the skin chars and blisters. Place in a bowl, cover with clear film (plastic wrap) and leave to stand until cool. Peel off the skin, dice and place in a bowl.

4 Brush the onions with 30ml/2 tbsp oil and grill for 5 minutes on each side, until browned. Cool, then chop.

5 Add the onions, tomatoes, chilli (if using) to taste, the mint, parsley, oregano or marjoram and half of the cumin and sumac to the peppers. Stir in the remaining oil and 30ml/2 tbsp of the lemon juice. Season with salt, pepper and sugar and leave to stand for 20–30 minutes.

6 Prepare a barbecue or heat a heavy frying pan or griddle over a high heat and grease with olive oil. Cook the burgers for about 5–6 minutes on each side, or until just cooked at the centre.

7 While the burgers are cooking, taste the relish and adjust the seasoning, adding more salt, pepper, sugar, chilli, cumin, sumac and lemon juice to taste. Serve the burgers as soon as they are cooked, with the relish.

Skewered Lamb with **Red Onion Salsa**

This summery tapas dish is ideal for outdoor eating, although, if the weather fails, the skewers can be grilled rather than barbecued. The simple salsa makes a refreshing accompaniment – make sure that you use a mild-flavoured red onion that is fresh and crisp, and a tomato which is ripe and full of flavour.

Serves 4

225g/8oz lean lamb, cubed
2.5ml/¹/₂ tsp ground cumin
5ml/1 tsp paprika
15ml/1 tbsp olive oil
salt and ground black pepper

For the salsa
1 red onion, very thinly sliced
1 large tomato, seeded and chopped
15ml/1 tbsp red wine vinegar
3–4 fresh basil or mint leaves,
   coarsely torn
small mint leaves, to garnish

1 Place the cubes of lamb in a bowl and add the cumin, paprika and olive oil and season with plenty of salt and pepper. Toss thoroughly until the lamb is coated with the spices.

2 Cover the bowl with clear film (plastic wrap) and set aside in a cool place for several hours, or in the refrigerator overnight, so that the lamb absorbs the flavours of the spices.

3 Thread the lamb cubes on to four small skewers – if using wooden skewers, soak them first in cold water for about 30 minutes to prevent them from burning during cooking.

4 To make the salsa, put the sliced onion, tomato, red wine vinegar and torn basil or mint leaves in a small bowl and stir together until thoroughly combined. Season to taste with salt, garnish with mint, then set aside while you cook the lamb skewers.

5 Cook the skewers over the barbecue or under a preheated grill (broiler), turning frequently, for 5–10 minutes, until the lamb is well browned but still slightly pink in the centre. Serve immediately, with the salsa.

Garlic and **Chilli Marinated Beef** with **Corn-crusted Onion Rings**

Fruity, smoky and mild Mexican chillies combine well with garlic in this marinade for grilled steak.

Serves 8

40g/1 1/2oz large mild dried red chillies, such as mulato or pasilla
4 garlic cloves, plain or smoked, finely chopped
10ml/2 tsp ground toasted cumin seeds
10ml/2 tsp dried oregano
120ml/4fl oz/1/2 cup olive oil
8 beef steaks, rump (round) or rib-eye, 175–225g/6–8oz each
salt and ground black pepper

For the onion rings
4 onions, sliced into rings
475ml/16fl oz/2 cups milk
175g/6oz/1 1/2 cup coarse corn meal
5ml/1 tsp dried red chilli flakes
10ml/2 tsp ground toasted cumin seeds
10ml/2 tsp dried oregano
vegetable oil, for deep-frying

1 Cut the stalks from the chillies and discard the seeds. Toast the chillies in a dry frying pan for 2–4 minutes. Place them in a bowl, cover with warm water and leave to soak for 20–30 minutes. Drain and reserve the water.

2 Process the chillies to a paste with the garlic, cumin, oregano and oil in a food processor. Add a little soaking water, if needed. Season with pepper.

3 Wash and dry the steaks, drizzle the chilli paste all over them and leave to marinate for up to 12 hours.

4 To make the onion rings, soak the onions in the milk for 30 minutes. Mix the corn meal, chilli, cumin and oregano and season to taste.

5 Heat the oil for deep-frying to 160–180°C/325–350°F, or until a cube of day-old bread turns brown in about 60 seconds.

6 Drain the onion rings and dip each one into the corn meal mixture, coating it thoroughly. Deep-fry for 2–4 minutes, or until browned and crisp. Do not overcrowd the pan, but cook in batches. Lift the onion rings out of the pan with a slotted spoon and drain on kitchen paper.

7 Heat a barbecue or griddle. Season the steaks with salt and cook for about 4 minutes on each side for a medium result.

diva desserts

Make sure that your guests leave the party on a high
note after sampling one (or more!) of these
superlative, mouthwatering sweet dishes.

Mint Chocolate Meringues

Omit the alcohol and these mini meringues are perfect for a child's birthday party.

Makes about 50

2 egg whites
115g/4oz/generous ½ cup caster (superfine) sugar
50g/2oz chocolate mint sticks, chopped
(unsweetened) cocoa powder, sifted (optional)

For the filling
150ml/¼ pint/⅔ cup double (heavy) or whipping cream
5–10ml/1–2 tsp crème de menthe, or mint essence (extract)

1 Preheat the oven to 110°C/225°F/ Gas ¼. Line two or three baking sheets with baking parchment. Whisk the egg whites until stiff, then gradually whisk in the sugar until it is thick and glossy.

2 Fold in the chopped mint sticks and then place teaspoons of the mixture on the prepared baking sheets.

3 Bake for 1 hour, or until crisp. Remove from the oven and leave to cool, then dust with cocoa, if using.

4 To make the filling whip the cream until it stands in soft peaks and stir in the crème de menthe or mint essence. Use the cream to sandwich the meringues together in pairs just before serving.

Chocolate Truffles

These irresistible, melt-in-the-mouth truffles will make a dainty addition to the buffet table as a dessert or as an after-dinner treat. Use a good quality chocolate with a high percentage of cocoa solids to give a real depth of flavour.

Makes 20–30

175ml/6fl oz/¾ cup double
(heavy) cream
1 egg yolk, beaten
275g/10oz plain (semisweet)
Belgian chocolate, chopped
25g/1oz/2 tbsp unsalted (sweet)
butter, cut into pieces
30–45ml/2–3 tbsp brandy (optional)

For the coatings
(unsweetened) cocoa powder
finely chopped pistachio nuts
or hazelnuts
400g/14oz plain (semisweet), milk
or white chocolate, or a mixture

1 Bring the cream to the boil, then remove the pan from the heat and beat in the egg yolk. Add the chocolate, then stir until melted and smooth. Stir in the butter and the brandy, if using, then pour into a bowl and leave to cool. Cover and chill in the refrigerator for 6–8 hours.

COOK'S TIP
Chocolate truffles will delight guests at a drinks party – serve them with coffee to follow all the savoury bites.

2 Line a large baking sheet with baking parchment. Using a very small ice cream scoop or two teaspoons, form the chocolate mixture into 20–30 balls and place on the parchment. Chill if the mixture becomes too soft.

3 To coat the truffles with cocoa, sift some powder into a small bowl, drop in the truffles, one at a time, and roll to coat well. To coat them with nuts, roll the truffles in finely chopped pistachio nuts or hazelnuts.

4 To coat with chocolate, freeze the truffles for at least 1 hour. In a small bowl, melt the plain, milk or white chocolate over a pan of barely simmering water, stirring until melted and smooth, then leave to cool slightly.

5 Using a fork, dip the frozen truffles into the cooled chocolate, one at a time, tapping the fork on the edge of the bowl to shake off the excess. Place on a baking sheet lined with baking parchment and chill. If the melted chocolate thickens, reheat until smooth. All the truffles can be stored, well wrapped, in the refrigerator for up to 10 days.

Tropical Scented Red and Orange Fruit Salad

This fresh fruit salad, with its bright colour and exotic flavour, is perfect after a rich, heavy meal or on the buffet table. It is also a refreshing dish to serve at a summer picnic or barbecue.

Serves 4–6

350–400g/12–14oz/3–3½ cups
   strawberries, hulled and halved
3 oranges, peeled and segmented
3 small blood oranges, peeled
   and segmented
1–2 passion fruit
120ml/4fl oz/½ cup dry white wine
sugar, to taste

1 Put the strawberries and oranges into a serving bowl. Halve the passion fruit and spoon the flesh into the bowl.

2 Pour the wine over the fruit and add sugar to taste. Toss gently and then chill until ready to serve.

COOK'S TIP

Omit the white wine if you like and replace with orange or tropical juice.

VARIATION

Other fruit that can be added include pear, kiwi fruit and banana.

Fig, Port and Clementine Sundaes

These exotic sundaes will make an ideal finale to a rich meal. The fresh flavours of figs and clementines contrast beautifully with the warm spices and port.

Serves 6

6 clementines
30ml/2 tbsp clear honey
1 cinnamon stick, halved
15ml/1 tbsp light muscovado
    (brown) sugar
60ml/4 tbsp port
6 fresh figs
about 500ml/17fl oz/2¼ cups orange
    sorbet (sherbet)

1 Finely grate the rind from two clementines and put it in a small, heavy pan. Cut the peel off the clementines, then slice the flesh thinly. Add the honey, cinnamon, sugar and port to the rind. Heat gently until the sugar has dissolved, to make a syrup.

2 Put the clementine slices in a heatproof bowl and pour over the syrup. Cool completely, then chill.

3 Slice the figs thinly and add to the clementines and syrup, tossing the ingredients together gently. Leave to stand for 10 minutes, then discard the cinnamon stick.

4 Arrange half the fig and clementine slices around the sides of six serving glasses. Half fill the glasses with scoops of sorbet. Arrange the remaining fruit slices around the sides of the glasses, then pile more sorbet into the centre. Pour over the port syrup and serve.

COOK'S TIP
A variety of different types of fresh figs are available. Dark purple skinned figs have a deep red flesh; the yellowy-green figs have a pink flesh and green skinned figs have an amber coloured flesh. All types can be eaten, complete with the skin, simply as they are or baked and served with Greek (US strained plain) yogurt and honey for a quick dessert. When they are ripe, you can split them open with your fingers to reveal the soft, sweet flesh full of edible seeds.

Passion Fruit Crème Caramels with Dipped Physalis

The aromatic flavour of the fruit permeates these crème caramels, which are perfect for a dinner party.

Serves 8

375g/13oz/generous 1¾ cups caster (superfine) sugar
150ml/¼ pint/⅔ cup water
8 passion fruit
8 physalis
6 eggs plus 2 egg yolks
300ml/½ pint/1¼ cups double (heavy) cream
300ml/½ pint/1¼ cups full-cream (whole) milk

1 Place 300g/11oz/1½ cups of the caster sugar in a heavy pan. Add the water and heat the mixture gently until the sugar has dissolved. Increase the heat and boil until the syrup turns a dark golden colour.

2 Meanwhile, cut each passion fruit in half. Scoop out the seeds from the passion fruit into a sieve set over a bowl. Press the seeds against the sieve to extract all their juice. Spoon a few of the seeds into each of eight 150ml/¼ pint/⅔ cup ramekins. Reserve the passion fruit juice.

3 Peel back the papery casing from each physalis and dip the orange berries into the caramel. Place on a sheet of baking parchment and set aside. Pour the remaining caramel carefully into the ramekins.

4 Preheat the oven to 150°C/300°F/Gas 2. Whisk the eggs, egg yolks and remaining sugar in a bowl. Whisk in the cream and milk, then the passion fruit juice. Strain through a sieve into each ramekin, then place the ramekins in a baking tin (pan). Pour in hot water to come halfway up the sides of the dishes and bake for 40–45 minutes, or until just set.

5 Remove the custards from the tin and leave to cool, then cover and chill them for 4 hours before serving. Run a knife between the edge of each ramekin and the custard and invert each, in turn, on to a dessert plate. Shake the ramekins firmly to release the custards before lifting them off the desserts. Decorate each with a dipped physalis.

Crème Brûlée

This dessert actually originated in the English city of Cambridge, but has become associated with France and is widely eaten there.

Serves 6

1 vanilla pod (bean)
1 litre/1¾ pints/4 cups double
 (heavy) cream
6 egg yolks
90g/3½oz/½ cup caster
 (superfine) sugar
30ml/2 tbsp orange liqueur (optional)
75g/3oz/⅓ cup soft light brown sugar

1 Preheat the oven to 150°C/300°F/ Gas 2. Place six 120ml/4fl oz/½ cup ramekins in a roasting pan and set aside until required.

2 With a small sharp knife, split the vanilla pod lengthways and scrape the black seeds into a medium pan. Add the cream and bring just to the boil over a medium heat, stirring constantly. Remove from the heat and cover. Set aside for 15–20 minutes.

VARIATION

You can omit the liqueur if you like. You could also substitute almond liqueur, such as Amaretto, if you prefer the flavour.

COOK'S TIP

To test if the custards are ready, push the point of a knife into centre of one – if it comes out clean, the custards are cooked.

3 Whisk the egg yolks, caster sugar and orange liqueur, if using, in a mixing bowl until thoroughly blended. Whisk in the hot cream and strain the mixture into a large jug (pitcher). Divide the custard equally among the six ramekins.

4 Pour enough boiling water into the roasting pan to come about halfway up the sides of the ramekins. Cover the pan with foil and bake for about 30 minutes, until the custards are just set. Remove the ramekins from the pan and leave to cool. Return to the dry roasting pan and chill.

5 Preheat the grill (broiler). Sprinkle the brown sugar evenly over the surface of each custard and grill (broil) for 30–60 seconds, until the sugar melts and caramelizes. (Do not let the sugar burn or the custard curdle.) Place in the refrigerator to set the crust and chill completely before serving.

Chocolate Mandarin Trifle

Trifle is always a tempting treat, but when a rich chocolate and mascarpone custard is combined with amaretto and mandarin oranges, it becomes irresistible.

Serves 6–8

4 trifle sponges
14 amaretti
60ml/4 tbsp Amaretto di Saronno or
*   sweet sherry*
8 mandarin oranges

For the custard

200g/7oz plain (semisweet) chocolate,
*   broken into squares*
30ml/2 tbsp cornflour (cornstarch) or
*   custard powder*
30ml/2 tbsp caster (superfine) sugar
2 egg yolks
200ml/7fl oz/⅞ cup milk
250g/9oz/generous 1 cup
*   mascarpone cheese*

For the topping

250g/9oz/generous 1 cup fromage
*   frais or farmer's cheese*
chocolate shapes
mandarin slices

1 Break up the trifle sponges and place them in the base of a large glass serving dish. Crumble the amaretti over and then sprinkle with Amaretto or sweet sherry.

2 Squeeze the juice from two of the mandarins and sprinkle into the dish. Segment the rest of the mandarins and put in the dish.

3 Make the custard. Melt the chocolate in a heatproof bowl set over a pan of barely simmering water. In a separate bowl, mix the cornflour or custard powder, sugar and egg yolks to a smooth paste.

4 Heat the milk in a small pan until almost boiling, then pour in a steady stream on to the egg yolk and cornflour or custard mixture, stirring constantly. Return the mixture to the clean pan and stir over a low heat until the custard has thickened slightly and is smooth.

5 Stir in the mascarpone until melted, then add the melted chocolate, mixing it thoroughly. Spread evenly over the trifle base, leave to cool, then chill in the refrigerator until set.

6 To finish, spread the fromage frais over the custard, using a spatula, then decorate with chocolate shapes and the remaining mandarin slices just before serving.

COOK'S TIP
Always use the best chocolate which has a high percentage of cocoa solids, and take care not to overheat the chocolate when melting as it will lose its gloss and look "grainy".

Chocolate Hazelnut Galettes

If only all sandwiches looked and tasted as good as these chocolate rounds.

Serves 4

175g/6oz plain (semisweet) chocolate, broken into squares
45ml/3 tbsp single (light) cream
30ml/2 tbsp flaked (sliced) hazelnuts
115g/4oz white chocolate, broken into squares
175g/6oz/³⁄₄ cup fromage frais or farmer's cheese
15ml/1 tbsp dry sherry
60ml/4 tbsp finely chopped hazelnuts, toasted
physalis, dipped in white chocolate, to decorate

1 Melt the plain chocolate in a bowl over hot water, then remove from the heat and stir in the cream.

2 Draw 12 × 7.5cm/3in circles on sheets of non-stick baking parchment. Turn the paper over and spread the plain chocolate over each marked circle, covering in a thin, even layer. Sprinkle flaked hazelnuts over four of the circles, then leave to set.

3 Melt the white chocolate in a heatproof bowl set over a pan of barely simmering water, then stir in the fromage frais and dry sherry. Gently fold in the chopped, toasted hazelnuts. Leave to cool until the mixture holds its shape.

4 Remove the chocolate rounds carefully from the paper and sandwich them together in stacks of three, spooning the hazelnut cream between each layer and using the hazelnut-covered rounds on top. Chill in the refrigerator before serving.

5 To serve, place the galettes on individual plates and decorate with chocolate-dipped physalis.

COOK'S TIP
Strictly speaking, white chocolate is not really chocolate. It is made from cocoa butter, but contains no cocoa solids.

VARIATION
The chocolate could be spread over heart shapes instead, for a special Valentine's Day dessert.

Chocolate and **Chestnut Pots**

Prepared in advance, these are the perfect ending for a dinner party. Remove them from the refrigerator about 30 minutes before serving, to allow them to "ripen".

Serves 6

250g/9oz plain (semisweet) chocolate
60ml/4 tbsp Madeira
25g/1oz/2 tbsp butter, diced
2 eggs, separated
225g/8oz/scant 1 cup unsweetened
   chestnut purée
crème fraîche or whipped double
   (heavy) cream, to decorate

1 Make a few chocolate curls for decoration, then break the rest of the chocolate into squares and melt it with the Madeira in a pan over a gentle heat. Remove from the heat and add the butter, a few pieces at a time, stirring until melted and smooth.

COOK'S TIPS

• The quickest and easiest way to make chocolate curls is to use a vegetable peeler. Make sure the chocolate is at room temperature, then hold it firmly and shave off curls from one side. Transfer them using a cocktail stick (toothpick) to avoid damaging them.
• If Madeira is not available, use brandy or rum instead.
• These chocolate pots can be frozen successfully for up to 2 months.

2 Beat the egg yolks quickly into the chocolate mixture, then beat in the chestnut purée, mixing well until completely smooth.

3 Whisk the egg whites in a clean, grease-free bowl until stiff. Stir about 15ml/1 tbsp of the whites into the chestnut mixture to lighten it, then fold in the rest smoothly and evenly, using a metal spoon or rubber spatula.

4 Spoon the mixture into six small ramekins and chill in the refrigerator until set. Serve the pots topped with a generous spoonful of crème fraîche or whipped double cream and decorated with the plain chocolate curls.

Bitter Chocolate Mousse

This is the quintessential French dessert – easy to prepare ahead, rich and extremely delicious. Use the darkest chocolate you can find for the most authentic and intense chocolate flavour.

Serves 8

225g/8oz plain (semisweet)
  chocolate, chopped
30ml/2 tbsp orange liqueur or brandy
25g/1oz/2 tbsp unsalted (sweet)
  butter, cut into small pieces
4 eggs, separated
90ml/6 tbsp whipping cream
1.5ml/¼ tsp cream of tartar
45ml/3 tbsp caster (superfine) sugar
crème fraîche or sour cream and
  chocolate curls, to decorate

1 Place the chocolate and 60ml/ 4 tbsp of water in a heavy pan. Melt over a low heat, stirring until smooth. Remove the pan from the heat and whisk in the liqueur and butter.

2 With an electric mixer, beat the egg yolks for 2–3 minutes, until thick and creamy, then slowly beat into the melted chocolate until well blended. Set aside.

COOK'S TIP
The world's most popular orange liqueur is cointreau, a triple sec that combines bitter orange peels from the Caribbean with sweet Mediterranean oranges. You could also use grand marnier.

3 Whip the cream until soft peaks form and stir a spoonful into the chocolate to lighten it. Fold in the remaining cream.

4 In a clean, grease-free bowl, using an electric mixer, beat the egg whites until they are frothy. Add the cream of tartar and continue beating until they form soft peaks. Gradually sprinkle over the sugar, while continuing to beat until the egg whites are stiff and very glossy.

5 Using a rubber spatula or large metal spoon, stir a quarter of the egg whites into the chocolate mixture to slacken, then gently fold in the remaining egg whites, cutting down to the bottom, along the sides and up to the top in a semicircular motion until they are just combined. (Don't worry about a few white streaks.)

6 Gently spoon the mousse into a 2 litre/3½ pint/8 cup dish or into eight individual dishes. Chill in the refrigerator for at least 2 hours until set and chilled.

7 Spoon a little crème fraîche or sour cream over the mousse and decorate with chocolate curls.

Mocha Cream Pots

The name of this rich baked custard, a classic French dessert, comes from the baking cups, called *pots de crème*. The addition of coffee gives the dessert an exotic touch.

Serves 8

15ml/1 tbsp instant coffee powder
475ml/16fl oz/2 cups milk
75g/3oz/⅓ cup caster (superfine) sugar
225g/8oz plain (semisweet)
　chocolate, chopped
10ml/2 tsp vanilla essence (extract)
30ml/2 tbsp coffee liqueur (optional)
7 egg yolks
whipped cream and crystallized
　mimosa balls, to decorate (optional)

1 Preheat the oven to 160°C/325°F/ Gas 3. Place eight 120ml/4fl oz/ ½ cup cups or ramekins in a roasting pan.

2 Put the instant coffee into a pan and stir in the milk, then add the sugar and set the pan over a medium-high heat. Bring to the boil, stirring constantly, until the coffee and sugar have completely dissolved.

3 Remove the pan from the heat and add the chocolate. Stir until the chocolate has melted and the sauce is smooth. Stir in the vanilla essence and coffee liqueur, if using.

COOK'S TIP
Kahlúa is a sweeter coffee liqueur than the other leading brand, Tia Maria.

4 In a bowl, whisk the egg yolks to blend them lightly. Gradually whisk in the chocolate mixture until thoroughly blended, then strain the mixture into a large jug (pitcher) and divide equally among the cups or ramekins. Pour enough boiling water into the roasting pan to come about halfway up the sides of the cups or ramekins. Cover the pan with foil.

5 Bake for 30–35 minutes, until the custard is just set and a knife inserted into it comes out clean. Remove the cups or ramekins from the roasting pan and leave to cool. Place the cups or ramekins on a baking sheet, cover with clear film (plastic wrap) and chill in the refrigerator. Decorate with the whipped cream and crystallized mimosa balls, if using.

Cold Lemon Soufflé with Almonds

Terrific to look at, yet easy to make, this dessert is mouthwatering, ideal for the end of any party meal.

Serves 6

vegetable oil, for greasing
grated rind and juice of 3 large lemons
5 large (US extra large) eggs, separated
115g/4oz/generous ½ cup caster
  (superfine) sugar
25ml/1½ tbsp powdered gelatine
450ml/¾ pint/scant 2 cups double
  (heavy) cream

For the almond topping
75g/3oz/¾ cup flaked (sliced) almonds
75g/3oz/¾ cup icing
  (confectioner's) sugar

1 To make the soufflé collar, cut a strip of baking parchment long enough to fit around a 900ml/1½ pint/3¾ cup soufflé dish and wide enough to extend 7.5cm/3in above the rim. Fit the strip around the dish, tape and then tie it around the top of the dish with string. Using a pastry brush, lightly coat the inside of the paper collar with oil.

2 Put the lemon rind and yolks in a bowl. Add 75g/3oz/6 tbsp of the caster sugar and whisk until the mixture is creamy.

COOK'S TIP
Heat the lemon juice and gelatine in a microwave, on full power, in 30-second bursts, stirring between each burst, until it is fully dissolved.

3 Place the lemon juice in a small heatproof bowl and sprinkle over the gelatine. Set aside for 5 minutes, then place the bowl in a pan of simmering water. Heat, stirring occasionally, until the gelatine has dissolved. Cool slightly, then stir the gelatine and lemon juice into the egg yolk mixture.

4 In a separate bowl, lightly whip the cream to soft peaks. Fold into the egg yolk mixture and set aside.

5 Whisk the whites to stiff peaks. Gradually whisk in the remaining caster sugar until stiff and glossy. Quickly and lightly fold the whites into the yolk mix. Pour into the prepared dish, smooth the surface and chill for 4–5 hours.

6 To make the almond topping, brush a baking tray lightly with oil. Preheat the grill (broiler). Sprinkle the flaked almonds over the baking tray and sift the icing sugar over. Grill (broil) until the nuts turn a rich golden colour and the sugar has caramelized.

7 Leave to cool, then remove the almond mixture from the tray with a palette knife or metal spatula and break it into pieces.

8 When the soufflé has set, carefully peel off the paper. If the paper does not come away easily, hold the blade of a knife against the set soufflé to help it keep its shape. Sprinkle the caramelized almonds over the top before serving.

VARIATIONS
• This soufflé is wonderfully refreshing when served semi-frozen. Place the undecorated, set soufflé in the freezer for about an hour. Just before serving, remove from the freezer and decorate with the caramelized almonds.
• You can also vary the flavour slightly by using the juice and rind of 5 limes.

Clementines in Cinnamon Caramel

The combination of sweet, yet sharp clementines and caramel sauce with a hint of spice is divine. Served with Greek yogurt or crème fraîche, this makes a delicious and refreshing dessert.

Serves 4–6

8–12 clementines
225g/8oz/generous 1 cup
*   granulated sugar*
2 cinnamon sticks
30ml/2 tbsp orange-flavoured liqueur
25g/1oz/¼ cup shelled pistachio nuts

1 Pare the rind from two clementines using a vegetable peeler and cut it into fine strips. Set aside.

2 Peel all the clementines, removing all traces of the bitter, white pith, but keeping them intact. Put the fruits in a serving bowl.

3 Gently heat the sugar in a small, heavy pan until it melts and turns a rich golden brown. Immediately turn off the heat.

4 Cover your hand with a dishtowel to protect it and pour in 300ml/½ pint/ 1¼ cups warm water (the mixture will bubble and splutter). Gradually bring to the boil, stirring constantly until the caramel has dissolved. Add the shredded clementine peel and cinnamon sticks, then simmer gently for 5 minutes. Stir in the orange-flavoured liqueur.

5 Leave the syrup to cool for about 10 minutes, then pour it over the clementines. Cover the bowl with clear film (plastic wrap) and chill for several hours or overnight.

6 Blanch the pistachio nuts in boiling water. Drain, cool and remove the dark outer skins. Sprinkle over the clementines and serve immediately.

White Chocolate Parfait

This dessert is everything you could
wish for in one mouthwatering slice.

Serves 10

225g/8oz white chocolate, chopped
600ml/1 pint/2½ cups whipping cream
120ml/4fl oz/½ cup milk
10 egg yolks
15ml/1 tbsp caster (superfine) sugar
25g/1oz/scant ½ cup desiccated (dry
    unsweetened shredded) coconut
120ml/4fl oz/½ cup canned sweetened
    coconut milk
150g/5oz/1¼ cups macadamia nuts

For the chocolate icing (frosting)
225g/8oz plain (semisweet) chocolate
75g/3oz/6 tbsp butter
20ml/generous 1 tbsp golden (light
    corn) syrup
175ml/6fl oz/¾ cup whipping cream
curls of fresh coconut, to decorate

1 Line the base and sides of a 1.4 litre/
2⅓ pint/6 cup terrine mould
(25 × 10cm/10 × 4in) with clear film
(plastic wrap).

2 Place the chopped white chocolate
and 50ml/2fl oz/¼ cup of the cream in
the top of a double boiler or in a
heatproof bowl set over a pan of
barely simmering water. Stir until
melted and smooth. Set aside.

3 Put 250ml/8fl oz/1 cup of the cream
and the milk in a pan and bring to
boiling point.

4 Meanwhile, whisk the egg yolks and
caster sugar together in a large bowl,
until thick and pale.

5 Add the hot cream mixture to the
egg yolks, beating constantly. Pour
back into the pan and cook over a low
heat for 2–3 minutes, until thickened.
Stir constantly and do not allow the
mixture to boil. Remove the pan from
the heat.

6 Add the melted chocolate,
desiccated coconut and coconut milk,
then stir well and leave to cool.

7 Whip the remaining cream until
thick, then fold into the chocolate and
coconut mixture.

8 Put 475ml/16fl oz/2 cups of the
parfait mixture in the prepared mould
and spread evenly. Cover and freeze
for about 2 hours, until just firm.
Cover the remaining mixture and chill.

9 Sprinkle the macadamia nuts evenly
over the frozen parfait. Pour in the
remaining parfait mixture. Cover the
terrine and freeze for 6–8 hours or
overnight, until the parfait is firm.

10 To make the icing, melt the
chocolate with the butter and syrup in
the top of a double boiler or in a
heatproof bowl set over a pan of
barely simmering water, stirring the
mixture occasionally.

11 Heat the cream in a pan, until just
simmering, then stir into the chocolate
mixture. Remove the pan from the
heat and leave to cool until lukewarm.

12 To turn out the parfait, wrap the
terrine in a hot towel and set it upside
down on a plate. Lift off the terrine
mould, then peel off the clear film.
Place the parfait on a rack over a
baking sheet and pour the chocolate
icing evenly over the top. Working
quickly, smooth the icing down the
sides with a palette knife or spatula.
Leave to set slightly, then freeze for a
further 3–4 hours.

13 Cut into slices using a knife dipped
in hot water. Serve, decorated with
curls of fresh coconut.

COOK'S TIP
When melting chocolate over a pan of hot
water, do not let the base of the bowl
touch the surface of the water. Keep the
water at simmering point.

Iced Lime Cheesecake

4 Press the cottage cheese through a sieve into a bowl. Beat in the mascarpone cheese, then the lime syrup. By hand, lightly whip the cream and then fold into the cheese mixture. Pour into a shallow container and freeze until thick. If you are using an ice cream maker, add the lightly-whipped cream and churn in an ice cream maker until thick.

5 Meanwhile, cut a slice off either end of each of the remaining limes, stand them on a board and slice off the skins. Cut them into very thin slices.

6 Arrange the lime slices around the sides of the tin, pressing them against the paper.

7 Pour the cheese mixture over the biscuit base in the tin and level the surface. Cover and freeze the cheesecake overnight.

8 About 1 hour before you are going to serve the cheesecake, carefully transfer it to a serving plate and put it in the refrigerator to soften slightly.

This frozen dessert has a deliciously tangy, sweet flavour but needs no gelatine to set the filling, unlike most unbaked cheesecakes. It is not difficult to prepare and an added advantage is that it can be made several days beforehand.

Serves 10

175g/6oz almond biscuits (cookies)
65g/2½oz/5 tbsp unsalted (sweet) butter
8 limes
115g/4oz/generous ½ cup caster (superfine) sugar
90ml/6 tbsp water
200g/7oz/scant 1 cup cottage cheese
250g/9oz/generous 1 cup mascarpone cheese
300ml/½ pint/1¼ cups double (heavy) cream

1 Lightly grease the sides of a 20cm/8in springform cake tin (pan) and line with a strip of baking parchment. Break up the almond biscuits slightly, put them in a strong plastic bag and crush them with a rolling pin.

2 Melt the butter in a small pan and stir in the biscuit crumbs until evenly combined. Spoon the mixture into the tin and pack it down with the back of a spoon. Freeze the biscuit mixture while you make the filling.

3 Finely grate the rind and squeeze the juice from five of the limes. Heat the sugar and water in a small pan, stirring until the sugar dissolves. Bring to the boil and boil for 2 minutes without stirring, then remove the syrup from the heat, stir in the lime juice and rind and leave to cool.

Frozen Grand Marnier Soufflés

2 Heat the milk until almost boiling and pour it on to the yolks, whisking constantly. Return to the pan and stir over a gentle heat until the custard is thick enough to coat the back of the spoon. Remove the pan from the heat. Stir the soaked gelatine into the custard. Pour the custard into a bowl and leave to cool. Whisk occasionally, until on the point of setting.

3 Put the remaining sugar in a pan with 45ml/3 tbsp water and dissolve it over a low heat. Bring to the boil and boil rapidly until it reaches the soft ball stage or 119°C/238°F on a sugar thermometer. Remove from the heat. In a clean bowl, whisk the egg whites until stiff. Pour the hot syrup on to the whites, whisking constantly. Leave the meringue to cool.

4 Add the Grand Marnier to the cold custard. Whisk the cream until it holds soft peaks and fold into the cooled meringue, with the custard. Pour into the prepared glasses or dishes. Freeze overnight. Remove the paper collars and leave at room temperature for 15 minutes before serving.

Light and fluffy, yet almost ice cream, these delicious soufflés are perfect and wonderfully easy for a special dinner. Start preparations the day before as the desserts have to be frozen overnight.

Serves 8

200g/7oz/1 cup caster
 (superfine) sugar
6 large (US extra large) eggs, separated
250ml/8fl oz/1 cup milk
15ml/1 tbsp powdered gelatine,
 soaked in 45ml/3 tbsp cold water
60ml/4 tbsp grand marnier
450ml/³/₄ pint/scant 2 cups double
 (heavy) cream

1 Wrap a double collar of baking parchment around eight dessert glasses or ramekins and tie with string. Whisk together 75g/3oz/scant ½ cup of the caster sugar with the egg yolks, until the yolks are pale. This will take about 5 minutes by hand or about 3 minutes with an electric hand mixer.

COOK'S TIPS
• The soft ball stage of a syrup is when a teaspoon of the mixture dropped into a glass of cold water sets into a ball.
• If you prefer, you can make just one dessert in a large soufflé dish, rather than eight individual ones, or serve in very small glasses for a buffet.

Lime Sorbet

This light, refreshing sorbet is a good dessert to serve after a substantial main course.

Serves 4

250g/9oz/1¼ cups sugar
grated rind of 1 lime
175ml/6fl oz/¾ cup freshly squeezed
  lime juice
15–30ml/1–2 tbsp freshly squeezed
  lemon juice
icing (confectioners') sugar,
  to taste
slivers of lime rind, to decorate

1 In a small, heavy pan, dissolve the sugar in 600ml/1 pint/2½ cups water, without stirring, over medium heat. When the sugar has dissolved, bring to the boil and continue to boil for 5–6 minutes. Remove the pan from the heat and leave to cool.

2 Combine the cooled sugar syrup and lime rind and juice in a measuring jug (cup) or bowl. Stir well. Taste and adjust the flavour by adding lemon juice or some icing sugar, if necessary. Do not over-sweeten.

3 Freeze the mixture in an ice-cream maker, following the manufacturer's instructions.

4 If you do not have an ice-cream maker, pour the mixture into a metal or plastic freezer container and freeze for about 3 hours, until softly set.

5 Remove the mixture from the container and chop coarsely into 7.5cm/3in pieces. Place in a food processor and process until smooth. Return the mixture to the freezer container and freeze again until set. Repeat this freezing and chopping process two or three times, until a smooth consistency is obtained.

6 Serve in scoops decorated with slivers of lime rind.

COOK'S TIP
If using an ice-cream maker for these sorbets (sherbets), check the manufacturer's instructions to find out the freezing capacity. If necessary, halve the recipe quantities.

Iced Christmas Torte

Not everyone likes traditional Christmas pudding. This makes an exciting alternative, but do not feel that you have to limit it to the festive season. Packed with dried fruit and nuts, it is perfect for any special occasion.

Serves 8–10

75g/3oz/¾ cup dried cranberries
75g/3oz/scant ½ cup pitted prunes
50g/2oz/⅓ cup sultanas (golden raisins)
175ml/6fl oz/¾ cup port
2 pieces preserved stem ginger,
  finely chopped
25g/1oz/2 tbsp unsalted (sweet) butter
45ml/3 tbsp light muscovado
  (brown) sugar
90g/3½ oz/scant 2 cups fresh
  white breadcrumbs
600ml/1 pint/2½ cups double
  (heavy) cream
30ml/2 tbsp icing (confectioners') sugar
5ml/1 tsp mixed (pumpkin pie) spice
75g/3oz/¾ cup brazil nuts,
  finely chopped
sugared bay leaves (see Cook's Tip)
  and fresh cherries, to decorate

1 Put the cranberries, prunes and sultanas in a food processor and process briefly. Tip them into a bowl and add the port and ginger. Leave to absorb the port for 2 hours.

2 Melt the butter in a frying pan. Add the sugar and heat gently until it has dissolved. Tip in the breadcrumbs, stir, then cook over a low heat for about 5 minutes, or until lightly coloured and turning crisp. Leave to cool.

COOK'S TIP
To make the sugared bay leaves wash and dry the leaves, then paint both sides with beaten egg white. Sprinkle with caster (superfine) sugar. Leave to dry on baking parchment for 2–3 hours.

3 Tip the breadcrumbs into a food processor or blender and process to finer crumbs. Sprinkle one-third into an 18cm/7in loose-based springform cake tin (pan) and spread them out to cover the base of the tin evenly. Freeze until firm.

4 Whip the cream with the icing sugar and mixed spice until it is thick but not yet standing in peaks. Fold in the brazil nuts with the fruit mixture and any port that has not been absorbed.

5 Spread a third of the mixture over the breadcrumb base in the tin, taking care not to dislodge the crumbs. Sprinkle with another layer of the breadcrumbs. Repeat the layering, finishing with a layer of the cream mixture. Freeze the torte overnight.

6 Chill the torte for about 1 hour before serving, decorated with sugared bay leaves and fresh cherries.

Blackforest Gâteau

Morello cherries and kirsch lend their distinctive flavours to this ever-popular gâteau.

Serves 8–10

6 eggs
200g/7oz/1 cup caster (superfine) sugar
5ml/1 tsp vanilla essence (extract)
50g/2oz/½ cup plain (all-purpose) flour
50g/2oz/½ cup (unsweetened)
   cocoa powder
115g/4oz/½ cup unsalted (sweet)
   butter, melted

For the filling and topping
60ml/4 tbsp kirsch
600ml/1 pint/2½ cups double
   (heavy) cream
30ml/2 tbsp icing (confectioners') sugar
2.5ml/½ tsp vanilla essence (extract)
675g/1½ lb jar pitted morello cherries,
   well drained

To decorate
icing (confectioner's) sugar, for dusting
grated chocolate
chocolate curls
fresh or drained canned morello cherries

1 Preheat the oven to 180°C/350°F/ Gas 4. Grease three 19cm/7½ in sandwich cake tins (layer pans). Line the bases with baking parchment. Combine the eggs, sugar and vanilla essence in a bowl and beat with a hand-held electric mixer until pale and thick.

2 Sift the flour and cocoa powder over the mixture and fold in lightly and evenly with a metal spoon. Gently stir in the melted butter.

COOK'S TIP
To make chocolate curls, spread melted chocolate over a marble slab to a depth of about 5mm/¼ in. Leave to set. Draw a knife across the chocolate at a 45° angle, using a seesaw action to make long curls.

3 Divide the mixture among the prepared cake tins, smoothing them level. Bake for 15–18 minutes, or until the cakes have risen and are springy to the touch. Leave them to cool in the tins for about 5 minutes, then turn out on to wire racks and leave to cool completely. Remove the lining paper from each cake layer.

4 Prick each layer all over with a skewer or fork, then sprinkle with kirsch. Using a hand-held electric mixer, whip the cream until it starts to thicken, then beat in the icing sugar and vanilla until the mixture begins to hold its shape.

5 To assemble, spread one cake layer with a thick layer of flavoured cream and top with about half the cherries.

6 Spread a second cake layer with cream, top with the remaining cherries, then place it on top of the first layer. Top with the final cake layer.

7 Spread the remaining cream all over the cake. Dust a serving plate with icing sugar, and position the cake carefully in the centre. Press grated chocolate over the sides and decorate the top of the cake with the chocolate curls and fresh or drained cherries.

Marbled Swiss Roll

Simply sensational – that's the only way to describe this superb cake.

Serves 6–8

90g/3½oz/scant 1 cup plain
   (all-purpose) flour
15ml/1 tbsp (unsweetened)
   cocoa powder
25g/1oz plain (semisweet)
   chocolate, grated
25g/1oz white chocolate, grated
3 eggs
115g/4oz/generous ½ cup caster
   (superfine) sugar

For the filling
75g/3oz/6 tbsp unsalted (sweet) butter
175g/6oz/1½ cups icing
   (confectioners') sugar
15ml/1 tbsp (unsweetened)
   cocoa powder
2.5ml/½ tsp vanilla essence (extract)
45ml/3 tbsp chopped walnuts
plain and white chocolate curls, to
   decorate (optional)

1 Sift half the flour with the cocoa powder into bowl. Stir in the grated plain chocolate. Sift the remaining flour into another bowl; stir in the grated white chocolate.

2 Preheat the oven to 200°C/400°F/ Gas 6. Grease and line a 30 x 20cm/ 12 x 8in Swiss roll tin (jelly roll pan). Whisk the eggs and sugar in a heatproof bowl then set over a pan of hot water until thickened.

3 Remove the bowl from the heat and tip half the mixture into a separate bowl. Fold the white chocolate mixture into one portion, then fold the plain chocolate mixture into the other. Stir 15ml/1 tbsp boiling water into each half to soften the mixtures.

4 Place alternate spoonfuls of the two mixtures in the prepared tin and swirl lightly together to create a marbled effect. Bake for about 12–15 minutes, or until firm. Turn out on to a sheet of non-stick baking parchment.

5 Trim the edges to neaten and cover with a damp, clean dishtowel and leave to cool.

6 To make the buttercream filling, beat the butter, icing sugar, cocoa powder and vanilla essence together in a bowl until smooth, then mix in the walnuts.

7 Uncover the sponge cake, lift off the baking parchment and spread the surface with the buttercream. Roll up carefully from a long side and place on a serving plate. Decorate with plain and white chocolate curls, if you like.

Chocolate Layer Cake

The cake layers can be made ahead, wrapped and frozen.

Serves 10–12

unsweetened cocoa, for dusting
225g/8oz can cooked whole beetroot
  (beet), drained and juice reserved
115g/4oz/¹⁄₂ cup unsalted (sweet)
  butter, softened
500g/1¹⁄₄lb/2¹⁄₂ cups light brown sugar,
  firmly packed
3 eggs
15ml/1 tbsp vanilla essence (extract)
75g/3oz cooking (unsweetened)
  chocolate, melted
275g/10oz/2¹⁄₄ cups plain
  (all-purpose) flour
10ml/2 tsp baking powder
2.5ml/¹⁄₂ tsp salt
120ml/4fl oz/¹⁄₂ cup buttermilk
chocolate curls (optional)

For the chocolate ganache frosting
475ml/16fl oz/2 cups whipping cream
500g/1¹⁄₄lb dark (bittersweet) or plain
  (semisweet) chocolate, chopped
15ml/1 tbsp vanilla essence (extract)

1 Preheat the oven to 180°C/350°F/ Gas 4. Grease two 23cm/9in cake tins (pans) and dust the bases and sides with cocoa powder. Grate the beetroot and add to the beetroot juice. With an electric mixer, beat the butter, brown sugar, eggs and vanilla essence for 3–5 minutes, until pale and fluffy. Reduce the speed of the mixer and beat in the chocolate.

2 Sift the flour, baking powder and salt into another bowl. With the mixer on low speed, alternately beat the flour mixture in quarters and the buttermilk in thirds into the egg mixture. Add the beetroot and juice and beat for 1 minute. Divide between the cake tins and bake for 30–35 minutes, or until a cake tester inserted in the centre comes out clean. Cool for 10 minutes in the tins, then turn out and cool completely.

3 To make the ganache frosting, heat the cream in a heavy pan over a medium heat until it just begins to boil, stirring occasionally to prevent it from scorching.

4 Remove the pan from the heat and add the chocolate, stirring constantly until it is until melted and smooth. Stir in the vanilla. Strain into a bowl and chill in the refrigerator, stirring every 10 minutes, for about 1 hour, until the frosting is spreadable.

5 Assemble the cake. Place one layer on a serving plate and spread with one-third of the chocolate ganache frosting. Turn the cake layer bottom side up and spread the remaining ganache over the top and side of the cake. If using, top with the chocolate curls. Leave the ganache to set for 20–30 minutes, then chill in the refrigerator before serving.

Raspberry and White Chocolate Cheesecake

Raspberries and white chocolate are an irresistible combination, especially when teamed with rich mascarpone on a crunchy ginger and pecan nut base.

Serves 8

50g/2oz/4 tbsp unsalted (sweet) butter
225g/8oz/2⅓ cups ginger nut biscuits, (gingersnaps) crushed
50g/2oz/½ cup chopped pecan nuts or walnuts

For the filling
275g/10oz/1¼ cups mascarpone cheese
175g/6oz/¾ cup fromage frais or farmer's cheese
2 eggs, beaten
45ml/3 tbsp caster (superfine) sugar
250g/9oz white chocolate
225g/8oz/1⅓ cups raspberries

For the topping
115g/4oz/½ cup mascarpone cheese
75g/3oz/⅓ cup fromage frais or farmer's cheese
white chocolate curls and raspberries, to decorate

1 Preheat the oven to 150°C/300°F/Gas 2. Melt the butter in a pan over a low heat, then stir in the crushed biscuits (cookies) and nuts. Press the mixture evenly into the base of a 23cm/9in springform cake tin (pan).

2 To make the filling, beat together the mascarpone and fromage frais in a bowl, then beat in the eggs and caster sugar until evenly mixed.

3 Break up the white chocolate and melt it gently in a heatproof bowl set over a pan of barely simmering water.

4 Stir the melted chocolate into the cheese mixture and gently fold in the raspberries.

5 Tip the filling into the prepared tin and spread it evenly with a palette knife or spatula, then bake for about 1 hour, or until just set. Switch off the oven, but do not remove the cheesecake. Leave it until cold and completely set.

6 Release the tin and lift the cheesecake on to a plate. Make the topping by mixing the mascarpone and fromage frais in a bowl and spread over the cheesecake. Decorate with chocolate curls and raspberries.

Chocolate and Cherry Polenta Cake

This delicious dessert has an unusual nutty texture.

Serves 8

50g/2oz/⅓ cup quick-cook polenta
200g/7oz plain (semisweet) chocolate
5 eggs, separated
175g/6oz/¾ cup caster
  (superfine) sugar
115g/4oz/1 cup ground almonds
60ml/4 tbsp plain (all-purpose) flour
finely grated rind of 1 orange
115g/4oz/½ cup glacé (candied)
  cherries, halved
icing (confectioners') sugar, for dusting

1 Place the polenta in a heatproof bowl and pour over just enough boiling water to cover, about 120ml/ 4fl oz/½ cup. Stir well, then cover the bowl and leave to stand for about 30 minutes, until the polenta has absorbed all the excess moisture.

2 Preheat the oven to 190°C/375°F/ Gas 5. Grease a deep 22cm/8½in round cake tin (pan) and line the base with non-stick baking parchment. Break the chocolate into squares and melt it in a heatproof bowl set over a pan of barely simmering water.

3 Whisk the egg yolks with the sugar in a bowl until thick and pale. Beat in the melted chocolate, then fold in the polenta, ground almonds, flour and orange rind.

COOK'S TIP
Citrus fruits are often "waxed" to preserve their appearance. For grating, use unwaxed fruit or thoroughly wash the orange in hot water first.

4 Whisk the egg whites in a clean, grease-free bowl until stiff. Stir 15ml/ 1 tbsp of the whites into the chocolate mixture, then fold in the remainder. Finally, fold in the cherries.

5 Scrape the mixture into the prepared tin and bake for 45–55 minutes, or until well risen and firm to the touch. Cool on a wire rack. Dust with icing sugar to serve.

Blueberry-hazelnut Cheesecake

The base for this cheesecake is
made with ground hazelnuts – a
tasty and unusual alternative to a
biscuit base.

Serves 6–8

350g/12oz blueberries
15ml/1 tbsp clear honey
75g/3oz/6 tbsp sugar
juice of 1 lemon
175g/6oz/¾ cup cream cheese, at
  room temperature
1 egg
5ml/1 tsp hazelnut liqueur (optional)
120ml/4fl oz/½ cup whipping cream

For the base
175g/6oz/1⅔ cups ground hazelnuts
75g/3oz/⅔ cup plain (all-purpose) flour
pinch of salt
50g/2oz/4 tbsp butter, softened
65g/2½oz/⅓ cup light brown sugar,
  firmly packed
1 egg yolk

1 For the base, put the hazelnuts in a
large bowl. Sift in the flour and salt,
and stir to mix. Set aside.

2 Beat the butter with the brown
sugar until light and fluffy. Beat in the
egg yolk. Gradually fold in the nut
mixture, in three batches, until
thoroughly combined.

3 Press the dough into a greased
23cm/9in pie tin (pan), spreading it
evenly against the sides. Form a rim
around the top edge that is slightly
thicker than the sides. Cover with clear
film (plastic wrap) and chill for at least
30 minutes.

4 Preheat the oven to 180°C/350°F/
Gas 4. Meanwhile, for the topping,
combine the blueberries, honey, 15ml/
1 tbsp of the sugar and 5ml/1 tsp
lemon juice in a heavy pan. Cook the
mixture over a low heat, stirring
occasionally, for 5–7 minutes, until
the berries have given off some liquid
but still retain their shape. Remove
the pan from the heat and set aside
to cool.

5 Place the pastry base (pie shell) in
the oven and bake for 15 minutes.
Remove from the oven and set aside to
cool completely while you are making
the filling.

6 Beat together the cream cheese
and remaining sugar until light and
fluffy. Add the egg, 15ml/1 tbsp
lemon juice, the liqueur, if using, and
the cream and beat until smooth
and thoroughly blended.

7 Pour the cheese mixture into the
pastry shell and spread evenly with a
palette knife or spatula. Bake for
20–25 minutes, until just set.

8 Let the cheesecake cool completely
on a wire rack, then cover with clear
film (plastic wrap) and chill in the
refrigerator for at least 1 hour.

9 Spread the blueberry mixture evenly
over the top of the cheesecake. Serve
at cool room temperature.

COOK'S TIP
The cheesecake can be prepared 1 day in
advance, but do not add the fruit topping
until just before serving.

Fresh Berry Pavlova

Pavlova is the simplest of desserts, but it can also be the most stunning. Fill with a mix of berry fruits if you like – raspberries and blueberries make a marvellous combination.

Serves 6–8

4 egg whites, at room temperature
225g/8oz/1 cup caster (superfine) sugar
5ml/1 tsp cornflour (cornstarch)
5ml/1 tsp cider vinegar
2.5ml/½ tsp pure vanilla
    essence (extract)
300ml/½ pint/1¼ cups double
    (heavy) cream
150ml/¼ pint/⅔ cup crème fraîche
175g/6oz/1 cup raspberries
175g/6oz/1½ cups blueberries
fresh mint sprigs, to decorate
icing (confectioners') sugar,
    for dusting

1 Preheat the oven to 140°C/275°F/ Gas 1. Line a baking sheet with baking parchment. Whisk the egg whites in a grease-free bowl to stiff peaks. Whisk in the sugar to make a stiff, glossy meringue. Sift the cornflour over and fold it in with the vinegar and vanilla.

2 Spoon the meringue mixture on to the paper-lined sheet. Spread into a round, swirling the top, and bake for 1¼ hours, or until the meringue is crisp and lightly golden. Switch off the oven, keeping the door closed, and leave the meringue to cool for 1–2 hours.

3 Carefully peel the paper from the meringue and transfer it to a serving plate. Whip the cream until it forms soft peaks, fold in the crème fraîche, then spoon the mixture into the centre of the meringue case. Top with the raspberries and blueberries and decorate with the mint sprigs. Sift icing sugar over the top and serve.

Fresh Cherry and Hazelnut Strudel

Serve this wonderful old-world treat as a warm dessert with crème fraîche or custard, or leave it to cool and offer it as a scrumptious cake as part of a buffet-style brunch.

Serves 6–8

75g/3oz/6 tbsp butter
90ml/6 tbsp light brown sugar
3 egg yolks
grated rind of 1 lemon
1.5ml/¼ tsp grated nutmeg
250g/9oz/generous 1 cup
  ricotta cheese
8 large sheets filo pastry
75g/3oz ratafias, crushed
450g/1lb/2½ cups cherries, pitted
30ml/2 tbsp chopped hazelnuts
icing (confectioners') sugar, for dusting

1 Preheat the oven to 190°C/375°F/ Gas 5. Soften 15g/½oz/1 tbsp of the butter in a bowl and beat in the sugar and egg yolks until light and fluffy. Beat in the lemon rind, nutmeg and ricotta.

2 Melt the remaining butter in a small pan. Working quickly, place a sheet of filo on a clean dishtowel and brush it generously with melted butter. Place a second sheet on top and repeat the process. Continue until all the filo has been layered and buttered, reserving some of the melted butter.

3 Sprinkle the crushed ratafias over the top, leaving a 5cm/2in border around the outside. Spoon the ricotta mixture over the ratafias, spread it lightly to cover, then sprinkle over the cherries.

4 Fold in the filo pastry border and use the dishtowel to help roll up the strudel, Swiss-roll (jelly-roll) style, beginning from one of the long sides of the pastry. Grease a baking sheet with the remaining melted butter.

5 Place the strudel on the baking sheet and sprinkle the hazelnuts over the surface. Bake for 35–40 minutes, or until the strudel is golden and crisp. Dust with icing sugar and serve immediately if serving hot.

Chocolate Chestnut Roulade

This is a dream dinner party finale to have chocoholics swooning. The combination of intense flavours produces a very rich dessert, so serve it well chilled and in thin slices. It slices better when it is cold.

Serves 10–12

vegetable oil, for greasing
175g/6oz dark (bittersweet)
    chocolate, chopped
30ml/2 tbsp (unsweetened) cocoa
    powder, sifted, plus extra for dusting
50ml/2fl oz/¼ cup freshly brewed
    strong coffee or espresso
6 eggs, separated
75g/3oz/6 tbsp caster (superfine) sugar
pinch of cream of tartar
5ml/1 tsp vanilla essence (extract)
glacé (candied) chestnuts,
    to decorate (optional)

For the chestnut cream filling
475ml/16fl oz/2 cups double
    (heavy) cream
30ml/2 tbsp rum or
    coffee-flavoured liqueur
350g/12oz can sweetened
    chestnut purée
115g/4oz dark (bittersweet)
    chocolate, grated
thick cream, to serve

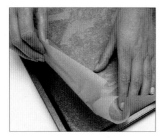

1 Preheat the oven to 180°C/350°F/ Gas 4. Oil the base and sides of a 38 × 25cm/15 × 10in Swiss roll tin (jelly roll pan). Line with baking parchment, allowing a 2.5cm/1in overhang.

2 Melt the chocolate in the top of a double boiler, over a low heat, stirring frequently. Set aside. Dissolve the cocoa in the coffee. Stir to make a smooth paste, and set aside.

3 In an electric mixer or in a bowl using a whisk, beat the egg yolks with half the sugar for about 3–5 minutes, or until pale and thick. Gradually beat in the melted chocolate and cocoa-coffee paste until just blended.

4 In another bowl, beat the egg whites and cream of tartar until stiff peaks form. Sprinkle the remaining sugar over in two batches incorporating each thoroughly, and continue to beat until the whites are stiff and glossy. Then beat in the vanilla essence.

5 Stir a spoonful of the whisked whites into the chocolate mixture to lighten it, then fold in the remainder.

6 Spoon the mixture into the tin and level the top. Bake for 20–25 minutes, or until the cake is firm, set and risen, and springs back when lightly pressed with the fingertips.

7 Meanwhile, dust a clean dishtowel with the extra cocoa powder. As soon as the cake is cooked, carefully turn it out on to the towel and gently peel off the baking parchment from the base. Starting at a narrow end, roll the cake and towel together Swiss-roll fashion. Leave to cool completely.

8 To make the filling, whip the cream and rum or liqueur until soft peaks form. Beat a spoonful of cream into the chestnut purée to lighten it, then fold in the remaining cream and most of the grated chocolate. Reserve a quarter of the chestnut cream mixture.

9 To assemble the roulade, unroll the cake and spread with the filling, to within 2.5cm/1in of the edges. Gently roll it up, using the towel for support.

10 Place the roulade on a plate. Spoon the reserved chestnut cream into an icing (pastry) bag and pipe rosettes along the top of the roulade. Dust with more cocoa and decorate with glacé chestnuts and grated chocolate.

Tarte au Citron

You can find this classic lemon tart in bistros all over France.

Serves 8–10

*350g/12oz unsweetened or sweet
  shortcrust pastry
grated rind of 2 or 3 lemons
150ml/¼ pint/⅔ cup freshly squeezed
  lemon juice
90g/3½oz/½ cup caster
  (superfine) sugar
60ml/4 tbsp crème fraîche
4 eggs, plus 3 egg yolks
icing (confectioners') sugar, for dusting*

1 Preheat the oven to 190°C/375°F/ Gas 5. Roll out the pastry thinly and use to line a 23cm/9in flan tin (tart pan). Prick the base of the pastry all over with a fork.

2 Line the pastry case (pie shell) with foil or baking parchment and fill with baking beans. Bake for about 15 minutes, until the edges are set and dry. Remove the foil and beans and continue baking for a further 5–7 minutes, until golden.

3 Place the lemon rind, juice and sugar in a bowl. Beat until combined and then gradually add the crème fraîche and beat until well blended.

4 Beat in the four eggs, one at a time, then beat in the remaining egg yolks and pour the filling into the pastry case. Bake for 15–20 minutes, until the filling is set. If the pastry begins to brown too much, cover the edges with foil. Leave to cool. Dust with a little icing sugar before serving.

Pear and Almond Cream Tart

This tart is equally successful made with other kinds of fruit, and some variation can be seen in almost every good French pâtisserie.

Serves 6

350g/12oz unsweetened or sweet
*   shortcrust pastry*
3 firm pears
lemon juice
15ml/1 tbsp peach brandy or water
60ml/4 tbsp peach preserve, strained

For the almond cream filling
115g/4oz/¾ cup blanched
*   whole almonds*
50g/2oz/¼ cup caster
*   (superfine) sugar*
65g/2½oz/5 tbsp butter
1 egg, plus 1 egg white
few drops almond essence (extract)

1 Roll out the pastry thinly and use to line a 23cm/9in flan tin (tart pan). Chill the pastry case (pie shell) while you make the filling. Put the almonds and sugar in a food processor and pulse until finely ground; they should not be pasty. Add the butter and process until creamy, then add the egg, egg white and almond essence and mix well.

2 Place a baking sheet in the oven and preheat to 190°C/375°F/Gas 5. Peel the pears, halve them, remove the cores and brush with lemon juice to prevent them from discolouring.

3 Put the pear halves, cut-side down, on a board and slice thinly crossways, keeping the slices together.

4 Pour the almond cream filling into the pastry case. Slide a palette knife or spatula under one pear half and press the top with your fingers to fan out the slices. Transfer to the tart, placing the fruit on the filling like the spokes of a wheel. If you like, remove a few slices from each half before arranging and use them to fill in any gaps in the centre.

5 Place the tart on the baking sheet and bake for about 50–55 minutes, until the filling is set and golden brown. Place the tart on a rack and leave to cool.

6 Meanwhile, heat the brandy or water and the preserve in a small pan over a low heat, then brush over the top of the hot tart to glaze. Serve the tart warm, at room temperature.

Boston Banoffee Pie

This is a simple but impressive party dish. You can press the wonderfully biscuity pastry into the tin, rather than rolling it out. You can make the pastry case and the fudge-toffee filling in advance and then arrange the sliced banana topping and cream before serving. It will prove irresistible.

Serves 6

115g/4oz/½ cup butter, diced
200g/7oz can skimmed, sweetened
    condensed milk
115g/4oz/½ cup soft brown sugar
30ml/2 tbsp golden (light corn) syrup
2 small bananas, sliced
a little lemon juice
whipped cream, to decorate
5ml/1 tsp grated plain
    (semisweet) chocolate

For the pastry
150g/5oz/1¼ cups plain
    (all-purpose) flour
115g/4oz/½ cup butter, diced
50g/2oz/¼ cup caster
    (superfine) sugar

1 Preheat the oven to 160°C/325°F/ Gas 3. In a food processor, process the flour and diced butter until crumbed. Stir in the caster sugar and mix to form a soft, pliable dough.

2 Press the dough into a 20cm/8in loose-based flan tin (tart pan). Bake for 30 minutes.

3 To make the filling, place the butter in a pan with the condensed milk, brown sugar and syrup. Heat gently, stirring, until the butter has melted and the sugar has completely dissolved.

4 Bring to a gentle boil and cook for 7–10 minutes, stirring constantly, until the mixture thickens and turns a light caramel colour.

5 Pour the hot caramel filling into the pastry case and leave until it is completely cold. Sprinkle the banana slices with lemon juice to stop them going brown and arrange them in overlapping circles on top of the filling, leaving a gap in the centre. Pipe a generous swirl of whipped cream in the centre and sprinkle with the grated chocolate.

Greek Chocolate Mousse Tartlets

The combination of chocolate and yogurt makes an irresistibly light, but not too sweet, filling.

Serves 6

175g/6oz/1½ cups plain
(all-purpose) flour
30ml/2 tbsp (unsweetened)
cocoa powder
30ml/2 tbsp icing
(confectioners') sugar
115g/4oz/½ cup butter
melted chocolate, to decorate

For the filling
200g/7oz white chocolate
120ml/4fl oz/½ cup milk
10ml/2 tsp powdered gelatine
30ml/2 tbsp caster (superfine) sugar
5ml/1 tsp vanilla essence (extract)
2 eggs, separated
250g/9oz/generous 1 cup Greek
(US strained plain) yogurt

1 Preheat the oven to 190°C/375°F/ Gas 5. Sift the flour, cocoa and icing sugar into a large bowl.

2 Place the butter in a pan with 60ml/4 tbsp water and heat gently until just melted. Leave to cool, then stir into the flour to make a smooth dough. Cover with clear film (plastic wrap) and chill until firm.

3 Roll out the pastry and use to line six deep 10cm/4in loose-based flan tins (tart pans).

4 Prick the base of each pastry case (pie shell) all over with a fork, cover with greaseproof (waxed) paper weighed down with baking beans and bake blind for 10 minutes. Remove the baking beans and paper, return to the oven and bake a further 15 minutes, or until the pastry is firm. Leave to cool in the tins.

5 Make the filling. Break the chocolate into squares and melt in a heatproof bowl over a pan of barely simmering water. Pour the milk into a pan, sprinkle over the gelatine and heat gently, stirring, until the gelatine has dissolved completely. Remove from the heat and stir in the chocolate.

6 Whisk the sugar, vanilla essence and egg yolks in a large bowl, then beat in the chocolate mixture. Beat in the yogurt until evenly mixed.

7 Whisk the egg whites in a clean, grease-free bowl until stiff, then fold into the mixture. Divide among the pastry cases and leave to set.

8 Drizzle the melted chocolate over the tartlets to decorate.

COOK'S TIP
You can decorate the tartlets with melted dark (bittersweet) or plain (semisweet) chocolate. Both provide an attractive contrast to the filling.

Chocolate Amaretti Peaches

This delicious dessert can also be made with fresh nectarines.

Serves 4

115g/4oz amaretti, crushed
50g/2oz plain (semisweet)
 chocolate, chopped
grated rind of ½ orange
15ml/1 tbsp clear honey
1.5ml/¼ tsp ground cinnamon
1 egg white, lightly beaten
4 firm ripe peaches
150ml/¼ pint/⅔ cup white wine
15ml/1 tbsp caster (superfine) sugar
whipped cream, to serve

1 Preheat the oven to 190°C/375°F/ Gas 5. Mix together the crushed amaretti, chopped chocolate, grated orange rind, honey and cinnamon in a bowl until well combined. Add the beaten egg white and mix to bind the mixture together.

2 Halve and stone (pit) the peaches and fill the resulting cavities with the chocolate and amaretti mixture, mounding it up slightly.

3 Arrange the stuffed peaches in a lightly buttered, shallow ovenproof dish that will just hold the peaches comfortably in a single layer. Pour the wine into a measuring jug (cup) and stir in the sugar.

4 Pour the wine mixture around the peaches. Bake for 30–40 minutes, until the peaches are tender. Serve them immediately with a little of the cooking juices spooned over and the whipped cream.

Pears in **Chocolate Fudge Blankets**

Warm poached pears coated in a
rich chocolate fudge sauce – who
could resist?

Serves 6

6 ripe eating pears
30ml/2 tbsp lemon juice
75g/3oz/scant ½ cup caster
(superfine) sugar
1 cinnamon stick

For the sauce
200ml/7fl oz/⅞ cup double
(heavy) cream
150g/5oz/scant 1 cup brown sugar
25g/1oz/2 tbsp unsalted (sweet) butter
60ml/4 tbsp golden (light corn) syrup
120ml/4fl oz/½ cup milk
200g/7oz plain (semisweet) chocolate

1 Peel the pears thinly, leaving the
stalks on. Scoop out the cores from
the base. Brush the cut surfaces with
lemon juice to prevent them from
turning brown.

2 Place the sugar and 300ml/½ pint/
1¼ cups of water in a large, heavy
pan. Heat gently, stirring constantly,
until the sugar dissolves. Add the
pears and cinnamon stick with any
remaining lemon juice, and, if
necessary, a little more water, so that
the pears are almost covered.

3 Bring to the boil, then lower the heat,
cover the pan and simmer the pears
gently for 15–20 minutes.

4 Meanwhile, make the sauce. Place
the cream, sugar, butter, golden syrup
and milk in a heavy pan. Heat gently,
stirring constantly, until the sugar has
completely dissolved and the butter
and syrup have melted, then bring to
the boil. Boil, stirring constantly, for
about 5 minutes, or until the sauce is
thick and smooth.

5 Remove the pan from the heat.
Break up the chocolate and stir in a
few squares at a time.

6 Using a slotted spoon, transfer the
poached pears to a dish and keep hot.
Boil the syrup rapidly to reduce to
about 45–60ml/3–4 tbsp. Remove and
discard the cinnamon stick and then
gently stir the syrup into the chocolate
fudge sauce.

7 Serve the pears in individual bowls
or on dessert plates, with the hot
chocolate fudge sauce spooned over.

Summer Berries in **Warm Sabayon Glaze**

This luxurious combination of summer berries under a light and fluffy alcoholic sauce is lightly grilled to form a deliciously crisp, caramelized topping.

Serves 8

900g/2lb/8 cups mixed summer berries, or soft fruit
8 egg yolks
115g/4oz/generous ½ cup vanilla sugar or caster (superfine) sugar
250ml/8fl oz/1 cup liqueur, such as Cointreau, Kirsch or Grand Marnier, or white dessert wine, plus extra for drizzling (optional)
a little icing (confectioners') sugar, sifted, and mint leaves, to decorate (optional)

1 Divide the fruit among eight individual heatproof glass dishes or ramekins. Preheat the grill (broiler).

2 Whisk the egg yolks in a large heatproof bowl with the sugar and liqueur or wine. Place the bowl over a pan of hot simmering water and whisk constantly until the yolks have become thick, fluffy and pale.

3 Pour equal quantities of the sauce into each dish. Place under the grill for 1–2 minutes, or until just turning brown. Sprinkle the fruit with icing sugar and decorate with mint leaves just before serving, if you like.

VARIATION

To omit the alcohol, use a juice substitute, such as grape, mango or apricot.

Hot Chocolate Zabaglione

A deliciously chocolate-flavoured variation of a classic Italian dessert, this is a perfect way to end a celebratory meal.

Serves 6

6 egg yolks
150g/5oz/³⁄₄ cup caster
(superfine) sugar
45ml/3 tbsp (unsweetened)
cocoa powder
200ml/7fl oz/⁷⁄₈ cup Marsala
(unsweetened) cocoa powder or icing
(confectioners') sugar, for dusting
almond biscuits (cookies), such as
amaretti, to serve

1 Half fill a medium pan with water and bring to the simmering point.

2 Place the egg yolks and sugar in a heatproof bowl and whisk well until the mixture is pale and all the sugar has dissolved.

3 Add the cocoa powder and Marsala, then place the bowl over the simmering water. Whisk until the consistency of the mixture is smooth, thick and foamy.

4 Pour quickly into tall heatproof glasses, dust lightly with cocoa powder or icing sugar and serve immediately with almond biscuits.

COOK'S TIP

Marsala is a fortified wine from Sicily. It may be dry or sweet and flavoured versions, including chocolate and coffee, are also produced.

Amaretto Soufflé

A mouthwatering and luxurious soufflé with rather more than a hint of Amaretto liqueur.

Serves 6

130g/3½oz/½ cup caster
  (superfine) sugar
6 amaretti, coarsely crushed
90ml/4 tbsp Amaretto liqueur
4 eggs, separated, plus 1 egg white
30ml/2 tbsp plain (all-purpose) flour
250ml/8fl oz/1 cup milk
pinch of cream of tartar (if needed)
icing (confectioners') sugar, for dusting

1 Butter a 1.5 litre/2½ pint/
6¼ cup soufflé dish and sprinkle it
with a little of the caster sugar.

2 Preheat the oven to 200°C/400°F/
Gas 6. Put the amaretti in a bowl.
Sprinkle them with 30ml/2 tbsp of the
Amaretto liqueur and set aside.

3 Using a wooden spoon, carefully mix
together the egg yolks, 30ml/ 2 tbsp of
the remaining caster sugar and all of
flour in another bowl.

4 Heat the milk to just below boiling
point in a heavy pan. Gradually add
the hot milk to the egg mixture,
stirring constantly.

5 Pour the mixture back into the pan.
Set over a low heat and simmer gently
for 3–4 minutes, or until thickened,
stirring occasionally.

6 Stir in the remaining Amaretto
liqueur, then remove the pan from the
heat and leave to cool slightly.

7 In a clean, grease-free bowl, whisk
all the egg whites until they will hold
soft peaks. (If not using a copper bowl,
add the cream of tartar as soon as the
whites are frothy.) Add the remaining
caster sugar and continue whisking
until stiff.

8 Add about one-quarter of the
whites to the liqueur mixture and stir
in with a rubber spatula to lighten.
Add the remaining egg whites and
fold in gently.

9 Spoon half of the mixture into the
prepared soufflé dish. Cover with a
layer of the moistened amaretti, then
spoon the remaining soufflé mixture on
top to cover.

10 Bake for 20 minutes, or until the
soufflé is well risen, just set and lightly
browned. Sprinkle with a little sifted
icing sugar to decorate and serve the
soufflé immediately.

Hot Mocha Rum Soufflés

Serve these superb soufflés as soon as they are cooked.

Serves 6

25g/1oz/2 tbsp butter, melted
65g/2½oz/generous ½ cup
(unsweetened) cocoa powder
75g/3oz/generous ⅓ cup caster
(superfine) sugar
60ml/4 tbsp strong black coffee
30ml/2 tbsp dark rum
6 egg whites
icing (confectioners') sugar, for dusting

1 Preheat the oven with a baking sheet inside to 190°C/375°F/ Gas 5. Grease six 250ml/8fl oz/1 cup soufflé dishes with the melted butter.

2 Mix 15ml/1 tbsp of the cocoa powder with 15ml/1 tbsp of the caster sugar in a bowl. Tip the mixture into each of the dishes in turn, rotating them so that they are evenly coated. Tip out any excess.

3 Mix the remaining cocoa with the coffee and rum.

4 Whisk the egg whites in a scrupulously clean, grease-free bowl until they form firm peaks. Gradually add the remaining caster sugar, whisking constantly. Stir a generous spoonful of the egg whites into the cocoa mixture to lighten it, then gently fold in the remaining whites.

5 Spoon the mixture into the prepared dishes, smoothing the tops. Place on the hot baking sheet, and bake for 12–15 minutes, or until well risen. Serve the soufflés immediately, lightly dusted with icing sugar.

COOK'S TIPS

• When serving the soufflés at the end of a dinner party, prepare them just before the meal is served. Pop in the oven as soon as the main course is finished and serve freshly baked.

• When whisking egg whites, use a glass, earthenware or stainless steel bowl or, best of all, a copper one. As a result of a chemical reaction with the copper, the foam is more stable. However, do not leave the egg whites in a copper bowl for more than about 15 minutes or they will turn grey. A plastic bowl is not suitable as it is difficult to be sure that it is completely grease-free.

Chocolate Crêpes with Plums and Port

This dish can be made in advance and always looks impressive.

Serves 6

50g/2oz plain (semisweet) chocolate
200ml/7fl oz/⅞ cup milk
120ml/4fl oz/½ cup single (light) cream
30ml/2 tbsp (unsweetened)
  cocoa powder
115g/4oz/1 cup plain
  (all-purpose) flour
2 eggs

For the filling

500g/1¼lb red or golden plums
50g/2oz/¼ cup caster (superfine) sugar
30ml/2 tbsp port
vegetable oil, for frying
175g/6oz/¾ cup crème fraîche

For the sauce

150g/5oz plain (semisweet) chocolate
175ml/6fl oz/¾ cup double (heavy)
  cream
30ml/2 tbsp port

1 Break the chocolate into squares and place in a pan with the milk. Heat gently until the chocolate has melted. Pour into a blender or food processor and add the cream, cocoa powder, flour and eggs. Process until smooth, then tip into a jug (pitcher) and chill for 30 minutes.

2 Meanwhile, make the filling. Halve and stone (pit) the plums. Place them in a pan and add the sugar and 30ml/ 2 tbsp of water. Bring to the boil, then lower the heat, cover and simmer gently for about 10 minutes, or until the plums are tender.

3 Stir in the port and simmer for a further 30 seconds. Remove the pan from the heat and keep warm.

4 Have ready a sheet of non-stick baking parchment. Heat a crêpe pan, grease it lightly with a little oil, then pour in just enough chocolate batter to cover the base of the pan, swirling to coat it evenly.

5 Cook until the crêpe has set, then flip it over to cook the other side. Slide the crêpe out on to the sheet of parchment, then cook 9–11 more crêpes in the same way.

6 To make the sauce, break the chocolate into squares and place in pan with the cream. Heat gently, stirring until smooth. Add the port and heat gently, stirring, for 1 minute.

7 Divide the plum filling between the crêpes, add a spoonful of crème fraîche to each and roll them up carefully. Serve immediately in shallow plates, with the chocolate sauce spooned over the top.

Chocolate and **Orange Scotch Pancakes**

Fabulous baby pancakes in a rich creamy orange liqueur sauce.

Serves 4

115g/4oz/1 cup self-raising
  (self-rising) flour
30ml/2 tbsp (unsweetened)
  cocoa powder
2 eggs
50g/2oz plain (semisweet) chocolate
200ml/7fl oz/⅞ cup milk
finely grated rind of 1 orange
30ml/2 tbsp orange juice
butter or oil for frying
60ml/4 tbsp chocolate curls

For the sauce
2 large oranges
30ml/2 tbsp unsalted (sweet) butter
45ml/3 tbsp light brown sugar
250ml/8fl oz/1 cup crème fraîche
30ml/2 tbsp grand marnier

1 Sift together the flour and cocoa powder into a large bowl and make a well in the centre. Add the eggs to the well and beat with a balloon whisk, gradually incorporating the surrounding dry ingredients to make a smooth batter.

2 Break the chocolate into squares and mix it with the milk in a pan. Heat gently, stirring occasionally, until the chocolate has melted, then beat the mixture into the batter until smooth and bubbly. Stir in the grated orange rind and orange juice.

3 Heat a large heavy frying pan or griddle. Grease with a little butter or oil. Drop large spoonfuls of the chocolate batter on to the hot surface. Cook over a medium heat. When the pancakes are lightly browned underneath and bubbly on top, flip them over to cook the other side. Slide on to a plate and keep hot, then make more pancakes in the same way until all the batter has been used.

4 To make the sauce, grate the rind of one of the oranges into a small bowl and set aside. Peel both oranges, taking care to remove all the pith, then slice the flesh fairly thinly. Remove any pips (seeds) if necessary.

5 Heat the butter and sugar in a wide, shallow pan over a low heat, stirring until the sugar dissolves. Stir in the crème fraîche and heat gently. Do not allow the sauce to boil.

6 Add the pancakes and orange slices to the sauce, warm through gently for 1–2 minutes, then spoon over the grand marnier. Sprinkle with the reserved orange rind. Transfer to warmed plates, sprinkle over the chocolate curls to decorate and serve the pancakes immediately.

Cherry Pancakes

These pancakes are virtually fat-free, and lower in calories and higher in fibre than traditional ones. Serve with a spoonful of natural yogurt or crème fraîche.

Serves 4

50g/2oz/¹/₂ cup plain
(all-purpose) flour
50g/2oz/¹/₂ cup plain wholemeal
(whole-wheat) flour
pinch of salt
1 egg white
150ml/¹/₄ pint/²/₃ cup skimmed milk
a little oil, for frying
425g/15oz can black cherries in juice
7.5ml/1¹/₂ tsp arrowroot

1 Sift the plain flour, wholemeal flour and salt into a large bowl, adding any bran remaining in the sieve to the bowl at the end.

2 Make a well in the centre of the flour and add the egg white. Gradually beat in the milk and 150ml/¹/₄ pint/²/₃ cup of water, whisking vigorously with a balloon whisk until all the liquid has been incorporated and the batter is smooth and bubbly.

3 Heat a non-stick pan with a small amount of oil until the pan is very hot. Pour in just enough batter to cover the base of the pan, swirling the pan to cover the base evenly.

4 Cook over a medium heat until the pancake is set and the underside is golden and then turn to cook the other side. Remove to a sheet of absorbent paper or baking parchment and then cook the remaining batter to make about eight pancakes.

5 Drain the cherries, reserving the juice. Set the cherries aside. Blend about 30ml/2 tbsp of the juice from the can of cherries with the arrowroot in a small pan. Stir in the remaining juice. Heat gently, stirring constantly, until boiling. Stir over a medium heat for about 2 minutes, until thickened and clear.

6 Add the cherries and stir until thoroughly heated. Spoon the cherries into the pancakes and fold them into quarters. Transfer to warm plates and serve immediately.

VARIATIONS
• Substitute 30ml/2 tbsp kirsch or brandy for the same quantity of juice from the can of cherries.
• You can use other canned fruits for the filling, such as chopped apricots.
• After spooning the cherry filling into the pancakes, sprinkle with a few toasted flaked (sliced) almonds before folding.

COOK'S TIP
The basic pancakes can be made in advance, as they freeze very successfully. Cook them and leave to cool, then interleave them with non-stick baking parchment or absorbent paper, wrap them in plastic and seal. Freeze for up to 6 months. Thaw thoroughly at room temperature before reheating.

Steamed Chocolate and Fruit Puddings

Some things always turn out well, including these wonderful little puddings. Fluffy chocolate sponge with tangy cranberries and apple is served with a chocolate syrup.

Serves 4

115g/4oz/⅔ cup dark muscovado
(molasses) sugar
1 eating apple
75g/3oz/¾ cup cranberries, thawed
if frozen
115g/4oz/½ cup soft margarine
2 eggs
75g/3oz/⅔ cup plain (all-purpose) flour
2.5ml/½ tsp baking powder
45ml/3 tbsp (unsweetened)
cocoa powder

For the chocolate syrup
115g/4oz plain (semisweet) chocolate
30ml/2 tbsp clear honey
15ml/1 tbsp unsalted (sweet) butter
2.5ml/½ tsp vanilla essence (extract)

1 Prepare a steamer or half fill a large pan with water and bring it to the boil. Grease four individual heatproof bowls and sprinkle each one with a little of the muscovado sugar to coat well all over. Tip out any excess muscovado sugar.

2 Peel and core the apple. Finely dice it into a bowl, add the cranberries and mix together well. Divide the fruit mixture equally among the prepared heatproof bowls.

3 Place the remaining muscovado sugar in a mixing bowl. Add the margarine, eggs, flour, baking powder and cocoa powder beat well until combined and smooth.

4 Spoon the mixture into the heatproof bowls and cover the top of each with a layer of greaseproof (waxed) paper and a double thickness of foil tied securely with string.

5 Steam in a covered pan for about 45 minutes, topping up the boiling water as required, until the puddings are well risen and firm.

6 Meanwhile, make the syrup. Break the chocolate into squares and place it in a small pan with the honey, butter and vanilla essence. Heat gently, stirring, until melted and smooth. Pour the syrup into a jug (pitcher).

7 Run a round-bladed knife around the edge of each pudding to loosen it, then turn out on to individual warm plates. Serve immediately, with the chocolate syrup.

COOK'S TIP
The puddings can be cooked very quickly in the microwave. Use non-metallic bowls and cover with greaseproof (waxed) paper instead of foil. Cook on High (100% power) for 5–6 minutes, then stand for 2–3 minutes before turning out.

Chocolate Chip and **Banana Pudding**

Hot and steamy, this superb light
pudding tastes extra special served
with chocolate sauce.

Serves 4

*200g/7oz/1¾ cups self-raising
  (self-rising) flour
75g/3oz/6 tbsp unsalted (sweet) butter
2 ripe bananas
75g/3oz/⅓ cup caster (superfine) sugar
60ml/4 tbsp milk
1 egg, beaten
60ml/4 tbsp plain (semisweet)
  chocolate chips
glossy chocolate sauce and whipped
  cream, to serve*

1 Prepare a steamer or half fill a pan
with water and bring it to the boil.
Grease a 1 litre/1¾ pint/4 cup
heatproof bowl. Sift the flour into a
bowl and rub in the butter with your
fingertips until the mixture resembles
breadcrumbs.

2 Mash the bananas in a bowl. Stir
them into the flour mixture, with the
caster sugar.

3 Whisk the milk with the egg in a
jug (pitcher) or small bowl, then beat
into the pudding mixture. Stir in the
chocolate chips and mix well until
thoroughly combined.

4 Spoon the mixture into the
heatproof bowl, cover closely with
greaseproof (waxed) paper and a double
thickness of foil, and steam for 2 hours,
topping up the water as required.

5 Run a knife around the top of the
pudding to loosen it, then turn it out
on to a warm serving dish. Serve hot,
with the chocolate sauce and a
spoonful of whipped cream.

COOK'S TIP

To make glossy chocolate sauce:
Place 130g/4½oz/scant ¾ cup caster
(superfine) sugar in a pan with
120ml/4fl oz/½ cup water, and heat until
the sugar has dissolved. Stir in
175g/6oz plain (semisweet) chocolate,
broken into squares, until melted. Then
add 25g/1oz/2 tbsp butter and melt in
the same way. Do not let the sauce boil.
Add 30ml/2 tbsp brandy or the grated
rind of an orange. Serve warm.

Hot Chocolate Cake

This is wonderful served as a
dessert with a chocolate sauce.

Makes 10–12 slices

*200g/7oz/1¾ cups self-raising
    (self-rising) wholemeal (whole-
    wheat) flour*
*25g/1oz/¼ cup (unsweetened)
    cocoa powder*
pinch of salt
175g/6oz/¾ cup soft margarine
175g/6oz/¾ cup soft light brown sugar
few drops vanilla essence (extract)
4 eggs
75g/3oz white chocolate
chocolate leaves and curls, to decorate

For the white chocolate sauce
75g/3oz white chocolate
*150ml/¼ pint/⅔ cup single
    (light) cream*
30–45ml/2–3 tbsp milk

1 Preheat the oven to 160°C/325°F/
Gas 3. Sift the flour, cocoa powder
and salt into a bowl, adding in any
bran remaining in the sieve.

2 In a separate bowl, cream the
margarine, sugar and vanilla essence
together with a wooden spoon until
light and fluffy, then gently beat in one
of the eggs.

3 Gradually stir in the remaining eggs,
one at a time, alternately folding in
some of the flour, until the mixture is
blended in.

4 Coarsely chop the white chocolate,
then stir it into the mixture. Spoon into
a 675–900g/ 1½–2lb loaf tin (pan) or
an 18cm/7in greased cake tin. Bake for
30–40 minutes, or until just firm to the
touch and beginning to shrink away
from the sides of the tin.

5 Meanwhile, prepare the sauce.
Break the white chocolate into squares
and place in a pan with the cream.
Heat very gently until the chocolate
has melted. Add the milk and stir until
the sauce is cool.

6 Slice the cake and serve in a pool of
sauce, decorated with chocolate leaves
and curls.

Chocolate Almond Meringue Pie

This dream dessert combines three very popular flavours.

Serves 6

175g/6oz/1½ cups plain
(all-purpose) flour
50g/2oz/⅓ cup ground rice
150g/5oz/⅔ cup unsalted
(sweet) butter
finely grated rind of 1 orange
1 egg yolk
flaked (sliced) almonds and melted
chocolate, to decorate

For the filling
150g/5oz plain (semisweet) chocolate
50g/2oz/4 tbsp unsalted (sweet)
butter, softened
75g/3oz/⅓ cup caster (superfine) sugar
10ml/2 tsp cornflour (cornstarch)
4 egg yolks
75g/3oz/¾ cup ground almonds

For the meringue
3 egg whites
150g/5oz/¾ cup caster
(superfine) sugar

1 Sift the flour and ground rice into a bowl. Add the butter and rub in with your fingertips until the mixture resembles breadcrumbs. Stir in the orange rind. Add the egg yolk, mix well and bring the dough together. Roll out on a lightly floured surface and use to line a 23cm/9in round flan tin (pie pan). Chill in the refrigerator for 30 minutes.

2 Preheat the oven to 190°C/375°F/ Gas 5. Prick the pastry base all over with a fork, cover with greaseproof (waxed) paper weighed down with baking beans and bake blind for 10 minutes. Remove the pastry case (pie shell).

3 To make the filling, break the chocolate into squares and melt in a heatproof bowl set over a pan of barely simmering water. Cream the butter with the sugar in a bowl, then beat in the cornflour and egg yolks. Fold in the almonds, then the chocolate. Spread in the pastry case. Bake for a further 10 minutes.

4 To make the meringue, whisk the egg whites until stiff, then gradually add half the sugar. Fold in the remaining sugar.

5 Spoon the meringue over the chocolate filling to cover it completely, lifting it up with the back of the spoon to form peaks. Reduce the oven temperature to 180°C/350°F/Gas 4 and bake the pie for 15–20 minutes, or until the topping is pale gold. Serve warm, sprinkled with almonds and drizzled with melted chocolate.

Christmas Pudding

This recipe makes enough to fill one 1.2 litre/2 pint/5 cup bowl or two 600ml/1 pint/2½ cup bowls. It can be made up to a month before Christmas and stored in a cool, dry place. Steam the pudding for 2 hours before serving.

Serves 8

115g/4oz/½ cup butter
225g/8oz/1 heaping cup soft dark brown sugar
50g/2oz/½ cup self-raising (self-rising) flour
5ml/1tsp ground mixed (apple pie) spice
1.5ml/¼ tsp grated nutmeg
2.5ml/½ tsp ground cinnamon
2 eggs
115g/4oz/2 cups fresh white breadcrumbs
175g/6oz/generous 1 cup sultanas (golden raisins)
175g/6oz/generous 1 cup raisins
115g/4oz/½ cup currants
25g/1oz/3 tbsp mixed (candied) peel, chopped finely
25g/1oz/¼ cup chopped almonds
1 small cooking apple, peeled, cored and coarsely grated
finely grated rind or 1 orange or lemon
juice of 1 orange or lemon, made up to 150ml/¼ pint/⅔ cup with brandy

1 Cut a disc of greaseproof (waxed) paper to fit the base of the heatproof bowl(s) and grease the disc and bowl(s) well with butter.

2 Beat the butter and sugar together until creamy and combined. Beat in the flour, spices and eggs. Stir in the remaining ingredients thoroughly. The mixture should have a soft dropping (pourable) consistency.

3 Turn the mixture into the prepared bowl(s) and level the surface with the back of a spoon.

4 Cover with another disc of buttered greaseproof paper.

5 Make a pleat across the centre of a large piece of greaseproof paper and cover the bowl(s) with it, tying it in place with string under the rim. Cut off the excess paper. Pleat a piece of foil in the same way and cover the bowl(s) with it, tucking it around the bowl neatly, under the greaseproof frill. Tie another piece of string around and across the top, as a handle.

6 Place the bowl(s) in a steamer over a pan of simmering water and steam for 6 hours. Alternatively, put the bowl(s) into a large pan and pour around enough boiling water to come halfway up the bowl(s) and cover the pan with a tight-fitting lid. Check the water is simmering and top it up with boiling water as it evaporates. When the pudding(s) have cooked, leave to cool completely. Then remove the foil and greaseproof paper. Wipe the bowl(s) clean and replace the greaseproof paper and foil with clean pieces, ready for reheating.

TO SERVE
Steam for 2 hours. Remove and discard the paper and foil, run a knife around the bowl(s) and turn the pudding out on to a warm plate. Leave it to stand for about 5 minutes before removing the pudding bowl(s) (the steam will rise to the top of the bowl and help to loosen the pudding). Decorate with a sprig of holly. Serve with brandy or rum butter, whipped cream or freshly made custard.

Index